The Road to Iraq

The Road to Iraq

The Making of a Neoconservative War

Muhammad Idrees Ahmad

EDINBURGH
University Press

This book is dedicated to my mom for all her sacrifices and my beloved late sister Mah'Jabeen for teaching us not to be ordinary.

© Muhammad Idrees Ahmad, 2014

Edinburgh University Press Ltd
The Tun – Holyrood Road
12 (2f) Jackson's Entry
Edinburgh EH8 8PJ
www.euppublishing.com

Typeset in 11/14 Sabon by
Servis Filmsetting Ltd, Stockport, Cheshire,
and printed and bound in Great Britain by
CPI Group (UK) Ltd, Croydon CR0 4YY

A CIP record for this book is available from the British Library

ISBN 978 0 7486 9302 3 (hardback)
ISBN 978 0 7486 9303 0 (paperback)
ISBN 978 0 7486 9304 7 (webready PDF)
ISBN 978 0 7486 9305 4 (epub)

The right of Muhammad Idrees Ahmad to be identified as author of this work
has been asserted in accordance with the Copyright, Designs and Patents Act
1988 and the Copyright and Related Rights Regulations 2003 (SI No. 2498).

Contents

Acknowledgements

For an autodidact who in the past has never given formal education its due in time, energy or attention, writing a scholarly book on international affairs could be a daunting task. But thanks to the advice, assistance and encouragement of some remarkable individuals the process for me proved a fruitful and stimulating one. I am pleased to record the debts I have incurred.

I am immensely grateful for the friendship of Robin Yassin-Kassab, Rebecca Gordon-Nesbitt, Kim Bizzarri, Ealasaid Munro, Marisa de Andrade, Tariq Kataria, Osama Saeed, Stuart Price, Henning Drager, Palash Dave and Iqbal Asaria. Without their support this work would not have been possible. Thanks are also due to Mitch Miller and Johnny Roger for launching me on a writing career; to Ziauddin Sardar, Faisal al Yafai, Philip Weiss, John Judis, Jim Lobe, Wendy Kristianesen, Leigh French, Tony Karon and the late Alexander Cockburn for providing me a platform; and to Greg Philo, David Miller and Will Dinan for their guidance and support.

Maria Teresa Martinez-Dominguez, Rani Dhanda, Jairo Lugo-Ocando, Dahr Jamail, Adam Shatz and Giovanna Fassetta are exemplary friends, the best anyone could ask for. Their generosity knows no bounds. They have always been there for me in times of need and often gone farther. To them I remain eternally grateful. I am also lucky to count among my closest friends exceptional individuals like Thomas Hacker and Corinne Fowler.

Thanks are also due to my PULSE collaborators David Thomson, Tali Shapiro, Huma Dar, M. Shahid Alam and Grant F. Smith; to my Strathclyde friends Ludek Stavinoha, Lucy Brown, Tommy Kane, Roy Revie, Kate Spence, Claire Harkins, Rizwaan

Sabir and Joseph Idegwu; and to the great Scottish philosopher, poet and environmentalist Alastair McIntosh for his friendship, support and advice.

I am indebted to Nicola Ramsey, John Watson, Michelle Houston and Jenny Peebles at Edinburgh University Press for their feedback and support; and to Eliza Wright for her stellar editing.

John J. Mearsheimer is a modern-day Thucydides. He is original and provocative as a thinker and gracious and magnanimous as a person. His approval is the greatest validation that any writer on international relations can hope for. To him I owe gratitude for inspiration and support.

No one, however, has impacted my life and work more in the past years than Jasmin, my friend, guide and anchor (and frequent saviour); and Acacia, who through her boundless love and *joie de vivre* gave me some of the happiest moments of my life.

Abbreviations

ABM	Anti-Ballistic Missile
ACDA	Arms Control and Disarmament Agency
ADL	Anti-Defamation League
AECA	Arms Export Control Act
AEI	American Enterprise Institute
AFL–CIO	American Federation of Labor and Congress of Industrial Organizations
AIPAC	American Israel Public Affairs Committee
APN	Americans for Peace Now
AVOT	Americans for Victory over Terrorism
AWACS	Airborne Warning and Control System
BICOM	Britain Israel Communications and Research Centre
BRT	Business Roundtable
CAMERA	Committee for Accuracy in Middle East Reporting in America
CDM	Coalition for Democratic Majority
CENTCOM	US Central Command
CEO	Chief Executive Officer
CLI	Committee for the Liberation of Iraq
CPD	Committee on the Present Danger
CPMAJO	Conference of Presidents of the Major American Jewish Organizations; also known as 'Presidents Conference'
CPSG	Committee for Peace and Security in the Gulf
CSP	Centre for Security Policy
CUFI	Christians United for Israel
CUSIME	Committee on US Interests in the Middle East

CWC	Chemical Weapons Convention
DIA	Defense Intelligence Agency
DPB	Defense Policy Board
DPG 92	Defense Policy Guidance 1992
FARA	Foreign Agents Registration Act
FDD	Foundation for Defense of Democracies
HRC	Human Rights Caucus
ILSA	Iran and Libya Sanctions Act
INC	Iraqi National Congress
INR	Bureau of Intelligence and Research
JINSA	Jewish Institute for National Security Affairs
MEMRI	Middle East Media Research Institute
MIC	Military–Industrial Complex
MPS	Mont Pelerin Society
NCRAC	National Jewish Community Relations Advisory Council
NESA	Near East and South Asia Bureau
NIE	National Intelligence Estimate
NSC	National Security Council
ONA	Office of Net Assessments
OPCW	Organisation for the Prohibition of Chemical Weapons
OPT	Occupied Palestinian Territories
OSP	Office of Special Plans
OVP	Office of the Vice President
PCEG	Policy Counterterrorism Evaluation Group
PFIAB	Presidential Foreign Intelligence Advisory Board
PNAC	Project for the New American Century
R&D	Research and Development
RMA	Revolution in Military Affairs
SAC	Strategic Air Command
UAV	Unmanned Aerial Vehicle
UN	United Nations
USIFTA	US–Israel Free Trade Agreement
WHIG	White House Iraq Group
WINEP	Washington Institute for Near East Policy
WINPAC	Weapons Intelligence Non-Proliferation and Arms Control

WJC	World Jewish Congress
WMD	Weapon of Mass Destruction
WZO	World Zionist Organization
ZOA	Zionist Organization of America

Part I The Argument

Introduction

On 1 May 2003, after a dramatic tail-hook landing on the air-craft carrier USS *Abraham Lincoln*, George W. Bush addressed sailors assembled on the ship's deck. Behind him was draped a banner that boldly proclaimed 'Mission Accomplished'. 'Major combat operations in Iraq have ended', he said, 'In the Battle of Iraq, the United States and our allies have prevailed.' The crowd exulted and the media echoed the applause. Baghdad had fallen with the same ease with which the Taliban were vanquished in 2001. The US military appeared invincible. Washington was triumphal. The success encouraged some neoconservatives into goading. Anyone can go to Baghdad, they said, 'real men go to Tehran'.[1]

Events of the following years frustrated this optimism. With 'shock and awe' giving way to the attrition of ambushes and improvised explosive devices, the vaunted US military proved not nearly as formidable. By December 2011, when it finally exited Iraq, it had suffered five thousand losses and caused the deaths of 461,000 Iraqis.[2] Iraq's ancient heritage was stolen, vandalised, or destroyed. The conflict nearly bankrupted the US economy and cost the world in excess of $6 trillion.[3] The public had long since switched channels.[4]

Much has been written about the war since 2003. The journal-istic accounts are understandably partial; they focus on specific individuals, isolated parts of the government or particular aspects of policy. Scholarly accounts are ballasted with the dead weight of deterministic grand theory, ignoring agency. Autobiographies are predictably self-serving. And though many have written about the role of the neoconservatives, their specific contributions and likely motivations are often mislaid. Salient among the latter is the security of Israel.

Since the end of World War II, US policy towards the Middle East has been guided by two competing concerns: oil and Israel.[5] The former mandates friendly relations with Arab states; the latter is mandated by domestic political imperatives.[6] That US interest in the region's oil and its support for Israel have remained constant leads some analysts to see the two concerns as complementary.[7] They are not. Over the past seven decades, on too many occasions, perceived US interests have collided with Israeli interests as defined by its vocal domestic supporters. The most vociferous among these are the neoconservatives.

Few dispute today that the neoconservatives played a leading role in pushing for war against Iraq.[8] In the heady days following the fall of Baghdad, many neoconservatives were themselves quick to claim credit. Some of the war's leading advocates are equally eager to complement the neoconservatives. In his sympathetic account of the neoconservative war, George Packer, for example, is effusive about the idealism of the war's supporters and derisive of anti-war voices like Edward Said, who he claims, were overtaken by history.[9] In an interview with *Haaretz*, liberal hawk Thomas Friedman was equally forthright about the neoconservatives' role:

> It's the war the neoconservatives wanted . . . It's the war the neoconservatives marketed. Those people had an idea to sell when September 11 came, and they sold it . . . So this is not a war that the masses demanded. This is a war of an elite . . . I could give you the names of 25 people (all of whom are at this moment within a five-block radius of this office) who, if you had exiled them to a desert island a year and a half ago, the Iraq war would not have happened.[10]

Joe Klein of *Time*, another former supporter of the war, argues that the neoconservatives led the US into a foolish war with Iraq because they were 'using U.S. military power, U.S. lives and money, to make the world safe for Israel'.[11]

Less noted, however, is the resistance the war faced within the establishment. As one journalist noted in the winter of 2002, inside the foreign-policy, defense and intelligence agencies, nearly the whole rank and file, along with many senior officials, are opposed to invading Iraq. But because the less than two dozen neoconservatives leading the war party have the support of Vice President Dick Cheney and Secretary of Defense Donald Rumsfeld, they are able to marginalize that opposition.[12]

Economist Robert Kuttner likewise observed that 'the vast foreign policy mainstream – Republican and Democratic ex-public officials, former ambassadors, military and intelligence people, academic experts – consider Bush's whole approach a disaster'.[13] Before the administration launched its public diplomacy, there was little enthusiasm for it even in Congress.[14]

Yet, despite widespread opposition, the neoconservatives prevailed. They helped manufacture the propaganda, amplified it in the media and 'stovepiped' it to decision makers. The invasion was sold as a 'pre-emptive' war to disarm Iraq, which, through the conjunction of its alleged weapons of mass destruction (WMDs) and terrorist ties, was presented as an imminent threat. The neoconservatives furnished both elements of the case.

These claims, which were doubted even before the invasion, collapsed soon afterwards. They were replaced by the new official rationale of 'democracy promotion'. A staple of neoconservative rhetoric for years, however, democracy promotion was publicly embraced only after the invasion. In her memoir, Condoleezza Rice rejects the notion that the war was waged 'to bring democracy'. Rumsfeld too denies that the war had anything to do with democracy – indeed, he suggests that the rhetoric of democracy promotion was used to cover the embarrassment of the absent WMDs.[15] But by the time Obama replaced Bush, the idea had crystallised into a consensus. The new president felt the need to pay it lip service even in repudiating the war.[16]

The question remains, however, how a small band of neoconservatives managed to hijack the foreign policy of the world's pre-eminent power. The answer lies in the salient position that the neoconservatives hold within the vast institutional network of the Israel lobby. Without the lobby's help, they would have struggled to secure the key advisory positions that enabled them to influence top decision makers and neutralise dissenting government agencies. Nor would they have been able to secure Congress's blessing and demoralise public opinion. The lobby's clout over Congress and its formidable organs of public influence were critical.

Though the ultimate target of the lobby and the neoconservatives was Tehran, Iraq was seen as a stepping stone. But before it was defanged in the 1991 Gulf War, Iraq too was seen as a potential rival by the Israeli defence establishment. There had been plans in place since the 1970s for the balkanisation of the country – plans that were adopted and assimilated by the neoconservatives. The Iraq war was conceived in Washington, but its inspiration came from Tel Aviv.

The war party

Though the neoconservatives have featured prominently in anti-war polemics, their specific role and motivations are often obscured. There is even confusion over neoconservative ideology and composition, which has at times led analysts to lump them with traditional conservatives like Dick Cheney and Donald Rumsfeld. Others have imputed to them economic motives largely inferred from the presumed material ends of the war. To the extent that distinctions are made between the neoconservatives and aggressive nationalists like Cheney and Rumsfeld, the former are assigned a subordinate role in the war's planning and execution. Not enough attention has been paid to the vast power structure – the network of think tanks, foundations and lobby groups – that lends the neoconservatives their political and ideological salience.

Some have used the signatures on the various open letters that the Project for the New American Century (PNAC) published as a catalogue of neoconservative membership. But not all the actors who signed these letters were neoconservatives, and some did not share the neoconservatives' preference for the use of military force. As Chapters 3–4 highlight, neoconservatism is more a biography than an ideology – that is, the members of the movement are bound together less by a coherent set of principles than by a shared experience in pursuit of common interests. The movement has an identifiable core and fuzzy borders. Each member of this core actively promoted the war before and after 9/11. This is not necessarily true of all PNAC signatories or members of the administration.

The key criteria for inclusion in the war party must therefore include (1) an actor's commitment to military intervention in Iraq before 9/11; and (2) their tangible contribution to the case for war afterwards. I do not include neoconservatives in government who played ancillary roles. Nor do I include leading neoconservatives outside the government who may have served a propaganda function but whose influence on policy is not directly obvious (Irving Kristol, Norman Podhoretz, et al.). This reduces the list of key actors to twenty-four, all of whom are neoconservatives except two aggressive nationalists (John Bolton and Newt Gingrich) and one Iraqi exile (Ahmed Chalabi) (Table 1). All these actors are embedded in the neoconservative institutional infrastructure; some have links to major arms producers.

Table 1 The war party

No.	Actor	Role
1	Richard Perle	'Clean break' and PNAC signatory; orchestrated letterhead groups; influenced post-9/11 rhetoric; facilitated Iraqi National Congress (INC) access; used Defense Policy Board (DPB) to push for war.
2	Michael Ledeen	Started advocating for war within hours of 9/11; assisted Office of Special Plans (OSP) with manufacturing evidence.
3	Paul Wolfowitz	Advocate of war against Iraq since 1970s; oversaw the production of the Defense Policy Guidance 1992 (DPG 92); PNAC signatory; claimed credit for winning over Bush on war at crucial 15 September National Security Council (NSC) meeting; helped establish Bletchley II and OSP.
4	Douglas Feith	'Clean break' signatory; key liaison with Israeli intelligence and the INC; established Policy Counterterrorism Evaluation Group (PCEG) and OSP.
5	Scooter Libby	One of the drafters of DPG 92; PNAC signatory; joined Wolfowitz to lobby for war against Iraq at crucial Camp David meeting on 15 September; lynchpin of OSP, DPB and Office of the Vice

No.	Actor	Role
5	Scooter Libby	President (OVP) coordination who 'stovepiped' propaganda to Cheney and Bush.
6	Judith Miller	Key conduit for neoconservative and INC propaganda; author of *New York Times* front-page articles making claims about Iraq's WMDs, which the administration used to make its case; co-author with Laurie Mylroie of a book on Iraq.
7	Laurie Mylroie	The leading proponent of the Iraq–Al-Qaeda link; co-author with Judith Miller of a book on Iraq's WMDs; close associate of Perle, Wolfowitz and Libby.
8	Elliott Abrams	PNAC signatory; veteran of various Israel lobby institutions; leading proponent of Jewish exceptionalism; key behind-the-scenes player who was placed at the NSC to keep watch over his boss Condoleezza Rice.
9	David Wurmser	Principal author of the 'clean break' and 'crumbling states' documents; author of the 'dual rollback' strategy; member of PCEG; later a Middle East adviser to Cheney; married to Middle East Media Research Institute (MEMRI) co-founder Meyrav Wurmser.
10	John Bolton	Signatory to Committee for Peace and Security in the Gulf (CPSG) and PNAC letters; the neoconservatives' key liaison at the State Department; helped suppress questions raised by the department's Bureau of Intelligence and Research (INR) about Iraq's alleged WMDs.
11	Bernard Lewis	Popularised the phrase 'clash of civilisations' and proposed the 'Lebanonisation' of Iraq as far back as 1979; key influence on Cheney; advised both the president and vice president in the immediate aftermath of 9/11 about the necessity of demonstrating American power in Iraq.
12	James Woolsey	PNAC signatory who used his credentials as a former CIA director to peddle Mylroie's thesis about the Iraq–Al-Qaeda link; his law firm Shea & Gardner lobbied for Ahmed Chalabi's INC.
13	Reuel Gerecht	PNAC signatory; key proponent of the 'demonstration effect'; advocate of regime change in Iraq and Iran; liaison between the INC and the PCEG and OSP.

No.	Actor	Role
14	William Kristol	Editor of *The Weekly Standard*; co-founder of PNAC; leading hawk particularly influential with the conservative republican government; his publication became the key conduit for OSP propaganda.
15	Robert Kagan	Kristol's close associate; key intellectual force behind PNAC's neo-militarism.
16	Frank Gaffney	Founder of Center for Security Policy (CSP); PNAC signatory; leading propagandist for war.
17	Charles Krauthammer	PNAC signatory; proponent of American unilateralism; recipient of frequent OSP leaks.
18	David Frum	Author of the key Bush speech on 9/11 in which he followed Perle's instructions to include a reference to 'states that harbour terrorists' as potential targets of US retaliation, opening the way for the invasion of Iraq.
19	Ken Adelman	PNAC signatory; DPB member; close friend of Cheney and Rumsfeld; proponent of the war as 'cakewalk' theory.
20	Newt Gingrich	PNAC signatory; ultra-reactionary hawk who used his DPB imprimatur to personally lobby the CIA, demanding a more hawkish National Intelligence Estimate (NIE).
21	Bruce Jackson	PNAC signatory; key liaison between the military–industrial complex (MIC) and the neoconservatives; rallied 'New Europe' with various forms of inducements to stand up to the recalcitrant 'Old Europe'.
22	Ahmed Chalabi	Leader of the INC; acolyte of Albert Wohlstetter and a close friend of Perle Wolfowitz, who provided much of the false intelligence which was subsequently stovepiped by the neoconservatives to top officials.
23	Stephen Hadley	Early advocate of war; became Libby's key liaison at the NSC; ignored CIA's warnings to repeatedly reinsert claims about Iraq's alleged purchase of uranium ore into Bush's 2003 State of the Union Speech.
24	Albert Wohlstetter	Original lynchpin of the neoconservative network who insinuated most members of the neoconservative core into government; leading advocate of the Revolution in Military Affairs (RMA); also helped draft the DPG 92.

Viewed out of context such linkages can be misleading. Individuals often serve in an organisation without necessarily sharing the politics of colleagues. Think tanks and letterhead organisations go out of their way to secure the signatures of individuals from outside the clique to foster the appearance of broader support. Only through a person's actions can one distinguish notional support from actual commitment. Linkages between Dick Cheney and Colin Powell are myriad, for example; but these would not have helped predict their respective attitudes towards the war. Likewise, Richard Armitage is a signatory to PNAC letters on Iraq and a former friend of Wolfowitz; they served in three different administrations together – but none of that would have helped predict the divergent positions both would take on the war.

The neoconservatives are best understood as what social anthropologist Janine Wedel calls a 'flex net'. Central to this form of power is a figure that 'serves at one and the same time as business consultant, think-tanker, TV pundit, and government adviser [who] glides in and around the organisations that enlist his services'.[17] These actors value personal relations over bureaucratic chains of command, put official information to private use and use private information to steer official policy. They owe no allegiance to the institution: their loyalties lie with the informal network – the flex net – whose close social bonds, ideological coherence, protean facility, and infiltration of official and corporate spheres serve as fulcrum for their influence. Their multiple overlapping roles and fluid identities allow them to navigate the public–private divide, co-opt public policy agendas, craft policy in their private interest, and undermine both public accountability and market competition. They are able to harness official authority and resources without subjecting themselves to the corresponding checks and balances.[18] They use official imprimatur for private gain and claim citizens' prerogatives when confronted with the possibility of public accountability. They also exploit the 24-hour news cycle by using official credentials to claim expertise while advancing sectional interests.

Wedel argues that the rise of this form of power has been facilitated by four key developments: (1) the redesign of government along business lines around the 1970s with the attendant consolidation of executive power and outsourcing of many of its functions; (2) the end of the Cold War and the proliferation of under-governed areas; (3) the rise of advanced communication technologies, complex information systems (particularly in finance) and the ascent of 'experts'; and (4) a transformed public sphere in which politics and entertainment blend, with performance valued over truth, self-serving claims over objectivity.[19] The chimera of 'big government' has long animated a bipartisan drive to control the number of civil servants in government by outsourcing inherently governmental functions to private contractors, leading to the rise of a massive 'shadow government'. The proportion of contractors in the US federal labour force, for example, increased from three-fifths in 1990 to three-quarters in 2008. The cost of contractor services soared from $125 billion in 2001 to $320 billion in 2008. Between 1996 and 2006, the services budget of the Pentagon (which accounts for 75 per cent of all federal procurements) increased by 78 per cent. Contracts currently account for 70 per cent of the intelligence budget, a quarter of whose core manpower is private. While efficiency was cited as the rationale for redesigning government along business lines, the blurring public–private divide has diminished both public accountability and market discipline.[20] The consequences for democracy have been deleterious. This habitat has been particularly conducive to 'institutional nomads' like the neoconservatives.

The neoconservative core is a small band of ideological kin brought together by common goals, shared personal histories and an Israel-centric worldview. Like all flex nets, writes Wedel, they are 'more amorphous and less transparent than conventional lobbies and interest groups, yet more coherent and less accountable . . . they are subject to no greater oversight than their own consciences and the social pressures of their own networks'.[21] They have a tendency to personalise and bypass bureaucracy, privatise official information and assume multiple overlapping roles. Their intense social and ideological bonds undergird their networks of think tanks, front groups and letterhead organisations. They have a record of relaxing or bending rules to their advantage.[22] These characteristics also distinguish them from the less

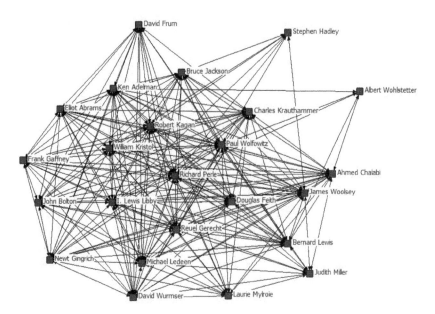

Figure 1 The neoconservative core and Ahmed Chalabi. Source: Data compiled by RightWeb (International Relations Center) and Powerbase. info (a project of Spinwatch). Richard Perle lies at the core of this unusually dense network with a direct, one-to-one relationship with every other member of the network. Albert Wohlstetter is the outlier mainly because he belongs to a previous generation. He is included because he played the crucial role in inserting apex neocons into government

versatile epistemic communities. The flex net does not have hard boundaries – to further specific causes, members form alliance with political actors of all stripes. But it does have a gravitational core (Figure 1).

The neoconservative core's coordination and ideological coherence allowed them to conceive and instigate the 2003 Iraq invasion despite strong reservations of the military and intelligence bureaucracies. Their capacity to undermine, circumvent or intimidate the professional intelligence community stretches back to their efforts to disrupt détente between the US and the Soviet Union in the mid-1970s. It has enabled them to insert dubious, even fabricated, information into the policy process, often under the imprimatur of ad hoc, quasi-governmental bodies. The ambiguity of their roles has in turn allowed them to evade scrutiny while preserving their reputations. Though their star has dimmed somewhat, their militarist imprint on foreign policy is only now beginning to fade. But the neoconservatives have tried to ensure continuity by enshrining their ideas in institutions. The cutting edge of their propaganda apparatus is a vast network of think tanks with overlapping and interlocking memberships.

On Capitol Hill, the think tanks target both the Congresspersons and their staffers, inviting them to seminars, keeping an eye on policy proposals, monitoring Congressional hearings and using Congressional testimonies to plant new ideas. By virtue of being uttered in an august official forum, these ideas are then amplified in the media. They exploit Congresspeople's perennial time and resource constraints by feeding them ideas and placing staffers and interns in their offices.[23] Think tanks also compete during presidential elections to provide advisers to candidates, who, if elected, will be responsible for filling up to ten thousand bureaucratic positions.[24] This is one way of improving an operative's chances of being appointed as a staffer to the White House after the elections.

Neoconservative think tanks have monitored the federal bureaucracy, with a special focus on the Departments of Defense, State and Homeland Security, producing studies and reports to influence policy.[25] They also target the media. The Washington Institute for Near East Policy (WINEP), the American Enterprise Institute (AEI), the Heritage Foundation and the Foundation for Defense of Democracies (FDD) have large funds allocated to PR.[26] The once centrist Brookings Institution has also become more hospitable to neoconservative opinion since 2002, when the Israeli-American media mogul Haim Saban used a $12 million donation to establish the Saban Center for Middle East Studies and install as its head the Israel lobby veteran Martin Indyk. In 2003, Brookings allocated $1 million and Heritage $6.6 million to media and government relations.[27] Brookings, AEI, Heritage and the Council on Foreign Relations (whose Middle East Program is dominated by neoconservatives like Elliott Abrams and Dan Senor) were the top-five most cited think tanks in 2006–7.[28]

Manufacturing compliance

The media may not always succeed in telling people *what to think*, but they *can* tell people *what to think about* by privileging one story over another through selective emphasis (for example, what appears on the front page of a newspaper with a striking image is far likelier to stay in most readers' minds than what appears in a side column of an inside page). The extent to which this agenda-setting function of the media is understood and manipulated by the powerful is evident from a telling statement in the biography of former White House press secretary Scott McClellan who described the presidency as a 'bully pulpit', a 'giant megaphone' through which a leader could easily set the daily news agenda given the media's proclivity for reporting and amplifying presidential statements. In the lead-up to the war as the Bush Administration engaged in 'a carefully-orchestrated campaign to shape and manipulate sources of public approval to our advantage', he notes, the overly 'deferential' media served as 'complicit enablers'. 'Their primary focus would be on covering the campaign to sell the war, rather than aggressively questioning the rationale for war or pursuing the truth behind it.' The press failed to apprise the public of the 'uncertainties, doubts, and caveats that underlay the intelligence about the regime of Saddam Hussein'. [29]

The failure of journalism in the lead-up to the Iraq war has been much remarked upon. For the most part, the media in the US, and to a lesser degree in the UK, echoed the claims of their respective governments. But they did not always succeed in persuading their audience. The fact that the elite have a desire to manufacture consent does not mean that they always succeed – nor do they have to. For it is not so much the manufacturing of consent they are after as the *appearance* of consent. The battle, sociologists Miller and Dinan note, is really for 'morale, advantage, freedom of action, and concrete outcomes'; the battle is for compliance rather than consent.[30] The aim is to demobilise popular opposition by presenting the *illusion* of a consensus – to convince the audience that it is *they* who are out of touch.

Polls and persuasion

A key weapon in the battle for public morale is the opinion poll. Using a forced-choice method, media polls shape public opinion by imposing preferences that are not the people's own. In their failure to take into account public apathy or ignorance, polls do not just measure public opinion, they also manufacture it. In his incisive study of the modern polling process, former Gallup senior editor David Moore argues that the polling system has an inherent power bias that manufactures public opinion to support elite policy. By making no distinction between superficially held views and cherished convictions, the polls insure that people who are largely ignorant or apathetic – the majority in the US when it comes to foreign affairs – respond to notions in the air. The media's agenda-setting role becomes crucial as poll results often mirror the views that already prevail in the media thereby according them a stamp of public approval.[31]

In February 2003, after Colin Powell's crucial speech at the UN, a CNN–USA Today–Gallup poll found 59 per cent of respondents supporting the forced toppling of Saddam Hussein. These figures more or less comported with the results of other polls carried out at the time. But these numbers were highly misleading: they failed to measure public apathy. Respondents were made to choose between options to which they might not have had any strong commitment. Presented with a forced choice, respondents often decide based on superficially held beliefs. These are no more than 'uncaring, unreflective, top-of-mind responses'.[32] These are precisely the types of belief that the media is able to engender through its emphasis and framing of issues. With headlines blaring Iraq's alleged links to Al-Qaeda, and front pages splashed with warnings of the threats posed by Iraq's alleged WMDs, it is not surprising that those who were indifferent to the issue would go with the choice that *appeared* to have more support. They opted for war when presented with a choice between action and inaction in the face of much-ballyhooed threats.

However, the aforementioned Gallup poll also chose to test the intensity of the opinion with a follow-up question asking each respondent how upset they would be if the government did not follow their preferred policy position. The results were dramatic. The support for war dropped to 29 per cent and opposition to 30 per cent; 41 per cent were without an opinion.

> Seventy percent would have been content with invading Iraq (the 41 percent who didn't care plus the 29 percent who supported the war and would have been upset if it hadn't occurred) and 71 percent would have been content with not going to war (the 41 percent who didn't care plus the 30 percent who opposed the invasion and said they would be upset if it did occur).[33]

The same poll could therefore be read as showing public consensus both for *going to war* as well as for *not going to war*. If the US public can be blamed for anything, it is for tolerating the invasion.

The overwhelming reliance of modern media polling on this format makes it easy for states to create the illusion of public support. For Moore, polls serve 'the media's power bias'; they 'provide closure to a cycle that legitimizes the policies of those in power'.[34] In Federalist No. 49, the author (believed to be James Madison or Alexander Hamilton) had perceptively noted:

> If it be true that all governments rest on opinion, it is no less true that the strength of opinion in each individual, and its practical influence on his conduct, depend much on the number which he supposes to have entertained the same opinion. The reason of man, like man himself, is timid and cautious when left alone, and acquires firmness and confidence in proportion to the number with which it is associated.[35]

In the case of Iraq, writes Moore, 'the public's apparently positive response to the Bush administration's campaign to war did, arguably, influence many others in the country, especially many Democrat political leaders, who were intimidated by public opinion into voting for war despite their reservations'.[36] The cycle began with the White House, which instituted a special outfit, the White House Iraq Group (WHIG), which fed the media stories about the alleged threat from Iraq; the media, with very few exceptions, reported these stories uncritically; and then, writes

Moore, 'the media conducted their polls to measure the public's top-of-mind reaction and discovered – surprise! – widespread support for the war'.[37]

This book is structured to proceed from the general to the specific, from context to event. But first of all, in Chapter 1, I examine the alternative theories that have been offered to explain the war, including oil, free-markets and military bases. In Chapter 2, I look at the affinities and distinctions between neoliberals and neoconservatives, the significance of Israel to the neoconservative worldview, and the movement's origin as a nexus between the Israel lobby and the military–industrial complex. In Chapter 3, I assess the various historical contingencies that aided the neo-conservatives through the 1990s and the manner in which the neoconservatives adapted to these changes and shaped post-Cold War discourse. I also examine the neoconservatives' interest in Iraq, which traces its origins to Israel's long-standing 'periphery doctrine'. The next two chapters deal specifically with events between 11 September 2001 and the invasion of Iraq in March 2003. They relate to two distinct aspects of the case for war. Chapter 4 deals with the agenda-setting aspect, how the neo-conservatives successfully put Iraq on the agenda by linking it to the events of 9/11; and Chapter 5 deals with the manufacturing of the evidence related to Iraq's alleged WMDs. Finally, in the Appendix, I revisit the debate occasioned by the publication of John Mearsheimer and Stephen Walt's *The Israel Lobby and US Foreign Policy*. As I argue, the evidence produced in this book vindicates their claim that absent the Israel lobby, the Iraq war would not have happened. I also rebut some of the common criticisms that were levelled against their argument.

1 Black Gold and Red Herrings

Journalists and scholars have frequently treated the Iraq war as the outcome of a coherent strategy rooted in a consensual elite, national or class interest. The explanations are often mono-causal: oil, imperialism, militarism, Israel, democracy promotion and the demonstrative use of power. But these are not mutually exclusive propositions. Each played some part in the calculus of decision makers, though not all are equally significant. Key actors were not driven by the same motives, nor did they reach their decisions simultaneously. Some had been committed to regime change for years, others embraced it after 9/11; still others accepted it after the war had become inevitable. Bush, Cheney and Rumsfeld were the war's chief executors, but they embraced its logic long after the neoconservatives first conceived it. They would not have had their war without the neoconservatives' enabling role. Chronology and function are significant. Some polemics have focused on the Oedipal roots of Bush's Iraq fixation, but this may only explain why advisers found it easy to persuade him of a war already conceived. Most in the administration shared an aversion for Saddam Hussein, but only a few saw war as the preferred means for toppling him. All these factors offer at best a partial explanation for the war and fail to address its determinative causes.

Oil

If Iraq was invaded for oil, then the US was remarkably negligent in securing the prize. In 2006, the new Iraqi government was already reviving Hussein-era deals with China. In late 2009, with over 200,000 US troops and mercenaries present, Iraq awarded its first major post-war oil concessions – and the biggest winners were Norway, France, China and Russia.[1] Of the eleven contracts signed, only one was secured by a US company, Exxon Mobil, as part of a consortium with Royal Dutch Shell. By November 2011, Exxon too was in negotiations with Shell and Russia's Lukoil to sell its shares.[2] Exxon's attempt to sign a separate contract with the Kurdish regional government in 2011 was peremptorily rejected by the Iraqi central government. The only sector in which US companies triumphed was oil services – but in that sector the US has always enjoyed a virtual monopoly, invasions or no.[3] By 2013, China had emerged as the largest buyer of Iraqi oil and one of the biggest investors in its oil sector. The irony did not escape one of the war's biggest enthusiasts. 'The Chinese had nothing to do with the war,' said Michael Makovsky, the neoconservative former Pentagon official, 'but from an economic standpoint they are benefiting from it, and our Fifth Fleet and air forces are helping to assure their supply.'[4]

Yet the 'war for oil' argument retains a powerful grip on popular imagination. After all, hasn't oil figured centrally in US relations with the Middle East? Hasn't the US engineered coups in oil-rich states in the past? Hasn't it asserted its right, and demonstrated its will to intervene militarily where its 'vital interests' are at stake? Hasn't Iraq one of the world's largest oil reserves? Wasn't the president of the United States a former oilman and his deputy the head of a major oil services company? Wasn't one of the war's very first combat operations a Navy commando raid on Iraq's two offshore oil terminals? Weren't the first locations that the US and UK forces seized during the invasion Iraq's oil installations? Didn't the US spare troops after the fall of Baghdad to protect the oil ministry even as Iraq's ancient heritage was plundered unimpeded? Haven't oil companies made record profits in the years since the invasion?

For all its prima facie plausibility, the 'war for oil' thesis is selective in fact and speculative in argument. Its two mutually contradictory claims collapse on closer reading.

The more pedestrian version of the thesis – that Iraq was invaded to maximise profits for US energy corporations – ignores the fact that these companies were being held back not by Saddam Hussein but by US-imposed sanctions. Indeed, for nearly a decade, the industry had been lobbying for an end to sanctions and resuming relations with Hussein, who was eager to do business.[5] In 1996, Texaco, Conoco, Mobil and Halliburton joined 670 other companies and trade associations to form USA*Engage, a lobbying coalition that worked closely with the US Chamber of Commerce to fight the sanctions. They lost the battle to the American Israel Public Affairs Committee (AIPAC), which successfully expanded the embargo with the Iran and Libya Sanctions Act (ILSA), a bill partially drafted by AIPAC's director of foreign policy issues Steven Rosen.[6] The oil industry's battle to repeal the bill continued well into the next decade (and efforts to repeal succeeding bills targeting Iran continue to this day).[7] In May 2001, according to *Business Week*, a proposal to ease sanctions again pitted 'powerful interests such as the pro-Israeli lobby and the U.S. oil industry against each other'.[8] In 1998, Cheney had disparaged the 'sanctions happy' policy of the Clinton Administration; it was hurting US businesses.[9] Cheney had no compunction about doing business with Iraq; he had overseen $23.8 million in sales to the country between 1998 and 1999.[10] Cheney's successor at Halliburton shared his view. In an 18 April 2001 letter to Senate Majority Leader Trent Lott, Halliburton's director of government affairs Donald A. Deline complained that because of the sanctions 'American farmers, workers, and companies have sacrificed without any progress toward U.S. foreign policy objectives.'[11] Conoco CEO Archie Dunham likewise protested that 'US companies, not rogue regimes, are the ones that suffer when the United States imposes economic sanctions.'[12]

The oil industry is aware that it can no longer rely on destabilising military adventures to open new markets. Since the 1970s, it has relied on agreements with host governments for its operations. Belligerence on the other hand has only jeopardised investments and brought uncertainty to future projects. Bush's withdrawal from the Anti-Ballistic Missile (ABM) Treaty resulted in US oil companies losing major contracts in Russia. ILSA kept them out of the lucrative Iranian and Libyan markets.[13] Meanwhile, European competitors such as Total, Gazprom and Petronas were able to dominate the market unchallenged. On 15 March 1995, when Clinton issued Executive Order 12957 banning US companies from developing Iran's oil resources, Conoco lost $1 billion worth of contracts that Total then picked up for a bargain.

The industry was also hurt by the pronounced pro-Israel tilt ushered in by the Bush Administration. The neoconservatives' hostility towards the Saudis alarmed oil companies, in particular Shell and Exxon Mobil, which had made huge investments in the Kingdom's natural gas.[14] US companies for the first time lost major contracts to European competitors in 2001, mainly due to the then Crown Prince Abdullah's anger over US indifference towards the Palestinians.[15] In May 2001, Abdullah declined an invitation to the White House because of continuing US support for Israel; later, on 27 August, he threatened to sever relations altogether.[16] According to Anthony Sampson, author of the acclaimed *The Seven Sisters*, oil companies feared finding themselves 'between the American-Israeli intervention and nationalists fearing reversion to a neo-colonial system'. The architects of the Iraq war presented oil security as one of the war's objectives, but oil companies were worried 'about the short-term danger and the supposed long-term benefits of intervention'.[17] They dreaded burning oilfields, saboteurs and political chaos interrupting supplies. Shares fell as the war approached.

Later in the war, oil companies did reap windfall profits from soaring prices.[18] But the price hikes were determined by internationally competitive oil markets that are subject as much to the laws of supply and demand as to the manipulations of speculators.[19] Prices reached a record high in the summer of 2008 even though Iran had 30 million barrels of oil in storage for lack of buyers. A June 2006 US Senate report found 'substantial evidence supporting the conclusion that the large amount of speculation in the current market has significantly increased prices'.[20]

However, after reaching a peak in July 2008, oil prices fell precipitately following a steep decline in demand. In March–May 2008, the US experienced its sharpest decline in miles driven as more and more people abandoned their personal vehicles in favour of public transportation.[21] The fate of the oil industry is tied to many others: higher oil prices mean fewer buyers of

American autos, less flying, reduced tourism, and so on. High prices also renewed calls for investment in alternative fuels, a scenario that the oil industry dreads. The oil services industry on the other hand did benefit from the war; but it would have benefited equally had sanctions been lifted. Even without the war, Iraq's decrepit oil infrastructure was in need of a major overhaul.

Oil companies no doubt gained from the price hikes following the invasion of Iraq. This makes Big Oil no more responsible for launching the war than Iran or Venezuela, which also reaped in windfall profits. That they did not launch the war does not mean that they would not try to benefit from it. 'If we go to war, it's not about oil,' said Larry Goldstein, president of the Petroleum Industry Research Foundation. 'But the day the war ends, it has everything to do with oil.'[22]

A second thesis maintains that the war was less 'about increasing the profits of Exxon' than 'about guaranteeing American hegemony'; less about access than about control.[23] For Noam Chomsky, controlling Iraq's vast oil reserves could enormously extend US strategic power over Europe and Asia.[24] For Michael Klare, the design for 'American world dominance' arises from two different sets of concerns: one energy driven, the other security driven. Controlling Iraq is for him about 'oil as power, rather than oil as fuel'; it 'translates into control over Europe, Japan, and China'.[25] David Harvey, using what he calls a 'historical-geographical materialist' approach, posits the war as a geopolitical inevitability.[26] It was the manifestation of a 'new imperialism' in which the logic of capital replaces the logic of territorial acquisition.[27]

However, in place of evidence, this thesis offers a deterministic view of US foreign policy that treats the war as a historical inevitability given the US interest in the region's resources. Chomsky, for example, adduces as evidence a 1945 State Department planning document that identifies Middle Eastern oil as 'a stupendous source of strategic power'. He cites a post-invasion article in which Zbigniew Brzezinski argued that US control over the Middle East 'gives it indirect but politically critical leverage on the European and Asian economies'.[28] This Chomsky finds is consistent with the conclusions of the post-World War II planner George

Kennan who 'recognized that control of the resources of the Gulf region would give the United States "veto power"'.[29]

What Chomsky overlooks, however, is that the State Department document in question is about Saudi Arabia, not Iraq; it prescribes friendly relations, not war.[30] It is also not clear how causation for a war in 2003 can be inferred from a document written in 1945. Chomsky also ignores the fact that neither Brzezinski nor Kennan supported the war. Brzezinski denounced the war as 'a historic, strategic, and moral calamity . . . driven by Manichean impulses and imperial hubris'.[31] Kennan saw it as a distraction from the fight against terrorism; it undermined the UN inspections regime.[32] Both noted its Israel-centric provenance.[33] They were not alone: among the figures most closely associated with Big Oil – Bush Sr., James Baker, Lawrence Eagleburger – none supported the war.

Chomsky has speculated that a post-invasion Iraq was to serve as 'an obedient client state' which would 'also house major US military bases'.[34] But Chomsky offers no evidence that the Bush Administration considered, much less planned for, a long-term presence. George Packer confirms that there was never a 'coherent postwar plan', because the people 'who mattered' – Rumsfeld, Wolfowitz and Feith – 'never intended to stay in Iraq'. Their plan was to 'turn it over to these [INC] exiles very quickly and let them deal with the messes that came up'.[35] Rumsfeld's 'shock and awe' did not contemplate a lengthy occupation: the large-scale military presence it would entail went against his vision of a sleek, hi-tech combat force. The official historian for the Iraq campaign Major Isaiah Wilson and the official Marine Corps historian Col. Nicholas Reynolds both confirm the absence of postwar plans.[36] The neoconservatives had wrested post-war planning from the State Department but had produced none of their own.[37] A briefing paper prepared for Tony Blair and his advisers for a 23 July 2002 meeting concluded that the US military was giving 'little thought' to what could be a 'protracted and costly' occupation or to 'the aftermath and how to shape it'.[38]

To the extent that oil factored in neoconservative calculations, it was mainly as a means to bring about the demise of OPEC, cut oil prices and weaken 'rogue states'.[39] The neo-conservatives were driven by 'the clearest vision for Iraqi oil', notes oil policy analyst Yahya Sadowski, to flood the market with it in order to drive prices to $15 a barrel or less. 'They hope that this collapse will stimulate economic growth in the US and the West, finally destroy OPEC, wreck the economies of "rogue states" (Iran, Syria, Libya), and create more opportunities for "regime change" and democratisation.'[40]

According to Sampson, many neoconservatives looked to 'a realignment of US foreign policy, to intervene in both Iran and Saudi Arabia, ensuring both the security of American oil supplies, and the security of Israel'. Iraqi oil would '[lessen] US dependence on Saudi Arabia' and thereby diminish its capacity to influence policies in Washington.[41] Wolfowitz, according to a *New York Times* profile, 'seems more pleased than not that democracy in Iraq (and a free flow of competing Iraqi oil) makes the Saudis uneasy', and is not averse to 'rocking the stability of tyrannies in the Arab world, even West-leaning tyrannies'.[42] But from a policy perspective, this made little sense since the US government would be jeopardising a reliable source of oil (Saudi Arabia) for a gamble whose outcome was at best uncertain. Low prices would also be detrimental to the interests of US domestic producers that extract at far higher costs.

The neoconservatives sold the war with the rosy prediction that its costs would not exceed $50–60 billion, part of which would be financed by other countries. But the rest of the government was less sanguine. Bush's economic adviser Lawrence Lindsey was banished from government after he suggested that the costs of war might reach $200 billion – an overly conservative estimate in retrospect. The State Department, the CIA, the Army War College's Strategic Studies Institute and the Pentagon's Energy Infrastructure Planning Group had all predicted post-war chaos and disruption.[43] The latter specifically warned that Iraq's decaying oil infrastructure would require years of repairs and billions in investment.[44] For conservative economist and Nobel laureate Gary Becker, 'if oil were the driving force behind the Bush Administration's hard line on Iraq, avoiding war would be the most appropriate policy'.[45]

Inferring oil as the war's presiding motive from the fact that

US forces showed extraordinary solicitude towards Iraq's energy infrastructure assumes that if the war was not for oil then the invaders would not care about it.[46] Gulf energy resources have always been a vital US interest. On no other occasion has the US had to occupy a country to secure them.[47] Regardless of why Iraq was invaded, it is reasonable to assume that an occupier would exploit rather than destroy its assets. Indeed, the neoconservatives used oil both as an incentive to get the energy industry onside and as a disincentive against dissent, threatening exclusion from future oil contracts. Oil may have played a part in the thinking of some policy makers – as Juan Cole argues it had in Dick Cheney's – but even Cole admits that Iraq was invaded only because the Israel lobby was blocking all other means of access to it.[48]

If oil were indeed the overriding concern, it is likelier that we would have US boots on Venezuelan ground. After all, nowhere were US interests more threatened than in Latin America, and few governments had a more provocative attitude towards the US than Hugo Chavez's. Yet, the US was able to do little when the Venezuelan government rewrote laws to claim 30 per cent (up from 16 per cent) of the oil profits for the national oil company.[49]

Much of the 'war for oil' speculation is driven by unfamiliarity with long-standing US policy. Inherently imperial, the policy has historically privileged stability over democracy and human rights. It has asserted the right to use 'any means necessary, including military force' should US vital interests – that is, stable access to oil – be at risk.[50] It informed the 1991 Gulf intervention. In the lead-up to the 2003 invasion, many 'war for oil' sleuths took routine statements of the doctrine in official documents as confirmation of the oil motive. There was much excitement when it was reported in the press that according to a Baker Institute for Public Policy report presented to the White House Energy Policy Development Group[51] (Cheney's infamous Energy Task Force), the Bush cabinet had 'agreed in April 2001 that "Iraq remains a destabilizing influence to the flow of oil to international markets from the Middle East" and because this is an unacceptable risk to the US "military intervention" is necessary'.[52]

However, there is only one reference to 'military intervention' in the report, and it is in relation to a hypothetical scenario unrelated to Iraq where it *may* become necessary to use force. This is a mere reiteration of the Carter Doctrine which stressed that the US would use 'any means necessary, including military force' to protect its 'vital interests' in the Persian Gulf.[53] But whereas Carter had emphasised conservation, Cheney stressed force and alternative sources of supply, particularly in West Africa and the Caspian.[54]

A report prepared for the Joint Chiefs of Staff by the Institute for National Strategic Studies (part of the National Defense University) was similarly used as proof of 'war for oil'. The report forecast that in the event of a disruption of energy supplies, 'US forces might be used to ensure adequate supplies'. This is a mere reiteration of the Carter Doctrine with no specific reference to Iraq.[55] The same report also warns that 'if the great powers return to the 19th century approach of securing resources and conquering suppliers, the world economy will suffer and world politics will become more tense'.[56]

The doctrine was first promulgated during Jimmy Carter's 1980 State of the Union Address in response to the Soviet invasion of Afghanistan (partly also to deflect accusations of weakness due to the hostage crisis in Iran).[57] The key line of the speech in which Carter outlined his doctrine was written by his National Security Advisor Zbigniew Brzezinski, later a leading opponent of the Iraq war. The war was also opposed by Brent Scowcroft, the National Security Advisor to Bush *père*, one of the main architects of the 1991 Gulf War, a textbook application of the Carter Doctrine.

Free markets

The obvious limits of 'war for oil' have led some analysts to aver that the war was 'bigger than oil'; it was an attempt to forcibly impose free-market capitalism on Iraq.[58] Naomi Klein, for example, sees the war as another instance of the 'Shock Doctrine', a new and frightful variation on Schumpeter's notion of 'creative destruction', which exploits the trauma of war to force free-market reforms on a disoriented polity.[59] Iraq exemplifies 'a careful and faithful application of unrestrained Chicago School ideology', which presupposes 'ferocious violence' for the implementation of its radical economic agenda.[60]

Like 'war for oil', this mode of analysis ignores the policy process. For these analysts, the state is no more than the ruling class's 'instrument for the domination of society' by virtue of the economic power conferred upon it by its ownership and control of the means of production.[61] It overlooks specific geopolitical concerns, which, as previously noted, are not always congruent with corporate interests. Political theorist Stephen Holmes observes:

> If [Cheney] followed any example in his dim plans for post-invasion Iraq, it was not Milton Friedman's but Ariel Sharon's. No one would suggest that Sharon aimed to 'redeem' the Palestinians or create a model market society in the West Bank and Gaza. What he aimed for, and achieved, was managed anarchy: a weak, internally divided and festering society unable to project power outwards but susceptible to periodic violent intrusions. Free-market orthodoxy was not on Sharon's mind, or on Cheney's either.[62]

Not all imperial projects are about economic predation: some simply aim to destroy political enemies. Chicago School ideology was certainly ascendant in the aftermath of the invasion, but there is no evidence that it played any part in the deliberations over war.

Beyond short-term gains for a few businesses, the war proved a disaster for the world capitalist system. Joseph Stiglitz and Linda Bilmes note that since the war was waged mostly on credit, the world will be paying the price for years to come.[63] The 'national chauvinism' and 'limitless ambition' of the Bush Administration, Lieven argues, only compromised 'the security and stability of the world capitalist system of which America is the custodian and greatest beneficiary. [They] have been irresponsible and dangerous not in Marxist terms, but in their own. They have offended against the Capitalist Peace.'[64] In 2006, Bechtel had already cut its losses and bailed out;[65] by 2009, Blackwater was also forced out.[66] Today US companies hold mainly subcontracting positions.

Hegemony and Dominance

If the war was driven by US geopolitical concerns, then it had few supporters in the US foreign policy establishment. Prominent geo-strategists like Zbigniew Brzezinski and Brent Scowcroft foresaw the invasion as undermining US strategic interests.[67] Brzezinski worried that the war would weaken US alliance with Western Europe, the 'anchor point of America's engagement in the world', leaving NATO unity in 'real jeopardy'. At no point, said Brzezinski, has the US been 'so isolated in the modern era'. Despite unparalleled military power, he warned, the US is 'not capable of simply dictating to the entire world'.[68] The Western European foreign policy establishment also echoed his concerns.[69] Scowcroft, the National Security Advisor under Bush *père* and chairman of the Presidential Foreign Intelligence Advisory Board (PFIAB) under Bush *fils*, used an op-ed in the *Wall Street Journal* to bluntly warn Bush: 'Don't attack Saddam'.[70] Reservations were also expressed by such titans of realpolitik as former Republican secretaries of state James Baker and Lawrence Eagleburger.[71] By far the most notable sceptic was Bush's own father who, while publicly avoiding confrontation with his son, encouraged Colin Powell, Brent Scowcroft and former Ambassador Joseph Wilson to resist the push to war.[72]

There was scepticism in Congress too. On 4 September 2002, when Bush convened a meeting of Congressional leaders to rally support for the war, both the Senate Majority Leader Tom Daschle, a Democrat, and House Majority Leader Dick Armey, a Republican, voiced reservations.[73]

The war also found little support among the realist intelligentsia. Thirty-three leading lights of the realist school – including such names as Thomas Schelling, John Mearsheimer, Stephen Walt, Robert Pape, Robert Jervis, Barry Posen and Stephen Van Evera – took out an ad in *The New York Times* on 26 September 2002 with the headline 'War with Iraq is not in America's national interest'. (Ironically, Donald Rumsfeld in his memoir would cite Schelling as one of his major intellectual influences.) Many of the same individuals would later form the Coalition for a Realistic Foreign Policy to check the administration's 'dangerous direction toward empire'.[74] Diplomats also opposed the war. Three US ambassadors – Ann Wright, Joseph Wilson and John Brady Kiesling – resigned in protest.[75]

The intelligence agencies were not keen on the war either. Many senior officers made attempts to impede the march to war. The head of the CIA George Tenet was more enabler than instigator.[76] Many senior US military officers also opposed the invasion. Among these, noted *The Washington Post*'s respected military correspondent Thomas Ricks, were 'some top generals and admirals in the military establishment, including members of the Joint Chiefs of Staff'. They favoured containment. In their view there was 'no evidence of an Iraqi intent to work with terrorists to attack the United States'.[77] Three former heads of the US Central Command (CENTCOM) – Gen. Anthony Zinni, Gen. Norman Schwarzkopf and Gen. Joseph Hoar – also opposed the war. Equally sceptical were two former NATO allied supreme commanders, Gen. Wesley Clark and Gen. James Jones. Even Gen. Merrill McPeak, the executor of the savage 1991 bombing campaign against Iraq, questioned its wisdom.[78] The former commander of US forces in Europe Gen. Frederick Kroesen warned that the 'campaign based on hope' would lead to a disastrous occupation.[79]

Other opponents included former secretary of the US Navy James Webb.[80] The then chairman of the Joint Chiefs of Staff Gen. Hugh Shelton had riled administration hawks by opposing action against Iraq at the crucial 15 September 2001 meeting at Camp David; a year later, he was still warning that the war would undermine the fight against terrorism.[81] He was replaced by the pliant Gen. Richard Myers.[82] Gen. Shinseki was expelled after he contradicted the Pentagon civilians' optimistic assessment of the scale of deployment necessary for the operation. The future head of the Joint Special Operations Command Gen. Stanley McChrystal also opposed the war. Military professionals spent the months leading up to the invasion urging caution in their publications;[83] by January 2003, *Time* could report that 'one officer estimates that as many as 1 in 3 senior officers questions the wisdom of a pre-emptive war with Iraq' and that according to one Pentagon official, there were 'hundreds of one-star generals and action officers who complain that Rumsfeld's not listening to the military'.[84]

If the war was being waged to advance US imperial interests, then it had remarkably few supporters among the traditional advocates of American primacy.

Military–industrial complex

Another popular theory maintains that the war in Iraq was waged at the behest of the Military–Industrial Complex (MIC). The MIC welcomed the war and no doubt benefited from it. It certainly egged on the war; but there is little evidence that it instigated it. Those who argue that the war was waged on behalf of the MIC infer its role from the inevitable profits that accrued to military contractors like SAIC and Lockheed Martin. But the MIC has been able to generate profits without actually needing a war. Its ability to secure new contracts was in no way diminished between the two Gulf Wars. The biggest boost to its profits came during the 1980s, courtesy of the Fulda Gap – a *potential* vulnerability in central Europe – rather than an actual war. The kind of money that is involved in hi-tech projects like the Strategic Defence Initiative and the RMA cannot be expected to be made from the mass production of body armour and assault rifles – the kind of equipment that an occupation mainly needs. The desire to make profits and invent new enemies, writes Anatol Lieven, is 'not the same, however, as having an actual desire for war, least of all for a major conflict which might ruin the international economy'.[85] If Iraq appeared like a 'doable' target, then an air campaign augmented by sophisticated surface-to-surface missile attacks *à la* Gulf '91 would have presented greater opportunities for profit making.

The case also fails on empirical grounds; it leaves unstated the question of agency. To the extent that evidence of lobbying is offered, it points to neoconservative think tanks such as PNAC, Centre for Security Policy (CSP) and the Jewish Institute for National Security Affairs (JINSA).[86] To be sure, a bevy of retired generals with links to arms manufacturers did parade on prime-time US television to promote the war.[87] But they were merely cheerleading a venture others had conceived.

Might the war have been waged to secure permanent military bases in the region? The most notable proponent of this thesis is the late political scientist Chalmers Johnson who in his *Blowback Trilogy* argued that the new unit of empire was no longer the colony but a military base – and that the imperial tendencies of the US were evident in its quest for new bases in regions where its material interests were at stake.[88] This thesis is broadly true, but most of these bases have been acquired through agreements with host governments. In the case of Iraq, Johnson acknowledged the role of oil, electoral politics *and* the Israel lobby in fomenting the Iraq war.[89] But he insisted that the 'more encompassing explanation' for the war was 'the inexorable pressures of imperialism and militarism'.[90] Yet his argument was qualified and at times contradictory.

If the war's aim was to secure permanent military bases, Johnson did not say why the US would jeopardise its existing secure base in Saudi Arabia to opt for a venture whose outcome was at best uncertain (recall that the administration neoconservatives had made openly anti-Saudi statements in the lead-up to war).[91] Johnson provides a comprehensive history of base acquisitions by the US in the Gulf region as part of a trend that explains the US intervention in Iraq. However, his evidence shows that all the bases in the region have been established through a consensual arrangement with the host government. Indeed, in some instances, as in the case of Qatar and Oman, the host countries actively vied for US troop presence. Many of them fear a distant hegemon less than a neighbouring foe. Moreover, wherever they have chosen to do so, the host countries have not found it hard to dislodge US bases (as in the case of the Prince Sultan Air Base in Saudi Arabia or Camp Snoopy in Qatar). It is not clear why the US – which, according to Johnson, 'always understood that the presence of our forces in Saudi Arabia was a root-cause of al-Qaeda's terrorist activities' – would want to vacate an existing base in a friendly country to seek more in another where it had every reason to expect hostility.[92] Though US interest in the region's oil is indisputable, Johnson acknowledges that 'the carrier task forces that have already turned the Persian Gulf into an American lake would be sufficient to protect those interests'.[93]

Indeed, the only arguments made in favour of military repositioning ostensibly to secure the region's oil came from the neoconservatives. Making the case for 'a major concentration of forces in the Middle East over a long period of time', Donald Kagan, father of neoconservative luminaries Robert and Frederick Kagan and co-founder of PNAC, averred that if there were US forces in Iraq, 'there will be no disruption in oil supplies'.[94] In a May 2003 interview, Wolfowitz presented the relocation of bases from Saudi Arabia to Iraq as an *ex post facto* justification for the war.[95] But if this was the plan, then the military was in the dark. They also knew that having a base is no guarantee that they would be allowed to use it in the manner they chose; in most cases, they have to remain subject to the host country's sensitivities. That is why the US was able to use neither Incirlik in Turkey nor the Prince Sultan airbase in Saudi Arabia for its invasion of Iraq. In the end, for all the fear-mongering about permanent US bases, even the otherwise pliant government of Nouri al-Maliki was forced by constituents and allies, mostly notably the Sadrist block, into demanding the complete withdrawal of US troops.[96]

Conclusion

Many, indeed all, of these concerns played some part in the thinking of key decision makers; but as we have seen, these were not the determinants of the Iraq war policy. Neither was it 'democracy promotion'. As noted earlier, Rice and Rumsfeld both reject the notion that the war had anything to do with democracy promotion. According to Rumsfeld, it was a functional dodge and Bush's democratisation rhetoric was merely echoing the views of Natan Sharansky, a far-right cabinet minister in Ariel Sharon's Likud government.[97] A proponent of the expulsion of Palestinians from their ancestral homes, and considered an obstructionist even by Ariel Sharon, Sharansky makes an unlikely candidate for democratic idealist. So does the neoconservatives' 'idealist-in-chief', Paul Wolfowitz. In the lead-up to the war, Wolfowitz went so far as to rebuke the Turkish military for refusing to overrule a civilian government that, responding to near unanimous public opinion, had declined an American request for the use of its territory for the attack against Iraq.[98]

In order to fix the agency for the war, one has to look at the origins, institutional architecture and ideological make-up of its key proponents. The following, the first of two chapters on the neoconservatives, is an analysis of the origins of the movement, the interests that animate their politics, and the institutions that have helped amplify their power despite their limited numbers.

Part 2 The Rise of the Neoconservatives

2 Origins and Interests

Decisions of state in modern democracies are rarely free from the influence of interest groups. The right to lobby is every citizen's prerogative in a functioning democracy, but no democracy guarantees a level playing field. Research shows that the success of lobby groups is commensurate with the amount of money they spend.[1] No less important is their capacity to work the shadows. 'A lobby is like a night flower,' said one former executive of the pro-Israel lobby group AIPAC, 'it thrives in the dark and dies in the sun.'[2] Visibility often constrains lobbyists' capacity to influence, especially if their demands are in overt conflict with public opinion. Lobbyists may therefore strive to redefine public interest to match their own: they invest in 'experts' who favour their point of view, or populate key government advisory or policy positions with allies.[3] If the neoconservatives were able to successfully appropriate the resources of state and instrumentalise its authority in the lead-up to the war, it was because their power was undergirded by institutional support, ideological momentum and historical contingency. Chief among the institutional forces were the corporate rich, the MIC and the Israel lobby; ideologically, they were aided by the Cold War and the 'war on terror'; and historically, they rode the waves of a new militarised humanitarianism.

This chapter explores the relationship between neoconservatism and neoliberalism. It traces the evolution of neoconservatism from its modest origins as an eccentric intellectual formation to a political force of global consequence. It highlights the role that the Nazi Holocaust and Israel play in shaping the neoconservative worldview. It examines the relationship between the neoconservatives and the MIC and the role it played in elevating the small group of ideologues from the margins of US politics to the heart of the national security establishment. The measure of neoconservatives' capacity to influence policy in the wake of 9/11 can only be taken by understanding the interests that drive them and the institutions that have nurtured them.

Neoconservatives and neoliberals

In a 1979 convocation address at McMaster University, Canadian media mogul Conrad Black lamented that the ravages of capitalism had for over a century driven intellectuals into the arms of socialism. 'Because intellectuals do dominate the power of the word,' he continued,

> the conservative philosophy of capitalism has made a very poor showing in the recent history of ideas. Businessmen largely have been unable or unwilling to defend themselves with words; and even when they tried, they have tended to bellow ultra-right clichés like wounded dinosaurs, much to the amusement of the intellectual left . . . The truth is that until recently conservative ideas were so poorly articulated that they simply were not taken seriously.[4]

But 'a development of great significance' was taking place, he noted: 'the left is being challenged by a group of right-wing thinkers, who have been labelled neo-conservatives because in many instances they are retreaded leftists.' As with academics and journalists, he noted, 'the conservatives now have intellectual credentials as impeccable as any on the left'.[5] Business always had economic power; it now had its myth makers.

Neoliberalism

Given the complementary relationship between business and neo-conservatism, the terms 'neoliberal' and 'neoconservative' are often used interchangeably.[6] The two constitute distinct political rationalities, even if their relationship is characterised more by concert than conflict. Political scientist Wendy Brown has distinguished neoconservatism as a 'moral-political rationality', as opposed to the 'market-political rationality' of neoliberalism.[7] The dominant strains of both political movements favour concentration of executive authority – neoliberals in a market state and neoconservatives in a national security state. Both thrive in an environment where governmental regulations are weak and inherently governmental functions are privatised. However, where neoliberals disdain social welfare programmes, neoconservatives remain ambivalent. Many first-generation neoconservatives were committed New Dealers. On the other hand, if neoliberalism celebrates individual rights and freedom of choice, neoconservatism envisions an intrusive state upholding public security and traditional morality.[8] Against the individualist *anarchy* on which neoliberalism thrives, neoconservatism seeks to restore *hierarchy* and authority.[9] Both seek global hegemony but for neoliberals the preferred means are multilateral institutions such as the International Monetary Fund, World Trade Organization and World Bank, and for the neoconservatives the barrel of an American gun.[10]

Neoliberalism has no canonical set of fixed doctrines, but it has converged over time on a shared political philosophy and a worldview.[11] As defined by David Harvey, it is 'a theory of political economic practices proposing that human well-being can best be advanced by the maximization of entrepreneurial freedoms within an institutional framework characterized by private property rights, individual liberty, unencumbered markets, and free trade'.[12]

The state's role in this system is to facilitate such practices by ensuring the quality of money, securing property rights, supporting functioning markets and creating markets where they do not exist. Beyond these tasks, neoliberalism envisages no role for the state and often sees it as a hindrance.[13]

Sociologists Mirowski and Plehwe see neoliberalism as a constructivist project that encompasses a plurality of philosophical and political tendencies. The Austrian School (Hayek, Mises, et al.) seeks to ground markets, as self-regulating engines of freedom and ingenuity in a purely rationalist version of natural necessity; the German/Swiss ordoliberals want the state to directly organise competition within a well-functioning market; and the Chicago School seeks to reconcile a version of neoclassical economic theory with a conception of state with concentrated executive power, diminished regulatory authority and privatised governmental functions.[14] (In contrast to classical liberalism's emphasis on competition, the Chicago School disdains anti-trust laws, preferring monopolies to 'big government'.) In the Anglo-Saxon world, the Chicago School backed by corporate power has eclipsed other tendencies. Friedmanite pragmatists have displaced Hayekian romanticists.[15]

The origins of neoliberalism can be traced back to the first meeting of the Mont Pelerin Society (MPS) on 1 April 1947, when, fresh from the success of his influential tract *The Road to Serfdom* (1944), Austrian economist Friedrich von Hayek convened a gathering of philosophers, historians and economists to devise a strategy for countering the prevailing Keynesian consensus (or 'creeping collectivism', as Hayek described it). Hayek claimed that the group's aim was to facilitate the 'exchange of views', to 'contribute to the preservation and improvement of the free society'. MPS members consciously avoided overt propaganda or political action. But this transnational 'thought collective' was at the centre of an 'elaborate social machinery designed to collect, create, debate, disseminate, and mobilize neoliberal ideas'. At its core were economists and philosophers at universities surrounded by expanding layers of special-purpose foundations, think tanks, letterhead organisations and astroturf (fake grassroots) organisations.[16] Over the next decades, with the backing of wealthy financiers, they would undertake a massive campaign to turn opinion against the Keynesian consensus using pressure groups, specialist foundations and think tanks. The University of Chicago and the London School of Economics became its intellectual hubs; and AEI, Brookings and the Heritage Foundation (and in Britain the Institute of Economic Affairs) its marketers.[17]

The Keynesian consensus collapsed amid the post-Vietnam War global recession and the Arab oil embargo.[18] Inflation and unemployment ('stagflation') had soared in the early 1970s, and labour and urban social movements across the West had been calling for reform and state intervention. An alarmed corporate elite moved to pre-empt more radical alternatives.[19] In a 1971 memo written for the US Chamber of Commerce, Lewis Powell, who would soon be appointed to the Supreme Court, urged business to 'buy the top academic reputations in the country to add credibility to corporate studies and give business a stronger voice on the campuses'.[20] A year later business pooled its resources to found the Business Roundtable (BRT), comprising 194 CEOs of the largest US corporations with a combined GNP greater than that of any other country in the world.[21] With the free-market ideologues providing intellectual legitimacy and with neoliberal think tanks marketing their ideas, the corporate elites launched one of the most successful propaganda campaigns in history that effectively turned the intellectual tide in favour of neoliberalism by 1976. Keynes yielded to Hayek, and neoliberal ideologues abandoned the fringes to occupy influential positions in education, media, policy, corporate boardrooms, financial institutions, key state bureaucracies (treasury departments, central banks), and multilateral institutions regulating global finance and commerce.[22]

Neoliberalism's greatest success was in restoring class power. But inequality is not its only consequence. The technocratic, managerial form of government it fosters relies on a passive, disempowered citizenry; it attacks public services and social welfare; it de-politicises class and disdains political autonomy. Its consolidation of media undermines freedom of the press and its amoral economic rationality contributes to cultural decline. Its utilitarian conception of law, stripped of moral legitimacy, creates the ground for its routine suspension. Political rights are subordinated to individual rights.[23] The resulting social fragmentation creates a new susceptibility for associations around identity and creed. It also creates a climate uniquely favourable to the rise of anti-Democratic statism.[24] Enter the neoconservatives.

Neoconservatism

Political scientist Michael Harrington derisively bestowed the label 'neoconservative' on a group of former Trotskyist radicals who had turned to the right to lead the Cold War anti-communist crusade.[25] The movement had its origins in the political convolutions of the 1930s Jewish émigré intellectual scene in New York, comprising figures such as Max Shachtman, Sidney Hook, James Burnham, Irving Kristol and Irving Howe. In the years following World War II, their radical anti-Stalinism gave way to liberal anti-communism. The Congress for Cultural Freedom – a CIA-funded operation engaged in culture war against the Soviet bloc – helped the neoconservatives develop the networks and political alliances that would later be used to battle domestic rivals.[26] By the end of the Vietnam War, the neoconservatives finally abandoned liberalism for 'neo'-conservatism.[27] They were alarmed by the rise of the New Left. Electoral reforms had diminished their influence in the Democratic Party and led to the rise of anti-war figures like George McGovern. They disparaged the anti-war sentiment as 'isolationism', its proponents as 'McGovernites', and defected in droves to join the Republican Party.[28]

The neoconservative movement, according to Heilbrunn, is best understood 'as an extended family based largely on the informal social networks patiently forged by [its] two patriarchs [Irving Kristol and Norman Podhoretz]'.[29] This social cohesion has also facilitated their quick rise in the national security establishment.[30] The neoconservatives have compensated for their meagre numbers by forming strategic alliances with various formations on the right. They made common cause with social conservatives and the Christian Right against the counterculture movement; with business entrepreneurs against Lyndon Johnson's Great Society programme; with aggressive nationalists against Kissinger and Nixon's détente; with weapons manufacturers against arms reduction treaties. They succeeded in establishing themselves as the 'intellectual light brigade' of what Blumenthal calls the Counter-Establishment.

Irving Kristol – often identified as the 'godfather' of the movement – described neoconservatism as a 'persuasion' rather than a 'movement' (which presupposes a significant following). The neoconservatives' success derives from joining a larger movement whose concerns broadly complement their own allowing them to use their intellectual authority to channel its currents. For Kristol, 'the historical task and political purpose of neoconservatism' has been 'to convert the Republican Party, and American conservatism in general, against their respective wills, into a new kind of conservative politics suitable to governing a modern democracy'. This conversion includes a rejection of the conservative scepticism of strong government and the 'Hayekian notion that we are on "the road to serfdom"'. Kristol adds: 'Neocons do not feel that kind of alarm or anxiety about the growth of the state in the past century, seeing it as natural, indeed inevitable'; they 'tend to be more interested in history than economics or sociology'. Kristol therefore finds the ideas propounded by libertarian anti-imperialist Herbert Spencer in his *The Man Versus the State* 'a historical eccentricity'.[31]

Neoconservatives also eschew traditional 'balanced-budget' conservative economics in favour of cutting tax rates 'to stimulate steady economic growth' and 'an attitude toward public finance that is far less risk averse than is the case among more traditional conservatives'. Though the neoconservatives count Democrat Franklin Roosevelt among their twentieth-century heroes, they pointedly spurn the Republican Dwight Eisenhower.[32]

The neoconservatives are also set apart from traditional conservatism by geography. Where most traditional conservatives are from Southern or Midwestern states, the neoconservatives with few exceptions all come from the northeast, particularly New York. Neoconservative publicist Adam Bellow uses geography to distinguish 'New York conservatives from the zealous "movement" types down in Washington' whom the neocons 'instinctively hold ... at arm's length, regarding them as not just a different branch of the movement but a different species altogether'.[33]

Still, the neoconservatives find common ground with traditional conservatives. Both decry what Kristol calls the 'steady decline in our democratic culture, sinking to new levels of vulgarity'. This puts the neoconservatives in synch with 'religious traditionalists' and 'since the Republican Party now has a substantial base among the religious, this gives neocons a certain influence and even power'. The neoconservatives also share traditional conservatives' disdain for international institutions; however, they reject what they deride as 'isolationism' and advocate an interventionist foreign policy. The neoconservatives emphasise military superiority, but unlike traditional conservatives, they are not abashed in advocating its offensive use. 'With power come responsibilities', writes Kristol, '[a]nd it is a fact that if you have the kind of power we now have, either you will find opportunities to use it, or the world will discover them for you.'[34]

Historian Tony Judt characterises neoconservatism as 'a practice in search of its theory'. It presents little in the way of a coherent ideology.[35] Joe Klein is dismissive of the neoconservatives' idealist self-image: neoconservatism in foreign policy, he writes, 'is best described as unilateral bellicosity cloaked in the utopian rhetoric of freedom and democracy'.[36]

The neoconservatives' political journey, writes Blumenthal, cannot be explained 'simply by reference to a calibrated ideological scale':

> Although they are frequently inclined to the formulaic, they are less coherent as an intellectual movement than a social group. Some are welfare-statists, others are free-marketeers; some proclaim the moral mission of America in global terms, others urge hardheaded realpolitik. What really binds them together is their common experience.[37]

Though neoconservatism originated as an intellectual phenomenon, by the mid-1990s, it was already being pronounced an anachronism.[38] Neoconservatism, the political phenomenon, however, was on the cusp of its greatest triumph. Since the 1970s, it had been building a formidable capacity to mobilise and coordinate the resources of a vast political infrastructure that included a network of foundations, think tanks, journals, friendly editors and well-placed individuals in the executive branch. Irving Kristol epitomised these interlocking and overlapping relationships. Blumenthal notes:

> His positions as co-editor of *The Public Interest*, professor at New York University, columnist for the *Wall Street Journal*, board member of five corporations, and senior fellow of the American Enterprise Institute merely hint at his activity. 'I raise money for conservative think tanks. I am a liaison to some degree between intellectuals and the business community,' he claimed modestly.[39]

Kristol embarked on his journey by reminding businessmen the limits of 'thinking economically' and urging them to learn the long-term benefits of 'thinking politically'. In his own words:

We had to tell businessmen that they needed us. They are still not convinced . . . The neoconservatives, the Republican politicians, and the business community do not make an easy mixture . . . But at least they mix, whereas they used not to mix at all. Business understands the need for intellectuals much more than trade unionists understand it, but not enough. Basically, it wants intellectuals to go out and justify profits and explain to people why corporations make a lot of money.[40]

Business obliged, and neoconservatives soon came to dominate conservative think tanks, such as the AEI and the Heritage Foundation, besides establishing their own, such as the Institute for Educational Affairs, which Kristol co-founded with William Simon.[41] Kristol also encouraged and promoted the work of Jude Wanniski, who had written 'The Mundell–Laffer Hypothesis' for *The Public Interest*, an article which for the first time spelled out the framework for supply-side economics – the macroeconomic theory that holds that economic growth is best spurred by lowering taxes and reducing regulation, which will benefit consumers with a greater supply of goods and services at lower prices.[42] Kristol had used his acquaintance with Randolph Richardson, heir to the Vicks VapoRub fortune, to secure a job for a young neoconservative, Leslie Lenkowsky, as chief programme officer of the Smith Richardson Foundation, responsible for dispensing yearly grants of about $3 million. Kristol helped Wanniski secure Lenkowsky's first grant and helped secure a berth for him at AEI as a 'resident journalist' to expand his ideas into a book. 'I was not certain of its economic merits,' writes Kristol, 'but quickly saw its political possibilities.'[43] At Kristol's urging, Wanniski tutored Congressman Jack Kemp who codified his ideas into the Kemp-Roth Bill. Kemp in turn facilitated Wanniski's appointment as an adviser to Ronald Reagan during the 1980 presidential campaign. For Wanniski, Kristol was 'the invisible hand'.[44]

The neoconservatives helped business entrepreneurs harness the political power of the Republican Party, and helped the Republican

Party capture the popular base of the largely white working-class voters. Disaffected, insecure and alienated, the white working class was especially susceptible to the neoconservative appeals to 'tradition', 'values' and 'national greatness'.[45] They were successful, writes Lieven, in combining

> both the civic nationalist belief in America's mission to lead the rest of the world towards democracy and freedom, and the chauvinist nationalist celebration of America's military might (and even brutality), and intense hostility to rivals and critics of the US.[46]

This political base, writes Harvey,

> could be mobilized through the positives of religion and cultural nationalism and negatively through coded, if not blatant, racism, homophobia, and anti-feminism. The problem was not capitalism and the neoliberalisation of culture, but the 'liberals' who had used excessive state power to provide for special groups (blacks, women, environmentalists, etc.).[47]

Tradition, religion and deference to authority would henceforth shield against 'the moral permissiveness' of the increasingly ungovernable individualist society. It would restore 'a sense of moral purpose, some higher-order values that will form the stable centre of the body politic'.[48] The GOP – the party of big business – was thus turned into a sanctuary of 'heartland American values'.[49]

The neoconservatives had emerged as the intellectual strata of big business, but none among its core were economists. Many were committed social democrats (including Daniel Bell, Allan Bloom and Henry 'Scoop' Jackson).[50] 'In economic and social policy', Kristol writes,

> [neoconservatism] feels no lingering hostility to the welfare state . . . it seeks not to dismantle the welfare state in the name of free-market economics but rather to reshape it so as to attach to it the conservative predispositions of the people.[51]

His son, William Kristol, echoes the same sentiment. He told the BBC: 'I'm much more interested in liberty and democracy than I am in capitalism. I was once a social democrat . . . social democracy is fine. It's about freedom and democracy. It's not about capitalism.'[52]

The neoconservative alliance with business was pragmatic, not ideological. They exploited the fissures between the corporate managers, the CEOs represented by the BRT, who cherish stability and avoid risk taking – and the new men of money, the entrepreneurs who came to prominence with Nixon and Reagan, who envied and resented the caste superiority and inherited entitlements of the 'establishment'.[53] Unlike the CEOs, who are keener to cultivate long-term, stable relationships, the entrepreneurs thrive on the opportunities that arise from crises. They became the neoconservatives' natural allies.

Kristol admitted that his discontent with social democracy and liberalism had 'absolutely nothing to do with economics, of which I was perfectly ignorant. It did have to do with foreign policy, where I was, on general principles, a "realist" to the core.'[54]

Kristol admits that 'there is no set of neoconservative beliefs concerning foreign policy, only a set of attitudes derived from historical experience'.[55] But despite his realist disposition, Kristol rejects the 'defensive' usage of 'national interest' as a geographical term – only a 'smaller nation' would do that. Great powers have 'ideological interests in addition to more material concerns', and 'complicated geopolitical calculations of national interest' should not prevent them from coming to the defence of 'a democratic nation under attack from nondemocratic forces'. That is why, he writes, 'we feel it necessary to defend Israel today, when its survival is threatened'.[56]

In his generous reading, Bacevich draws on Podhoretz to summarise the essence of neoconservatism in six propositions. They include: (1) a theory of history based in the events of the 1930s and the legacy of the Holocaust which serves as a parable for present times; (2) a preference for the use of military force; (3) a messianic view of the American role in the world; (4) a focus on 'traditional values' and appreciation for authority; (5) a capacity to see crisis as a permanent condition and the alternatives as stark, requiring urgent and decisive action; and (6) the faith in strong leadership as the antidote to crisis, exhibited in men such as Winston Churchill, Ronald Reagan and George W. Bush.[57] Irwin Stelzer sums up the neoconservative approach as 'diplomacy if possible, force if necessary; the UN if possible, ad hoc coalitions or unilateral action if necessary; pre-emptive strikes if it is reasonable to anticipate hostile action on the part of America's enemies'.[58]

Putative neoconservative principles serve as a system of justification and legitimation and are often discarded when they come into conflict with concrete political objectives.[59] The idealist image is functional. Neoconservatives have happily accepted the traditional conservatives' dismissal of them as 'liberal internationalists' even though they share none of the liberal internationalists' preference for multilateral institutions.[60] They were likewise bothered by the internationalism of the New Left because it called for cuts in military spending and an end to foreign interventions. Norman Podhoretz summed up neoconservative fears thus: it is a 'fact', he said,

> that continued American support for Israel depended upon continued American involvement in international affairs – from which it followed that an American withdrawal into the kind of isolationist mood that had prevailed most recently between the two world wars, and that now looked as though it might soon prevail again, represented a direct threat to the security of Israel.[61]

Murray Friedman notes that with Podhoretz's intensifying sense of his own Jewishness, *Commentary* articles 'came to emphasize threats to Jews and the safety and security of the Jewish state. By the 1980s, nearly half of Podhoretz's writings on international affairs centered on Israel and these dangers.'[62] Political scientist Benjamin Ginsberg observes:

> In the Reaganite right's hard-line anti-communism, commitment to American military strength, and willingness to intervene politically and militarily in the affairs of other nations to promote democratic values (and American interests), neocons found a political movement that would guarantee Israel's security.[63]

Neoconservatism and Israel

Following the Iraq debacle, some neoconservatives disowned the 'neoconservative' label. Some declared it anti-Semitic.[64] To pre-empt the anticipated abuse, critics have been reluctant to point up the Jewish origins of neoconservatism. In his acclaimed biography of the movement, Justin Vaïsse finds 'unconvincing' the idea that 'neoconservatism is "in essence" a Jewish movement' because 'many of the most prominent neoconservatives are not Jewish, and the overwhelming majority of American Jews are not neoconservatives'.[65] Vaïsse is partially right. It is true that neoconservatism is a minority flavour among American Jews – but the neoconservative core is exclusively Jewish.

A Jewish movement

For the former American Jewish Committee official Murray Friedman, neoconservatism is an essentially Jewish phenomenon; historian Peter Novick sees it as 'almost exclusively a Jewish affair'; British neoconservative Melanie Phillips as a 'quintessentially Jewish project'.[66] Most neoconservatives, notes Blumenthal, 'are second-generation Jews, torn between cultures . . . They are a minority within a minority in one city: neoconservatives among conservatives, conservative Jews among liberal Jews, and parochial New Yorkers.'[67] Goldberg describes them as 'an anomaly: a school of thought dominated by Jews on the American right which had always been alien territory to Jews'.[68] 'If there is an intellectual movement in America to whose invention Jews can lay sole claim,' writes Gal Beckerman in the Jewish daily *Forward*, 'neoconservatism is it.'[69] '[H]owever much they may deny it,' writes Heilbrunn, another alumnus, 'neoconservatism is in a decisive respect a Jewish phenomenon, reflecting a subset of Jewish concerns.'[70] The American Jewish Committee publishes the movement's flagship journal, *Commentary*.

Neoconservatism, writes Heilbrunn, 'is as much a reflection of Jewish immigrant social resentments and status anxiety as a legitimate movement of ideas. It is a 'mindset', rather than an ideology – one that has been 'decisively shaped by the Jewish immigrant experience, by the Holocaust, and by the twentieth century struggle against totalitarianism'.[71] For Weiss, they are 'propelled by resentments against WASP elites – the men who had ignored the Holocaust, they felt, and "frozen out" Jews from the establishment'.[72] Social exclusion was a key factor in shaping the thinking of first-generation neoconservatives.[73]

To be sure, the movement has attracted gentiles: Jeane Kirkpatrick, Daniel Patrick Moynihan, Francis Fukuyama and Zalmay Khalilzad are but the most prominent. It has also found influential patrons in Henry Jackson and Dick Cheney (of the two, only Jackson fully accepted neoconservative ideology); and allies in the likes of Samuel Huntington. But none of these figures is part of the socially cohesive neoconservative core. Both Jackson and Cheney were influenced in their views on foreign policy by the neoconservatives, rather than the other way around. The neoconservatives' implacable militarism and inability to distinguish Israeli interests from those of the US eventually led to the defection of non-Jewish neoconservatives such as Moynihan and Fukuyama. Moynihan complained that the neoconservatives 'wished for a military posture approaching mobilisation' and 'would create or invent whatever crises were required to bring this about'.[74] Both Fuykuyama and Huntington opposed the 2003 war (Fukuyama was in turn branded an anti-Semite by Charles Krauthammer for allegedly suggesting that the neoconservatives were placing Israeli security over US interests).[75]

The Holocaust and neoconservative memory

Journalist Jim Lobe points to the Nazi Holocaust as a seminal experience in shaping the neoconservative worldview.[76] Perle told the BBC:

> [T]he defining moment in our history was certainly the Holocaust. It was the destruction, the genocide of a whole people, and it was the failure to respond in a timely fashion to a threat that was clearly gathering. We don't want that to happen again. When we have the ability to stop totalitarian regimes we should do so, because when we fail to do so, the results are catastrophic.[77]

Both Wolfowitz and Feith lost family members in the Nazi Holocaust; they are sensitive about the subject.[78] Feith's father Dalck survived the Holocaust but lost his parents, three brothers and four sisters in the death camps. He later joined Betar, the youth wing of Ze'ev Jabotinsky's Revisionist Zionists, the forerunners of Israel's Likud.[79] Douglas Feith inherited his father's politics and has been active in Zionist causes since his youth.[80] In an interview with Jeffrey Goldberg, Feith admitted the extent to which the Holocaust has shaped his worldview: 'The surprising thing is not that there are so many Jews who are neocons,' he added, 'but that there are so many who are not.'[81]

'To be neoconservative,' Timothy Noah observes, 'is to bear almost daily witness to the resurrection of Adolf Hitler.' 'New Hitler', 'appeasement' and 'isolationism' are staples of neoconservative rhetoric. For Charles Krauthammer, Saddam Hussein is Hitler; for Wolfowitz, Hitler is Osama bin Laden and Al-Qaeda; for Podhoretz, it is Iranian president Mahmoud Ahmadinejad; for Richard Perle, Yasser Arafat.[82] In their 2004 book *An End to Evil*, David Frum and Perle write that the war against terrorism had no room for a middle way: it was 'victory or holocaust'.[83] Conversely, anyone unwilling to toe the neoconservative line is an appeaser. Jimmy Carter was one; and, in the end, so was Reagan.[84]

According to Novick, the Nazi Holocaust did not figure much in American Jewish life until 1967, but since then it has been conspicuous.[85] Opinions vary as to the cause of this resurgence. For Novick, it was Israel's isolation following the wars of 1967 and 1973 that revived fears of a 'second Holocaust'. For Finkelstein, it is the political leverage it afforded after Israel's stunning victory over Soviet clients. 'Israel's military prowess suddenly became a springboard for Jews to acquire more power in the US', he argues, and invoking the Holocaust turned into 'a powerful way to delegitimize criticism of Jews'.[86] Were the fear of the Jewish State's destruction really behind this resurgence, Finkelstein argues, it would have occurred in 1948, when Israel was significantly weaker, or in 1956, when its isolation was more complete.[87]

But American Jewish opinion was responding to the *perception* rather than the reality of Israel's weakness. Israel has enjoyed military superiority over its Arab adversaries in every war since its founding; it outnumbered the combined Arab forces even in 1948.[88] However, the 1967 war was preceded by the Israel lobby's unprecedented propaganda campaign, which rallied public support by presenting Israel as on the verge of annihilation.[89] So successful was the campaign that even Noam Chomsky could write: 'I personally believed that the threat of genocide was real and reacted with virtually uncritical support for Israel at what appeared to be a desperate moment.'[90] There is no reason to assume that American Jewry was any less sincere in its fear for Israel's survival.[91]

Historian Tony Judt argues that with the rise of identity politics, a mostly secular American Jewish community formed its identity around two external tags: Israel and the Holocaust – one in space, another in time.[92] But the neoconservatives, Heilbrunn warns, 'have invested the Holocaust with a contemporary political significance that warrants caution'.[93] David Biale notes that: 'There is a difference between remembrance and constructing a collective identity around an event and an experience alien to the realities of American Jewish life.'[94] To sustain this identity, Novick argues, much is invested in the reification of the Holocaust – in monuments, rituals and literature. No less important to this identity, however, is the State of Israel, which, according to neoconservative sociologist Nathan Glazer emerged since 1967 as the 'religion of the American Jews'.[95]

The Israel connection

For all the globalist and idealist rhetoric, write Halper and Clarke, in actual practice the neoconservatives' focus can be distilled to 'the Middle East and military power, most of all the use of military power in the Middle East'.[96] In Kagan and Kristol's 2000 collection of essays *Present Dangers: Crisis and Opportunities in American Foreign and Defense Policy* – a book which, according to Halper and Clarke, 'provides something close to the contemporary neo-conservatism canon' featuring contributions from the leading lights of the movement – they find 'no mention of Latin America, Mexico, or Africa', the 'economic dimension is almost entirely absent', and fully '80 percent of the book deals with the Middle East or the need for a strong military'.[97] Pressure groups like PNAC and Americans for Victory over Terrorism (AVOT) focus mainly on the Middle East.[98] 'The closer you examine it,' writes former *New Republic* editor Andrew Sullivan, once a neo-conservative ally,

> the clearer it is that neoconservatism, in large part, is simply about enabling the most irredentist elements in Israel and sustaining a permanent war against anyone or any country who disagrees with the Israeli right ... And to insist that America adopt exactly the same constant-war-as-survival that Israelis have been slowly forced into.[99]

The neoconservatives' attachment to Israel predates 1967; it has always loomed large in their concerns.[100] Before 1967, writes Goldberg, *Commentary* offered 'an odd mix, combining Jewish scholarship of narrow appeal with contemporary issues of no Jewish content'; the only time Jewish concerns would combine with current affairs was in articles dealing with 'foreign policy, the Middle East crisis, and the problem of Communism'.[101]

The neoconservatives' opposition to the USSR was in part a function of their residual Trotskyism, but, as noted earlier, it also helped promote US support for Israel. The neoconservatives' unilateralist impulse and disdain for international law is likewise informed by Israel's fraught relationship with multilateral institutions such as the UN and International Court of Justice.[102] The doctrine of pre-emption, which became part of the National Security Strategy of 2002 and was used in the case of Iraq, was also inspired by a tendentious reading of the June 1967 war.

Leo Strauss, one of the more influential figures in the neoconservative pantheon, saw much to admire in the ethnic exclusivism of the ascendant German right in the 1930s, which dovetailed with his own ideological inclinations.[103] He was a staunch opponent of Jewish assimilation and an ardent follower of Vladimir Jabotinsky's Revisionist Zionism. Like Jabotinsky, he did not believe in accommodation with the indigenous Palestinians – a view he would bequeath to key followers.[104] He was a frequent contributor to *Commentary* and Israel figured significantly in his writings. As far back as 5 January 1957, a strong letter can be found that he wrote to the *National Review* in response to an article that described Israel as a 'racist state'.[105] Strauss's anxieties about the 'dangers of assimilation', which he feared could destroy the 'Jewish people', also informed his defence of the Israeli prohibition of civil unions.[106] Second-generation neoconservatives have inherited this ethnocentrism. Elliott Abrams – the Iran–Contra felon and Podhoretz's son-in-law who would later play a leading role in the Bush Administration – wrote in 1997:

> Outside the land of Israel, there can be no doubt that Jews, faithful to the covenant between God and Abraham, are to stand apart from the nation in which they live. It is the very nature of being Jewish to be apart – except in Israel – from the rest of the population.[107]

The events of the 1930s had also left a deep imprint on the thinking of Albert Wohlstetter, the intellectual mentor to Wolfowitz and Perle. A staunch Zionist, he maintained close ties to Israel. He procured top-secret Israeli documents alleging that Egypt was diverting civilian nuclear technology to build a weapon, which became the basis for Wolfowitz's doctoral dissertation on nuclear proliferation in the Middle East. Under his tutelage, writes Anthony David, 'Perle and Wolfowitz had carried with them the spectre of a Middle-Eastern-madman-with-a-nuke as they rose through the ranks of the Nixon, Ford, and Carter administrations.'[108]

For a neoconservative such as David Wurmser, 'Israel is the driving force', according to one of his friends, a Bush Administration official. 'He is the son of two émigré Jews ... He met his wife, Meyrav, in Israel and they are the dynamic duo of think-tank Zionism. His wife writes about Israel losing its Zionist view.'[109] It is certainly true, writes Podhoretz, that 'all neoconservatives are strong supporters of Israel' and the US has 'a vital interest' in the survival of Israel, the 'loneliest outpost' of 'the free world'.[110] According to Gerson, Moynihan and Kirkpatrick were both appointed as US ambassadors to the UN – under Ford and Reagan, respectively – based on articles they wrote for *Commentary*. Both went on 'to defend Podhoretz's ideals from the floor of the United Nations'. After the UN had passed a resolution equating Zionism with racism, Moynihan responded with a speech excoriating Third World and Soviet 'anti-Semitism'. Podhoretz drafted much of the speech.[111] To protect Israel, Moynihan and Kirkpatrick did much to undercut the UN; so, three decades later, would John Bolton.[112]

Some neoconservatives' ties go beyond mere advocacy. Richard Perle, Paul Wolfowitz, Douglas Feith, Michael Ledeen and Stephen Bryen (who also served as the executive director of JINSA) have been under FBI investigation at various points in their careers on suspicion of spying for Israel. Wolfowitz was the subject of an FBI probe for passing classified documents to an Israeli official through a conduit while serving on the Arms Control and Disarmament Agency (ACDA) during the Carter Administration. In 1978, Perle was caught on FBI wiretap passing classified information to the Israeli embassy. In 1982, Feith was fired from his post as a Middle East analyst at the NSC after supplying classified material to an Israeli embassy official. (He was immediately rehired by Perle at the Defense Department.)[113] In 2005, Feith would resign his Defense Department position amid yet another FBI investigation into the transfer of classified material to Israeli embassy officials by one of his subordinates.[114] Michael Ledeen has likewise been the subject of a long-standing FBI investigation into the identity of a certain 'Mr. X' who assisted convicted Israeli spy Jonathan Pollard, currently serving a life sentence.[115] The FBI probe also focused on Harold Rhode, a Ledeen protégé working in the Office of Net Assessment, who served as the neoconservatives' key liaison with Iraqi exile Ahmed Chalabi.[116]

The foreign policy preferences of neoconservatives, however, would find little support if they were merely benefiting a foreign ally. Couched in the rhetoric of American nationalism, they have found greater resonance. Through a network of institutions and 'citizens' groups' with overlapping memberships, writes Heilbrunn, the neoconservatives have created their own parallel national security establishment that, after 9/11, was successful in displacing the traditional foreign policy elite.[117] Among their myriad alliances, none has proved more consequential than their association with the MIC.

Neoconservatives and the military–industrial complex

In the wake of the Vietnam debacle, interventionism had been largely discredited in the US and the prestige of the military was at an all-time low.[118] Conscious of diminishing US power and an ailing economy, Nixon was seeking détente with the Soviet Union. The liberal internationalists who until then dominated the Democratic Party were losing ground to a growing anti-imperialist sentiment rallying around the presidential campaign of George McGovern. In the cultural arena, the New Left was making gains and support was growing for Third World liberation movements, including the Palestinians.[119] This alarmed many – the aggressive nationalists, ideological cold warriors, the liberal hawks and the Christian Right – but none more so than the Israel lobby and the MIC. Both saw in détente and the 'New Politics' of progressive Democrats a threat to their interests. The lobby worried that a growing isolationist tendency might leave Israel in the cold; the MIC feared that détente and its attendant arms reduction treaties would adversely affect its profits. Together these concerns contributed to the rise of neoconservatism as a political force – a nexus of the Israel lobby's right wing and the MIC. With *Commentary* and *The New Republic* as sounding boards, this 'military–intellectual complex' began campaigning for increased military spending and rolling back détente.[120]

Wohlstetter, Nitze and the arms race

If the MIC was the lever for the neoconservatives' ascent to power, the fulcrum was Albert Wohlstetter – secular Jewish mathematician, former Trotskyist, committed Zionist. Wohlstetter made his name working for the RAND Corporation with a study highlighting the vulnerability of Strategic Air Command (SAC) bases to a surprise Soviet attack. Following the Air Force's adoption of his prescriptions on basing and 'fail-safe' nuclear deployment, Wohlstetter gained direct access to the top strata of government. He used his influence to populate the Kennedy and Johnson Administrations with protégés and made thinkable the idea of a winnable nuclear war.[121] Such a war, he argued, could be waged and won through a graduated escalation until the enemy was forced to the negotiating table. In an influential article for *Foreign Affairs*, Wohlstetter emphasised that deterrence was possible only through the stockpiling of weapons so that in the event of a surprise attack there were enough left for a 'second strike'.[122] This, writes author Alex Abella, would serve as 'the groundwork for the constant escalation of the nuclear race that would result in each side having enough armaments to destroy the world thousands of times'.[123] Wohlstetter and RAND's 'counterforce' strategy, which mandated a large nuclear reserve for second-strike capability, became official US nuclear strategy.

Wohlstetter was an advocate of modern non-nuclear technology and precision weaponry, anticipating the RMA.[124] He was also an early proponent of missile defence, testifying against the signing of the ABM Treaty in 1969. For him, the Soviets were unappeasable.[125] According to Abella, '[Wohlstetter's] pessimistic worldview, in which the worst was always possible, would profit him for the next four decades in a variety of ways – through the commissioning of books and articles, government panel appointments, consulting work, and university positions.' (Wohlstetter and his acolyte, the 'futurologist' Herman Kahn, would serve as inspirations for Stanley Kubrick's *Dr. Strangelove* and Sidney Lumet's *Fail-Safe*.) After he was fired from RAND for the unauthorised transfer of classified documents to an associate, Wohlstetter accepted an offer to teach political science at the University of Chicago, where he would go on to mentor figures such as Perle, Wolfowitz, Khalilzad and Ahmed Chalabi.[126] Doom-mongering was for him a career, Abella writes: '[H]e found a racket and exploited it all his life.'[127]

Another figure pivotal to the rise of the neoconservatives was Paul Nitze, the director of the State Department's policy planning staff under Truman. He replaced the realist George Kennan, who had repeatedly clashed with Secretary of State Dean Acheson over the nature of the Soviet threat. Under Acheson's directions, Nitze drafted the infamous national security directive NSC-68 that replaced Kennan's containment policy with one of aggressive militarisation.[128] The language of NSC-68 was deliberately hyped, according to Acheson, because its purpose was to 'bludgeon the mass mind of "top government"'.[129] It succeeded. After the start of the Korean War, on 30 September 1950, Truman dropped his initial scepticism to make NSC-68 official US policy. He increased the defence budget for the next fiscal year from \$13.5 billion to \$48.2 billion.[130] The policy reversed post-World War II demobilisation, kicked off the arms race and ushered in the Cold War.[131]

But Truman's successor Dwight D. Eisenhower – who had opposed the dropping of atomic bombs on Japan during World War II – was pessimistic about the prospect of surviving a nuclear war. He was even less enthusiastic about the arms race. 'I hate war,' he confessed 'as only a soldier who has lived it can, as one who has seen its brutality, its futility, its stupidity.'[132] On 16 April 1953, he told a gathering of the American Society of Newspaper Editors:

> Every gun that is made, every warship launched, every rocket fired, signifies in the final sense a theft from those who hunger and are not fed, those who are cold and not clothed. The world in arms is not spending money alone. It is spending the sweat of its labourers, the genius of its scientists, the hope of its children.[133]

Eisenhower's 'New Look' strategy rolled back Truman's military spending and emphasised a long-term approach to defence calibrated to the US economy. He had just ended the Korean War and was leery of engaging in more (though overtly he maintained an aggressive posture, including the authorisation to use tactical nuclear weapons).[134] The cold warriors were dismayed, and Democrats took to blaming the fiscally conservative Republicans for weakening US defences. But things changed on 4 October 1957 after the successful launch of the Soviet *Sputnik*.[135]

On 7 November 1957, President Eisenhower received an alarmist report from an independent commission headed by RAND chairman H. Rowan Gaither, which warned of 'spectacular progress' in Soviet missile technology and the vulnerability of SAC bases to a surprise attack. It also recommended allocating \$44 billion for the construction of civil defence shelters. Its principal author was Paul Nitze.[136] Instituted by Eisenhower in a bid to placate critics, the commission brought together leading lights from the corporate, academic and defence worlds. Wohlstetter, Kahn and Andrew Marshall served as advisers. The final report predictably bore Wohlstetter's imprint: drawing on his wife Roberta's study on Pearl Harbor, it played up US vulnerability and advocated 'second strike' capability. Eisenhower, who doubted the logistical possibility of a surprise attack, was dismissive of the report's claims and tried to quietly bury it.[137] A month later, dejected members of the committee and other influential figures gathered at a dinner hosted by deputy chairman William Foster at which Nitze proposed going public with the findings of the top-secret report. Though the committee chairman officially declined, the conclusions of the report soon found their way into the national press.[138] Thus was born the 'missile gap' myth.[139]

John F. Kennedy, who had hired Wohlstetter as an adviser, used 'missile gap' during his presidential campaign to attack the incumbent for spending too little on the military. (The attacks on the Eisenhower administration had already led the CIA to make its NIEs more ominous.)[140] Once in office, Defense Secretary Robert McNamara made 'counterforce' and 'second strike' official military doctrine, even though he soon came to realise that the missile gap was a myth. The Soviets only had four land-based operational intercontinental ballistic missiles – the gap was in the US's favour.[141] When in the wake of the Cuban missile crisis Kennedy and later Lyndon Johnson started pursuing arms-control agreements with the Soviet Union, they were criticised by Nitze and the hawkish Senator Henry 'Scoop' Jackson.[142] Though Nitze served as an assistant secretary of defense under Kennedy and as a deputy secretary of defense under Johnson, both were wary of his intransigence and the former kept him at arm's length.[143]

Following Lyndon Johnson's overtures towards a moratorium on the ABM programme, Nitze, Wohlstetter and Jackson fought back with the Committee to Maintain a Prudent Defense Policy, the first of many letterhead organisations that the neoconservatives would use to press for a more hawkish foreign policy. Headed by Nitze and Acheson, the committee's staff included Perle, Wolfowitz and Edward Luttwak among others. The group went on to provide Congress with many position papers on the need for missile defence as well as formulating responses to the press and doves such as J. William Fulbright, Edward Kennedy and George McGovern. In the end Jackson succeeded in getting the Senate to approve the Safeguard ABM system. 'The successful campaign became a model for Perle and other budding neoconservatives', Heilbrunn writes. 'A small guerrilla organization could run rings around the establishment experts.'[144]

Killing détente

Following McGovern's defeat in the 1972 presidential elections, a group of neoconservatives calling themselves 'Scoop Jackson Democrats' established the Coalition for Democratic Majority (CDM). Led by Podhoretz, and with Jackson as a figurehead, the group aimed to reclaim the Democratic Party from the 'isolationism' of the 'McGovernites'. In Jackson the neoconservatives had gained an influential patron, and in CDM a vehicle for their political ascent. Known as the 'Senator from Boeing', Jackson's staunch support for Israel and visceral hatred of the Soviet Union had been influenced by a braintrust put together by foreign policy adviser Dorothy Fosdick, which included Wohlstetter, Harvard Sovietologist Richard Pipes and the influential Orientalist Bernard Lewis.[145] Key neoconservatives who played a central role in selling the Iraq war – Perle, Abrams, Feith, Wolfowitz, Gaffney – all served as his aides. Nixon and Kissinger's détente suffered a crippling blow when at Perle's instigation, Jackson, with the help of Charles Vanik, introduced the Jackson–Vanik amendment linking the Soviet Union's 'most-favored-nation' status with Jewish emigration, upsetting the delicate trade negotiations which were at the centre of the rapprochement.[146] Perle was joined in lobbying by AIPAC founder I. L. Kennan, future AIPAC executive director Morris Amitay, and American Federation of Labor and Congress of Industrial Organizations (AFL–CIO) head George Meany (a right-wing supporter of Latin American dictators and a key supporter of the Vietnam War).[147] Nixon's arms control programmes likewise suffered a setback when, under assault from the neoconservatives, Nixon purged the ACDA of moderates. The Republican hard-liner was unprepared for an attack from the right.[148]

Nor was Henry Kissinger, who had emerged as a bête noire of the neoconservatives because of his 'realism' and 'amoral' balance-of-power politics. He was deemed insufficiently committed to Israel, labelled a *Hofjude* – a court Jew of the WASP establishment – who ignored the interests of Jewry, particularly the plight of the Soviet Jews.[149] The ferocity of the neoconservatives' attacks on Kissinger increased with the resignation of Nixon; Podhoretz went so far as to accuse him of 'Making the World Safe for Communism'.[150] An ambitious young Donald Rumsfeld, who was determined to displace Kissinger, encouraged the neoconservatives. Along with loyal deputy Dick Cheney, Rumsfeld managed a successful palace coup – the infamous 'Halloween Massacre' – when he engineered the exit of the Defense Secretary James Schlesinger and wrested the NSC portfolio from Kissinger. Rumsfeld replaced Schlesinger, and Cheney took over as the president's chief of staff. Gerald Ford believed that the hawkish Schlesinger's exit would allow him to pursue a less belligerent foreign policy. The neoconservatives had different ideas.[151]

In a replay of the Gaither Commission, Nitze and Wohlstetter campaigned against the CIA's 1974 NIE, alleging that it consistently underestimated the extent of Soviet advances in military technology.[152] Wohlstetter gave lectures and penned columns attacking its cautious conclusions.[153] The criticism found favour with militarists and cold warriors who wanted to scuttle détente and the on-going Strategic Arms Limitations Treaty negotiations. With Rumsfeld and Bechtel president George Schultz's support, Nitze and CDM member Eugene Rostow successfully lobbied Ford to submit the NIE to independent evaluation.[154] Bush relented and authorised the creation of a Team B comprising of external analysts to evaluate the assessments of the CIA's Team A. Three parallel panels were entrusted with the review; only one – the Strategic Objectives Panel – became the source of contention. Put together by Perle, its bevy of Wohlstetter acolytes (Pipes, Nitze, Marshall, Wolfowitz, et al.) ensured appropriately alarmist conclusions.[155] According to ACDA official Paul Warnke, the panel 'was composed entirely of individuals who made careers of viewing the Soviet menace with alarm'.[156] Unlike the other two panels, this one focused on 'intentions', allowing the neoconservative hawks to make dubious claims that could not be empirically challenged.[157] The group accused the CIA of consistently underestimating the 'intensity, scope, and implicit threat' posed by the Soviet Union, relying on technical or 'hard' data rather than 'intentions . . . ideas, motives and aspirations'.[158] A dismissive Bush quietly shelved the report; and in a repeat of earlier events, the neoconservatives leaked it to the media as an 'October Surprise' to derail Jimmy Carter's presidential bid.[159] It failed to influence the election, but it again pressured the CIA into inflating its threat assessment. *The New York Times* reported that the 1976 NIE was 'more sombre than any in more than a decade'.[160]

Carter started his term committed to détente with his foreign policy oriented to the multilateral vision of the Trilateral Commission, from whose ranks he drew much of his foreign policy team. His administration pointedly excluded members of CDM.[161] He even used Team B's claims about the impenetrability of Soviet air defences to cancel the production of a planned new bomber.[162] Administration members spoke openly of the 'inordinate fear of Communism' and shunned the likes of Nitze.[163] Neoconservatives were incensed. The Team B report soon resurfaced as 'What Is the Soviet Union Up To?', the first policy statement of the Committee on the Present Danger (CPD), a Cold War relic resuscitated by Nitze three days after the election. It brought together an odd cast of cold warriors, aggressive nationalists, trade union leaders, corporate executives and liberal hawks under a neoconservative umbrella.[164] 'Appeasement' became a common motif. The majority of CPD's 141 members were Democrats who rejected Carter's 'human rights agenda', preferring a policy of 'peace through strength'.[165] The committee received ideological reinforcement from JINSA, which boasted an impressive roster of military brass and weapons manufacturers. Meanwhile, the neoconservatives progressively colonised AEI's upper tier.[166]

Leading neoconservatives and many Jewish Democrats were wary of Carter's wish to see the creation of a Palestinian 'homeland'.[167] They were alarmed to learn that Carter's UN ambassador Andrew Young, a former aide to Martin Luther King Jr., had been in secret contact with the PLO. He was forced to resign.

Carter's thorny relations with Israeli Prime Minister Menachem Begin and his commitment to impose a settlement on reluctant Israel did little to endear him to the neoconservatives.[168] He would be at odds with the Israel lobby throughout his presidency. Golda Meir, Rabin and Moshe Dayan disliked him. Dayan would frequently use the Israel lobby's clout over Congress to constrain Carter. But Carter successfully forced Israel to withdraw after its 1978 invasion of Lebanon by threatening to use the Arms Export Control Act (AECA) to cancel US aid. Carter's pressure on Begin during the Camp David summit and his indecisiveness during the Iranian revolution further inflamed neoconservative opinion against him.[169]

In stark contrast to the carefully cultivated 'idealist' image of late neoconservatism, Carter was criticised in realist terms for his 'crackpot moralism'. The neoconservatives were happy to use human rights as a stick to beat the Soviet Union with, but did not want it to constrain allies.[170] Jeane Kirkpatrick provided an intellectual rationale for the attacks in her infamous *Commentary* essay 'Dictatorships and Double Standards' in which she distinguished between left-wing totalitarian regimes, to be confronted and defeated, and right-wing authoritarian regimes, to be shored up and assisted. The latter, she argued, 'are less repressive than revolutionary autocracies'; it was therefore a mistake for the US to constrain friendly dictators like Somoza in Nicaragua and the Shah of Iran.[171] Kirkpatrick had furnished hard-liners with what Heilbrunn calls a 'fig-leaf of justification' for supporting human rights abusers from Argentina, Nicaragua and Chile to El Salvador.[172]

Following Carter's fruitless attempt at rapprochement after the Soviet invasion of Afghanistan, many neoconservatives abandoned the Democratic Party to join Reagan.[173] Reagan was CPD's prize recruit. His election was a validation of their belligerent, unilateral philosophy of power. By 1980, forty-six CPD members had joined Reagan's foreign policy advisory group. Fifty CPD members, including four Team B alumnae, would go on to serve in the higher reaches of the Reagan national security apparatus.[174] Reagan's aggressive anti-communism, affinity for the Israeli right and promises of increased military spending had turned his administration into a haven for Jackson Democrats (since rebranded Reagan Democrats). He would adapt his foreign policy doctrine – support for proxy forces to 'rollback' Communism, unilateralism and the tactical use of human rights – directly from Kirkpatrick's *Commentary* article. He appointed Kirkpatrick as his ambassador to the UN, where she would rail against the Third World, and defend the US invasion of Grenada and the Israeli invasion of Lebanon.[175] To keep Reagan in line, the neo-conservatives launched a new pressure group, the Committee for the Free World, with a $125,000 grant from the conservative Scaife, John M. Olin and Smith Richard Foundations. Donald Rumsfeld and William Simon used their corporate connections to secure further funding from Sears, Roebuck and Mobil Oil. Inevitably, the organisation also launched its own publication called *Contentions*.[176] 'The committee served as a clearinghouse for neoconservative activists,' writes John Ehrman,

> putting them in touch with one another and helping them find support. It was especially eager to help campus groups, providing help to conservative student groups, especially those trying to establish conservative campus newspapers. According to [Midge] Decter, the committee also helped set up the National Association of Scholars.[177]

But Reagan disappointed the neoconservatives. Within two years Podhoretz would brand him an 'appeaser'.[178] For Podhoretz and the neoconservatives, Reagan was far too solicitous of the Saudis, whom the neoconservatives saw as contenders with Israel for the status of 'strategic asset'. The neoconservatives campaigned hard to derail the sale of the Airborne Warning and Control System (AWACS) to Saudi Arabia – and nearly succeeded (see Appendix).[179] But eager to court Saudi support for the proxy wars in Afghanistan and Central America, and dependent on Saudi arms purchases to help US economic recovery, Reagan pulled out all stops to ram through the sale.[180] Despite Reagan's solidly pro-Israel credentials, the neoconservatives excoriated him. He was accused of loving commerce more than hating communism, and indicted for falling into a 'habit of appeasing' Saudis. For Podhoretz, this was 'all the more disturbing in its implications for the American connection with Israel'.[181] Reagan lost so much political capital in the AWACS battle that during his second term in office, when King Fahd came to Washington to buy $70 billion worth of arms, Reagan volunteered to broker a deal with Britain rather than confront the lobby again.[182]

Neoconservative attempts to wean Reagan away from the Saudis meanwhile continued apace, culminating in the bizarre Iran–Contra affair. Throughout the early 1980s, Saudis had been underwriting American proxy operations in Nicaragua, Angola and Afghanistan, thereby helping Reagan bypass Congressional scrutiny.[183] Riled by the growing US–Saudi ties, Michael Ledeen engineered the sale of Israeli military hardware to Iran in return for the release of American hostages in Lebanon, with the money thus raised used to fund the Contra rebels fighting Nicaragua's leftist Sandinista government. A key neoconservative concern, writes Trita Parsi, was to mastermind a rapprochement with the Iranian government as a counterweight to Iraq.[184] The resulting scandal nearly sank the presidency of Ronald Reagan, who in a bid to assuage outraged Arab allies intensified covert support for Iraq.[185]

Dominating national security discourse

In Reagan the neoconservatives had found a president with a genuine commitment to Israel. But given Israeli Prime Minister Menachem Begin's intransigence and his disregard for US interests, the moral and strategic case for supporting Israel was growing increasingly thin. The neoconservatives had long disdained State Department 'Arabists' for their indifference to Israel; they were growing equally wary of the foreign policy mavens at the centrist Brookings Institution, whom they deemed insufficiently supportive of Israel.[186] Around this time, their AIPAC allies began targeting policy makers more directly. In 1982, writes Edward Tivnan, AIPAC began publishing a series of heavily footnoted 'position papers' under the editorship of Steven Rosen – a former RAND analyst who had joined AIPAC as a director of foreign policy[187] – aimed at policy makers in the White House, the Pentagon and the State Department. The papers focused on Israel's strategic value to the US.[188] To counter Brookings' influence and to gain 501(c)3 tax-exempt status, AIPAC also established WINEP with Rosen's deputy Martin Indyk as executive director and Barbi Weinberg, who had served as an AIPAC director and as a former president of the Jewish Federation in Los Angeles (she was also the wife of AIPAC Chairman Emeritus Lawrence Weinberg), as president.[189]

WINEP helped extend AIPAC's influence from the legislative to the executive branch. It also shaped public discourse through the media.[190] Dennis Ross, who would go on to play a key role in the Bush I, Clinton and Obama Administrations, wrote its first policy paper.[191] Ahead of the 1988 presidential election, WINEP published a report – *Building for Peace: An American Strategy for the Middle East* – that urged the incoming administration to 'resist pressures for a procedural breakthrough' in Israel–Palestine, where the first Intifada had erupted the year before.[192] According to Middle East scholar Joel Beinin,

> Six members of the study group responsible for the report joined the Bush I administration, which adopted this stalemate recipe not to change until change was unavoidable. Hence, it acceded to Israel's refusal to negotiate with the Palestine Liberation Organization despite the PLO's recognition of Israel at the November 1988 session of the Palestine National Council.[193]

In 1990, following Iraq's invasion of Kuwait, the neoconservatives were among the leading voices calling for intervention.[194] Though support for the war was broader, neoconservatives were central to the propaganda campaign. They founded the CPSG, headed by Richard Perle and former New York Congressman Stephen Solarz, to build bipartisan support.[195] The group coordinated its efforts with Citizens for a Free Kuwait, a front group financed by the Kuwaiti monarchy.[196] CPSG was funded primarily by the conservative Lynde and Harry Bradley Foundation, which would later also underwrite PNAC.[197] Tom Lantos, the Hungarian-born pro-Israel Congressman, organised a hearing of the Human Rights Caucus (HRC) – a front for Hill and Knowlton, the PR firm hired by the Kuwaiti government – to furnish the centrepiece of war propaganda: a teary testimony by a 14-year-old girl named Nayirah about atrocities, including Kuwaiti babies being thrown out of incubators by Iraqi soldiers. (The girl was in fact the Kuwaiti ambassador's daughter and a Hill and Knowlton executive had prepped her for the testimony.)[198] The media soon picked up the story and Amnesty International published it as part of its 1990 annual report; Bush and pro-war lawmakers used it to make their case for war.[199] Public opinion remained divided, but Congress was swayed.

For the US, the war was an unqualified success. But neoconservatives like Wolfowitz, Wohlstetter, Perle, et al., who wanted to see Hussein toppled, were less thrilled. Their dismay grew when, after the war, Bush felt obliged to reward the Arab members of the war coalition by making an effort to resolve the Arab–Israeli conflict.[200] An international conference was convened in Madrid in October 1991, followed by eleven sessions of bilateral Palestinian–Israeli negotiations in Washington.[201] The talks failed, ending prematurely with Bush's loss to Bill Clinton in the 1992 election. Bush's decision to withhold loan guarantees, demanded by the Israeli government to underwrite the resettlement of Russian Jews, played a part in his defeat.[202] The Israel lobby mobilised against the president who, having just concluded a successful war, was at the peak of his popularity. Several neoconservatives returned to the Democratic Party fold to campaign against Bush. Perle, Abrams, Feith, et al. formed the Committee on US Interests in the Middle East (CUSIME), another one of their myriad letterhead organisations. Its purpose, according to Feith, was to 'help determine what is in the US national interest', unlike Bush's policy of 'antagonism toward Israel', which clearly was not.[203] On 26 February 1992, CUSIME took out an ad in *The New York Times* that lambasted Bush for veering from the 'traditional, strong American support for the legitimacy, security and general well-being of the Jewish State'. Some neoconservatives also endorsed Clinton in a subsequent ad that appeared in *The New York Times* on 17 August 1992. David Ifshin of AIPAC helped rally them in support of Clinton who was publicly endorsed by Nitze, Amitay and James Woolsey.[204]

The neoconservatives' disappointment with Bush was relieved by the arrival of Clinton who on foreign policy had outflanked his opponent from the right.[205] Although no neoconservative was hired to any position of significance (with the exception of Woolsey, who briefly served as the head of the CIA), Clinton continued an interventionist policy.[206] Controversy had preceded Clinton's election when AIPAC president David Steiner was taped by Harry Katz, a Jewish real estate investor posing as a prospective donor, saying that the lobby had

> a dozen people in the campaign, in the headquarters ... and they're all going to get big jobs ... I also work with a think tank [WINEP]. I have Michael Mandelbaum and Martin Indyk being foreign policy advisers ... We're more interested right now in the secretary of state and the secretary of National Security Agency ... I've got a list ... We'll have access.[207]

Steiner also boasted that he had 'cut a deal' with the Bush Administration to provide more aid to Israel.[208] He was forced to resign when the controversy broke, but what sounded like exaggeration proved mere candour.[209] Clinton's foreign policy team was, according Joel Beinin, 'thoroughly colonised by WINEP affiliates':

> Eleven signatories of the final report of WINEP's 1992 commission on US–Israeli relations, *Enduring Partnership*, joined the Clinton administration. Among them were National Security Adviser Anthony Lake; the UN ambassador and later Secretary of State, Madeleine Albright; the Undersecretary of Commerce, Stuart Eizenstat; and the Secretary of Defense, the late Les Aspin.[210]

Prominent among these recruits were WINEP founder Martin Indyk and Dennis Ross, the Israel lobbyist who started his career under Wolfowitz.[211] An Australian by birth, Indyk would be granted an American citizenship overnight and appointed as the US ambassador to Israel.[212] His influence over Clinton's Middle East policy was palpable: he masterminded Clinton's 'dual containment' policy.[213] With Ross, he would scuttle several peace negotiations by acting as what one of their subordinates, Aaron David Miller, called 'Israel's lawyers'.[214] The Oslo process faced formidable challenges not just from within but also from the Israel lobby and its neoconservative vanguard.[215] The neoconservatives also staved off efforts by US businesses represented by USA*Engage to revoke sanctions against Iran and Iraq.[216]

Conclusion

Neoconservatism started as an intellectual movement whose goals reflected its Jewish and Trotskyist origins. Its staunch anti-communism had endeared it to Cold War hawks; some like Sidney Hook, Irving Kristol and Melvin Lasky even collaborated with the CIA.[217] But it was the rise of the New Left and the spectre of détente that severed the neoconservatives' remaining ties with the left. The neoconservatives feared that the growing anti-war sentiment would erode the US government's resolve to stand behind Israel. They abandoned their socialist and social democratic ideals to secure berths at free market think tanks and emerged as the ablest cheerleaders for corporate America. In turn they redefined conservatism, which has always been unilateralist, also as reflexively interventionist and solidly pro-Israel. Their aggressive posture made them the natural allies of the MIC, which was also leery of the growing isolationism. Together they helped derail détente and assisted Ronald Reagan's ascent. When the Cold War ended in triumph for the US, the neoconservatives were quick to claim credit. But even as some rejoiced, others were already on a quest for new enemies. The neoconservative capacity for nemesis creation was proven; a new one was quickly found for the post-Cold War era. How the Red menace came to be replaced by the 'Islamic threat' is the subject of the next chapter.

3   Ideology and Institutions

Strategic alliances cultivated over the past four decades have given the neoconservatives influence out of proportion to their small numbers. The previous chapter highlighted the various institutional scaffoldings that afford them their proximity to power. However, their history is not one of uninterrupted success. They have often had to battle the US foreign policy establishment, and even within the pro-Israel community their position was until recently marginal and is again in decline. There was nothing inevitable about the Iraq war. There were strong institutional forces that held neoconservative ambitions in check. But the neoconservatives' response to the end of the Cold War was robust: they tried to dominate the national security discourse and generated an interventionist momentum which, accelerated by the contingency of 9/11, succeeded in overwhelming institutional barriers.

This chapter looks at the various historical factors – some willed, some contingent – that contributed to the unique circumstances that led to the Iraq war. It starts with the post-Cold War search for a new national security paradigm; the technological advances that made the use of force cheap and palatable; the rise of human rights as an interventionist doctrine; the emergence of a shadow military establishment that turned crisis into a permanent state; and, most important, the attacks of 11 September 2001.

From the end of history to the clash of civilisations

The introspection occasioned by the Vietnam debacle had alarmed the neoconservatives. Uncertainty also followed the fall of the

Berlin Wall. For the duration of the Cold War it had been possible for the Israel lobby to justify the transfer of extraordinary amounts of cash and hardware to Israel on the grounds that it served a US strategic interest keeping Soviet proxies at bay.[1] With the collapse of the Soviet Union the argument was no longer tenable. A new paradigm had to be found to preserve Israel's privileged status. A state of conflict in the Middle East was the *sine qua non* for the 'special relationship' and, as the leading advocates of a Pax Americana, the neoconservatives were eager to find new demons to slay.

The end of history

In 1989, Francis Fukuyama, a former State Department official and a protégé of Strauss, Bloom and Wolfowitz, wrote 'The End of History?', an article in which he argued that the end of the Cold War signalled the 'total exhaustion of viable systematic alternatives [heralding] an unabashed victory of economic and political liberalism'. He was channelling the French-Russian philosopher Alexandre Kojève's idiosyncratic reading of Hegel.[2] This triumph, Fukuyama argued, would lead to 'the growing "Common Marketization" of international relations and the diminution of the likelihood of large-scale conflict between states'. It was 'the end of history as such: that is, the end of point of mankind's ideological evolution and the universalization of Western liberal democracy as the final form of human government'.[3] Though Fukuyama's triumphalism was at odds with the functional pessimism of dominant neoconservative thought, its sunny conclusions were taken as a validation of the role the neoconservatives believed they had played in vanquishing Communism.

The article appeared in *The National Interest*, the journal Irving Kristol founded in 1985 as a foreign policy counterpart to his other creation, *The Public Interest*. Circulation had been dwindling since the end of the Cold War, the publication's *raison d'être*. In a bid to revive its fortunes, editor Owen Harries decided to use Fukuyama's article as a vehicle, deploying what Heilbrunn calls 'an old editor's trick to try to gain some attention':

He solicited a symposium of contributors to respond to it, including Bloom, Kristol, Gertrude Himmelfarb, and Pierre Hassner. Kristol, as usual, had the best crack: 'I am delighted to welcome G. W. F. Hegel to Washington, D.C.'

Embassies, governments, and journalists from all over the globe contacted the *National Interest*, desperate to obtain a faxed copy.[4]

Fukuyama soon secured a book contract, rid the title of the tentative question mark, and published it as *The End of History and the Last Man*. It soon became *de rigueur* for political scientists to engage with it, if only to refute its arguments. Fukuyama's success also heralded the ascendance of *The National Interest* over *Commentary*, and the shift of the neoconservative centre of gravity from New York to Washington, DC.[5]

Among Fukuyama's many critics was Samuel P. Huntington, the controversial Harvard political scientist who had gained notoriety during the Vietnam War for his advocacy of what he called 'forced urbanisation' – the 'direct application of mechanical and conventional power ... on such a massive scale as to produce a massive migration from countryside to city'[6] – and for his speculations on the post-1960s 'excess of democracy'.[7] In his 1993 article for *Foreign Affairs* 'The Clash of Civilizations?', Huntington agreed with Fukuyama that primarily ideological or economic conflicts were over, but argued that the future 'dominating source of conflict will be cultural' and global politics will be overshadowed by 'the clash of civilizations', with 'Islam' as the chief adversary. 'Islam's borders are bloody,' he claimed, 'and so are its innards.'[8] By the time he expanded the article into a book, Huntington, like Fukuyama, had discarded the speculative title in favour of the affirmative *The Clash of Civilizations and the Remaking of the World Order*. If the *End of History* was a victory lap, *The Clash of Civilizations* signalled battles to come.

The clash of civilisations

Samuel Huntington intended his article to do for the post-Cold War era what the realist George Kennan's 'X article' (a *Foreign Affairs* article based on his famous 'Long Telegram' in which he proposed the 'containment' policy) did for the Cold War.[9] But it was not until after 9/11 that it became the dominant framework defining relations between the West and the Arab-Muslim world.[10] Although it had been the subject of much academic debate during the 1990s, its impact on policy was minimal. Its logical and empirical shortcomings had been noted.[11] And Huntington, like Fukuyama, later retreated from his more radical claims (both also opposed the Iraq war). But the neoconservatives embraced the 'clash' thesis, much as they had the 'end of history'. Re-branded as 'World War IV', it replaced 'anti-communism' as a mobilising tool.[12]

Unlike Fukuyama, Huntington was not a neoconservative. But like Cheney, Rumsfeld and other proponents of 'robust nationalism', he shared the neoconservatives' Hobbesian conception of human nature and commitment to US primacy.[13] The ultra-conservative John M. Olin Foundation underwrote the ideological endeavours of both.[14] Huntington drew his title from a 1990 Bernard Lewis article in which the influential Orientalist had spoken of 'the irrational reaction' of 'an ancient rival against our Judeo-Christian heritage' heralding a 'clash of civilizations'.[15] This was by no means the first iteration of the concept: Lewis had been speaking about it since 1957 when in a speech at The Johns Hopkins University he described the conflict in the Middle East as 'a clash between civilizations'.[16]

Though Huntington popularised the 'clash' thesis, it was Lewis's interventionist views that prevailed after 9/11. The thesis had been reified into a foreign policy paradigm even though Huntington himself had grown sceptical. He rejected the notion that 9/11 confirmed his thesis, and encouraged realism and restraint. If he had once called Islam a problem, he now contended that Islam was not 'any more violent than any other religion'.[17] Where his 'clash' thesis had excused US culpability in recent conflicts, he now pointed to the US support for Israel, its military presence in Saudi Arabia, and its support for authoritarian governments as the potential trigger for civilisational conflict.[18] In short, he had made himself irrelevant to post-9/11 Washington.

Not so Bernard Lewis. A friend to several Israeli prime ministers, a mentor to Henry 'Scoop' Jackson and Daniel Patrick Moynihan, and father to AIPAC's disinformation specialist Michael Lewis, Bernard Lewis is arguably the Israel lobby's most influential intellectual.[19] Several Lewis protégés populated key positions in the Bush Administration. (His 2003 book, *The Crisis of Islam* was dedicated to the Pentagon's Harold Rhode.) Unlike Huntington, Lewis disdains realism. In an echo of Nitze's claims about the Soviets, Lewis postulated that the US was no longer confronted with a 'rational' actor. Islam, Lewis argued, has been licking its wounds since the Ottomans were defeated at the gates of Vienna in 1683; it watched in humiliation as the West overtook it 'militarily, economically and culturally'.[20] In his post-9/11 best-seller *What Went Wrong?*, Lewis attributed the clash between 'Islam' and the West to the former's failure to modernise.[21] 'I have no doubt,' he told journalist Michael Hirsh, 'that September 11 was the opening salvo of the final battle.'[22] Lewis told C-SPAN shortly after 9/11 that 'the question people are asking is why they hate us. That's the wrong question' – because for Lewis this hate was 'axiomatic', 'natural' and 'centuries' old. 'The question which we should be asking,' he suggested, 'is why do they neither fear nor respect us?'[23] A decisive show of American power was necessary to restore respect; and, notes Hirsh, 'the most obvious place to seize the offensive and end the age-old struggle was in the heart of the Arab world, in Iraq'.[24] (Lewis's view that political cultures can be remade through force also inspired Ariel Sharon's 1982 invasion of Lebanon.)[25] Lewis's ideas would assume lethal significance after 9/11 when he would gain privileged access to Vice President Dick Cheney.

Lewis's influence notwithstanding, the permissive atmosphere that would enable Cheney and Bush to wage an unprovoked war was the outcome of many contingent factors, among them the technological advances that engendered the illusion that force could be deployed for humanitarian ends at minimal cost.

Revolution in military affairs

Following the humiliation in Vietnam, a chastened US military had foresworn the piecemeal use of force as a means of resolving political problems. Marine General Creighton Abrams and later Defense Secretary Casper Weinberger tried to reconstitute the military in a manner that would prevent easy recourse to force. This concern found expression in the Weinberger Doctrine, which prioritised diplomacy without ruling out force. Indeed, in its evolved form as the Powell Doctrine, it prescribed 'overwhelming force'[26] – but only after diplomatic options had been exhausted and an exit strategy laid out. This did not sit well with a central tenet of neoconservatism – pre-emption; neither did the legacy of Vietnam. 'Of all the disasters of Vietnam,' Wohlstetter had warned, 'the worst may be the "lessons" that we'll draw from it.'[27] Neoconservatives, Heilbrunn writes, 'sought to overturn what has come to be called the Vietnam syndrome' and were eager to resurrect the legend of World War II – the good war.[28]

The Gulf War of 1991 rehabilitated war as a tool of statecraft. It was a successful test case for the Powell Doctrine, though Powell was himself a reluctant participant. The war had other champions. Within days of Iraq invading Kuwait, Wohlstetter was calling for bold offensive action using 'precise weapons, stealth and other advanced techniques'.[29] The war would come to be characterised as much for the use of hi-tech, precision weaponry as it would for the so-called 'CNN effect', the real-time delivery of sanitised war footage to television screens across America and the world.[30] Over 100,000 Iraqis were killed, but viewers saw only carefully selected, grainy images of concrete buildings being blown up.[31] Between the video-game images of destruction and the 24-hour news cycle, war had become a bloodless spectacle.[32] It helped neoconservative columnist Charles Krauthammer to cheerfully refute the myth that the US was being overtaken by Japan. 'Is making a superior Walkman a better index of technological sophistication than making laser bombs that enter through the front door?' he exulted.[33] It was a 'surgical' war, waged by skilled professionals using 'smart' weapons; it could be experienced vicariously. 'In the right circumstances, for the right cause,' writes Bacevich, 'it now turned out, war could actually offer an attractive option – cost effective, humane, even thrilling.'[34]

It was called the Revolution in Military Affairs (RMA). Its architect Andrew Marshall described it as 'a major change in the nature of warfare brought about by the innovative application of new technologies which, combined with dramatic changes in military doctrine and operational and organizational concepts, fundamentally alters the character and conduct of military operations'.[35] It emphasises long-range precision weapons, command and control, battlefield surveillance, advanced communications and intelligence processing. An old Wohlstetter associate from RAND, Marshall has headed the Pentagon's Office of Net Assessments (ONA) since its founding in 1972.[36] He was institutionalising ideas Wohlstetter first conceived in his quest for serviceable means of waging preventive war. Already in 1974, Wohlstetter was celebrating the 'revolution in microelectronics' which allowed 'an expanding family of precision guided munitions' to more effectively apply force in 'an increasingly wider variety of political and operational circumstances'.[37] In 1987, Wohlstetter co-chaired the bipartisan Commission on Integrated Long-Term Strategy that advocated making anticipatory use of force part of the national security strategy. Published in January 1988, the Commission's report *Discriminate Deterrence* was, according to Bacevich, 'an important milestone on the road to the Bush Doctrine'. In 2003, Wolfowitz paid tribute to Wohlstetter as the first major figure to grasp that 'accuracy translates into a whole transformation of strategy and politics'.[38]

Yet the military itself remained hesitant. From its success in the Gulf, it came away with the expectation that in the future it would participate only in large-scale conventional warfare consistent with the Powell Doctrine. To remain pre-eminent, the military brass agreed to maintain sufficient forces to fight and win two major wars simultaneously. This led to a situation where the Pentagon's budget was often higher than the Cold War average. By 2010, US military spending would account for 44.32 per cent of the world total of $1.57 trillion.[39] Liberal hawks in the Clinton Administration were mystified by the gap between this capability and the military's willingness to deploy it. During the Bosnian crisis, Madeleine Albright lashed out at the Chairman of the Joint Chiefs of Staff Colin Powell: 'What's the point of having this superb military you're always talking about if we can't use it?'[40]

The administration got its way. Its foreign policy under Albright grew progressively more interventionist. From its early setback in Somalia, where an American military intervention went disastrously awry, the administration recovered by reverting to a nineteenth-century colonial practice. Instead of overwhelming force, it would rely on what Bacevich calls 'gunboats and gurkhas' – that is, cruise missiles and other airborne precision weaponry, and mercenaries euphemistically rebranded as 'private military contractors'.[41] The check that the Powell Doctrine was supposed to serve was ultimately undercut by Powell's own unchecked enthusiasm for strengthening the military.[42] The 1991 Gulf War had helped bury the spectre of Vietnam, but the limited interventions of the 1990s helped bury the Powell Doctrine. A commission appointed by the US government in 1999 reported that 'since the end of the Cold War, the United States has embarked upon nearly four dozen military interventions . . . as opposed to only 16 during the entire period of the Cold War'.[43]

From humanitarian intervention to shock and awe

It is rare to find a historical instance where an aggressor has not been motivated by noble intent. Nineteenth-century European imperialists claimed to be preventing female genital mutilation in Africa, *sati* in India, slavery in the Caribbean, and so on.[44] But after World War II, anti-communism became the overarching paradigm in which interstate rivalries unfolded. With the end of the Cold War, the interests invested in maintaining the military primacy of the world's surviving superpower were bereft of a rationale. They found one in human rights.

The right to intervene

The 1991 Gulf War led some politicians to eye limited use of force as a cost-effective means for resolving political crises. The conceptual and institutional barriers that remained were eventually overcome by *droit d'ingérence* – the doctrine of intervention. The doctrine was developed in France between 1985 and 1987 by Mario Bettati, a professor of international law, at the urging of Bernard Kouchner, a founding member of Médecins Sans Frontières who would later serve as France's foreign minister.[45] On 8 December 1988, the UN General Assembly encoded this right into Resolution 43/131 – initially limited to doctors and aid workers to deliver emergency aid across borders – and French president François Mitterrand created a post for Kouchner as secretary of state for humanitarian affairs.[46] But as the Cold War ended and the checks on the use of force diminished, the right to 'humanitarian access' in Kouchner's hands became the 'right to intervene'.[47] The measure, which had affirmed the sovereignty and territorial integrity of states, had with these developments rendered them conditional.[48] 'The sovereignty of states can be respected only if it emanates from the people inside the state', Kouchner countered. 'If a state is a dictatorship, then it is absolutely not worthy of the international community's respect.'[49]

A key influence on Kouchner's thought was Bernard-Henri Lévy.[50] Due to Lévy's influence, notes French investigative journalist Pierre Péan, 'Kouchner's worldview is schematised in the extreme . . . It is a sort of subtitled version of the American neoconservative ideology, every platitude of which he espouses.'[51] For Kouchner, whose grandparents perished at Auschwitz, the Holocaust was a formative experience, as it was for most neoconservatives. And *ingérence*, writes Traub, was the answer to the terrible question it raised.[52]

Kouchner broke with the French government in 2003 to declare Iraq 'a legitimate war on the basis of bad and false reasons'.[53] Once in government, Kouchner would be equally supportive of the neoconservative campaigns against Iran, at one point even threatening war.[54] This led Péan to accuse Kouchner and the French *nouveaux philosophes* of signing on to neoconservative ideology. The resemblance is not superficial. All are former leftists and committed Zionists for whom the Holocaust looms large as an emotional reference – they wage war against the same enemies.

The liberal hawks

'In today's America,' historian Tony Judt argues, 'neo-conservatives generate brutish policies for which liberals provide the ethical fig-leaf.'[55] Judt excoriates the liberal interventionists for abdicating 'personal and ethical responsibility', especially in their 'failure to think independently about the Middle East'. Their support for Bush's preventive war makes more sense, he writes, 'when one recalls their backing for Israel: a country which for fifty years has rested its entire national strategy on preventive wars, disproportionate retaliation, and efforts to redesign the map of the whole Middle East'. It was because the US had adopted 'an Israeli-style foreign policy' that the liberal interventionists overwhelmingly supported it.[56] Anatol Lieven found the statements in the Progressive Policy Institute's publication *Progressive Internationalism: A Democratic National Security Strategy*, calling for a muscular foreign policy, 'indistinguishable from neoconservative tracts'. Signatories such as Michael Tomasky, Michael McFaul and Kenneth Pollack had staked out positions that aligned them 'with neoconservative hardliners and the Israeli lobby . . . against both Colin Powell's State Department and the view of leading European allies'. They were 'simply following a path already marked out by Richard Perle, Irving Kristol and others a generation before'.[57]

For Heilbrunn, the second-generation neoconservatives 'inherited the Manichaean worldview of their elders, but lacked their skepticism about actually altering the state of current affairs'.[58] *Droit d'ingérence* served as the nexus between the neoconservatives and liberal interventionists; and together they laid the foundation of a new international order that subordinated state sovereignty to the whims of powerful states. The concept found new champions in individuals such as Paul Berman and Michael Ignatieff, and it became respectable for celebrated dissidents like Václav Havel, Adam Michnik and José Ramos-Horta to sign on to the neoconservative project.[59]

The new humanitarian order

The attraction of humanitarian intervention lay in its de-politicisation of the use of force, Wendy Brown observes.[60] It replaced the profoundly political language of law, sovereignty and citizenship with the profoundly apolitical – at times anti-political – language of 'humanitarianism'. 'Humanitarianism does not claim to reinforce agency,' Mamdani asserts, 'only to sustain bare life.'[61] It also leads to a relativisation of international law. This has led to a situation where 'state sovereignty obtains in large parts of the world but is suspended in more and more countries in Africa and the Middle East'.[62]

Critics of humanitarian intervention, however, overstate their case. That humanitarian concerns have been – and can be – used to justify illegal intervention is beyond question. But this does not mean that there are not crises where predatory states use the cover of sovereignty to tyrannise vulnerable populations. Indeed, it was the failure of realism in the face of genuine crises as in Bosnia and Rwanda that gave the neoconservatives the moral leverage that they were able to use in Iraq. Their motives might have been insincere, but their position had the merit of not appearing indifferent. Bosnia was critical in earning them the respect of liberal internationalists. It was an intervention that Wolfowitz, Perle and Kristol supported while Powell opposed.[63] On the significance of Bosnia, George Packer observes:

> Suddenly the model was no longer Vietnam, it was World War II – armed American power was all that stood in the way of genocide. Without the cold war to distort the debate, and with the inspiring example of the East bloc revolutions of 1989 still fresh, a number of liberal intellectuals in this country had a new idea . . . to use American military power to serve goals like human rights and democracy . . . they advocated a new role for America in the world, which came down to American power on behalf of American ideals.[64]

Consequently, the neoconservative–liberal alliance solidified over the expansion of NATO:

The longtime neocon backer Bruce P. Jackson – a protégé ... of Paul Wolfowitz – who worked as a lobbyist at Lockheed Martin, established a group called the US Committee on NATO that helped garner conservative support for the Clinton administration's move to include the Baltic States in NATO. The effort was spearheaded by Richard Holbrooke ... Jackson would go on to create the Committee for the Liberation of Iraq, which included liberal members like Will Marshall, head of the Progressive Policy Institute, and former senator Bob Kerrey.[65]

In 1998, Kerrey co-sponsored with Joe Lieberman the Iraq Liberation Act that turned regime change into official US policy. Randy Scheunemann of the US Committee on NATO and Steve Rademaker of AEI drafted the bill (Scheunemann would later head Jackson's Committee for the Liberation of Iraq – CLI) and Clinton signed it into law on 31 October 1998.[66] It was the basis on which Congress authorised the use of military force in 2002.[67]

To be sure, the liberal interventionist argument had played a determining role in Bosnia and Kosovo. In Iraq, it was significant but not crucial. Its real importance was in shaping the climate of debate. The Wilsonian conceits of the liberal hawks were useful in easing the inhibitions of some about the use of force.[68] The war found able advocates in Berman, Ignatieff, Packer, Jeffrey Goldberg, Kenneth Pollack, Thomas Friedman, Peter Beinart, David Remnick, Christopher Hitchens, Jean Bethke Elshtain, Bill Keller and Leon Wieseltier.[69] Berman, Elshtain and Pollack rushed out books in time for the invasion.[70] Packer followed with an edited collection in which he joined Todd Gitlin and Michael Tomasky to denounce anti-war voices.[71] The editorial pages of the *New Yorker*, the *New Republic*, *The Washington Post* and *The New York Times* supported the war.

On the function of the liberal hawks, Packer writes:

These liberal hawks could give a voice to [Bush's] war aims, which he has largely kept to himself. They could make the case for war to suspicious Europeans and to wavering fellow Americans. They might even be able to explain the connection between Iraq and the war on terrorism.[72]

The connection, as will be shown later, was indeed explained by Kenneth Pollack and Jeffrey Goldberg. Like the neoconservatives, both see the Middle East through an Israeli prism.[73]

The periphery doctrine

The circumstances of Israel's birth – the expulsion of over 750,000 Palestinians and the expropriation of their land – have left Israel, for all its power, with an existential anxiety. It is surrounded by hostile states that see it as a usurper. The capture of the remaining Palestinian territories in 1967 and the creeping colonisation of the West Bank have intensified regional hostility.[74] Israeli strategists have therefore considered thwarting the emergence of regional rivals as necessary for the state's long-term survival. This concern informed David Ben-Gurion's 'doctrine of the periphery'. Middle East scholar Trita Parsi explains that

> the improbability of achieving peace with the surrounding Arab states forced Israel to build alliances with the non-Arab states of the periphery – primarily Iran, Turkey and Ethiopia – as well as non-Arab minorities such as the Kurds and Lebanese Christians. This network of alliances would drive a wedge between Israel's enemies, weaken the Arab bloc, and halt the spread of pan-Arabism in the region.[75]

Israel also had territorial ambitions. During secret discussions with his French and British counterparts in Sèvres, ahead of the 1956 Suez invasion, Ben-Gurion proposed regime change in Egypt and the annexation of Sinai, the West Bank and Lebanese territory up to the Litani, with the eastern quarter handed to Syria and a Maronite Christian state established in the rest; and in the south assuming control of the Gulf of Aqaba and the Straits of Tiran. Guy Mollet, the French prime minister, shot down the plan.[76] But part of this ambition was fulfilled in the pre-emptive war that Israel launched in 1967.[77] After his accession as prime minister in 1977, writes Israeli historian Ilan Peleg, Menachem Begin 'adopted an offensive posture characterized by grandiose expansionist goals': Begin 'was determined to establish Israeli hegemony in the area, a new balance of power in which Israel would be completely dominant'.[78] Constraints on Israel's regional ambitions were eroded with the signing of the Camp David treaty, which removed Egypt, the main Arab deterrent, from the equation. Begin's second cabinet brought in hard-liners like Ariel Sharon who argued that Israel must establish regional hegemony by dissolving the surrounding states into their tribal units. Military action was seen as a catalyst for such destabilisation.

Yinon's strategy for the Middle East

The strategic vision of the hard-liners was summed up in an article by veteran Israeli diplomat Oded Yinon in the February 1982 issue of *Kivunim*, the journal of the World Zionist Organization (WZO).[79] For Yinon, the surrounding Muslim Arab world was a 'temporary house of cards put together by foreigners'; it was made up of 'combinations of minorities and ethnic groups which are hostile to one another'. It could be easily dissolved into feuding tribal fiefdoms without the capacity to challenge Israel. He identified several Arab states, including Egypt, Syria, Saudi Arabia and Iraq, as ripe for dismemberment. He held what he saw as Lebanon's imminent dissolution into five provinces as a precedent for the rest of the Arab world:

> Iraq, rich in oil on the one hand and internally torn on the other, is guaranteed as a candidate for Israel's targets . . . In the short run it is Iraqi power which constitutes the greatest threat to Israel . . . Every kind of inter-Arab confrontation will assist us in the short run and will shorten the way to the more important aim of breaking up Iraq into denominations as in Syria and in Lebanon. In Iraq, a division into provinces along ethnic/religious lines as in Syria during Ottoman times is possible.[80]

For Yinon, this plan would also cause 'the termination of the problem of the territories densely populated with Arabs', who could then be spirited away into Jordan. Israel Shahak, who translated the article, noted a 'strong connection with neoconservative thought in the USA' in the author's proposals to turn 'an Imperial Israel into a world power'.[81]

Israel's subsequent invasion of Lebanon and the 'new order' it tried to impose were based on 'a conception not unlike what Yinon expresses,' writes Chomsky.[82] Begin, according to Tyler, saw 'a unique opportunity to shape the strategic landscape in the Middle East'. 'Sharon believed that in one stroke, Israel could destroy the PLO, humiliate and weaken Syria, create a Jewish–Christian alliance with Lebanon, and orchestrate the migration of Palestinian refugees to Jordan.'[83] According to Chomsky, the new hegemonic conception saw Israel using its military dominance to deliberately undermine the status quo in search of what it defined as a 'new reality', or a 'new order'. It was only natural to expect

> that Israel will seek to destabilize the surrounding states . . . A plausible long-term goal might be what some have called an 'Ottomanization' of the region, that is, a return to something like the system of the Ottoman empire, with a powerful centre (Turkey then, Israel with US-backing now) and much of the region fragmented into ethnic religions communities, preferably mutually hostile.[84]

The invasion of Lebanon proved a disaster. It led to an abortive US intervention that ended with retaliatory attacks on the US embassy and marine barracks. Begin was soon at loggerheads with Reagan.[85] Sharon also lost his key backer in the Reagan Administration when Alexander Haig, who without Reagan's approval had given a green light to the operation, was relieved of his duties.[86] Opinion in Israel turned against the war when news of the massacre at the Sabra and Shatila refugee camps drew international condemnation. Sharon, writes sociologist Baruch Kimmerling, was constrained from 'fully implementing his grand design' by 'American pressure and Israeli public opinion'.[87]

The destabilisation plan worked at cross-purposes with the US emphasis on stability and balance of power. The plan could work only if destabilisation also became an American priority. Through the mediation of the neoconservatives, observes Kaplan, Israeli preferences were gradually translated into American policy. 'As they spelled out in the PNAC report,' he writes, 'they were interested, above all, in preserving an international environment conducive to "American pre-eminence" – a goal consistent with preserving Israel's pre-eminence in the Middle East.'[88]

The Iraq obsession

Iraq has loomed large as a threat in the Israeli consciousness since their first encounter during the war for 1948. Iraq's role was limited, but it was the only country that refused to participate in the 1949 armistice.[89] Second only to Egypt as an Arab military power and rich in resources, Iraq maintained its hostility towards Israel, sending reinforcements to Jordan in 1967 and to Syria and Egypt in 1973 (its tanks played a critical role in checking the Israeli advance on Damascus).[90] In 1991, Iraqi Scuds targeted Tel Aviv, and during the Al-Aqsa Intifada, Saddam Hussein pledged support to the families of Palestinian *fidayeen*.[91]

Zionist contacts with Iraqi Kurds were established a decade before Israel's founding by Reuven Shiloah, an officer of the Zionist secret service. They were later used to facilitate the resettlement of Iraqi Jews to Israel. By the 1960s, Israel had become the primary source of weapons and training for Kurdish rebels, and Israel was using Iraqi Kurdistan as the base for a vast intelligence network engaged in undercover operations against Iraq.[92] Israeli intelligence also assisted in the establishment of the *Parastin*, the intelligence service of the Kurdish Democratic Party. Israel was able to manipulate the Kurds against both Iraq and Syria to keep their forces engaged away from the Israeli front line in times of war.[93] The relationship finally collapsed when the Shah of Iran withdrew his support from the Kurds as part of the Algiers Accords signed to end the rivalry with Iraq.[94] Israel was also using its alliance with the Shah to cover Iraq's eastern flank, selling weapons and training his infamous intelligence service, the SAVAK. A 1979 CIA report described the relationship thus:

> The main goal of the Israeli–Iranian relations was to boost pro-Israeli and anti-Arab policy in the Iranian government. Mossad had been involved in joint operations with the SAVAK for many years, since the late 1950s. Mossad assisted SAVAK and supported the Kurds in Iraq.[95]

Although the overt alliance ended with the accession of Ayatollah Khomeini, Israel maintained covert links.[96]

The Periphery Doctrine was accompanied also by direct action focused on Iraq's nuclear programme. Israel sabotaged an Iraqi reactor during assembly in France in 1977, assassinated Iraqi nuclear scientists, and carried out an airstrike on the Osirak reactor shortly before its activation.[97] Israel also assassinated the Canadian artillery expert Gerald Bull who was helping Iraq develop a long-range cannon.[98]

Iraq remained an Israeli-neoconservative obsession throughout the 1980s. In the wake of the Shah's overthrow, the US turned its support to Iraq as a bulwark against the spread of the Islamic revolution. The neoconservatives looked on with alarm when on 12 July 1983 Reagan signed National Security Decision Directive 99, signalling a tilt towards Iraq, which was suffering serious reverses in its war with Iran.[99] The neoconservatives resented the rapprochement, not least because it was mediated by Saudi Arabia – a country long seen by establishment realists as an indispensable ally, a status to which Israel aspired.[100] It was the neoconservatives' determination to wean the US away from the Saudis and Iraq that led to the Iran–Contra affair. In an attempt to give Israel an opportunity to serve as a 'strategic asset' and simultaneously trying to revive its links with Iran, Michael Ledeen arranged for Israelis to sell arms to Iran in return for the release of US hostages in Lebanon – and the revenue from the sales (instead of Saudi money) was used to fund the Nicaraguan Contras, bypassing restrictions put in place by the Boland Amendment.[101]

The neoconservatives were marginalised in the George H. W. Bush Administration, but the Iraqi invasion of Kuwait revived their fortunes. Bush, Baker and the Joint Chiefs of Staff were initially reluctant to intervene, as were the Saudis and Jordanians.[102] But hard-liners led by Brent Scowcroft, Dick Cheney, and his deputies Wolfowitz and Libby favoured a strong military response.[103] Foreshadowing the role played by PNAC in pushing for the war in 2003, the neoconservatives set up the CPSG under the joint chairmanship of Richard Perle and Stephen Solarz. In Congress and the media, much of the support emanated from the pro-

Israel camp. In his 3 January 1991 column, E. J. Dionne of *The Washington Post* observed:

> Israel and its supporters would like to see Saddam weakened or destroyed, and many of the strongest Democratic supporters of Bush's policy on the gulf, such as Solarz, are long-time backers of Israel. Similarly, critics of Israel – among conservatives as well as liberals – are among the leading critics of Bush's gulf policy.[104]

The neoconservative synergy with the Bush Administration soon evaporated when Bush chose to abide by the UN mandate to confine the war to ousting Iraqi forces from Kuwait. Many switched their loyalties to Clinton during the 1992 election. Under Clinton, the US would abandon the long-standing 'balance of power' policy in favour of 'dual containment', a strategy designed by AIPAC veteran Martin Indyk.[105] But the neoconservatives had different ideas.

A clean break

In 1996, core neoconservatives reprised most tenets of Yinon's grand strategy in two policy papers produced for the incoming Likud government of Benjamin Netanyahu. The papers, which advised the prime minister to directly challenge US policy, were written under the auspices of the Jerusalem-based Institute for Advanced Strategic and Political Studies, a Likud think tank run by the CPD and Team B veteran William van Cleave. Their principal author was David Wurmser, former director of Middle East studies at AEI and a veteran of WINEP. Signatories included Wurmser's Israeli-born wife Meyrav, the ubiquitous Perle and Wurmser's long-time associate Douglas Feith.[106] Besides advising Benjamin Netanyahu to make a 'clean break' with the Oslo peace process, the first paper identified the removal of Saddam Hussein as an important Israeli strategic goal in its own right. Since the end of the 1991 Gulf War, Israel had come to see Iraq as a spent force and Iran as the main rival. The document acknowledged Iraq's weakness but averred that eliminating it as a threat would improve Israel's strategic position vis-à-vis Iran and Syria. 'Whoever inherits Iraq,' the authors wrote, 'dominates the entire Levant strategically.'[107] A follow-up paper called for the redrawing of the map of the Middle East along tribal and familial lines given 'the crumbling of Arab secular-nationalist nations'.[108]

In a potential breach of the 1798 Logan Act – a law that prohibits US citizens from unauthorised interference in relations between the US and foreign governments – the 'clean break' document advised Netanyahu on ways to stave off US pressure. (Akiva Eldar, the chief political columnist for Israeli daily *Haaretz*, observed that Perle and Feith were 'walking a fine line between their loyalty to American governments and Israeli interests'.[109]) It also advised Netanyahu to use language that would resonate with an American audience with references to 'Western values and traditions' and to tap into 'themes of American administrations during the Cold War which apply well to Israel'. It introduced the doctrine of pre-emption, which would later become part of the 2002 US National Security Strategy. In relation to Iraq, it did not mention democracy – indeed, it advocated the restoration of the Hashemite monarchy. 'Were the Hashemites to control Iraq,' Wurmser argued, 'they could use their influence over Najf to help Israel wean the south Lebanese Shia away from Hizballah, Iran, and Syria.'[110]

Perle personally delivered the report to Netanyahu two days before his 10 July 1996 speech to the US Congress, in which he incorporated several of its proposals. Netanyahu embellished its focus on Iraq and Syria with the additional threat of Iran. *The Wall Street Journal* published excerpts from the paper to coincide with Netanyahu's speech before endorsing it editorially the next day.[111] Wurmser reinforced the message in a column for *The Wall Street Journal* a year later.[112] The following year he co-signed with Perle a letter exhorting the US government to support an insurgency in Iraq led by Chalabi's INC. Wurmser developed his ideas into the 1999 book, *Tyranny's Ally: America's Failure to Defeat Saddam Hussein*, the most detailed critique of Indyk's 'dual containment' policy, which instead recommended a policy of 'dual rollback' to overthrow both Hussein and the Islamic Republic in Iran. Perle wrote the foreword.[113]

Dual rollback in Iraq

Wurmser dismissed one of the central concerns of 'balance of power' and 'dual containment': that the predictable ascendancy of the majority Shia in Iraq would 'enable Iran to extend its influence through its coreligionists' and undermine Saudi Arabia's 'precarious stability' by spreading 'its fervor into Saudi Arabia's predominantly Shi'ite northeastern provinces', with the upheaval spreading 'to predominantly Shi'ite Bahrain, or to other gulf states with large Shi'ite minorities'. Far from serving as 'Iran's fifth column', he wrote, Iraq's Shia majority 'can be expected to present a challenge to Iran's influence and revolution' once liberated from Saddam's tyranny.[114] 'Shi'ite Islam is plagued by fissures', writes Wurmser, 'none of which has been carefully examined, let alone exploited.' He points to the concept of *Wilayat al-Faqih* – literally, the 'rule of the jurisprudent', Ayatollah Khomeini's innovation that gave clerics a central political role – and notes that it is 'rejected by most Shi'ite clerics outside Iran (and probably many of those within Iran, too)', most notably by Iraq's leading cleric Ayatollah Ali al-Sistani. (Sistani confirmed this when he later told a visiting Sunni leader that he did not believe in *Wilayat al-Faqih* and repeatedly stressed that 'religion has to be separated from government'.)[115] 'Liberating the Shi'ite centers in Najaf and Karbala, with their clerics who reject the *wilayat al-faqih*', Wurmser argued, the US 'could allow Iraqi Shi'ites to challenge and perhaps fatally derail the Iranian revolution', thereby achieving a 'Regional Rollback of Shi'ite Fundamentalism'. 'For the first time in half a century, Iraq has the chance to replace Iran as the center of Shi'ite thought, thus resuming its historic place', he writes. By shifting the 'Shi'ite center of gravity toward Iraq', the US could pry the Lebanese Shi'ite away from 'a defunct Iranian revolution' and reacquaint them with the Iraqi Shi'ites, to shift 'the region's balance and to whittle away at Syria's power'.[116]

Tehran University political scientist Mohammed Hadi Semati concurs. While the clerical doctrines may or may not become the basis for genuine rivalry, in the end 'Iraq influences Iran, not the other way around'.[117] Reuel Marc Gerecht – Wurmser's successor at AEI and formerly a CIA agent in Iran – likewise dismissed the notion of a 'fraternity between Iraqi and Iranian Shi'ites' and argued that the ascendance of the Iraqi Shia 'will be brutal for the mullahs'.[118] Ledeen assured that 'the Iraqi Shi'ites will fight alongside us against the Iranian terrorists'.[119] Wilfried Buchta of WINEP predicted that Ayatollah Sistani would emerge as Iranian Ayatollah Ali Khamenei's 'most serious competitor for the religious leadership of Shi'is' since the latter, unlike Sistani, is not a Grand Ayatollah.[120] Feith too believed that Sistani would eclipse Iranian clerical authority.[121] The policy would also have the additional benefit of weakening Saudi Arabia. In *An End to Evil*, Frum and Perle observe that Saudi oil is 'located on the eastern, Persian Gulf side' where 'one-third of the people' are Shia. 'Independence for the Eastern Province would obviously be a catastrophic outcome for the Saudi state.'[122]

Sociologist Jonathan Cutler finds striking parallels between the policies proposed by Wurmser and those enacted by the Bush Administration at the beginning of the war. Policies like de-Baathification may therefore appear like the work of 'blundering fools who would *unwittingly* hand Iraq to Iranian clerics', he writes, but in Wurmser's scheme 'the road to Tehran begins in Najaf'.[123] This analysis was partially borne out when in the aftermath of the invasion even an Iran-friendly group such as the Islamic Supreme Council of Iraq began distancing itself from Tehran to boost its appeal among the Iraqi Shia. Though Muqtada al-Sadr still subscribes to *Wilayat al-Faqih*, his staunchly nationalist disposition precludes him turning into a lackey of Iran. He has repeatedly made public his resentment of Iranian influence in Iraq.[124]

Ballistic missile defence

The 'clean break' document also provided unique insight into the motivation guiding the neoconservative obsession with military spending. It advised Netanyahu to cooperate closely with the US on anti-missile defence because

> Not only would such cooperation on missile defense counter a tangible physical threat to Israel's survival, but it would *broaden Israel's base of support among many in the United States Congress* who may

know little about Israel, but care very much about missile defense. Such broad support could be helpful in the effort to move the U.S. embassy in Israel to Jerusalem.[125]

The preoccupation with ballistic missile defence began with Wohlstetter in the 1960s and has remained part of the conversation on national security ever since. No one has done more to keep it alive than Frank Gaffney, Jr., a Henry Jackson protégé and a Perle associate.[126] Gaffney, a Senate staffer, was appointed Deputy Assistant Secretary of Defense for Nuclear Forces and Arms Control Policy under Perle. In his capacity, he opposed all arms control agreements. After he was relieved of his position in 1987 (along with Perle) by Reagan's new Secretary of Defense Frank Carlucci, Gaffney founded CSP and went on single-handedly to create the Congressional missile defence lobby. A prolific writer and ubiquitous in the media, Gaffney has churned out a steady stream of fear-mongering reports whose prescriptions, according to Jason Vest, have been simple:

> Gut all arms control treaties, push ahead with weapons systems virtually everyone agrees should be killed (such as the V-22 Osprey [manufactured by Boeing]), give no quarter to the Palestinians and . . . go full steam ahead on just about every national missile defense program.[127]

According to Peter Stone, Gaffney 'bombards 1,000 or so national reporters, policymakers and talk-radio hosts with two or three faxes a week'. Perle described the operation as a 'Domino's Pizza of the policy business'.[128]

The aerospace industry, with a stake in the star wars programme, is heavily represented on CSP's board of advisers. It also provides a quarter of CSP's funding. In turn, CSP has successfully lobbied to secure hundreds of billions of dollars' worth of contracts for missile defence, a project former Assistant Secretary of Defense Philip Coyle described as a 'high-tech scarecrow'.[129] The rest of CSP's funding comes from conservative foundations (Olin, Smith Richardson, Sarah Scaife, Carthage, and Bradley) and right-wing Zionist donors such as the California gambling magnate Irving Moskowitz, a director of JINSA and funder of right-wing Jewish settlers in the occupied West Bank; New York investment banker Lawrence Kadish, key funder of the Republican Jewish Coalition and AVOT (on whose board Gaffney serves as a 'senior adviser'); and casino magnate Poju Zabludowicz, owner of the arms manufacturer Soltam (Perle's former employer), and funder of the Conservative Friends of Israel and Britain Israel Communications and Research Centre (BICOM).[130]

In 1994, Gaffney persuaded Newt Gingrich to include missile defence as a plank in 'Contract with America', the Republican Party's platform for the upcoming mid-term elections.[131] Despite the Republican victory, however, there was little advance on the project given its forbidding cost. In 1997, this led CSP advisory board member Curt Weldon and a group of Congressional staffers associated with PNAC to sponsor the creation of the Commission to Assess the Ballistic Missile Threat to the United States. They chose Donald Rumsfeld as its chairman and Wolfowitz as his principal adviser. The Commission self-consciously followed the Team B precedent and on 15 July 1998 issued a report that once again contradicted the CIA's NIE (1995) with wildly alarmist claims. It identified the principle threats to the US as Iraq, Iran and North Korea – the soon-to-be 'axis of evil'. Earlier the same year, CSP had revived the CPSG for a letter to the president calling for the overthrow of Hussein. The letter reinforced PNAC's message and included most of the same signatories.[132]

On 16 July 1998, a day after the Rumsfeld Commission issued its report, Gary Schmitt of PNAC used it in a memo addressed to 'opinion leaders' blaming the Clinton Administration for pursuing a policy which left the US and its allies 'unprotected against attacks by ballistic missiles'.[133] For some analysts, the Commission was instituted to do little more than pressure the administration into increasing military spending.[134] It succeeded. In March 1999, Congress passed the National Missile Defence Act that made the deployment of 'national missile defence' the declared policy of the US government.[135] Rumsfeld, who had delivered a ninety-minute briefing to 250 Congresspeople before the vote, was given the CSP's 'Keeper of the Flame' award.[136] Later the same year, the CIA issued a new NIE with remarkably alarmist forecasts. According to Michael Dobbs of *The Washington Post*, this was in part due to 'a concerted campaign by the Republican-dominated Congress, supported by Israel, to focus attention on the potential leakage of missile technology from Russia to Iran'.[137]

The neoconservatives capitalised on the success by instituting the Commission to Assess US National Security Space Management and Organization, again headed by Rumsfeld. On 11 January 2001, the Rumsfeld Space Commission echoed PNAC's 'Rebuilding America's Defenses' in recommending the militarisation of space lest the US fall prey to a 'Space Pearl Harbor'.[138] Later in December, a 1995 CSP memo co-authored by Douglas Feith advocating withdrawal from ABM became policy when Bush announced that the US would no longer be bound by the treaty's obligations. The administration also followed CSP's recommendations in opposing the Comprehensive Test Ban Treaty, the Chemical Weapons Convention (CWC) and the International Criminal Court.[139]

JINSA and CSP's passionate attachment

Despite CSP's extraordinary success, according to Vest, White House political adviser Karl Rove was casting about in 2002 'for someone to start a new, more mainstream defence group that would counter the influence of CSP'. CSP, according to its conservative critics, was 'less concerned with the threat to America than to Israel'. It shared many board members, including Perle, Feith, Ledeen and former AIPAC executive director Morris Amitay, with JINSA.[140] Founded in 1976, JINSA's *raison d'être* is to ensure a steady supply of US arms to Israel. According to its website, JINSA strives to 'inform the American defense and foreign affairs community about the important role Israel can and does play in bolstering democratic interests in the Mediterranean and the Middle East'.[141] This is achieved through a stream of columns in newspapers, production of policy papers, and junkets for retired US military brass to Israel where, according to Vest,

> JINSA facilitates meetings between Israeli officials and the still-influential US flag officers, who, upon their return to the States, write op-eds and sign letters and advertisements championing the

93

Likudnik line. (Sowing seeds for the future, JINSA also takes US service academy cadets to Israel each summer and sponsors a lecture series at the Army, Navy and Air Force academies.)[142]

The officers are chosen for their ties with military contractors, particularly those that work closely with Israel. The military industry itself is well represented on JINSA's advisory board, which includes contractors from Northrop Grumman, Lockheed Martin, General Dynamics and Tamam (a subsidiary of Israeli Aircraft Industries, to produce an unmanned aerial vehicle – UAV).[143]

Both JINSA and CSP have devoted much of their resources to passing off Israel's enemies as enemies of the US. They presented Arafat as an abettor of Saddam Hussein in order to link the Palestinian issue with Iraq. This recurring focus has led some in military and intelligence circles to refer to JINSA, CSP, AEI and their allies as the 'axis of evil' who do not let pass any opportunity 'to advance other aspects of the far-right agenda by intertwining them with Israeli interests'.[144] In one report, Vest shows, JINSA advocates tapping the Arctic National Wildlife Refuge because Arab oil producers have 'interests inimical to ours' and tapping the wildlife reservations will 'limit [the Arabs'] ability to do damage to either of us'.[145]

With overlapping memberships, PNAC, JINSA and CSP emerged as a shadow defence establishment that reprised under Clinton the role that CPD had played under Carter. Many of their members would eventually end up in key posts in the Bush Administration. They would pursue from inside the goals that they had long advocated from outside.

A new Pearl Harbor

In 1995, William Kristol, John Podhoretz (Norman's son) and *New York Times* columnist David Brooks conceived of a publication that they could use to gain influence in Washington. Kristol secured media mogul Rupert Murdoch's backing and *The Weekly Standard* soon became the cutting edge of the Republican right's assault on Clinton. So influential was the publication that it led arch-conservative William Buckley, Jr. to fashion his well-established *National Review* along the same lines, replacing its realist editor with the neoconservative Rich Lowry, who would go on to support the Iraq war. Meanwhile, in *Commentary*, Norman Podhoretz started attacking Irving Kristol and Jeane Kirkpatrick for their 'neo-realism' and for losing their political bearings in the post-Cold War era.[146] But Kristol's progeny remained firmly in the neoconservative camp. In 1996, William Kristol joined Robert Kagan to write an article for *Foreign Affairs* entitled 'Toward a Neo-Reaganite Foreign Policy', which argued that the US should establish a 'benevolent global hegemony' and advocated 'change of regime' in China, Cuba and Iran.[147] Kristol, a foreign policy novice, had been influenced by Kagan, a veteran of neoconservative propaganda wars. In 1985, Kagan had been chosen by Elliott Abrams to head the Office of Public Diplomacy, which was engaged in drumming up support for the Nicaraguan Contras.[148]

In 1997, Kagan and Kristol gave their ideas an institutional basis with PNAC, a letterhead organisation operating out of the AEI offices. Its stated aim was to promote 'American global leadership' through 'a Reaganite policy of military strength and moral clarity'.[149] Its statement of principles was signed by proponents of US military pre-eminence, many of them neoconservatives, some not. Iraq became PNAC's primary focus. On 26 January 1998, it sent a letter to President Clinton outlining a plan for the overthrow of Saddam Hussein through unilateral action.[150] Perle and Stephen Solarz hand-delivered the letter to Clinton's National Security Advisor Sandy Berger.[151] The administration's response was dismissive. The neoconservatives pressed on. A copy was faxed to Donald Rumsfeld who at the time was trying to escape political irrelevance through the various Commissions. Rumsfeld duly signed.[152] The letter was made public on 19 February 1998 with an expanded list of signatories including Feith, Wolfowitz, Wurmser, Abrams and John Bolton. Letters were also dispatched on 29 May 1998 to the Republican Speaker of the House Newt Gingrich and Senate Majority Leader Trent Lott. PNAC, along with CSP and JINSA, became one of the key sponsors of the Iraq Liberation Act of 1998, which made regime change official US policy.[153]

Later, in 2000, Kagan and Kristol would edit *Present Dangers: Crisis and Opportunities in American Foreign and Defense Policy*, a collection of essays by apex neoconservatives that Clarke and Halper describe as 'the contemporary neo-conservatism canon'. The book attacked the realists' narrow definition of 'vital interests' and called for 'a foreign and defence policy that is unapologetic, idealistic, assertive and funded well beyond existing appropriations'.[154]

In the year of PNAC's launch, Wolfowitz contributed a cover story to *The Weekly Standard*, co-authored with Zalmay Khalilzad, encouraging Clinton to 'Overthrow Him' (that is, Saddam Hussein).[155] Wolfowitz had started his campaign for regime change tentatively mere months after leaving the Bush Administration with a lengthy essay in *The National Interest*. In the interim he had served as the principal foreign policy adviser to Robert Dole's 1996 presidential bid under campaign chairman Donald Rumsfeld.[156] During the campaign, he made an appearance before the Senate Foreign Relations Committee castigating Clinton for abandoning Iraq to a 'bloodthirsty dictator', a message he echoed in a subsequent column in *The Wall Street Journal*.[157] Michael Ledeen borrowed Wolfowitz's title and repeated the argument in *The Weekly Standard*.[158] Wolfowitz developed the case for regime change in a lengthy contribution to a book on Iraq's future. Conscious of the declining international support for US Iraq policy, he encouraged Clinton to 'act unilaterally'.[159] PNAC echoed the same message in a 26 January 1998 letter warning Clinton against the 'misguided insistence on unanimity in the UN Security Council'.

According to his friend and neighbour Rolf Ekeus, the former Swedish ambassador and UNSCOM chief, Wolfowitz would spend hours discussing Iraq's weapons programmes. It is therefore inconceivable that he was unaware of the destruction of Iraq's weapons. Saddam's son-in-law Hussein Kamel, the former head of Iraq's weapons programme, had personally confirmed it to Ekeus after his defection in 1995.[160] However, this did not deter Wolfowitz from advocating regime change in an appearance before the House International Relations Committee in February 1998 – because it was the 'only way to rescue the

96

region and the world from the threat that will continue to be posed by Saddam's unrelenting effort to acquire weapons of mass destruction'.[161] Wolfowitz repeated his case in front of the House National Security Committee. He criticised Clinton for failing to back Iraqi guerrillas who were trying to overthrow Hussein, comparing it to the Bay of Pigs incident.[162] The military was unimpressed: CENTCOM chairman Gen. Anthony Zinni dismissed Wolfowitz's proposals as recipe for a 'Bay of Goats'.[163] But the message was not lost on all. James Mann writes: 'Wolfowitz's arguments in these late-1990s articles helped persuade other prominent Republicans to support the overthrow of Saddam Hussein without worrying too much about the allies and friends who had proved helpful during the Gulf War.'[164]

The neoconservatives had covered Clinton's right flank during his various interventions, which were opposed by traditional Republicans. Clinton in turn appeased the unilateralist impulses of both by opposing the international treaty banning land mines (1997) and the International Criminal Court (1998), and by declining to submit the Kyoto treaty to Congress (1999).[165]

Between hawks and super-hawks

In 1998, after Bush announced his presidency, he decided to take Condoleezza Rice, a Brent Scowcroft protégé, as his principal foreign policy adviser. He later added Wolfowitz, who had formerly served as an aide to both George Schultz and Dick Cheney, the two early influences over Bush's foreign policy. In 1999, Rice and Wolfowitz put together a formal team of foreign policy advisers, later dubbed 'the Vulcans', comprising both realists and neoconservatives. All worked off the common premise of unrivalled US military superiority.[166] The group's membership overlapped with a clandestine campaign group headed by Rumsfeld at the Hoover Institution lobbying for 'missile defence'. Rice, Wolfowitz, Perle and Stephen Hadley all participated in it. Powell – who in his biography had made jocular reference to Cheney and his aides (including Wolfowitz) as 'right-wing nuts'[167] – remained external to the campaign.[168] The neoconservatives were even then trying to steer the focus towards Iraq. In a spring 2000 briefing,

Hadley had told a group of prominent GOP policy makers that the 'number-one foreign-policy agenda' of a Bush Administration would be regime change in Iraq.[169] But in a *Foreign Affairs* article, Rice struck a decidedly realist note declaring that 'rogue regimes' such as Iraq and North Korea could be easily deterred even if they possessed WMDs.[170] Meanwhile, Cheney had recommended himself as running mate for Bush, and once in office started populating key advisory positions with his neoconservative allies. He was worried that the popular and respected secretary of state would have too much influence over foreign policy. To rein him in, he appointed his old ally Donald Rumsfeld as the Secretary of Defense. His attempt to give Wolfowitz the number two position at the State Department was resisted by Powell. Instead Wolfowitz was installed as the second in command at the Pentagon despite Rumsfeld's reservations.[171]

The personnel choices were significant. For Mann, they determined 'the way in which foreign policy institutions would operate and the conceptual framework through which the administration would view the world'.[172] As State and Defense feuded over foreign policy, the NSC, which is traditionally entrusted with arbitrating such disputes, proved ineffectual under Rice. As more and more power accrued to Cheney, all such disputes were resolved in favour of the Defense Department. However, prior to September 11, Cheney's robust nationalism showed more shades of neoliberalism than of neoconservatism. In the contest between traditional Republicans demanding tax cuts and neoconservatives demanding increased military spending, Cheney sided with the former.[173] And while Powell was frequently outmatched by the superior coordination of his neoconservative adversaries, his popularity and stature allowed him to check the neoconservatives' more ambitious designs. Former Treasury Secretary Paul O'Neill has claimed that Bush was committed to regime change in Iraq as early as 30 January when the president raised the question of 'hitting Saddam' during the first meeting of the NSC.[174] Patrick Clawson, a key neoconservative supporter of the war, dismisses this claim. 'What O'Neill doesn't notice is that those who wanted to go to war lost,' he told Ricks, 'and those who supported "smart sanctions" won'. Before 9/11 there was not a 'war party' inside the Bush Administration, 'there really was just Wolfowitz' and his former aide Irving Libby.[175] Richard Armitage, Powell's loyal deputy, agrees: 'Prior to 9/11 we certainly were prevailing', he later recalled.[176] Feith too admits that the neoconservatives' call for action in Iraq was failing to gain traction before 9/11.[177] Powell was serving as the moderating influence, and in the months leading up to the attacks, Bush's unilateralism was more isolationist than interventionist.

The catalysing event

There was nothing inevitable about the course chosen after 9/11. Nearly all the prominent signatories to PNAC had taken top positions in the Bush Administration, but the neoconservatives only secured second-tier jobs. State, Defense and the NSC were headed by Powell, Rumsfeld, and Rice: all traditional conservatives. Before September 11, the neoconservative influence was palpable only to the extent that it accorded with the 'robust nationalism' of Cheney, Rumsfeld and Bush: the decision to withdraw from the ABM Treaty was consensual, as was the retreat from the Kyoto Protocols. Where interests diverged, as over China, realism prevailed. On 1 April 2001, a Chinese jet had crashed into the sea after it collided with a US EP-3 spy plane patrolling the Chinese coastline. The plane landed on Hainan Island and China refused to release its twenty-four-man crew unless the US apologised. Following Powell's intensive diplomacy, the crew was repatriated after Bush agreed to sign a letter of regret. The neoconservatives were incensed, especially since Saudis facilitated the negotiations.[178] In *The Weekly Standard*, Kristol and Kagan went so far as to accuse Bush of bringing about 'profound national humiliation'. (Bush placated the neoconservatives by authorising a massive arms shipment to Taiwan).[179]

Paul Wolfowitz had reiterated his desire for regime change in front of the Senate Arms Services Committee at his confirmation hearing. He, according to one analyst, 'was genuinely obsessed with the Middle East'.[180] According to Feith, in deputies' meetings, Wolfowitz and 'Scooter' Libby's call for intervention in Iraq was being blunted by Richard Armitage and the CIA Deputy

Director John McLaughlin. Even as the neocons pushed for war, Powell and Armitage were busy drafting a new, smarter sanctions programme aimed at alleviating the humanitarian catastrophe brought about by the earlier, indiscriminate sanctions regime under Clinton.[181] Powell was winning. For Powell, containment had worked:

> [Hussein] has not developed any significant capability with respect to weapons of mass destruction. He is unable to project conventional power against his neighbors. So, in effect, our policies have strengthened the security of the neighbors of Iraq, and these are the policies that we are going to keep in place.[182]

Even Rumsfeld was not biting. Feith notes that a memo that he and Wolfowitz sent to the Defense Secretary failed to elicit a favourable response. Indeed, Rumsfeld responded with a memo on 17 July, outlining three options, including dialogue.[183] Speculation was rife by the end of summer 2001 that Rumsfeld – who was busy fighting the Pentagon bureaucracy – was on his way out.[184] On the eve of 9/11, at a town hall style meeting, he declared the Department of Defense's hidebound bureaucracy the greatest threat to American security. September 11 rescued Donald Rumsfeld and the neoconservatives.

Conclusion

'The decisive element in every situation', Gramsci observed,

> is the permanently organized and long prepared force which can be put into the field when it is judged that a situation is favourable (and it can be favourable only in so far as such a force exists, and is full of fighting spirit). Therefore the essential task is that of systematically and patiently ensuring that this force is formed, developed and rendered ever more homogeneous, compact and self-aware.[185]

The events of 11 September 2001 changed the balance of power in the administration, if not the world. The neoconservatives, who had hitherto remained marginal, successfully used the trauma to focus policy on Iran, Iraq and Syria: countries that had been in their sight for at least a decade. They were prepared in a way the realists were not. Anticipation, superior coordination and ideological coherence allowed the neoconservatives to overcome the fragmentary opposition of the realists in the post-9/11 struggle over foreign policy. It was their capacity to frame the conflict expansively as a contest between good and evil, turning a political struggle into a global morality play, that gave their view the resonance that their opponents lacked. Their supporters in the media, academia and think tanks reinforced the message.

As the next chapter demonstrates, the neoconservatives waged a sustained campaign – both inside and outside the administration – to successfully place Iraq on the administration's agenda after September 11. They manufactured the bogus evidence that was used by the administration to make its case. They used their informal network to coordinate and short-circuit the policy process. And they manufactured and instrumentalised favourable public opinion to overwhelm dissent. Their sustained efforts to lay the ideological pretexts for a clash of civilisations had finally borne fruit. The amorphous Islamic threat had been hypostatised into an identifiable enemy. For almost everyone else, the name was Osama bin Laden. For the neoconservatives, it was Saddam Hussein.

Part 3   The Case for War

4 Setting the Agenda

In 2002, the Bush Administration was embarking on a war to pre-empt a 'grave and gathering threat'. The administration alleged that Iraq possessed WMDs, including nuclear, chemical and biological munitions. It also alleged that Iraq had links to Al-Qaeda. The conjunction of the two made the threat imminent as Iraq could at any time pass its weapons to terrorists committed to the destruction of the US.[1] The evidence of intention and capability was scant, but, in the evocative words of one administration official, they did not want the smoking gun to be a mushroom cloud.[2]

The pre-emption two-step

That Iraq had no WMDs is now well established. The Iraq Survey Group's comprehensive investigation failed to turn up any weapon or a weapons programme.[3] But all of this could have been ascertained without an invasion. Hussein Kamel – the Iraqi dictator's son-in-law and head of his weapons programme – had defected to Jordan in 1995 where he confirmed to his UN interrogators that he had 'ordered destruction of all chemical weapons. All weapons – biological, chemical, missile, nuclear – were destroyed.' The weapons programmes had been dismantled.[4] Both Condoleezza Rice and Colin Powell had admitted in 2001 that Iraq had been effectively disarmed and contained.[5] This view was also shared by the IAEA and later confirmed by renewed inspections.[6] Multiple intelligence sources had also confirmed ahead of the war that Iraq had no WMDs.[7]

Nor did Iraq have links to Al-Qaeda. Exhaustive studies by

both the 9/11 Commission and the Pentagon have failed to turn up any operational links between the two.[8] This was also known before the war. The State Department's annual 'Patterns of Global Terrorism' report for 2000 states that Iraq had 'not attempted an anti-Western terrorist attack since its failed plot to assassinate former President Bush in 1993 in Kuwait' (the specifics of which are disputed).[9] Though it mentions Iraq hosting several terrorist organisations, all of them targeted either Israel (Arab Liberation Front, Palestine Liberation Front, Abu Nidal Organization) or Iran (Mujahideen-e-Khalq). Immediately after 9/11, the White House Counter Terrorism Coordinator and the CIA had confirmed that no such links existed. The various claims about Iraq's alleged links to Al-Qaeda had also been comprehensively debunked by a CIA study headed by Michael Scheuer long before the war.[10]

Yet it was the Iraq–Al-Qaeda link that sold the war. It was central to Colin Powell's address to the UN Security Council in which he highlighted the 'potentially much more sinister nexus between Iraq and the al Qaeda terrorist network'. In key speeches in the lead-up to war – at the UN (12 September 2002), in Cincinnati (8 October 2002), at the State of the Union address (28 January 2003) – Bush referred to Iraq's alleged WMDs in the same breath as its presumed links to Al-Qaeda. As late as 1 March 2003, Bush was assuring Americans that Iraq 'will not be allowed to intimidate and blackmail the civilized world, or *supply his terrible weapons to terrorist groups*' (emphasis added). Indeed, even forty-eight hours before the invasion, in his final ultimatum to Saddam Hussein and his sons to leave Iraq, Bush asserted that the Iraqi regime had 'aided, trained, and harboured terrorists, including operatives of Al Qaeda'.

The attempt to link a WMD-armed Iraq with Al-Qaeda was deliberate and sustained – and it worked. A *Washington Post* poll showed in September 2003 that 69 per cent of Americans believed Iraq was behind the 9/11 attacks.[11] A Harris poll in February 2004 showed that 74 per cent of respondents still believed Iraq had 'certain' or 'likely' links to Al-Qaeda.[12] A February 2006 Zogby poll found that 85 per cent of the soldiers serving in Iraq believed their mission was mainly 'to retaliate for Saddam's role in the 9-11 attacks'.[13]

Much of the blame for the exaggerations has since been laid at the CIA's door by the neoconservatives, some journalists and the Senate's Silberman–Robb Commission.[14] Douglas Feith has pinned the blame on Colin Powell, claiming that he oversold the threat.[15] Powell and Tenet's acquiescence no doubt gave the case for war credibility that it would have otherwise lacked; however, only part of the intelligence used to sell the war originated with the CIA. Key elements of it came from self-interested Iraqi exiles via the neoconservatives. It was given an official imprimatur by two ad hoc groups set up inside the government: the PCEG and the OSP. More important, however, was the neoconservatives' success in putting Iraq on the agenda in the immediate aftermath of 9/11.

The following is an investigation into the origins of the Iraq–Al-Qaeda link; the role of the quasi-official Defense Policy Board (DPB) in promoting neoconservative preferences within the government and in coordinating the message with media allies; the part played by neoconservatives in the Pentagon and the OVP; the specific role played by the PCEG in rubberstamping neoconservative propaganda; and, finally, the enabling role and motivations of the vice president.

Laurie Mylroie and the unified field theory of terrorism

The neoconservative response to 9/11 was immediate. Within hours, several were pointing fingers at Saddam Hussein, whom they had long tried to implicate in terrorist attacks against the US. They based their claims on the theories of AEI's Laurie Mylroie who, in her 2000 book *Study of Revenge* and in myriad articles, had argued that Iraq was behind the 1993 WTC bombing, the Oklahoma City bombing and several other attacks.[16] As one of the very few 'Iraq experts' in the neoconservative ranks, she had a cult following. Mylroie's association with Iraq had begun in the 1980s as an unabashed apologist for Saddam Hussein.[17] In 1987, she co-authored an article with Daniel Pipes encouraging the Reagan Administration to adopt Hussein because he had significantly moderated his views on Israel.[18] In the same year, she

met the Israeli president Ezer Weizman, and, with Israeli blessing, visited Iraq to lobby Hussein for rapprochement between
the two states. Following Iraq's gassing of Kurds at Halabja, she
penned an article for the *Jerusalem Post* advising the US and Israel
against criticising Iraq. She continued her advocacy as late as
March 1990. She turned against Hussein only after the invasion
of Kuwait.[19]

None of this diminished neoconservative enthusiasm for
Mylroie's theories. In blurbs, it was called 'splendid and wholly
convincing' by Richard Perle, 'provocative and disturbing' by
Paul Wolfowitz, and 'superb' by James Woolsey.[20] Wolfowitz,
according to a *Vanity Fair* interview, was completely convinced
of its claims about Iraqi involvement in the WTC and Oklahoma
bombings.[21] In his foreword to the book, Woolsey, the former
CIA director, dared readers to 'try to think of a living American
to whom you would owe more' for future security.

People familiar with the subject were less generous, however.
Former White House counterterrorism coordinator Richard
Clarke called her theories 'totally discredited'.[22] Terrorism expert
Peter Bergen called her a 'crackpot' and an 'armchair provoca-
teur', whose 'unified field theory of terrorism' defied 'virtually
all evidence and expert opinion' – including that of the Joint
Terrorism Task Force, the FBI, the CIA, the NSC and the State
Department.[23] Bergen noted that in her book,

> Lewis 'Scooter' Libby ... is thanked for his 'generous and timely
> assistance.' And it appears that Paul Wolfowitz himself was instru-
> mental in the genesis of *Study of Revenge*: His then-wife is credited
> with having 'fundamentally shaped the book,' while of Wolfowitz, she
> says: 'At critical times, he provided crucial support for a project that
> is inherently difficult.'[24]

On 9/11, these friends in high places were quick to amplify her
message and her theories percolated up to the highest reaches
of the Pentagon and the OVP.[25] The fact that the Pentagon was
caught completely unprepared made it all the more receptive to
Mylroie's seemingly all-encompassing theories. Through official,
semi-official and private channels, and with help from allies in

the media, the neoconservatives used Mylroie's theories to bring a sense of certainty and authority to a situation in which confusion and chaos reigned. At a time when intelligence agencies were groping for answers, they were offering definitive answers.

Shortly after the Pentagon was attacked, Donald Rumsfeld was querying Gen. Richard Myers to find whether good enough information was available to link the attacks to Iraq. He advised Myers to 'go massive' and 'sweep it all up . . . [t]hings related and not'.[26] Between his much-publicised trip to Iraq in 1982 and his signing of PNAC's statement of principles, Rumsfeld had shown little interest in the country.[27] Lacking foreign policy experience, Rumsfeld was more interested in bureaucratic reform, a subject that preoccupied him even on the eve of the attacks. The neoconservatives were his main window onto the world.[28] Known for his intellectual arrogance, Rumsfeld was reportedly condescending towards Wolfowitz, Feith and Ahmed Chalabi.[29] But he deferred to Richard Perle, who was the lynchpin of the neoconservative campaign to implicate Iraq.[30]

Hours after the attacks, Perle suggested to the press that Iraq might be responsible. 'This could not have happened without the help of governments that back terrorists,' he stressed. According to Fitchett, Perle predicted that the shock of the attacks 'would galvanize U.S. policy into a systematic policy of retaliating severely against any foreign governments that have helped terrorists working against the United States'.[31] Perle's message was reinforced by Michael Ledeen who, within four hours of the attack, wrote an article for the *National Review* website blaming administration 'realists' for being indirectly responsible for the attacks: 9/11 happened because in 1991 the elder Bush and advisers such as Colin Powell and Brent Scowcroft shied away from 'finishing the job and liberating Iraq'.[32] Perle also used allies inside the administration to skew the discourse in favour of regime change. At his instigation, Bush's neoconservative speechwriter David Frum introduced a sentence in the President's speech that would also allow action against Iraq. 'We will make no distinction', Bush declared in his speech the next day, 'between the terrorists who committed these acts *and those who harbor them*' (emphasis added). With this barely noticed shift in rhetoric,

Bush had changed decades-old policy on terrorism and created the space for the neoconservative campaign against Iraq.[33] The neoconservatives' informal network allowed them to repeatedly outmanoeuvre the State Department, even encroach on its authority. Powell, according to *The New York Times*, was 'surprised' and 'distressed' to discover that without his approval, Stephen Hadley – the Deputy National Security Advisor, part of the neoconservative network – had inserted 'a far-reaching sentence' into a diplomatic letter to the UN security council which again paved the way for invading Iraq'.[34] It read: 'We may find that our self-defense requires further action with respect to other organizations and other states.'[35]

On 12 September, Mylroie, Woolsey and Charles Krauthammer wrote articles pointing fingers at Iraq. They repeated the emerging neoconservative meme that the US must go after the states that sponsored the attack.[36] Influential journalist – and neoconservative fellow traveller – Jim Hoagland reinforced this message, citing Mylroie to suggest Iraqi complicity.[37] Mylroie repeated her charges the next day; so did Woolsey and British neoconservative (and future Education Secretary) Michael Gove, both referencing Mylroie's work.[38] On 14 September, Gingrich, Kirkpatrick and Wurmser joined Mylroie at an AEI forum to make the case against Iraq.[39] Later the same day, Mylroie appeared on Fox's *O'Reilly Factor* to allege that Iraq carried out the 1993 WTC bombing. 'It would be good to get rid of Bin Laden,' she opined, but 'It wouldn't be as meaningful as getting rid of Saddam Hussein's regime.'[40] On 17 September, Mylroie once more targeted Iraq; so did Woolsey, referencing her work.[41] The story by then had a life of its own.

On 12 September, when Bush ordered his counterterrorism coordinator Richard Clarke to find out if Iraq was involved in the attacks, it made one participant at the meeting reportedly quip, 'Wolfowitz got to him.'[42] The deputy secretary had been insisting on an Iraq–Al-Qaeda link since before September 11. Bush brought up the Iraqi connection again in a telephone conversation with Tony Blair on 14 September, according to David Manning, the British prime minister's foreign policy adviser.[43] On 19 September, Bush asked Tenet to find out if there was a Saddam–Al-Qaeda link, adding: 'Vice President knows some things that might be helpful.' Cheney told Tenet that one of his staffers had picked up a report about a meeting between the September 11 hijacker Muhammad Atta and Ahmed Khalil Ibrahim Samir al-Ani, an Iraqi intelligence officer in Prague. Two days later, Tenet confirmed that FBI and CIA records showed that Atta was in north Virginia at the time the alleged meeting was to have taken place. The Prague Meeting was a myth.[44]

But by this time the story had taken off. The neoconservative case was further bolstered by a string of defectors furnished by Ahmad Chalabi, chairman of the INC. The group was established at the CIA's behest by the PR firm Rendon Group after the first Gulf War as an umbrella for the various organisations of Iraqi exiles seeking regime change.[45] The defectors would calibrate their statements to match the neoconservatives' claims. James Woolsey's law firm Shea & Gardner lobbied on behalf of the INC[46] – and after he had failed to substantiate Mylroie's claims in his two trips to the UK, he resorted to referencing INC defectors to back up his allegations.[47] In an article dated 12 October, the claims were given credence by Jim Hoagland, who relied exclusively on INC defectors.[48] The message was amplified ten days later by former Nixon speechwriter and influential neoconservative columnist William Safire in *The New York Times*, who in turn referenced Hoagland. Safire would harp on this theme in his columns and media appearances well into 2003, long after it had been discarded by others.[49]

The allegation got a further boost in November, when PBS's acclaimed *Frontline* series broadcast 'Gunning for Saddam', a documentary which gave platform to Woolsey, Perle, Chalabi, Dennis Ross and several INC defectors to press the case against Iraq.[50] On 21 December, the neoconservative case received an unexpected boost from David Rose, a British journalist long favoured by neoconservatives and intelligence agencies as a conduit.[51] He published a story in *Vanity Fair* alleging that Iraq was involved in 9/11 based on the testimony of a defector furnished by the INC. On the same night he appeared on CNN and NBC to repeat his allegations. He told NBC's Chris Matthews that 9/11 was **'a joint operation'** between **Al-Qaeda** and **Iraq**, which was training 'a super elite special forces offensive commando' unit of terrorists to target the US.[52] In the months leading up to the war Rose would produce three more equally fantastic reports, all referencing INC defectors.[53] Rose also wrote or co-authored five articles for the *Observer* alleging that Iraq supported Al-Qaeda and that the anthrax attacks in October 2001 had 'an ultimate Iraqi origin'.[54] He would also publish a glowing review of Mylroie's book – reissued for the occasion – in which he reprised her most outlandish claims.[55]

Defense Policy Board and the PNAC ultimatum

As chairman of the Defense Policy Board (DPB), Richard Perle was ideally placed to orchestrate the neoconservative campaign. The DPB is an advisory body that provides top Pentagon officials with 'independent, informed advice and opinion concerning major matters of defense policy'. Its members are appointed by the Under Secretary of Defense for Policy, a position held under Bush by Feith. The board comprises 'primarily of private sector individuals with distinguished backgrounds in national security affairs'.[56] In the months leading up to the war, its thirty members were mostly neoconservatives and aggressive militarists including many signatories to the PNAC charter.[57] Nine members of the board, including Perle, had links to defence contractors. Several of them would go on to profit significantly from the war.[58] Though nearly all members of the board were of hawkish disposition, only a select few played an active role in pressing for war. None, however, was more significant than the chairman Richard Perle.

Perle began agitating for war early. Former CIA director George Tenet recalls meeting him at the White House one morning after the attacks. 'Iraq has to pay a price for what happened yesterday,' he told Tenet, 'They bear responsibility.'[59] Though Dick Cheney had told NBC's 'Meet the Press' on 16 September that there was no evidence of Iraqi involvement in the attacks,[60] Perle took to the airwaves the same day to contradict the Vice President. He told CNN, We do know ... that Saddam Hussein has ties to

Osama bin Laden. That can be documented.' 'As long as [Saddam Hussein] is around with his desire for vengeance, he will be supporting international terrorism,' he argued. 'And we need to take this fight to the countries that harbor terrorists.'[61]

Represented by the Benador Associates – influential publicists favoured by the neoconservatives – Perle and company would find easy access to major networks and publications in the lead-up to war.[62] Access was also assured by Perle's position as a board member of Hollinger International (since renamed Sun-Times Media Group), then owned by Canadian media mogul Conrad Black.[63] Only Rupert Murdoch outdid Black in his eagerness to broadcast neoconservative opinion. Fox News and *The Weekly Standard* in particular set the tone.[64]

On 19–20 September, Richard Perle convened a nineteen-hour session of the DPB in a conference room at the Pentagon to discuss the threat posed by Saddam Hussein.[65] Both Wolfowitz and Feith attended, though the State Department was kept in the dark. Feith, known to officials as Perle's 'catspaw', had already been telling military officers to prepare plans for war against Iraq. Perle was upping the ante by inviting Bernard Lewis and Ahmad Chalabi to make the case for regime change. Chalabi argued that the Bush Administration must skip Afghanistan and make Iraq its top priority. Lewis invited the group to consider how much worse 9/11's devastation would have been had the terrorists used a weapon of mass destruction, which he suggested Iraq possessed or was developing.[66] Lewis had been conferring with Cheney as far back as the first Gulf War, but in the wake of 9/11 his jaundiced view of the Middle East found a particularly receptive audience at the White House. His views, according to Hirsh, 'had the remarkable virtue of appealing powerfully to both the hard-power enthusiasts in the administration . . . and to neoconservatives from the first Bush Administration such as Paul Wolfowitz'. He became a 'persona grata', Hirsh adds, delivering 'spine-stiffening lectures to Cheney over dinner in undisclosed locations'.[67] Cheney acknowledged Lewis's influence in an appearance on *Meet the Press*:

> I firmly believe, along with men like Bernard Lewis, who is one of the great students of that part of the world, that strong, firm U.S. response

to terror and to threats to the United States would go a long way, frankly, toward calming things in that part of the world.[68]

In a televised address to the Hebrew University's 2002 annual conference celebrating Lewis's birthday, Wolfowitz too acknowledged his influence: 'Bernard has taught how to understand the complex and important history of the Middle East, and use it to guide us where we will go next to build a better world for generations to come.' On 21 November, Lewis was also invited to the White House by Karl Rove to lecture Bush and Rice on the Islamic World.[69] David Frum, the president's neoconservative speechwriter and a Lewis admirer, reports noticing 'a marked-up copy of one of Bernard Lewis's articles' in Bush's hand shortly afterwards.[70] Lewis used various public fora to press for war.[71] According to an admiring profile in *The Wall Street Journal*, at a time when the administration was debating the appropriate response to the attack, it was Lewis who swayed views in favour of force. Frum concurs: 'Bernard comes with a very powerful explanation for why 9/11 happened,' he writes. 'Once you understand it, the policy presents itself afterward.'[72] For Lewis, writes Hirsh, 'Bin Laden's supposedly broad Muslim base, and Saddam's recalcitrance to the West, were part of the same pathology.'[73] For Lewis, Arabs only understand the language of force. This became the dominant view in the Bush Administration, particularly with Cheney and Rumsfeld. It guided 'shock and awe'. For Waldman, this heralded 'a decisive break' with the Cold War doctrine of containment: 'The Lewis Doctrine, in effect, had become U.S. policy.'[74]

For the finale of the 20 September meeting, Rumsfeld made a brief appearance to address the board.[75] He talked 'not about democracy', Heilbrunn reports, 'but about the need to demonstrate America power'.[76] (Though the next day Rumsfeld drafted a memo in which he proposed an alternative way: 'we may want to give Saddam Hussein a way out for his family to live in comfort'.[77]) The meeting concluded with attendees drafting a letter under the banner of PNAC that demanded action against Iraq, 'even if evidence does not link Iraq directly to the attack'.[78] It stressed that 'any strategy aiming at the eradication of terrorism and its sponsors must include a determined effort to remove Saddam Hussein from power in Iraq'. Significantly, it warned Bush that '[f]ailure to undertake such an effort will constitute an early and perhaps decisive surrender in the war on international terrorism.' The letter drew a direct link to the Israel–Palestine conflict and went on to focus on groups and countries that were unrelated to the attacks but at war with Israel. The letter stressed that 'any war against terrorism must target Hezbollah', and if Iran and Syria did not comply with its suggested demand to 'immediately cease all military, financial, and political support for Hezbollah and its operations', then the US 'should consider appropriate measures of retaliation against these known state sponsors of terrorism'. (The letter also recommended withholding assistance from the Palestinian Authority.)

Signatories to the letter included Perle, Podhoretz, William Kristol, Eliot Cohen, Kenneth Adelman, Robert and Donald Kagan, Reuel Marc Gerecht, Bruce Jackson, Randy Scheunemann, Martin Peretz and Clifford May. They also included Charles Krauthammer, who would become the main conduit for strategic leaks in the lead-up to war. Notably, not all attendees signed the letter, and some who signed were not attendees. Everyone who signed was a neoconservative, and those who did not were wary of its motivations. According to *The New York Times*, some members 'expressed concern that they might be pawns in what had become a bureaucratic battle' between the State and Defense Departments.[79]

Neoconservative members of the DPB were speaking with a unified voice at a time when sceptics were in disarray. Adelman – a friend of Cheney and Rumsfeld (and their respective families) and a former deputy to Jeane Kirkpatrick, who, as an arms control specialist in the Reagan Defense Department, had helped Perle and Wolfowitz secure jobs – was quick to take to the airwaves to allege Iraq's terrorist links and advocate military action.[80] In the months immediately after 9/11, he was a fixture on Fox News and was hosted almost weekly by CNN's Wolf Blitzer (a former editor of AIPAC's *Near East Report*).[81] Shortly after Bush's 2002 State of the Union address, he wrote a much-discussed article suggesting that war in Iraq would be a 'cakewalk'.[82] In April 2002, he signed another PNAC letter that asserted that the US and Israel confront a 'common enemy' which targets Israel because it is a friend of the US and shares 'American principles'. It added:

> As Secretary of Defense Rumsfeld has pointed out, Iran, Iraq, and Syria are all engaged in 'inspiring and financing a culture of political murder and suicide bombing' against Israel, just as they have aided campaigns of terrorism against the United States over the past two decades. You have declared war on international terrorism, Mr. President. Israel is fighting the same war.

To fight Israel's enemies, in other words, was to fight for America.

Adelman followed up in July with an article in which he slammed critics of US policy. 'Without excellence in any endeavors today, the Arabs should avoid criticizing others for much of anything,' he sneered, 'And without being able to offer much militarily or intellectually, European criticism of our policies becomes bitter carping, and little more.'[83] Adelman next intervened two days after Cheney's crucial 26 August speech to issue a ringing endorsement of the war.[84] Cheney was so pleased that he personally called Adelman to thank him. In October, he would use the pages of *Time* magazine to deride the administration for prolonging military action, a charge he would repeat two weeks before the invasion, in an article ridiculing Bush's pusillanimity. 'Give Saddam Hussein, a last, last, last, last, last chance. Oh please,' he taunted.[85] Adelman capped his pro-war run with an article published shortly after the fall of Baghdad in which he ridiculed those who doubted his claim that the war would be a cakewalk.[86] The significance of the Adelman contribution to the war effort is highlighted by the fact that after Baghdad fell, he was the only person besides Libby and Wolfowitz that Cheney invited to a private dinner to celebrate the victory (in her memoir, Rice is indignant at being excluded).[87]

Less influential, yet more persistent in pushing for war, was Reuel Marc Gerecht, a former CIA analyst and the director of PNAC's 'Middle East Initiative'. A protégé of Perle and Lewis, he had turned on the CIA for being overly cautious. Perle helped Gerecht financially, got him a fellowship at AEI and lent him his villa in France to write a book on Iran. He maintained close ties to the INC, serving as its unofficial intelligence handler, later funnelling its bogus claims to Feith's PCEG and OSP.[88] He and Bernard Lewis were members of a secret, quasi-official study group (Bletchley II) instituted by Wolfowitz in November 2001 to link 9/11 to Islamic history and strategise about the war. Unsurprisingly, it identified Iraq as a prime target.[89] Like his mentor Lewis, Gerecht is a subscriber to the Zionist dictum that Arabs only understand the language of force. His campaign against Iraq began long before 9/11 and intensified afterwards.[90] As the war looked more certain, he began pushing for Iran to also be included in the invasion plan.[91]

Others, including Eliot Cohen and Norman Podhoretz, also made their respective contributions to the pro-war drumbeat. Cohen had argued in a 20 November 2001 *Wall Street Journal* op-ed that Iraq was an 'obvious candidate' for retaliation because it 'not only helped al-Qaeda, but attacked Americans directly . . . and developed weapons of mass destruction'.[92] Podhoretz argued in *Commentary* that 'there can be no victory in this war if it ends with Saddam Hussein still in power'.[93] Some DPB members were more action oriented: Newt Gingrich made several trips to the CIA headquarters at Langley to cow analysts into producing intelligence that matched neoconservative policy goals.[94]

During this period, it also emerged that while Perle was pushing for war as the head of DPB, he was simultaneously trying to secure lucrative contracts for Trireme Partners L.P., a venture capital company he co-founded two months after 9/11. The firm's promotional material emphasised this privileged access to the highest echelons of the government.[95] After calls for an investigation by the chair of the House Judiciary Committee, Perle resigned as chairman of the board on 27 March 2003, though he would remain a member for another year.[96]

The board's biggest success was in helping the Pentagon triumph over bureaucratic rivals at the State Department and the CIA. It put its imprimatur behind dubious intelligence from the INC to pressure sceptics at rival agencies.[97] Rumsfeld and Wolfowitz resented the prominent role the CIA and State were assigned in the war against Afghanistan and they were eager to wrest control away. Rumsfeld saw Iraq as a means to reassert the Pentagon's authority over war making and to that end the neoconservatives proved indispensable as allies. It had been rumoured in the Pentagon for a year that Iraq might be attacked, but, according to Cockburn, 'this had been wishful thinking rather than any firm decision'. Following the attacks, the convergence of his hard-line worldview and the administration's desire for a forceful response would present him the opportunity to move centre stage. It would also elevate Paul Wolfowitz.[98]

Wolfowitz, Libby and their *idée fixe*

Dubbed the 'velociraptor' by *The Economist*, Wolfowitz had a long-standing interest in Iraq. He had first identified it as a threat in a study he prepared with Dennis Ross for the Carter Administration in 1979.[99] However, it was only in the wake of the 1991 Gulf War – in which he favoured toppling Saddam Hussein – that he turned into 'a man in the grip of an *idée fixe*'.[100] According to Bill Keller of *The New York Times*, 'in an administration that is not exactly a hotbed of Saddam coddlers, Wolfowitz has been on the case longer, more consistently, more persistently, than anyone'.[101] On 13 September, Wolfowitz declared that that the US response would include 'ending states who sponsor terrorism'. The statement drew a sharp rebuke from Powell: 'Ending terrorism is where I would like to leave it, and let Mr. Wolfowitz speak for himself,' he countered.[102]

On 15 September, Bush's top advisers gathered at Camp David to discuss the path ahead. Wolfowitz broached the subject of attacking Iraq, suggesting, without evidence, that there was a 10–50 per cent chance that it was involved in the 9/11 attacks. During a coffee break, when Bush joined Cheney, Wolfowitz and Libby for a chat, Wolfowitz pressed his case, arguing, according to Woodward, that 'war against Iraq might be easier than against Afghanistan'. His persistence annoyed both Rumsfeld and Bush, who instructed Andrew Card to tell him not to interject. According to Rice, he was also rebuked by Cheney.[103] Yet, writes Woodward, the 'intellectual godfather' of the Iraq war was 'like a drum that wouldn't stop'.[104] Cheney at this point shared Powell, Tenet and White House Chief of Staff Andrew Card's reservations about going to war with Iraq, even though he had not ruled out the possibility of a future attack.[105] General Hugh Shelton, the Chairman of the Joint Chiefs of Staff, was firmly opposed to any action against Iraq. At the end of this crucial meeting, the tally was four to nil votes against attacking Iraq. Rumsfeld abstained.[106] However, according to Tanenhaus, Woodward's account is incomplete: 'In fact, according to an informed source, Wolfowitz not only engaged Bush much more directly over coffee than has been reported, but also may have sold him on an eventual reckoning with Saddam.'[107]

Wolfowitz sent memos to Rumsfeld on 17 and 18 September, promoting Laurie Mylroie's theories about the Iraq–Al-Qaeda link.[108] After the administration decided against including Iraq in the president's 20 September speech to both houses of Congress, Cheney had to tell Wolfowitz to 'stop agitating for targeting Saddam'.[109]

Like David Frum, Wolfowitz was also working private channels in the immediate aftermath of 9/11. An official who reviewed the Pentagon's communication logs told Cockburn that

> every night, there were a lot of calls to Richard Perle, calls to Scooter Libby . . . I always felt that the Perles of this world knew where Paul was coming from, and could get them to do what they wanted.[110]

In his eagerness to implicate Iraq, Wolfowitz was stepping on the State Department's and the CIA's toes. Following the 19–20 September DPB meeting, Wolfowitz sent neoconservative hawk James Woolsey aboard a government plane on a personal intelligence mission to London to seek out Iraqi exiles who might corroborate Mylroie's theories and the Prague Meeting.[111] Woolsey, the former CIA director, had in the past served as an unofficial liaison to the INC and other Iraqi opposition groups.[112] Powell and CIA Director George Tenet found out about Woolsey's freelance sleuthing only after police in Wales called the US embassy to confirm if he was indeed on an official mission as he claimed.[113]

Shortly after the military campaign against Afghanistan got

underway, Wolfowitz recruited AEI head Christopher DeMuth to develop strategies for policy makers and explanations as to how terrorist acts relate to 'Islamic history, the history of the Middle East, and contemporary Middle East tensions'. The group he put together once again featured Bernard Lewis. Dubbed Bletchley II (after the World War II group of mathematicians based at Bletchley Park tasked with breaking the German ULTRA code), it included a dozen panellists who were required to work under conditions of strict secrecy.[114] (This was a potential a breach of the Federal Advisory Committee Act's disclosure requirements for federal government policy advisers.[115]) Lewis was joined by other neoconservative hard-liners such as Fouad Ajami and Reuel Marc Gerecht. Convened in Virginia on 29 November 2001, the group's deliberations were distilled into a seven-page report entitled *The Delta of Terrorism* that reproduced a recurring theme in Lewis's writings: a war 'within Islam'. September 11 'was not an isolated action that called for policing and crime fighting', it concluded; the 'United States was likely in for a two-generation battle with radical Islam'. It identified Egypt, Saudi Arabia and Iran as problems, but it settled on Iraq as the target because it was 'different, weaker, more vulnerable'. However, it saw no contradiction in at the same time declaring Iraq 'the most menacing, active and unavoidable threat'.[116] According to Woodward, 'Cheney was pleased with the memo, and it had a strong impact on President Bush, causing him to focus on the "malignancy" of the Middle East.'[117]

Wolfowitz's most significant ally in the crusade against Iraq was Irving Libby, his former Yale student whom he had reportedly 'helped climb the Washington escalator of success'.[118] Libby had served on the board of the RAND Corporation and as a consultant to the weapons manufacturer Northrop Grumman; he owned shares in several armaments companies.[119] A former anti-war radical, he transformed, according to a one-time friend, after his exposure to what she called the 'The Dark Side' – Paul Wolfowitz. She compared his neoconservative association to joining 'a secret society'.[120] Referred to as 'Cheney's Cheney', Libby's position, power and access were unprecedented. He had accepted the appointment as Cheney's chief of staff on the condition that he also be given the additional titles of National Security Adviser to the Vice President and Assistant to the President in order to 'give him more clout at interagency meetings'.[121] He was a member of the DPB, and, along with fellow neoconservative Stephen Hadley, the only non-principal to attend NSC meetings. 'It was a trifecta of positions probably never held before by a single person,' writes Woodward.[122] Libby sat atop two separate and parallel hierarchies in the White House. 'No one save Cheney and Bush themselves were his superiors', notes Gellman.[123] Libby would do 'so much of the preparation for the vice president's meetings and events, and so much of the hard work' that many of the vice president's close associates saw him as 'almost part of Cheney's brain'. The vice president, according to them, was 'lost without Libby'.[124]

If Libby's relationship with Cheney was close, it was closer still with Wolfowitz, and as result the degree of coordination between the two was higher than between Cheney and Rumsfeld.[125] In the lead-up to war, Libby became the lynchpin for all neoconservative activity in the Bush Administration. He coordinated the neoconservatives scattered in the different departments to enforce unanimity. Like Wolfowitz he also maintained close working relations with the Israelis. 'Israeli officials liked Libby', writes Ori Nir of the Jewish daily *Forward*. 'They described him as an important contact who was accessible, genuinely interested in Israel-related issues and very sympathetic to their cause.'[126] His loyalties to Israel were such that the British Foreign Secretary Jack Straw remarked: 'It's a toss-up whether Libby is working for the Israelis or the Americans on any given day.'[127] (In an unusual departure from established protocol, in 2003 when the president held meetings with Ariel Sharon's aides, he was joined by Libby, Feith and Abrams.[128]) During the 1991 Gulf crisis, Libby had proposed putting Special Forces into western Iraq to protect Israel. After the war, he was one of the principal authors of the infamous Defense Policy Guidance 1992, which would morph into PNAC's statement of principles and eventually into Bush's National Security Strategy of 2002.[129] Before returning to the limelight, Libby made a fortune as a partner of Leonard Garment (Richard Nixon's personal attorney), representing fugitive swindler and Mossad agent

Marc Rich.[130] In 2000, he joined Wolfowitz, Kristol and Kagan to author PNAC's 'Rebuilding America's Defenses'.[131]

Libby also helped Laurie Mylroie develop and promote her fantastic theories.[132] In the days after 9/11, Libby appears to have brought Cheney, who had earlier rejected Iraqi involvement in the attacks, to the Mylroiean view. According to Tenet, he joined Cheney to push the CIA hard on the issue: 'our answers never satisfied [Cheney] or some of our other regular "customers." Paul Wolfowitz and Scooter Libby, for example, were relentless in asking us to check, recheck, and re-recheck.'[133] Richard Clarke's experience was similar: he recalls an incident where Libby grabbed him in the White House driveway to say, 'I hear you don't believe this report that Mohammed Atta was talking to Iraqi people in Prague.'

> And I said, 'I don't believe it because it's not true.' And he said, 'You're wrong. You know you're wrong. Go back . . . Look at the rest of the reports and find out that you're wrong.' And I understood what he was saying, which was, 'This is a report that we want to believe, and stop saying it's not true. It's a real problem for the vice president's office that you, the counterterrorism coordinator, are walking around saying that this isn't a true report.'[134]

In April 2002, Libby also tried to convince MI6 chief Richard Dearlove of the Iraq–Al-Qaeda connection.[135]

After the CIA was asked by the Senate to produce an NIE on Iraq, Cheney would make around a dozen trips to the CIA headquarters to demand a more 'forward-leaning' interpretation of the threat. He was always accompanied by Libby, but sometimes Libby would also go on his own. Libby played the 'bad cop' to Cheney's polite 'good cop'.[136] In one instance, the overbearing pressure from Libby and Hadley reportedly reduced the generally pliable head of the Directorate of Intelligence Jami Miscik to tears.[137] Cheney, according to the *Los Angeles Times*, 'was insistent, sometimes asking the same question again and again as if he hoped the answer would change'.[138] Given Cheney's strident posture on regime change, the message was not lost on the analysts.[139] Where the intelligence agencies did not oblige, Cheney simply presented the neoconservatives' claims as the consensus view. Despite warnings from the CIA and FBI, for example, Cheney went on NBC's *Meet the Press* on 9 December 2002 to claim that the Prague Meeting had been 'pretty well confirmed'.

The CIA's caution enraged the neoconservatives. According to investigative journalist James Risen, 'Israeli intelligence played a hidden role in convincing Wolfowitz that he couldn't trust the CIA', which led him to turn to Chalabi and to establish units at the Pentagon modelled after Team B to produce intelligence that accorded with the administration's aims.[140] The first of these was the Policy Counterterrorism Evaluation Group.

PCEG and Feith-based intelligence

Douglas Feith set up the Policy Counterterrorism Evaluation Group (PCEG) in the immediate aftermath of 9/11 for the sole purpose of implicating Iraq. Feith's worldview had been shaped early by the Revisionist Zionism of his father, the lectures he took with Richard Pipes at Harvard, and the internship former NSC staffer and future secretary of the US Navy John Lehman arranged for him at ACDA (where he would work with Wolfowitz and Fukuyama among others) and another that Perle arranged for him at Henry Jackson's office.[141] Pipes, who joined the Reagan Administration, arranged a short-lived appointment for Feith at the NSC, which ended under suspicions of espionage. But Feith was soon rehabilitated and brought back to government in 1982 by Perle, who was working at Reagan's Defense Department. After leaving government service, Feith started a law firm with L. Marc Zell, representing the Israeli embassy in Washington among others (his partner Zell meanwhile represented West Bank Israeli settlers).[142] After spending the 1990s consulting for Israel's Likud and lobbying against the Oslo Peace Process, Feith returned to government when Perle recommended him for the Pentagon post.

PCEG would provide Rumsfeld, Wolfowitz and Feith with data they could use to disparage, undermine and contradict the CIA's analysis. It was run by David Wurmser and Michael Maloof.[143]

According to Paul Pillar, the former National Intelligence Officer for Near East and South Asia, PCEG

> seemed to be devoted overwhelmingly, perhaps exclusively, to the purpose of assembling these scraps of information that would point to links between Iraq and Al Qaida . . . the driving force here, quite clear, was the attempt . . . at the policy level to link the whole Iraq war to the idea of terrorism and the mood of the public after 9/11.[144]

The group eschewed traditional intelligence techniques in favour of dubious sources furnished by the INC's Chalabi, who has since admitted that the intelligence he produced was deliberately aimed at precipitating an invasion.[145] With access to raw intelligence, it frequently inserted into its reports claims that had been discarded by the CIA and DIA. The most prominent among these was the testimony of Ibn al-Shaykh al-Libi, an Al-Qaeda operative who under Egyptian torture had said that Iraq trained terrorists in the use of proscribed weapons. Only a month later, in February 2002, the claim had been discarded by the Defense Intelligence Agency (DIA); they believed that al-Libi was 'intentionally misleading the debriefers'. Yet, administration officials would reference this claim right up to the time of the invasion.[146]

Each week the group would brief the Undersecretary of Defense for Intelligence Stephen Cambone on its appropriately alarmist conclusions. According to Risen,

> Old ethnic, religious and political divides between terrorist groups were breaking down, the two men warned, posing an ominous new threat. They saw alliances among a wide range of Islamic terrorists, and theorized about a convergence of Sunni and Shiite extremist groups and secular Arab governments. Their conclusions, delivered to senior Bush administration officials, connected Iraq and Al Qaeda, Saddam Hussein and Osama bin Laden.[147]

The group produced a 'sociometric diagram' of links between disparate organisations with little in common. Describing it as the '[l]eave no dot unconnected' approach, both the CIA and the DIA remained sceptical that governments as diverse as those in Iraq, Syria, Saudi Arabia, Lebanon and Iran could be linked to anything like a cohesive terrorist network . . . The CIA saw little evidence, for example, that the Sunni-dominated Qaeda and the Shiite-dominated Hezbollah had worked together on terrorist attacks.[148]

However, as Bamford points out, 'the primary purpose of the unit was to come up with the basis to counter the CIA, whose analysts had consistently found no credible links between Al Qaeda and Hussein'.[149] Rumsfeld acknowledged as much in an October 2002 press briefing, according to Dreyfuss and Vest, who say that the 'primary purpose of the unit was to cull factoids, which were then used to disparage, undermine, and contradict the CIA'.[150] So did Wolfowitz when he told *The New York Times* that the 'lens through which you're looking for facts affects what you look for'.[151] The CIA was already wary that Pentagon civilians were 'politicizing intelligence to fit their hawkish views on Iraq'.[152] Wurmser was subsequently transferred to the State Department to join the hard-line undersecretary John Bolton and keep an eye on Colin Powell.[153]

Maloof, a Lebanese-American former journalist, who earlier had to give up his reporting career as a result of a conflict-of-interest issue, had served under Perle during the Reagan Administration. A long-time Pentagon contractor, his security clearance had been suspended under the Clinton Administration. Feith and Perle restored it, only for it to be revoked again after an FBI probe linked him to Imad el-Hage, a Lebanese-American businessman under investigation for arms trafficking.[154] He was also suspected of having leaked classified information to the news media.

Before the end of 2001, the PCEG had briefed Perle, Bolton, Wolfowitz and other Pentagon officials. According to Maloof, the findings led Wolfowitz to exclaim, 'How come I'm not hearing this from anybody else?'[155] On 21 September, the CIA daily brief had informed Bush in no uncertain terms that 'there was scant credible evidence that Iraq had any significant collaborative ties with Al Qaeda'.[156] However, it appears that by late November, the neoconservative propaganda barrage had overridden all scepticism. On 21 November 2001 Bush authorised Donald Rumsfeld to begin planning for an attack on Iraq. At this stage it was still a tentative proposal since Bush advised Rumsfeld not to tell anyone else, including the CIA director.[157] Cheney, who in his 16 September appearance on *Meet the Press* had denied links between Iraq and the 9/11 attacks, eventually changed his tune. He also began invoking the Mylroie thesis of an Iraqi involvement in the 1993 WTC attacks.

VP and the 'one percent doctrine'

Col. (ret.) Lawrence Wilkerson, Colin Powell's chief of staff, summed up the reasons why the neoconservatives were able to triumph over administration realists thus: 'The Vice President'.[158] Richard 'Dick' Cheney is widely considered the most powerful vice president in US history.[159] He was second only to Wolfowitz in his zeal for the war.[160] He played a central role in expanding executive power, eroding checks and balances, pushing an aggressive war and sanctioning torture.[161] Secrecy was one of his hallmarks: he continually avoided official scrutiny by refusing to disclose his office's workings. According to *The Washington Post*, 'the vice president's office goes to unusual lengths to avoid transparency. Cheney declines to disclose the names or even the size of his staff, generally releases no public calendar, and ordered the Secret Service to destroy his visitor logs'.[162] His legal flank was protected by his combative general counsel David Addington, according to whose interpretation 'the vice presidency is a unique office that is neither a part of the executive branch nor a part of the legislative branch', and is therefore exempt from the rules governing either.[163]

Insiders have suggested that Bush, a foreign policy novice, only had views on 'basic principles'; in making dozens of complex decisions he relied 'on pre-determined staff papers'.[164] One official involved in US policy towards North Korea told Dreyfuss:

> The president is given only the most basic notions about the Korea issue. They tell him, 'Above South Korea is a country called North Korea. It is an evil regime.' . . . So that translates into a presidential decision: Why enter into any agreement with an evil regime?[165]

According to one Pentagon official, Bush served more as a 'master-of-ceremonies, attending to the morale of the management team and focusing on narrow issues'.[166] Canny advisers found it easy to shape Bush's preferences.[167]

A seasoned politician adept at bureaucratic intrigue, Cheney was able to dominate the executive branch.[168] While some of Cheney's former colleagues have tried to exonerate him by suggesting that his radicalism is a result of the trauma of 9/11, others maintain that his quiet demeanour only concealed the extremist he always was.[169] His hard-line views were already in evidence when he joined Rumsfeld and the neoconservatives opposing détente in the 1970s. Cheney continued to espouse radical views during his subsequent stints in Congress, including his belief in untrammelled executive power. However, despite his association with AEI and JINSA, his foreign policy outlook remained realist, if overly hard-line. As the CEO of Halliburton, on several occasions he had complained about US sanctions on Iraq, which he considered detrimental to US commercial interests. He also maintained close ties with Saudi Arabia, a neoconservative bugbear. But beyond the realm of self-interest, the long association with the neoconservatives had shaped his worldview to favour one-sided policies towards Israel.[170] Like Bernard Lewis, he believed that Arabs only understand the language of force. Though in 1991 as defense secretary he joined Bush Administration realists to decide against overthrowing Hussein, Mann suggests that he privately sympathised with the neoconservatives.[171] Cheney resented what he considered Bush and his cabinet's pusillanimity.[172]

There were few people Cheney resented more than Colin Powell, the former chairman of the Joint Chiefs of Staff whose reputation was built on a war that he had initially opposed. Cheney tried to constrain Powell by placing his loyalists all around the secretary of state. Though he failed to install Wolfowitz as Powell's deputy, he overrode the secretary of state's objections to place Bolton, Wurmser, Robert Zoellick and his daughter Elizabeth Cheney at the State Department. He placed neoconservatives Stephen Hadley and Elliott Abrams at the NSC.[173] (He failed to get Wolfowitz the top job at the CIA due to the national security issues raised by the latter's on-going illicit relationship with foreign national Shaha

Ali Riza.)[174] All the appointments had one thing in common: their affiliation to PNAC, JINSA and AEI (where Cheney's wife, Lynne, is a fellow).[175]

Having failed to install loyalists at the CIA, Cheney's total control over the national security apparatus remained uncertain.[176] In a move unprecedented for a vice president, he established his own parallel national security council, with fifteen regional and military experts.[177] It was headed by Libby, who populated it with think tankers from AEI, WINEP and the Hudson Institute and with Cheney loyalists from Washington law firms.[178] The NSC and the CIA had been created by the National Security Act of 1947 at the beginning of the Cold War. But Cheney was building his shadow government without enabling legislation and thereby deliberately operating beyond the oversight of Congress and the courts.[179] Cheney was pursuing a foreign policy completely separate from the NSC's, and its primary preoccupation was to find the Iraq–Al-Qaeda link.[180]

This network was the key to his influence. It served not only as his 'eyes and ears' but at times also 'as his fists'.[181] The coordination between OVP and the other departments rendered the rest of the government so ineffectual that in order to avoid interference, they often had to operate outside the normal interagency process. Cheney even had the entire NSC computer system set up so that his staff would receive a blind copy of every email sent by government officials without their knowledge.[182] According to Wilkerson,

> [Cheney] set up a staff that knew what the statutory NSC was doing, but the NSC statutory staff didn't know what *his* staff was doing. The vice president's staff could read the statutory NSC's e-mail, but the NSC couldn't read *their* e-mail. So, once someone on the statutory NSC figured it out, they used various work-arounds. Like, for example, they would walk to someone's office, rather than send an e-mail, if what they were going to talk about they didn't want to reveal to the vice president's very powerful staff.[183]

However, Cheney's spies within the bureaucracy made such interaction exceedingly risky.[184] Cheney also set another precedent: he not only received a daily briefing from the CIA, he also sat in on the president's and attended all NSC principals' meetings.[185]

The NSC, which generally handles interagency disputes, had been enervated by resignations and reassignments. It was headed by Rice, who, according to one former top CIA official, was a 'very, very weak national security advisor [who] didn't really manage anything ... I think the real national security advisor was Cheney, and so Cheney and Rumsfeld could do what they wanted.'[186] Rice was distrusted because of her mentor Brent Scowcroft's known opposition to war. And to keep her in check the hawks installed Hadley – a close associate of Wolfowitz, Libby and Ledeen – as her deputy.[187] There were very few senior Iraq experts on the NSC staff, and those who remained left because of policy disputes with the neoconservatives.[188] Alina Romanowski, a Middle East expert, had her appointment held up by the neo-conservatives because she was suspected of being 'insufficiently supportive of the Jewish state'.[189] The void was filled in December 2002 by the appointment of Iran–Contra felon Elliott Abrams as top Middle East adviser.[190] '[The neoconservatives] worked really hard for Abrams', says former Pentagon desk officer Lt Col Karen Kwiatkowski (USAF);[191] and both Iran and Iraq became part of his portfolio. 'I have two-thirds of the axis of evil!' he reportedly enthused to one well-wisher.[192] It led one senior official to quip that 'the Likudniks are really in charge now'.[193]

If for the neoconservatives his appointment was cause for 'jubilation', for Israel it was 'a gift from heaven'.[194] His appointment came, according to one State Department official, as 'a signal victory for those who have argued that the road to peace in the Middle East runs through Baghdad, rather than Jerusalem'.[195] Former ambassador Joseph Wilson called it 'a very major move, both for Iraq and the Mideast peace process'. Abrams, he said, 'serves his constituency's interest', meaning the pro-Likud neo-conservatives.[196] He also led a task force that called for the US to take direct control of Iraq's oil fields after an invasion. A Russia specialist with little competence in other regions, Rice ended up relying on Abrams for all things Middle East. Because of his 'unambiguous views', according to one friend, Rice saw him 'not just as a good manager but a good strategist'.[197]

Abrams was joined at the NSC by the new Deputy National Security Adviser Wayne Downing, who had once served as a consultant to the INC and was a member of the CLI. With former CIA operative Duane 'Dewey' Clarridge, Downing had prepared a military plan for the overthrow of Saddam Hussein by US-trained INC guerrillas. The plan called for the presence of US military advisers on the ground and warplanes overhead. According to Scott Ritter,

> The 'Downing Plan' was a nice bit of trickery, plotting what was ostensibly an Iraqi opposition military force with minor U.S. military involvement, but masking what was in reality a much larger U.S. military effort with a minor role played by Chalabi's INC 'army.'[198]

Downing also served on the boards of several military contractors including SAIC, which would go on to receive major reconstruction contracts in Iraq.[199] He was a frequent commentator on NBC; a 2008 *New York Times* investigation would reveal him as one of the seventy-five 'message force multipliers' – military shills hired to relay Pentagon propaganda in the guise of authoritative professional analysis.[200]

Meanwhile, Powell was shadowed by Undersecretary of State for Arms Control and International Security Affairs John Bolton. A radical nationalist in the Rumsfeld–Cheney mould, Bolton had come to espouse neoconservative views, including fervent Zionism, through his association with AEI, JINSA and PNAC.[201] An unabashed unilateralist, Bolton questioned the legitimacy of the UN and led a campaign to rescind multilateral treaties. Early in the campaign against Iraq, Bolton would orchestrate the sacking of José Bustani, the head of the Organisation for the Prohibition of Chemical Weapons (OPCW), for offering to resolve the dispute over Iraq's alleged WMDs by persuading Iraq to sign the CWC. This would have allowed OPCW to conduct the inspections, instead of UNMOVIC, which the Iraqis (rightly) suspected of being infiltrated by the CIA.[202] After much manoeuvring, Bolton succeeded in terminating Bustani's appointment by threatening to withhold US dues from OPCW.[203]

According to the Jewish daily *Forward*, Bolton participated in meetings with Israeli officials, including members of Mossad, without first seeking 'country clearance' as the rules required. He also travelled to Israel two months ahead of the invasion to meet with Benjamin Netanyahu and Ariel Sharon to discuss strategies for 'preventing the spread' of WMDs. Already in February 2003, Bolton had started calling for future targeting of Syria, Iran and North Korea.[204] According to officials, Bolton often blocked Powell and, on one occasion, his successor Condoleezza Rice 'from receiving information vital to US strategies on Iran'.[205]

Equally chilling was the presence of Elizabeth Cheney, whose role, according to insiders, was to serve as 'an ace-in-the-hole' for the OVP.[206] Her presence had a sobering effect on the department's Middle East specialists, most of whom opposed the war, hence were distrusted by the neoconservatives.[207] 'With the unspoken support of her father,' writes Dreyfuss,

> Cheney has kept a hawk's eye on Iraq policy within the department, intimidating opponents of the neoconservative axis within the administration. And, less visibly, according to former officials who've worked with her, she has made her influence felt in choosing officials, selecting (or blocking) the appointment of ambassadors and other foreign service officers, and weighing in on other bureaucratic battles at the department.[208]

The Near East Affairs bureau, according to Parker Borg, a thirty-year State Department veteran and deputy chief of counterterrorism, was 'chilled' by her presence. 'How vocal would you be about commenting on Middle East policy with the vice president's daughter there?'[209] Timothy Phelps of *Newsday* reported that she operates what was essentially a 'shadow Middle East policy', separate from the rest of the State Department.[210]

The September 11 attacks had caught the Pentagon flat-footed. The neoconservatives watched with increasing exasperation as the CIA and State Department took charge of the administration's response. Significantly, even Cheney had disappointed them: to their dismay, he first rejected the Iraq connection, and then he endorsed the CIA's plan for Afghanistan. But as the Afghan war dragged on, Cheney was slowly brought around. In the process, he promulgated his infamous 'one percent doctrine' that, as described by investigative journalist Ron Suskind, mandated that 'even if there's just a one percent chance of the unimaginable coming due, act if it is a certainty'.[211] Powell also noted, writes Woodward, that 'Cheney took intelligence and converted uncertainty and ambiguity into fact.'[212] Cheney was keen to thwart the possibility, however marginal, that Iraq might reconstitute its nuclear programme, it might hand those weapons to terrorists, and they might detonate them in the US. It was therefore not necessary for the administration to produce conclusive proof: it needed only enough to plausibly argue the necessity of preventive war. Since the CIA's institutional constraints would frustrate any such effort, Cheney instead endorsed Wolfowitz, Libby and Feith's ad hoc intelligence operation. It was time to put the fear of America's God back into the Arabs.

On 29 January 2002 Bush delivered his State of the Union address in which he for the first time broached the subject of pre-emption. Bush warned that he would not 'wait on events as dangers gather' or 'stand by as peril draws closer'. Significantly, he branded Iraq, Iran and North Korea – the same three states identified by the Rumsfeld Commission three years earlier – as an 'axis of evil'. The phrase originated with David Frum, whose more prosaic suggestion 'axis of hatred' was given theological resonance by Bush's born-again evangelical lead speechwriter Michael Gerson. The 'axis of evil' speech was the triumph of a deliberate policy. The neoconservatives had won the first leg of the battle: Iraq was on the official agenda. They now had to manufacture a case to overcome bureaucratic inertia and public scepticism.

Conclusion

Since 1990, the desire to unseat Saddam Hussein had been common to both Republican and Democratic administrations. It was also shared by a substantial part of the US public. But since the Gulf War of 1991, every administration had considered Iraq contained and Hussein little more than a nuisance. Few believed that Iraq posed a direct threat to the US; fewer saw the threat as imminent. Though some uncertainty existed with regards to Iraq's illicit weapons programmes, few considered it capable of striking the US. The only conceivable scenario in which it could do that was by passing dangerous weapons to terrorists committed to harming the US. That Iraq possessed such weapons and that Iraq would pass them on to terrorists were both dubious propositions. But beginning in the early 1990s, a neoconservative campaign had tried to link Iraq to various terrorist attacks against the US. In alliance with the INC, the neoconservatives had also been busy disseminating claims about Iraq's alleged quest for nuclear weapons. In 1998, they had successfully lobbied to make the regime change the official policy of the United States with the Iraq Liberation Act. But before September 2001, they had been unable to overcome the institutional barriers towards the use of military force. The terrorist attacks and the resulting shock presented an opportunity that the neoconservatives were able to fully exploit. As this chapter has shown, the neoconservatives used both official and private channels to bring Iraq – a country that had no role in the 9/11 attacks – into the ambit of the 'war on terror'. With the internal battle thus won, the neoconservatives now had to get the machinery of state behind the war policy. For this the administration needed a case plausible enough to make the war seem one of necessity rather than of choice. The key component of the case – evidence of Iraq's alleged WMDs – was entirely furnished by the neoconservatives or their allies, as the next chapter will demonstrate.

5 Selling the War

By the end of 2001, the neoconservatives had successfully put Iraq on the agenda. Administration hawks were now determined to topple Saddam Hussein. But they still needed a convincing rationale to show that Iraq posed an imminent threat. The quick collapse of the Taliban regime in Afghanistan had quieted some of the revanchist fury. The trauma of 9/11 was wearing off. The flurry of false alarms, beginning with the anthrax scare, and the frequent tweaking of colour-coded terror warnings were meeting with increasing scepticism. Grumbling was getting louder inside the government. The war party was losing momentum.

But by autumn 2002, the hawks had defeated internal opposition, secured Congressional authorisation, and cowed the public into endorsing the war. After his April 2002 visit to Washington, the head of Britain's MI6 Richard Dearlove had reported that, 'intelligence and facts were being fixed around [the policy of regime change]'.[1] Bush had already embraced the idea of pre-emption in his 29 January 2002 State of the Union speech. He reiterated it in his promulgation of the 'Bush Doctrine' during his 1 June 2002 speech at West Point. Pre-emption became official policy with the National Security Strategy of September 2002.

The turnaround had come as a result of a coordinated effort by the neoconservatives and their allies to manufacture a case that presented Iraq as an imminent threat. The campaign used government and private channels to circumvent institutional barriers. It began with an unlikely source.

The great terror of a threatening storm

The administration's case got an early boost from articles appearing in the liberal press, from publications ostensibly critical of the conservative administration. The authors were not neoconservatives, but, like the neoconservatives, viewed the Middle East through the Israeli prism. In March 2002, the *New Yorker* published 'The Great Terror', an 18,000-word article by Jeffrey Goldberg that invoked the Nazi Holocaust to emphasise the scale of Saddam Hussein's crimes.[2] The core of the story was an interview with a prisoner, Muhammad Mansour Shahab, being held by the Patriotic Union of Kurdistan in the Kurdish-held Iraqi town of Sulaimaniya. Shahab claimed to be a gunrunner for Al-Qaeda who had relayed lethal materiel from Iraq to Afghanistan. Both Bush and Cheney cited the article as proof of the connection between Iraq and Al-Qaeda. The piece, according to one analyst, provided 'an eloquent set of images for the Bush administration's Iraq policy'.[3] The timing was propitious: a joint FBI and CIA investigation had just shown definitively that Muhammad Atta was in the US at the time when he was alleged to have been meeting an Iraqi intelligence officer in Prague. That much of the story focused on the threat to Israel elicited little comment. Months later, when the same prisoner was interviewed by British journalist Jason Burke, he was able to quickly establish the falsity of the claims. However, by then the story had taken off, giving the Iraq–Al-Qaeda link a new lease of life.[4]

'The Great Terror' merely proved the beginning of a campaign; later in October, Goldberg would openly advocate for war, because the Iraq–Al-Qaeda link was 'beyond doubt'; and 'naive' were those who had concluded that 'an invasion of Iraq will cause America to be loathed in the Middle East, rather than respected'.[5] Hours after Bush had signed a Congressional resolution authorising the use of force against Iraq, Goldberg appeared on CNN reiterating the threat from Iraq's 'weaponized aflatoxin'.[6] On 10 February – a day after 'The Great Terror' had been debunked – Goldberg published another story reviving the Saddam–Al-Qaeda link, a claim he then repeated on NPR's *All Things Considered*.[7]

The same month Goldberg published 'The Great Terror', a

strident call for war also appeared in the influential establish-ment journal *Foreign Affairs*. It argued that the US had 'no choice left but to invade Iraq itself'.[8] The author was Kenneth Pollack, the director of research at the Saban Center for Middle East Policy. Pollack was using his pedigree as a former NSC official in the Clinton Administration and as a liberal critic of the con-servative administration. In September 2002, he rushed out *The Threatening Storm: The Case for Invading Iraq* in which he dis-paraged the IAEA and the efficacy of UN weapons inspectors, who he argued had failed to thwart Iraq's nuclear ambitions. Short of a full-scale invasion, deterrence was impossible, he argued.[9] The book received two glowing reviews in *The New York Times*[10] fol-lowed by fulsome praise from the paper's editor Bill Keller, who called it 'the most influential book of this season' for providing 'intellectual cover for every liberal who finds himself inclining toward war but uneasy about Mr. Bush'.[11]

Based on dubious claims from defectors, exiles and some intel-ligence sources, the book presented few facts to challenge the IAEA's published record of nuclear disarmament in Iraq.[12] *The New York Times* subsequently invited Pollack to make the case for war in its opinion pages, relaxing its conventional 800-word limit. Pollack wrote or co-authored three op-eds – on 26 September 2002 (1,371 words), on 27 January 2003 with Martin Indyk of the Saban Centre (1,345 words) and on 21 February 2003 (1,760 words) – each more belligerent than the previous one.[13] The articles asserted Iraq's possession of nuclear weapons as fact, recommended avoiding the 'inspections trap' and advocated invasion. Besides his frequent appearances on CNN as a consult-ant, Pollack expounded his case on NPR, CBS, Fox, MSNBC, Charlie Rose and even Oprah. Pollack's familial ties helped. He is married to Andrea Koppel of CNN and his father-in-law is Ted Koppel, the star anchor of ABC's *Nightline* and a fellow war booster. (Embedded within the 3rd Infantry Division, Koppel would exhort soldiers, misquoting Shakespeare, to 'Wreak havoc and unleash the dogs of war!'[14]) Shortly after the war *The New York Times* would give Pollack a generous 1,900 words to insist that the WMDs would be found, and in case they were not, it still would not invalidate his pro-war argument.[15] Later in 2007, the paper would allow Pollack to reinvent himself as a 'critic' of the war who had turned into a grudging advocate for an escalation.[16]

Cheney declares war

George Bush ordered Donald Rumsfeld to start preparing plans for war two months after the 9/11 attacks, but according to Woodward, he was dithering as late as 5 August 2002 when Powell made a last-bid effort to dissuade him (Feith places Bush's decision even later, in December 2002).[17] Powell's effort proved futile. On 26 August, in a hawkish speech to a gathering of the Veterans of Foreign Wars in Nashville, Cheney pre-empted any possibility of de-escalation. 'Simply stated,' he asserted, 'there is no doubt that Saddam Hussein now has weapons of mass destruction, there is no doubt that he is amassing them to use against our friends, against our allies and against us.' Renewed sanctions would be 'futile'. He was followed the next day by Rumsfeld with a similarly hard-line message.[18] On 29 August, in San Antonio, Cheney repeated his claims, this time to the Veterans of the Korean War. ('As for the reaction of the Arab street,' he assured, 'the Middle East expert Professor Fouad Ajami [member of Wolfowitz's Bletchley II] predicts that after liberation in Basra and Baghdad, the streets are sure to erupt in joy.')

The speeches were widely interpreted as official policy and Cheney's claims about Iraq's illicit weapons were believed to represent the consensus of the intelligence agencies.[19] In fact, the speech was never vetted by the CIA, as is mandated for all White House speeches on national security issues.[20] Neither was it approved by Bush.[21] But the gambit paid: Bush's hand was forced and Powell neutralised.[22] On 7 September, in a news conference with Tony Blair, Bush claimed that according to an IAEA report, Iraq was six months from developing a nuclear weapon; no such report existed. The debate between hawks and sceptics had been settled in favour of the Pentagon and the OVP. It was time now to furnish the evidence.

Over a decade of propaganda had left little doubt in US minds that Iraq had WMDs.[23] Congress was no less credulous, but for it to approve the massive appropriations for war, it would have to be presented with a case that met the minimal standards of evidence. More significant than Congress, however, was the resistance the policy was likely to face within the state bureaucracy. Every state evolves structures to keep in check politicians' tendency to allow short-term political considerations to undermine long-term interests. The reservations of the State Department, the CIA, the Joint Chiefs of Staff and the diplomatic corps could potentially derail the campaign for war. The war party had to cajole, deceive or browbeat them. Administration hawks would also have to construct a case plausible enough to give allies legal cover. This would not have been possible without the neoconservatives.

By early 2002, with the help of Chris Carney and Christina Shelton, two DIA analysts detailed to Feith, PCEG had prepared a 150-page briefing and slide presentation which was taken to Rumsfeld.[24] Rumsfeld advised Feith to make the presentation to CIA Director George Tenet, whom he visited on 15 August. According to Tenet, the presentation entitled 'Iraq and al-Qa'ida – Making the Case' was made by Shelton, who

> started out by saying that there should be 'no more debate' on the Iraq–al-Qa'ida relationship. 'It is an open-and-shut case,' she said. 'No further analysis is required.' [. . .] The briefing slides she used were equally self-certain. One slide said that Iraq and al-Qa'ida had a 'mature, symbiotic relationship'. . . Another slide said there were 'some indications of possible Iraq coordination with Al Qaeda specifically related to 9/11.'[25]

Those present, according to one attendee, were 'nonplussed'. 'Much of it', according to one participant's notes, 'we had discounted already'.[26] For Tenet it was 'complete crap'.[27] Undeterred, Feith went behind Tenet's back to make the same presentation to Hadley and Libby.[28] Cheney used this briefing to later allege that 'there have been a number of contacts [between Iraq and Al-Qaeda] over the years'.[29] Tenet, who had earlier disparaged 'Team Feith' for its 'Feith-based intelligence', would himself change his tune, dispatching a letter to the Senate Select Committee on Intelligence on 7 October 2002 echoing Feith's claims.[30]

Office of Special Plans

In August 2002, with Wolfowitz's blessing, the modestly resourced PCEG was absorbed into a more sophisticated operation: the OSP. Feith set it up at the Pentagon Policy Directorate's Near East and South Asia Bureau (NESA).[31] Powell privately called it Feith's 'Gestapo office'[32] and the men who ran it the 'JINSA crowd'.[33] Almost all of the evidence for the claims about Iraq's alleged WMDs and its ties to Al-Qaeda would originate here. The propaganda it produced was crucial in deciding the intramural debates on Iraq.[34] 'If the president and Congress were to be sold the need for war,' writes former DIA analyst Patrick Lang,

> information had to be available with which to argue against what was seen as the lack of imagination and timidity of regular intelligence analysts. To facilitate the flow of such 'information' to the president, a dedicated apparatus centered in the [OVP] created [the OSP] to 'stovepipe' raw data to the White House.[35]

The aim of the unit was to avoid established vetting procedures that require rigorous scrutiny of intelligence before it reaches higher authorities. Instead, the unit would channel the intelligence directly to top officials. Coordinating closely with the OVP and DPB, the unit was able to circumvent the intelligence community, which according to Hersh, was in 'full retreat'.[36] Cherry picking facts from the vast amount of raw intelligence at its disposal or presenting them out of context was not the only way in which the OSP succeeded in politicising intelligence. It also gave the ammunition for Cheney, Libby, Hadley and Gingrich to pressure report officers in the CIA's directorate of operations whose job it is to vet input from agents around the world for 'the unsubstantiated and the incredible'.[37] As a result, the officers became reluctant to discard anything, however far-fetched.[38]

The operation was overseen by William Luti, whom some considered extreme, others 'downright irrational'. Israeli generals with whom he liaised closely concluded, 'Luti is insane.'[39] Luti's upward trajectory began in the 1990s when, as a Wohlstetter protégé, he came into the orbit of Perle and Wolfowitz.[40] A former aide to Cheney and Gingrich, Luti was sent to NESA from OVP where he was serving as special adviser on the Middle East under Libby. While the normal chain of command ran through Feith and Wolfowitz up to Rumsfeld, 'Luti made it clear that his chain of command principally ran directly up to Scooter Libby', writes Lang.[41] In some cases the office ignored institutional boundaries altogether to prepare memos specifically for Cheney and Libby, a practice unheard of in previous administrations. Kwiatkowski, who served at NESA from June 2002 to March 2003, reports her shock at learning that 'Luti was effectively working for Libby.'[42] Luti ordered NESA, and later OSP, to produce 'talking points', which he insisted were to be the only briefings provided on Iraq. Comprising of what Kwiatkowski calls 'propagandistic bullets', the talking points were distributed with orders that they be used verbatim in briefing papers for higher officials and people outside the Pentagon. From hearing 'many of those same phrases and assumptions and tones' in Cheney and Bush's speeches, Kwiatkowski got the impression that

> those talking points were not just for us, but were the core of an overall agenda for a disciplined product, beyond the Pentagon. Over at the vice president's office and the *Weekly Standard*, the media, and the neoconservative talking heads and that kind of thing, all on the same sheet of music.[43]

Many of the talking points were reproduced in the columns of Krauthammer in *The Washington Post* and *The Weekly Standard*.[44] The office also fed information 'directly and indirectly' to Fox News and *The Wall Street Journal*.[45] Among other things, the talking points included statements about Saddam Hussein's widely publicised aid to the Palestinians. Besides war planning guidance, the talking points were OSP's sole product.[46]

The principal author of the talking points was OSP director, Abram Shulsky, a former RAND analyst, a former staffer for Daniel Patrick Moynihan, and another beneficiary of Wohlstetter and Henry Jackson's tutelage. He studied under Leo Strauss and, like Wolfowitz, was a proponent of the 'noble lie' – the notion that deception by wise elites is morally acceptable in the pursuit of the public interest.[47] In 1993, he co-authored *Silent Warfare: Understanding the World of Intelligence* with PNAC director Gary Schmitt (republished in 2002) in which they argued that the goal of intelligence operations was victory, not truth.[48] They reprised the argument in the 1999 essay 'Leo Strauss and the World of Intelligence', which attacked the US intelligence community's analytical approach. They wrote:

> Strauss's view certainly alerts one to the possibility that political life may be closely linked to deception. Indeed, it suggests that deception is the norm in political life, and the hope, to say nothing of the expectation, of establishing a politics that can dispense with it is the exception.[49]

Other OSP members included Michael Rubin, a Zionist ideologue associated with WINEP, AEI and Daniel Pipes's Middle East Forum.[50] Rubin would later be embroiled in an FBI espionage investigation targeting Pentagon officials who in cahoots with Israel were trying to effect regime change in Iran.[51] Lawrence Franklin, the analyst who served as the conduit, would go on to serve a prison sentence on charges of spying after being caught in the act by the FBI.[52]

The unit added more recruits throughout the summer of 2002. Though OSP itself had fewer than ten full-time staff, it would go on to hire scores of temporary 'consultants' that included lawyers, Congressional staffers, and policy wonks from WINEP, AEI and JINSA. Numbering over a hundred at one point, most were 'off the books, on personal services contracts'.[53] Few of the new recruits had any intelligence experience. These included David Schenker, a WINEP veteran, brought in to replace the civilian head of the Israel, Lebanon and Syria desk office because of his predecessor's perceived even-handedness; Michael Makovsky, an Israeli-American who had worked for Shimon Peres, brought in to work on 'Iraqi oil issues' (his elder brother David Makovsky, the former executive editor of *Jerusalem Post*, also took up Israeli citizenship before joining WINEP as a senior fellow); Chris Lehman, brother of Reagan's neoconservative Secretary of the US Navy and CSP board member John Lehman; and William Bruner, a former

Gingrich staffer who served as 'Chalabi's handler'. In short, the office was a Likud beachhead inside the US government.[54]

Meanwhile, NESA was purged of existing professionals and Middle East policy experts. The rationale, according to Kwiatkowski, was to purge those 'who might have inadvertently developed sympathies for the people of the region'.[55]

The OSP, according to a *Guardian* investigation, also served as 'an open and largely unfiltered conduit' for transnational propaganda. It relayed dubious Israeli intelligence from a parallel, ad hoc intelligence operation inside Ariel Sharon's office directly to the White House. The outfit provided the Bush Administration with reports that were more alarmist than what Mossad was prepared to authorise.[56] Israelis also made frequent visits to Feith's office without being cleared into the Pentagon through normal channels.[57]

Equally significant to the Pentagon propaganda operation was the Iraq National Congress (INC). Headed by Ahmed Chalabi, the group had lost favour with the CIA and the State Department, the latter terminating its contract after it embezzled $2 million out of the $4.5 million allocated for an intelligence-gathering programme. Wolfowitz, who had a long-standing relationship with Chalabi, turned the Pentagon into the INC's new patron. In the months leading up to the war, Pentagon spokesman David Lapan noted that 'whatever intelligence the INC collects goes straight to the Defense Department'.[58] The CIA distrusted the information provided by the INC. 'Much of it is telling the Defense Department what they want to hear', said the former CIA official Vince Cannistraro. 'And much of it is used to support Chalabi's own presidential ambitions.'[59] 'Curveball', the supposed Iraqi engineer whose testimony Powell would rely on for his claims regarding Iraq's alleged mobile biological weapons labs, was the younger brother of an aide to Chalabi.[60]

Not everyone in the Pentagon supported the operation. Indeed, according to Cockburn, Stephen Cambone tried to wrest it from Feith. The State Department was also wary. But it had the crucial support of Perle and Wolfowitz. The office did not suffer criticism lightly: Luti, according to Kwiatkowski, labelled former Marine General and head of CENTCOM Anthony Zinni a 'traitor' for his public criticism of the rush to war; Schenker suggested that 'the best service' the reluctant Secretary of State Powell could offer 'would be to quit right now'.[61] When the Defense Intelligence Officer for Near East, South Asia and Counterterrorism Bruce Hardcastle expressed doubts over Iraq's alleged WMDs, Luti dismantled the position altogether.[62]

Months after the invasion, a letter surfaced seemingly confirming the Iraq–Al-Qaeda link. Dated 1 July 2001, the letter was addressed to Saddam Hussein from the Iraqi intelligence chief Tahir Jalil Habbush al-Tikriti. It stated that Muhammad Atta had completed his training for a mission in Iraq and also mentioned Iraq's purchase of yellowcake from Niger. However, journalist Ron Suskind revealed that Habbush had been on the US payroll since before the invasion and that the letter was forged on orders from the OVP. The letter was subsequently passed on to Con Coughlin of Conrad Black's *Sunday Telegraph* – a favourite conduit for neoconservative leaks – from where its claims were picked up and reproduced in *The New York Times* by William Safire and on Fox News by Israel lobby-linked 'terrorism expert' Evan Kohlmann.[63]

After the invasion, the OSP became the subject of an investigation by the Senate Select Committee on Intelligence. Phase two of the investigation also singled out PCEG and OSP for scrutiny.

Ledeen's Roman caper

OSP used an informal network across various departments and agencies to bypass official channels. At the State Department, instead of working with the Bureau of Intelligence and Research, the Near Eastern Affairs bureau or even its Iraq desk, it liaised directly with allies such as Bolton, Wurmser and Elizabeth Cheney. At the NSC, it liaised with Hadley and Abrams. It also made sure that its classified 'intelligence' would reach a wider audience by sharing it with allies at the quasi-governmental DPB who were not bound by secrecy laws.[64] One other person who, according to Kwiatkowski, 'was in and out of [OSP] all the time' was Michael Ledeen.[65]

Ledeen was wired into the Bush inner circle long before the administration took office. Karl Rove had asked Ledeen to funnel ideas to the White House, many of which became 'official policy or rhetoric', according to Edsall and Milbank.[66] Through his ties to Hadley, he also had influence over the WHIG, the marketing arm of the administration. Once the OSP was established, Feith hired him as a consultant. Both had worked together in the Reagan NSC, and both were members of JINSA (Feith drafted its charter; Ledeen was its first executive director).[67] At different times in their careers, both had been the subject of espionage investigations. In 1980, when Ledeen was serving as a correspondent for *The New Republic* in Rome, he was considered to be 'an agent of influence of a foreign government [Israel]' by the CIA station chief.[68] In 1988, his former superior, Assistant Secretary of Defense Noel Koch, had also asked the House Judiciary Committee to investigate him because as a 'terrorism consultant' at the Pentagon he 'lied about efforts to acquire by ruse classified information for which he had no legitimate claim'.[69]

During his stint in Rome, Ledeen had collaborated with the Italian military intelligence SISMI in two black propaganda operations.[70] He returned in 1981 to join the Reagan Administration as an adviser on terrorism to Secretary of State Alexander Haig. During this period, he would promote the thesis that all terrorist organisations around the world were part of a network with a hub in the former Soviet Union. He also played a central role in the Iran–Contra affair. His main collaborator was the Iranian conman Manuchehr Ghorbanifar.[71]

In November 2001, Ledeen met Ghorbanifar again, this time accompanied by the Pentagon's Harold Rhode and Larry Franklin. According to the Senate Select Committee investigation, Hadley consulted Ledeen when selecting the individuals for the meeting.[72] The aim was to undercut the developing rapprochement between the US and Iran, whose interests had temporarily converged in the Afghan war. Investigative journalist Craig Unger, however, suggests reasonable grounds to suspect that Ledeen collaborated with SISMI to produce the forged documents that alleged Iraq's attempted purchase of yellowcake – concentrated uranium oxide that can be enriched for use in nuclear weapons – from Niger. The documents were relayed to the French DGSE and the CIA. Both concluded they were bogus.[73]

Yet the documents would somehow make their way to Cheney (likely 'stovepiped' by the OSP), who pressed the CIA to verify the claims. The agency sent Joseph Wilson, the former ambassador to Iraq who had good relations with the prime minister of Niger, to investigate. Wilson soon established that the claims were bogus. By the time Wilson returned in March, the Niger report had been discredited by the DGSE, the CIA in Rome and in Langley, by the INR (twice), by the DIA and by the ambassador to Niger. Yet, in September when the White House launched its marketing campaign for war, it would use the Niger dossier as its key piece of evidence. It would eventually make its way into Tony Blair's dodgy dossier, and more significantly, into Bush's 2003 State of the Union address. Meanwhile, Ledeen would continue to use the editorial pages of *The Wall Street Journal* to call for 'total war,' against not just Iraq, but also Iran, Syria and Saudi Arabia.[74]

Judith Miller and WHIG's 'new products'

On 6 September 2002, White House Chief of Staff Andrew Card told the press, apropos the anticipated campaign for war against Iraq, that '[f]rom a marketing point of view, you don't introduce new products in August'.[75] The administration was planning to use the coming anniversary of 9/11 to bolster its campaign. Days earlier the WHIG had been instituted as the marketing arm of the war effort, to coordinate and streamline the message. Chaired by Karl Rove, it comprised political strategists (Michael Gerson, Karen Hughes, Mary Matalin, James Wilkinson and Nicholas Calio) and policy advisers (Rice and Hadley).[76] Libby served as the lynchpin, coordinating the message with the OSP and leaking dubious claims as 'scoops' to journalists. Faced with the challenge of making an unprovoked war appear like an act of self-defence, Michael Gerson came up with a phrase that turned uncertainty into a justification for war. Because the 'smoking gun' might be a 'mushroom cloud', to insist on conclusive evidence was to risk catastrophe.[77] However, there still had to be some basis for the uncertainty, since Iraq was weak and contained. A sophisticated propaganda apparatus was set up to supply this lack:

> First OSP supplies false or exaggerated intelligence; then members of the WHIG leak it to friendly reporters, complete with prepackaged vivid imagery; finally, when the story breaks, senior officials point to it as proof and parrot the unnamed quotes they or their colleagues previously supplied.[78]

On 8 September, the day the administration launched its coordinated media campaign, the front page of *The New York Times* carried a story by Judith Miller and Michael Gordon, which claimed, based on the testimony of Iraqi defectors and unnamed officials, that Iraq had 'stepped up its quest for nuclear weapons' and had 'embarked on a worldwide hunt for materials to make an atomic bomb'. By way of evidence, it added: 'Iraq has sought to buy thousands of specially designed aluminum tubes, which American officials believe were intended as components of centrifuges to enrich uranium.'[79] The article debuted the 'smoking gun/mushroom cloud' sound bite.[80]

The administration's case rested heavily on Iraq's alleged determination to reconstitute its nuclear programme: here was seemingly independent confirmation of its claims. The timing was propitious: it was the day the administration launched its promised 'marketing' campaign. As top officials fanned across evening talk shows to make the case for war, several referenced Miller's story. On CNN's *Late Edition with Wolf Blitzer*, Rice invoked Miller's claims and dismissed uncertainties because: 'We don't want the smoking gun to be a mushroom cloud.' On NBC's *Meet the Press*, Dick Cheney said he knew with 'absolute certainty' that Saddam Hussein was 'using his procurement system to acquire the equipment he needs to build a nuclear weapon'. He referenced Miller's piece and reprised the Prague Meeting. Bush himself went on CBS to claim that before leaving in 1998, UN weapons inspectors had concluded that Iraq was 'six months away from developing a weapon'. In his 12 September address to the UN General assembly, Bush declared Iraq a 'grave and gathering danger' that had made 'several attempts to buy high-strength aluminum tubes used to enrich uranium for a nuclear weapon'. Bush repeated the claim in his 8 October speech in Cincinnati. He concluded: 'We cannot wait for the final proof – the smoking gun – that could come in the form of a mushroom cloud.'

Ever since 1977, when she first joined *The New York Times*, Judith Miller had established a reputation as a neoconservative propagandist, implacably hostile to Arabs and Muslims.[81] In a trade publication, William E. Jackson, Jr. noted:

> She is known inside the paper to be very pro-Israel. She has had an extensive relationship with Daniel Pipes' Mideast Forum. Benador Associates lists her as a speaker. She has participated in conferences funded in part by departments of the Israeli government. Israeli security services funnel information through her, sources she occasionally cites.[82]

Miller's abiding preoccupation with Iraq began in 1990 when, shortly after the invasion of Kuwait, she joined Laurie Mylroie to produce *Saddam Hussein and the Crisis in the Gulf*, a book written in forty days that became an instant best-seller.[83] Miller and Mylroie aggressively promoted the war. During the 1990s, Miller developed a close relationship with the INC. In a candid email to her *New York Times* colleague John Burns, Miller wrote that she had been 'covering Chalabi for about 10 years ... He has provided most of the front page exclusives on WMD to our paper.'[84] In a front-page story in 1998, Miller helped launch the career of what would be the first in a series of Iraqi defectors furnished by the INC. After his defection in 1994, Khidir Hamza had tried unsuccessfully to interest publishers in a book co-authored with David Albright in which he revealed that Iraq's nuclear programme had 'fizzled out'. There were no takers. After a run-in with the INC, he revised his story to match the prevailing mood in Washington; and the INC in turn passed him on to Miller, who mined him for stories for the next five years.

In the aftermath of 9/11, Miller was once again quick to rush out an alarmist book, *Germs: Biological Weapons and America's Secret War*, co-authored with her NYT colleagues William Broad and Stephen Engelberg. A flurry of stories followed, hyping biological warfare. Sales were brisk. But the biggest boost came on 12 October, when Miller received an anthrax-laced letter as part of a series of attacks, which began in the immediate aftermath of the 9/11 attacks. Miller was the only prominent journalist targeted. The attacks proved to be a hoax, later traced to an Army research institute in Fort Detrick, Maryland, but the publicity sent Miller's book to number 1 on the best-seller list.

Miller began her pitch for war with a front-page story on 20 December with INC defector Adnan Ihsan Saeed al-Haideri, who claimed that he had 'personally worked on renovations of secret facilities for biological, chemical and nuclear weapons' as recently as 'a year ago'. 'If verified,' she wrote, 'the allegations would provide Administration hawks with the rationale for regime change.' However, a mere three days earlier, the CIA, according to Bamford, had concluded after a polygraph test that al-Haideri 'had made up the entire story, apparently in the hopes of securing a visa'. [85] Undaunted, Miller sought out anonymous 'government experts' who found al-Haideri's information 'reliable and significant'.[86]

Miller was relentless. On 13 September, she joined Michael Gordon to falsely claim that it was the 'unanimous view' of the intelligence agencies that the captured shipment of aluminium tubes was meant for Iraq's nuclear centrifuges.[87] Five days later, in anticipation of the results of renewed UN inspection, she declared that the verification of Iraq's disarmament 'may not be feasible' according to unnamed 'officials and former weapons inspectors'. Khidir Hamza was given a cameo to declare Iraq 'within two to three years' of a bomb.[88] On 3 December, she claimed that the CIA was investigating 'an informant's accusation that Iraq obtained a particularly virulent strain of smallpox from a Russian scientist'.[89] On 24 January 2003, Miller challenged UN weapons inspectors with testimony from Iraqi defectors, which in her words, was 'starkly at odds with the findings so far of the United Nations weapons inspectors'. Among the defectors was Al-Haideri, who Miller said was being credited by intelligence officials with supplying 'some of the most valuable information'.[90] After the invasion, in yet another front-page story, she claimed that 'American weapons experts' had confirmed that

Iraq had an active WMD programme. Their evidence was claims made by an alleged Iraqi scientist whom she 'could not interview', but was 'permitted to see ... from a distance' as 'he pointed to several spots in the sand where he said chemical precursors and other weapons material were buried'. She was told that 'Iraq had secretly sent unconventional weapons and technology to Syria, ... and that more recently Iraq was cooperating with Al Qaeda'.[91] All her claims proved false.[92]

For over two decades, Miller's career had remained unblemished by her persistent capacity for error. Her editors never examined her neoconservative pedigree or potential conflicts of interest.[93] She eventually fell from grace only after she had become the subject of an investigation into the outing of a covert CIA operative, whose husband (Joe Wilson) had challenged the administration's claims about Iraq's alleged WMDs. One again Miller had been leaked classified information by a fellow neoconservative – Irving Libby – to advance political aims.

Beginning in September 2002, the administration's message would dominate the twenty-four-hour news cycle until the commencement of hostilities. Journalists' need for access and officials' need for message control neatly dovetailed. Though there were many sceptics, the propaganda always managed to stay ahead: by the time one falsehood was debunked, several more would have entered the public discourse. Center for Public Integrity research from 2008 lists at least 935 false statements about the national security threat posed by Iraq made by Bush and seven top administration officials in the two years following 11 September 2001. The false statements first spiked in September 2002 – coinciding with the establishment of the OSP and WHIG – reaching their apogee with Colin Powell's speech to the UN in February 2002, as the graph (Figure 2) from a report by Charles Lewis and Mark Reading-Smith of the Center for Public Integrity illustrates.[94]

CIA, NIE and the White Paper

George Tenet, the CIA director, knew that the alleged Iraqi threat was bogus. A holdover from the Clinton Administration, Tenet

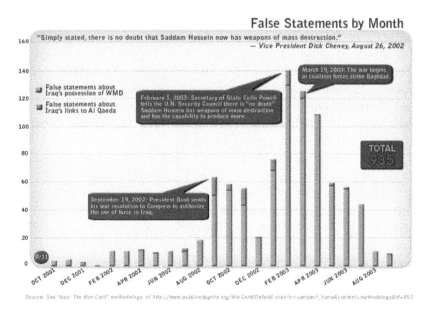

Figure 2 False statements top administration officials made, by month.
Source: Center for Public Integrity

had worked hard to keep his job.[95] His professional relationship with the president had also evolved into a friendship that many at the CIA feared would compromise the objectivity of the analysis delivered.[96] The concerns were borne out as Tenet's politician's instincts began to trump his professional judgement. As war looked increasingly likely, Tenet began siding with administration hawks against his own analysts. The CIA was further disadvantaged by the fact that the Pentagon controlled 80 per cent of the intelligence budget. Many inside the agency also resented Tenet's deferential attitude towards Rumsfeld.[97] Tenet did not resist when Rumsfeld seized many of his functions and handed them over to Cambone, Pentagon's 'intelligence czar', a newly invented position. He also remained silent about the OSP.[98] Meanwhile Libby and Cheney continued to pressure the CIA on the Iraq–Al-Qaeda link, which few at the agency believed existed.[99]

Top CIA officials believed Saddam Hussein was 'contained' and was 'unlikely to unleash weapons of mass destruction unless he [was] attacked'.[100] The neoconservatives resented the CIA's caution. 'There is a great deal of hesitancy if not opposition to the war at the [CIA]', complained Gerecht.[101] Richard Perle used the INC's dubious intelligence to attack what he called the 'status-quo oriented' CIA which was afraid of rocking the ark in the Middle East. 'They don't want to take risks. They don't like the INC because they only like to work with people they can control.'[102]

To avoid a rift with the White House, Tenet started tailoring the CIA's output to the administration's needs. Along with his senior lieutenants he created a climate in which analysts often suppressed reservations, and censored warnings about weak intelligence. Dissenters and sceptics were shunted aside. Ambitious analysts found their hawkish estimates rewarded.[103] On 1 August, for example, Tenet delivered a classified report to the White House that claimed that Iraq's attempted purchase of aluminium tubes from China was proof that it was reconstituting its uranium enrichment programme in order to develop a nuclear weapon. However, this conclusion was drawn from the assertion of a single junior WINPAC (Weapons Intelligence Non-Proliferation and Arms Control) analyst despite the contrary opinion of Department of Energy analysts.[104]

One hint that the administration was keen to wage war regardless of the actual threat is in the Bush Administration's reluctance to ask the CIA for an NIE (an authoritative report that encompasses the consensus of the US intelligence community) on Iraq's alleged WMDs.[105] Senate Intelligence Committee chair Senator Bob Graham was surprised when during a 5 September hearing, Tenet revealed that the CIA had not produced an NIE since the White House had not requested one.[106] Tenet and the administration were both reluctant to produce one since the findings were certain to be at odds with the administration's claims. The administration eventually authorised Tenet to produce an NIE, a task he delegated to Robert Walpole, an analyst who had previously collaborated with neoconservatives on the Rumsfeld Ballistic Missile Commission to produce a grossly alarmist report.[107] The assessment 'was sheep-herded by a national intelligence officer who works very closely with the vice president's office,' says Cannistraro. 'It's a flawed – fatally flawed – document and it should never have seen the light of day.'[108] Determined to control the content, Cheney and Libby visited Langley to badger low-level analysts to come up with evidence supportive of the administration's claims.[109]

Generally prepared over a period of months, the NIE was produced in less than three weeks. Tenet approved it after a single review meeting. The ninety-page classified document that Tenet delivered to the White House on 1 October affirmed that Iraq was procuring aluminium tubes from China and uranium ore from Niger to reconstitute its nuclear weapons programme; it had chemical and biological weapons programmes and mobile labs for clandestine production; it was developing UAVs possibly capable of carrying their load of deadly germs to the east coast of the US.[110]

But the document came with what Senator Graham calls 'vigorous dissents', even if they were mostly relegated to footnotes. Department of Energy experts, for example, did not think the aluminium tubes were meant for centrifuges; neither did the State Department. The Air Force did not believe the UAVs carried weapons, rather that they were most likely meant for reconnaissance. Significantly, the NIE asserted that Iraq was several years away from developing a nuclear weapon – and that whatever weapons Iraq might have, it would not use unless first attacked. Under questioning, Tenet also revealed that the alarmist claims in the NIE mostly came from third countries and exiles with an interest in overthrowing Iraq, and had not been independently verified by US intelligence.[111]

Senator Graham was eager to make the caveats in the classified document public. He asked Tenet to produce a white paper – an unclassified document for legislators to use in their public deliberations. On 4 October, Tenet presented a twenty-five-page document titled *Iraq's Weapons of Mass Destruction Programs*, which ostensibly condensed the findings of the NIE.[112] But the new document had dispensed with all the qualifications and presented even more dramatic conclusions. Cautious evaluations were turned into assertions of fact and conclusions were revised to make the strongest possible case for war. 'It represented an unqualified case that Hussein possessed [WMDs]', wrote Graham; it 'avoided a discussion of whether he had the will to use them and omitted the dissenting opinions contained in the classified version'. Additionally, it also suggested that Iraq might be purchasing 'weapons-grade fissile material from abroad'. Graham noted that the white paper was of 'a very high production level', it was an 'advocacy piece'; the decision to go to war had been made already, and the intelligence community was being used as 'almost a public relations operation to validate the war'.[113]

Paul Pillar – one of the primary authors of the white paper – concurs. 'It was clearly requested and published for policy advocacy purposes . . . The purpose was to strengthen the case for going to war with the American public . . . I regret having had a role in that.'[114] In his testimony to the Senate, Pillar noted: 'Instead of intelligence being used to inform policy decisions, it was used primarily to justify a decision already made.'[115] It has also since emerged that the white paper in fact predated the NIE and was part of the administration's effort to mobilise support for the war. Furthermore, national security analyst John Prados has revealed that the declassified earlier drafts of the white paper show a remarkable resemblance to Blair and Alastair Campbell's dodgy dossier, suggesting a high degree of coordination.[116]

But the NIE's significance in the case of Congressional authorisation can be overstated. No more than six senators read it, and most contented themselves with the five-page executive summary.[117] Nor did it influence the president's decision: the White House has acknowledged that the president did not read the document.[118] The public was largely unaware of its conclusions and reservations. On the other hand defence 'experts' were always at hand to present their own interpretations of the alleged threat. Most vocal were the neoconservatives.

WMD and the known unknowns

Since 1998, when the UN weapons inspectors were withdrawn from Iraq in anticipation of Operation Desert Fox, US intelligence received little in the way of new information. But in 2002, there had been key intelligence breakthroughs confirming Iraq's disarmament. The highest-level confirmation came from Naji Sabri, the Iraqi foreign minister, who was cooperating with French intelligence as a paid spy.[119] The French had turned him over to the CIA. Sabri revealed that Saddam neither possessed, nor was trying to develop, WMDs. Tenet personally delivered this news to Bush the next day (18 September), who dismissed it as disinformation.[120] The CIA persevered, and soon the French, who were monitoring Sabri's calls, sent recordings that backed the Iraqi's revelations. The fact that two of Sabri's brothers had been killed by Hussein helped explain his willingness to cooperate.[121] The CIA prepared a report on the operation which was passed on to the CIA station in New York; but the new document that emerged distorted the reports filed from France; they included an introductory paragraph that directly contradicted Sabri's disclosures. It claimed that Iraq possessed biological and chemical weapons and that it was also 'aggressively and covertly developing' nuclear weapons.[122] Suskind reports: 'This erroneous report – almost certainly altered under pressure from Washington – was guarded so closely that it was never shown to the teams, at CIA and elsewhere, hurriedly assembling the October 2002 NIE on Iraq's WMD.'[123] After further manipulation, the report was passed on to Tony Blair through Richard Dearlove, the head of MI6. Powell was never notified.[124]

A second confirmation came through Saad Tawfiq, a British-trained electrical engineer identified by the CIA as a 'key figure in Saddam Hussein's clandestine nuclear weapons program'.[125] In May 2002, the CIA recruited Tawfiq's sister Dr Sawsan Alhaddad, based in Cleveland, Ohio, to obtain details from her brother about Saddam's alleged nuclear weapons. She flew in to Iraq on 9 September to meet Tawfiq, who confirmed that Iraq's nuclear programme had been abandoned in 1991 and that the chemical and biological weapons programmes had been dismantled in 1995. According to Risen, Tawfiq was merely one of thirty former Iraqi WMD experts with relatives in the US who cooperated with the CIA to provide information on Iraq's weapons programmes.[126] They all confirmed it had been dismantled.[127] But afraid to contradict the administration, CIA officials withheld this information from the NIE, which conclusively stated that Iraq 'is reconstituting its nuclear program'.[128]

The third breakthrough came in December 2002, when Rob Richer, the head of the CIA's Near East Division, was passed a lead by Michael Shipster, the Middle East intelligence chief for the MI6, that he had a source inside Iraq – Tahir Jalil Habbush al-Tikriti, the head of the Iraqi Mukhabarat. Richer arranged a rendezvous through Saad Khayr, the head of Jordanian intelligence. Shipster met Habbush in Amman, Jordan in January 2003, and Habbush confirmed that Iraq had no WMDs. The White House was not pleased. A frustrated Bush asked: 'Why don't they ask him to give us something we can use to help us make our case?'[129] The weekly meetings with Habbush continued until early February, but the problem according to Richer was that Habbush had to 'prove a negative to testify to his credibility'.[130] The same month, Richard Dearlove, the head of MI6, personally flew to Washington to present Tenet with the report on which the British had worked hard. It stated that according to Habbush, Iraq's nuclear weapons programme had been discontinued in 1991; in the same year, it had also destroyed its chemical weapons stockpile; and the biological weapons programme had ended with the destruction of the Al Hakam biological weapons facility in 1996.[131]

Tenet worried this report would displease a White House set on going to war. When he briefed Bush and Rice, the latter reportedly responded: 'What the hell are we supposed to do with this?' Tenet retreated, instead highlighting how much of the already assembled 'case' contradicted Habbush.[132] Thus an opportunity to forestall war was lost. CIA sources later told Suskind that after the war, Habbush was paid $5m in 'hush money' and resettled in Jordan to conceal what the administration knew before the war.[133]

The administration also rebuffed an Iraqi offer to allow 'several thousand US troops into the country to take part in the search for banned weapons' and to allow '2,000 FBI agents to look wherever they wanted'.[134] This series of 'increasingly desperate peace offers', made amongst others through Syrian intelligence, and French, German and Russian diplomatic channels, 'were all

rejected by the Bush administration', according to the interme-
diaries involved.[135] They began in December with an approach
made by Habbush to the CIA's former head of counter-terrorism,
Vincent Cannistraro, who relayed it to the State Department.
He was subsequently informed that the offer had been 'killed'.
Another attempt was made between January and February 2003
in the meetings between Habbush and Michael Shipster. Again this
was rebuffed.[136] Next an offer was made through Imad el-Hage,
a Lebanese-American businessman and a friend of the PCEG's
Michael Maloof.[137] El-Hage was approached by Habbush's chief
of foreign operations Hassan al-Obeidi through the Syrian intelligence, and after receiving Habbush's message in Baghdad, he
relayed it first to Maloof and then directly to Richard Perle at a
meeting in London's Marlborough Hotel on 7 March 2003. The
White House chose not to negotiate.[138]

In the aftermath of the war, Bush chided those in Congress
making 'irresponsible comments' that the administration manipulated intelligence because they 'saw the same intelligence I saw
[the NIE and the White Paper] and then voted to authorize the use
of force against Saddam Hussein'.[139] This statement is false. Bush
had received several briefings both before and after the vote. A
report released by the Congressional Research Service a day after
Bush's speech concluded: 'The President and a small number of
presidentially designated cabinet-level officials, including the vice
president . . . have access to a far greater overall volume of intelligence and to more sensitive information, including intelligence
sources and methods' that included 'nine key U.S. intelligence
"products" not generally shared with Congress'.[140]

However, most of these investigations miss the point. There is a
straightforward reason why the war cannot be blamed on 'intelligence failure'. Iraq was not invaded merely because it possessed
WMDs; the administration claimed that in Iraq's hands these
weapons posed an *imminent* threat to the US. Even in their most
exaggerated estimates, this was a claim consistently disputed by
the CIA (as were the claims about Iraq's alleged ties to Al-Qaeda).
Indeed, a letter John McLaughlin sent to the Senate on Tenet's
behalf days before Bush's 7 October speech explicitly stated that
Iraq did not pose an imminent threat, and whatever weapons it

might have, it would not use them unless first attacked.[141] Both the claims about Iraq's alleged links to Al-Qaeda, and the imminent threat it posed originated with the neoconservatives.

On 21 December, Tenet and McLaughlin presented the CIA's best case to the president, which left him and the cabinet decidedly unimpressed. 'I've been told all this intelligence about having WMD,' Bush complained, 'and this is the best we've got?' Tenet instead promised that the case would be a 'slam dunk'.[142] Bush was sceptical. The CIA's forty-page report was instead handed over to Hadley and Libby, who embellished its already inflated conclusions with dubious claims from the OSP, including the discredited Prague Meeting.

Powell's sales pitch

Bush informed Powell of his decision to go to war in a one-to-one meeting on 13 January 2003, long after he had informed the Israelis and Saudis. Though Powell warned him of the consequences, Bush made it clear that he was not there to debate: he was only making a personal appeal for the secretary of state's support. Despite private misgivings, Powell obliged.[143] Powell had been the subject of intense pressure from the start, and his neoconservative detractors repeatedly impugned his caution as cowardice.[144] But once he fell in line, he took to selling the war with gusto. On 26 January, when he addressed the World Economic Forum in Davos, he repeated the lies about Iraq's attempts to purchase uranium from Niger and the alleged purpose of the aluminium tubes. This was contrary to the judgement of the State Department, which knew the allegations were false.[145]

On 25 January, when Libby and Hadley presented their case to top officials, some were appalled. Richard Armitage thought it was full of 'overreaching and hyperbole'; Bush's spin doctor Karen Hughes found it full of 'sweeping conclusions' that were 'too much'.[146] They wanted something less outrageous and more persuasive. Bush turned to Powell to make the public case for war, adding: 'You have the credibility to do it.' Powell would be selling a war he had fought hard to prevent, but the military careerist was, according to Woodward, 'flattered' by Bush's trust.[147] Cheney pressed further: 'Your poll numbers are in the 70s,' he mocked. 'You can afford to lose a few points.'[148] Cheney also asked him to use the forty-eight-page, single-spaced dossier with pictures of Iraq's 'nuclear mujahideen', which Libby and Hannah had prepared. He especially wanted Powell to emphasise Iraq's links to 9/11. Powell, according to Woodward, was appalled by the document: he threw out the 'oddball stuff' born of Cheney's 'unhealthy fixation' with the Iraq–Al-Qaeda link.[149]

As Powell's Chief of Staff Lawrence Wilkerson started tracking down sources for its various claims, he realised that 'the context was not quite what the cherry-picked item imported'.[150] Following Tenet's suggestion, a frustrated Powell decided to use the CIA's October NIE as a template for his speech instead. Powell instructed Wilkerson to visit Langley to prepare the speech. However, Libby, Hannah and Hadley continued to lurk around: they were also joined by Bolton who had earlier pressured the State Department's Bureau of Non-proliferation to produce a fact sheet that resurrected the claims about Iraq's alleged attempts to purchase uranium from Niger.[151] Libby, Hadley and Bolton brought considerable pressure to bear on CIA analysts to toe the line.[152] Libby and Hadley insisted that Powell link Iraq to Al-Qaeda in his speech. On one occasion when a reference to the Prague Meeting mysteriously reappeared after Powell had removed it from the draft, Hadley admitted that he had reinserted it.[153] 'They were just relentless,' says Wilkerson, 'you would take it out and they would stick it back in. That was their favourite bureaucratic technique – ruthless relentlessness.'[154] An extensive search carried out by a CIA team headed by Michael Scheuer turned up no links between Iraq and Al-Qaeda. Powell therefore dropped references to the Prague Meeting, but he obliged Cheney by alleging operational links between Iraq and Al-Qaeda.

Meanwhile, Hadley was busy on another front. On 9 September, a day after the administration launched its public campaign for war, Hadley contravened established protocol, which requires the chiefs of foreign intelligence agencies to coordinate only through their US counterpart, to meet Nicolo Pollari, the head of Italian intelligence and a Ledeen associate. Intelligence professionals interviewed by Unger found it doubtful that he would not have revealed that Iraq was using the aluminium tubes for their Italian-designed Medusa air-to-ground missile systems.[155] Two days later, he would try to insert the claim about Iraq's purchase of yellowcake from Niger into the president's statement on the first anniversary of 9/11. The CIA advised Hadley to delete the sentence. He would insert it again into the draft of another Bush speech in October. When on 5 October Hadley ignored a memo asking him to remove the reference, Tenet personally intervened to have it deleted.[156] The claim resurfaced on 19 December in a fact sheet produced by the State Department on Bolton's instructions. However, in early January, the National Intelligence Council, the body that oversees all fifteen intelligence agencies, confirmed that the 'the Niger story was baseless and should be laid to rest'.[157] Yet, despite all the warnings, the claim would reappear on 28 January 2003 in Bush's annual State of the Union Address. After repeating a litany of Iraqi crimes, he told to the joint session of Congress: 'The British government has learned that Saddam Hussein recently sought significant quantities of uranium from Africa' – the infamous 'sixteen words' that would serve as the casus belli. Hadley had inserted the claim into Bush's speech, attributing it to the British, after securing the assent of a low-level CIA officer to deliberately bypass requisite high-level vetting.[158] Hadley would later accept responsibility for inserting the sentence in the speech, claiming that he had 'forgotten' the earlier warnings.[159]

Bush's speech also included the claim that Iraq had 'several mobile biological weapons labs'. Tenet claims that he never read the speech before it was delivered. This may be true. But both Tenet and Powell accepted claims about which they were clearly warned by their respective agencies.[160]

In a 31 January memo to Powell, the INR had highlighted thirty-eight allegations in an early draft of his UN speech that it found 'unsubstantiated' or 'weak'. Only twenty-eight were removed.[161] Powell kept the reference to the aluminium tubes story in his speech even though he had been told by both the INR and the Department of Energy that the case was dubious. According to Greg Thielmann, a former director of the INR's Strategic,

Proliferation, and Military Affairs, the bureau had already concluded that 'the purchases were implausible – and made that point clear to Powell's office'.[162] After much deliberation, Powell had concluded that the CIA's best evidence was for the mobile germ factories. Tenet assured him that it was 'totally reliable information' for which he had four solid sources.[163]

As a matter of fact, the mobile lab claims originated with a single source, Rafid Ahmed Alwan, an Iraqi defector with ties to the INC.[164] Designated 'Curveball', the Iraqi, who was in the custody of the German intelligence service BND, was never interviewed by the CIA before the war. The reports that were relayed to the CIA third-hand through the Defence HUMINT Service came with warnings from the Germans that the source was unreliable, he was psychologically unstable and likely a fraud. Tyler Drumheller, the head of the European Division in the CIA's Directorate of Operations, was personally warned. Drumheller relayed the information up the chain of command, to Tenet among others.[165]

Despite their warnings, the Germans did not disavow Curveball outright: the BND was reluctant to admit that they had been conned and oversold his contributions.[166] But the more important story relates to the reason why the Germans denied the CIA access to Curveball. Suskind reveals that the Germans were in fact acting under the advice of Joe Wippl, the CIA station chief for Germany, who at the time was under internal investigation for questionable activities and was due to be relieved of his position. Working closely with the Pentagon, Wippl ensured that the CIA would not be given direct access to Curveball. CIA officers speculate that Wippl was acting at the behest of the OVP, since soon after his departure, he was handed the plum job as the head of CIA's Congressional Liaison Office at Cheney's recommendation.[167]

Shortly before Powell's speech, when a draft was circulated at the CIA, Drumheller was surprised to find extensive references to Curveball. He personally intervened with CIA Deputy Director John McLaughlin to have these excised and called Tenet the night before the speech to ensure their removal.[168] Regardless, Powell would go on to use Curveball's testimony, attributing his claims to 'solid . . . multiple' sources. To emphasise the CIA's support for his claims, Powell would make Tenet sit right behind him during the presentation.[169] The presentation left the Germans embarrassed and diplomats unimpressed.[170] 'Everyone felt uncomfortable', said one UN official, 'to see a man saying these lies. You knew it was bullshit.' Even the British ambassador was dismayed.[171] But in the US, the speech was a hit. Powell's performance was hailed in editorials: over a hundred media outlets compared it to Adlai Stevenson's dramatic presentation during the Cuban Missile Crisis, a precedent Powell had consciously tried to emulate.[172] A Washington Post/ABC News poll found that 67 per cent of respondents felt that the US was justified in going to war because of Iraq's illegal weapons.[173]

Within three days of the speech, on 8 February, a UN team led by US biological weapons experts would debunk Powell's claims after finding no evidence of mobile labs at their alleged location (Djerf al-Naddaf).[174] On 14 February, Hans Blix and Muhammad ElBaradei further demolished Powell's case in front of the UN Security Council. They revealed that in eleven weeks of unimpeded search through over three hundred suspected sites, their inspectors had not found a single prohibited weapon.[175] Richard Perle was unimpressed: 'UN weapons inspectors are being seriously deceived', he declared. 'It reminds me of the way the Nazis hoodwinked Red Cross officials inspecting the concentration camp at Theresienstadt in 1944.'[176] Perle and Bolton promised that Iraq would be only the first step in what Michael Ledeen called this 'war to remake the world'.[177] Iran, Syria, Saudi Arabia, Lebanon, North Korea and the PLO were next.[178]

On 25 February, in an appearance before the Senate Arms Services Committee, Army Chief of Staff Gen. Eric Shinseki made a last-ditch effort to restrain the war party. He stated that the Pentagon's estimate for the troops needed in Iraq was too optimistic: a few hundred thousand more would be needed.[179] Wolfowitz was outraged: he sent a message via Secretary of the Army Thomas White that the general had been out of line in challenging the administration's estimates. He made an appearance before the committee just two days later to stress that the general's estimate was wrong. No major deployments would be necessary, because: 'they will greet us as liberators'.[180] Undeterred,

Shinseki would appear before the House Defense Appropriations Subcommittee a month later to reiterate his original estimate. He was relieved of his duties three months later.

On 7 March, Blix and ElBaradei appeared before the Security Council again to confirm that Iraq was cooperating with the inspections. Blix confirmed that there were no mobile biological labs, and ElBaradei attested that the Niger documents were 'not authentic'. He added: 'After three months of intrusive inspections, we have to date found no evidence or plausible indication of the revival of a nuclear weapon program in Iraq.'[181]

Meanwhile, the war effort continued apace. On 6 March, Bush invoked Al-Qaeda and 9/11 a dozen times while talking about Iraq. On 9 March, Rice also repeated the allegation, based on the confessions under torture of Sheikh al-Libi, which had been doubted since February 2002.[182] Bush would also reiterate the link in his final ultimatum to Saddam Hussein and his sons forty-eight hours before the war. Earlier, the US had tried to cajole, bribe or strong-arm several nations on the UN Security Council to support its position. It even tried to bug the phones and emails of Security Council members.[183] But after France, Russia and China threatened to veto a resolution authorising the use of force, the US abandoned the UN track. Bush, Blair and Spanish Prime Minister José María Aznar instead gathered in the Azores to give the UN an ultimatum to support the war or risk irrelevance.[184] The UN failed to oblige. On 19 March, a US-led coalition initiated an illegal and unprovoked invasion of Iraq.

Conclusion

'The war of choice in Iraq could never have gained the Congressional support it got without the psychological linkage between the shock of 9/11 and the postulated existence of Iraqi weapons of mass destruction', writes Zbigniew Brzezinski, the former Cold War hawk who in the months leading up to war emerged as one of its most outspoken critics. 'The sense of a pervasive but otherwise imprecise danger was thus channelled in a politically expedient direction by the mobilizing appeal of being "at war"', he added.[185] In the immediate aftermath of 9/11, the neoconservatives succeeded in using the shock and disorientation of the attacks to place Iraq, a country to which many in the administration already bore some hostility, on the agenda and helped manufacture the case for invading it.

On 9/11, the US had lost more than blood and treasure: it had also lost its aura of invincibility. For a state that has so much invested in maintaining its military dominance, it was unlikely that it would confine itself to police action. It would have to re-establish deterrence. Afghanistan was the obvious target, but the neoconservatives used the revanchist momentum to successfully push Iraq on the agenda. For Cheney and Rumsfeld, who both wanted a demonstration of US power, this presented an attractive option. Iraq was weak, it was led by a notoriously cruel and demonised figure, and it sat on a colossal material prize which the status quo prevented US companies from exploiting. But to the extent that Cheney and Rumsfeld wanted to hit Iraq as a demonstration of US power, their interest was in itself the product of an environment created by a 'determined band of neo-conservatives far outside the foreign policy mainstream'; they persuaded Bush, Cheney and Rumsfeld that 'invading Iraq would demonstrate American power to tens of millions shocked and awed Arabs'.[186] Following his infamous 'one percent doctrine', Cheney was committed to treating the mere suspicion of Iraq's links to Al-Qaeda as a certainty. 'Terrorists are hard to find, maybe impossible to deter', writes Gellman. 'States were neither.'[187] So Cheney, following the neoconservative line, wanted to concentrate on states. It did not matter to him if the state was Iraq or Iran or North Korea; he loathed and suspected them all. But Iran had a large, motivated and well-equipped army and the capacity to retaliate beyond its borders. North Korea had ten thousand artillery pieces along its Southern border, long-range missiles and possibly nuclear weapons. It also had China on its border whose reaction was hard to predict. The US could not potentially confront either, but it could make an example of one as a message to the others. The aim was to show the willingness and capacity to destroy a foe; it was to re-establish deterrence:

Cheney, in the end, did not press for war with Iraq because Saddam really topped the list of 'grave and gathering threats,' as he had led the Bush administration in asserting. The United States would take him down because it could.[188]

Cheney had confirmed this. When asked by the Saudi Foreign Minister Saud Al-Faisal why the US was determined to invade Iraq, he replied, 'Because it's doable.'[189] Middle East scholar Olivier Roy concurs:

> the rationale for the military campaign in Iraq was not that Iraq was the biggest threat but, on the contrary, that it was the weakest and hence the easiest to take care of. The invasion was largely aimed at demonstrating America's political will and commitment to go to war.[190]

For Roy, the origins of this policy are traceable to 'many professional thinkers at the American Enterprise Institute' for whom 'the Israeli-Palestinian stalemate is America's most worrisome foreign entanglement, and can be broken only if the overall existing order in the Middle East is shaken up first'.[191] But it is one thing to desire a war, quite another to prosecute it when significant parts of the state bureaucracy are opposed. Cheney's 'one percent' approach was unlikely to overcome bureaucratic obstacles without help from the neoconservative network. The neoconservatives did not just conceive the war, they also enabled it.

Part 4   The Debate

Conclusions

The Iraq war cannot be explained by reference to economic or ideological structures alone. It had its agents (the neoconservatives) and its trigger (9/11). It was executed by Bush, Cheney and Rumsfeld, but Iraq in the end was a neoconservative war not only because the neoconservatives had wanted it longer, but also because without their specific contributions to the case for war – the Iraq–Al-Qaeda a link, the mythical WMDs – the war would not have happened. The neoconservatives' interest in toppling Iraq preceded Bush's, Cheney's or Rumsfeld's. Regime change had been official US policy since 1998 and unofficial policy even longer. But the means for this were understood to be diplomatic pressure, economic strangulation and covert action – not invasion and occupation. Bush only started receiving briefings on the subject in the run-up to his presidential campaign by an advisory group led by Condoleezza Rice, who in a position paper for *Foreign Affairs* had argued that Iraq's military power was 'severely weakened' and that the US could even live with a nuclear Iraq.[1] Sometime between then and the winter of 2001, Bush and aggressive nationalists like Cheney and Rumsfeld were persuaded of the war's merit. For Cheney and Rumsfeld, the primary motivation was the war's demonstrative effect – a sanguine assertion of US military power. For Bush, according to most insiders, the chief motor was his simplistic, messianic belief in fighting what he considered an 'evil' regime, one that had bedevilled his father and was capable of, if not responsible for, attacks like the ones on 9/11. The three may have believed that the war would also benefit Israel, but that was not their overriding concern.[2]

It is true that war cannot be blamed on warmongers alone.

The neoconservatives succeeded because they operate within a political consensus that sees US global dominance as the desired end and military force as the necessary, if not preferred, means. The public is by disposition isolationist, but through a combination of fear and appeals to national chauvinism can be induced to tolerate, if not acquiesce in, foreign adventures. The MIC is always enthusiastic about war, even if its profits do not necessarily rely on it (since its birth after World War II, it has relied more on the *threat* of war). Some corporations do welcome the chance to turn a quick profit, even if most prize the stability of long-term relationships and security for their investments. The oil services industry and the energy corporations also profited from the war even if they did not directly lobby for it. These interests combined to create fertile grounds for military adventurism.

But wars would *not* happen without the warmongers. Imperialism never occurs in a fit of forgetfulness: it has its agents. It is therefore less significant who supported or benefited from the war than who conceived, enabled and executed it. The subject-less structuralism of many analysts on the left and some on the right may help us discern the enabling circumstance but cannot adequately explain why a particular war happens at a particular time. There is no inevitability to war; it is an act of volition. It is no more possible to understand the Iraq war without understanding the role of the neoconservatives than it is to understand the overthrow of Jacobo Árbenz in Guatemala and Mohammad Mossadegh in Iran without taking into account the roles of United Fruit and Anglo-Iranian Petroleum.

One cannot infer agency from the consequences of war. If *cui bono* were the only criteria by which one could assign responsibility, then a plausible case could be made that the US invaded Iraq to empower Iran and China. Companies such as Halliburton and Bechtel doubtless profited from the war, exploiting the free-for-all that followed the fall of Baghdad. But that is what all businesses do in similar circumstances. The question, however, is whether the war was waged on their behalf. By adopting a state instrumentalist approach, proponents of this argument have divested themselves of the need for evidence.

Using culture to explain political actions is likewise fraught with the danger of inverting causation. Cultures are rarely monolithic and they carry within them the potential for multiple expressions. US exceptionalism and the messianic belief in the duty of the US to right global wrongs have often given licence to interventions abroad. But the US also has a strong tradition of isolationism and, indeed, anti-imperialism. Which of these latent resources is elaborated is ultimately a function of power.[3] It was in response to the perceived 'isolationist' tilt of the Democratic Party that the neoconservatives first picked up arms; because for them iso-lationism was redolent of the amorality that led everyone from the conservative Charles Lindbergh to the leftist Charles Beard to oppose US participation in World War II. Their full-scale assault on the concept – which equates it with narrow-mindedness and provincialism as opposed to the broad-mindedness, wisdom and responsibility of the 'internationalists'[4] – was given added impetus by Clinton's 'humanitarian' interventions of the 1990s. Anti-war voices have therefore had to fight not only the arguments for war, but also the charges of isolationism and Chamberlain-like appeasement.

The debacle of Iraq has finally created some pushback. Waves from the conversation begun by Mearsheimer and Walt with their essay in the *London Review of Books* have been rippling out even as neoconservative think tanks, pressure groups and letterhead organisations continue to sprout to foster the illusion of wide-spread support for military action against Iran. Yet the actual roster of actors remains the same. From their myriad perches, the neoconservatives have also argued against withdrawal from Afghanistan for fear that it would make intervention in Iran less likely. Meanwhile, a steady assault on civil liberties at home coupled with a culture of secrecy and surveillance have steadily eroded the democratic foundations of the US republic. As the US government is pushed towards a potentially more disastrous confrontation with Iran, the need to scrutinise the methods and composition of its leading backers assumes greater urgency. So does a revision of the theoretical premises on which much of the extant analysis is based.

Organisation and hierarchy are critical to the functioning of social power. But also significant are the non-hierarchical social networks, which, through extra-governmental affiliations, enable or constrain political action. Social networks which are not based in popular movements may not themselves possess the power to effect political change, but by harnessing the resources and authority of state they can enhance their efficacy. The true measure of their significance is their proximity to power and their influence over, or the control of, the decision-making process. However, the degree to which a network can dominate a state relies on the architecture of power and the political opportunities available at a given moment. Capturing the higher echelons of government is itself not a sufficient condition for wielding absolute power, especially in democratic states with functioning systems of checks and balances. But in authoritarian states, where power is concentrated in the executive branch, a network could easily command absolute authority merely by replacing or influencing the ruling elite. In Egypt and Iraq in the 1950s, networks of mid-level 'free officers' were able to assume power just by replacing the top ranks of the executive branch. This could not happen in a democratic state.

Or so it would seem.

From ancient Greece to the US republic, fear of tyrannical rule has led to the separation of powers to serve as a check on unrestrained executive authority. Even in parliamentary systems like the UK's, where there is a weak separation of powers – indeed a fusion of powers – the executive is in theory subservient to the legislative branch. However, in practice a tendency has always existed for power to concentrate in the executive, especially in times of crisis. This tendency was given ideological reinforcement by the neoliberal worldview ushered in by Reagan and Thatcher. Executive authority was consolidated – albeit with an increasingly managerial purpose – and more and more inherently governmental functions were privatised. The vacuum was filled by non-governmental actors who owed little loyalty to the institutions they were contracted to serve. Public and private functions were blurred, and the state bureaucracy, designed to be insulated from the vagaries of partisan politics, was progressively emasculated, sometimes replaced by unabashedly ideological actors who traversed the public/private divide at will. In times of crisis, as more power accrued to the executive branch, the power of these actors was also magnified.

The privatisation and outsourcing of more and more governmental functions has led to the decline of Weberian bureaucracy and the proliferation of sparsely regulated areas. This has created an ideal environment for the emergence of new configurations of power of the kind anthropologist Janine Wedel calls a 'flex net', whose aim is to capture and exploit the state's authority and resources while evading its accountability.[5] Its obvious target is the executive branch. Few have been more adept at navigating this environment than the neoconservatives. Though small in number, the neoconservatives have used their social cohesion, ideological coherence, professional malleability and political access to colonise parts of the national security apparatus. Following the 9/11 attacks, as the Bush Administration used the opportunity to concentrate power in the executive, the neoconservatives' influence was amplified; through superior coordination they were able to outmanoeuvre the more cautious and fragmented national security bureaucracy. Agile and resilient, they were able to evolve new political vehicles, both within and outside the government, to advance their aims. In the end, they not only got their war but also managed to leave an indelible imprint on the national security infrastructure.[6]

By fixating on the PNAC, the Vulcans or the OSP, most analysts have merely addressed the symptoms of this new political phenomenon without addressing its causes. However, it is more fruitful to look at the underlying network – its composition, its ideological make-up, its financial resources and its modus operandi – than to study each new political vehicle it spawns, whether a think tank, letterhead organisation, political campaign, Congressional commission or publication. No less important is an investigation of the normative power that actors like the neoconservatives possess through strategic alliances that help them appropriate the significant symbols of nation, tribe and civilisation, which they can selectively deploy depending on the intended audience. Their promotional expertise allows them to ease themselves from one role to another.

However, none of these actors operates in a vacuum. They are constrained by the structures within which they operate. But explanations of war that focus exclusively on larger structures have only limited utility. The world is too complex to be explained by all-encompassing models. History does not always bend to the deterministic laws of grand theory. From Marx to Bourdieu, theorists have recognised that the existence of broader structures might constrain or enable the choices of actors, but do not preclude their agency. 'Men make their own history,' writes Marx, 'but they do not make it as they please; they do not make it under self-selected circumstances, but under circumstances existing already, given and transmitted from the past.'[7] The neoconservatives were successful because within the extant system of dispositions – what Bourdieu calls 'habitus' – they found tendencies that could be nurtured and intensified to support their ends. Structures, as history reminds us, are not static: they evolve in relation to the balance of forces in society. Bourdieu, Berger and Luckman, and Giddens have all recognised the dialectical relationship between structure and agency.[8] However, as Margaret Archer notes, such conflation of structure and agency precludes the possibility of investigating the relative influence of each. Archer instead proposes what she calls analytical dualism, which, while mindful of the interdependence of structure and agency, sees the two operating on different timescales.[9]

A permissive environment is not in itself a sufficient condition for war; it has to be willed. If within the same structure it is possible for actors to either support *or* oppose a policy, then structure alone cannot plausibly explain the outcome. Unless there is a consensus, it should therefore be possible to identify agency. The agents of a policy include more than just the decision makers; they also include those who influence the decisions. The ones deciding an issue are not always the ones who conceive it. Their choices are sometimes constrained. These constraints work on multiple levels, taking ideological, economic or political form, often with significant overlaps. Interest groups have over the years evolved various means to formalise them into enduring structures of domination.[10] These include everything from lobbying organisations, political action committees and charitable foundations to letterhead organisations. For decision makers, these institutions set parameters whose breadth depends on the density of their interconnections.

In summary, this research shows that for the concept of power to be meaningful, it cannot be understood simply in terms of paramount agents dominating subordinate ones in overt conflict. As sociologist Steven Lukes suggests, it must take into account observable as well as non-observable conflict; acts of decision making as well as non-decision making; issues as well as potential issues; and subjective as well as real interests of subordinate agents.[11] Power, as theorists from Weber to Gramsci to Mann have argued, cannot be reduced solely to a function of economics; it also has ideological and political components, often with significant overlaps. One must therefore reject the economism associated with some vulgar interpretations of Marxism. To see the state as merely an instrument of economic interests is to give insufficient attention to political and ideological forces.

Theorists beginning with Marx, but especially Gramsci, Mills and Miliband, have recognised the potential autonomy of states, especially in times of crisis. In such times, the balance of power can shift, within limits, to those who are best prepared for the contingency (or at least *seem* best prepared). This has implications for the study of international relations. If pluralists have failed to take stock of hierarchies, state-centric theorists – Marxists as well as realists – have given insufficient attention to power struggles within states. There is a belated recognition of the influence of domestic interests on foreign policy in the work of realists like Mearsheimer and Walt. But despite the worthy interventions of Gramsci, dominant Marxism still remains confined to an excessively structuralist mode of analysis. This has often led to analytical failures in identifying agency (to the extent that it is acknowledged). This polarisation between structure and agency is obfuscatory; both can be understood only in relation to the other. But that does not mean that the relative primacy of one over the other at a given moment cannot be established. This balance is situational.

Power, as Mann argues, lies in hierarchy and organisation, but hierarchy in the neoliberal order has been detached from organisation as the boundaries between the public and private have steadily dissolved and parallel hierarchies have emerged. Elite interests have traditionally been reinforced by class-consciousness and social cohesion. But this does not mean that the elite are a unified bloc; their myriad factions are often at odds with each other, and, as Gramsci observed, they seek the support of civil society to gain advantage over competitors. Command is ultimately exercised through formal structures of authority, underpinned to some degree by public legitimacy and value commitment; but the decisions frequently reflect the interests of the broader elites and the dominant faction within them. And the factions that are best integrated, and most densely networked, are usually the ones that dominate. However, writes Gramsci, since government in theory remains accountable to the people, there is an attempt by the elites to appropriate the language of public interest and to shape public opinion in advance so that it accords with their own interests. Public opinion is manufactured (which, as noted earlier, is not the same as manufacturing 'consent') using sophisticated means that have been developed over the past century to manufacture it. However, for ideas to endure, they must be amplified and promoted and preserved through institutions. This explains the recent proliferation of advocacy think tanks as the focus of propaganda has shifted from grassroots (the public) to treetops (the decision makers).[12]

Yet, information dominance alone cannot guarantee influence. Decision makers can always rely on alternative sources. To ensure maximum influence, think tanks, like most interest groups, work the revolving door by granting sinecures to former government officials and placing their own alumnae in high office. But contrary to the pluralists' contention, think tanks do not operate on a level playing field, nor do they get heard based solely on the quality of their expertise. Think tanks are often themselves part of the elite power structure; and the ones that represent the most powerful interests usually have the greatest access and influence. As studies of policy networks have shown, the political system does not comprise a single discreet unit called 'state', but myriad policy domains in which power relations over specific issues are asserted through stable and enduring inter- and extra-organisational relations. Think tanks play a key role in this. Laumann and Knoke therefore contend that the relevant unit of analysis in the study of policy formation is 'not the state understood in the institutional sense, but the state as a collection of policy arenas incorporating *both* governmental and private actors'.[13]

Within these arenas, the policy communities that have the highest shared interests and policy consensus are usually most effective. Janine Wedel's 'flex net' conceptualises one such formation which operates in the interstices of official and private power and exploits the ambiguity of their multiple overlapping roles to evade public oversight and private competition. Individual members of the flex net are able to override bureaucratic chains of command through personal relations, putting official information to private use, and using private information to steer official policy. Their primary allegiance is to their private network rather than the public office they occupy. But Wedel appears to overlook the more traditional means through which flex nets exercise influence. They already have roots in one or more of the overlapping spheres – ideological, economic and political – that according to Michael Mann constitute social power.[14] They stand poised to exploit opportunities such as crisis situations when democratic checks are frayed and the public is disoriented, making it easier to steer policy in directions which would normally be resisted. The specific changes are not always irreversible, but they stretch perimeters which permanently affect future scope of legitimate action. Thus did the neoconservatives succeed in using the crisis of 9/11 to engender an environment which, despite their exit, has left US national security discourse permanently affected, more amenable to militarism, less democratic and too ready to dispense with civil liberties.

Appendix

Mearsheimer and Walt, redux

In *The Israel Lobby and U.S. Foreign Policy*, John Mearsheimer and Stephen Walt argue that a 'critical element' in the Bush Administration's decision to attack Iraq was pressure from 'Israel and the lobby', especially 'a group of neoconservative policy makers and pundits who had been pushing the United States to attack Iraq since well before 9/11'.[1] While the pressure was 'a necessary but not sufficient condition for the war' – 9/11 being a critical factor – without it 'the war would almost certainly not have occurred'. It was motivated 'at least in good part by a desire to make Israel more secure'.[2] For many, these claims were unexceptional. It was well known that although opposition to war was higher among American Jews than the rest of the population, organised Jewry – that is, American Jewish organisations – enthusiastically backed the war; and the lobby's neoconservative spearhead played a significant role in conceiving and selling the war. The book was frequently misrepresented, misinterpreted or misunderstood, but there were also substantive criticisms relating to questions of scope, balance of power, agency and motivation.[3]

Mearsheimer and Walt had defined the lobby broadly, including even groups like Americans for Peace Now (APN) – yet APN was opposed to the war. Organisations such as AIPAC did lobby for war, but mostly behind the scenes. The neoconservatives were indeed the leading advocates of the war, though Mearsheimer and Walt were less clear on their sources of power and their motivations in seeking regime change. But Mearsheimer and Walt were correct to note that the war would not have happened without the lobby. The fact that there were organisations within the lobby that opposed the war does not undermine their thesis. As they note, the lobby 'is not a single, unified movement with a central leadership . . . and the individuals and groups that make up this broad coalition sometimes disagree on specific policy issues'.[4] What is significant is not that a group like APN dissented, but the vigour with which the pro-war factions, especially the neoconservatives, lobbied for and enabled the war. If the neoconservatives have been able to harness the authority and resources of the US state, it is because they ride the scaffolding of a larger power structure: the Israel lobby.

The aim of this appendix is first, to address the sociological reality of the lobby, summarise its history, and map the network of its agents, institutions and power sources. Despite its visible presence in US political life, such an exercise becomes necessary because, as the late historian Tony Judt observed, what makes the Israel lobby distinctive is that unlike other lobbies, it is not content with achieving its desired political outcomes; it also had an interest in denying its own existence and enforcing silence on the subject of its lobbying. It exists 'to silence as well as to voice, to suppress as well as to secure'.[5] The second object is to address the explanations commonly put forth by those who deny the lobby's significance in ensuring unstinting support for Israel: (1) that supporting Israel is popular cause; and (2) that Israel is an indispensable ally, a strategic asset.

The Israel lobby

'Before Israel existed as a state,' writes Tivnan, 'it existed as a political lobby first in the capitals of Europe and then in Washington.'[6] The nascent lobby that had existed in the US since the 1910s established the American Zionist Emergency Council in 1939 to use the crisis in Europe to unite American Jews in support of the Zionist cause. In 1943, the American Jewish Conference was founded as an umbrella of sixty-two Jewish organisations, which for Tivnan marked the birth of the 'Jewish lobby'.[7] By the end of World War II, it was already a significant force, playing a decisive role in US recognition of the State of Israel.[8] By the early 1960s, its power was significant enough to merit an extensive Senate investigation led by J. William Fulbright and attempts under both the Eisenhower and Kennedy Administrations to have it registered under the Foreign Agents Registration Act (FARA).[9] But all that power pales in comparison with the formidable institutional network it has developed since then, which Alan Dershowitz describes as 'perhaps the most effective lobbying and fund-raising effort in the history of democracy'.[10]

As defined by Mearsheimer and Walt, the Israel lobby is 'a loose coalition of individuals and organizations that actively works to move US foreign policy in a pro-Israel direction'. It comprises 'Jews and gentiles', it is 'not a single, unified movement with a central leadership', and the 'various groups that make up the lobby do not agree on every issue, although they share the desire to promote a special relationship between the United States and Israel'.[11] At its epicentre is AIPAC, the most visible organisation registered to lobby Congress on behalf of Israel; it has been joined in recent decades by the more hawkish Zionist Organization of America (ZOA).[12] But AIPAC and ZOA are just two of the fifty-two organisations that constitute the Conference of Presidents of the Major American Jewish Organizations (CPMAJO – known to insiders as the 'Presidents Conference'), a coordinating body that lobbies the executive branch.[13] CPMAJO is not the only coordinating body of national Jewish organisations: there is also the National Jewish Community Relations Advisory Council (NCRAC).[14]

The Israel lobby has a large gentile component, comprising Christian Zionists and the US right, but at its core lies the Jewish lobby, which consists of major national Jewish organisations.[15] These include the big three 'defence' agencies – the American Jewish Committee, the American Jewish Congress and the Anti-Defamation League (ADL); women's groups like Hadassah; campus groups like Hillel; and the vast federations of Jewish charities. These organisations do not agree on every issue: some such as the American Jewish Committee were once non-, even anti-Zionist. But according to Tivnan, after 1967, 'few Jewish leaders were willing to risk the favor of the Israeli government, and thus their status as Jewish leaders. Total support of Israel had become a requirement of leadership in local Jewish communities throughout America.'[16] The American Jewish establishment would brook no criticism of Israel, however mild. As a consequence, even pro-peace organisations like J-Street, APN, Meretz USA and the Israel Policy Forum are impelled to couch their criticisms of specific policies in general affirmations of steadfast support for Israel. They all oppose withholding aid to Israel, or making it conditional on conduct.[17] The Israel lobby is not monolithic, but since at least the 1970s, its foreign policy agenda has been set by its most hawkish element: the neoconservatives.

The Israel lobby uses all the instruments of modern political lobbying: pressure groups, think tanks, media watchdogs, letterhead organisations, astroturf movements, front groups and ad hoc alliances. The lobby has insulated itself with a network of satellite institutions and alliances all invested in cultivating the view that Israeli and US interests are identical. It may be impossible to define the borders of the lobby, but its gravitational core is identifiable. It consists of lobbying organisations like AIPAC, American Jewish Committee, ADL, CPMAJO, ZOA and Christians United for Israel (CUFI); think tanks such as WINEP, JINSA, AEI, CSP, the Saban Center for Middle East Policy, FDD, and the defence/national security programmes of the Hudson Institute and the Heritage Foundation; letterhead organisations like PNAC, CLI, Committee for Democracy in Iran and CPSG; campus groups like Hillel, StandWithUS and Israel on Campus Coalition; media watchdogs like Committee for Accuracy in Middle East Reporting in America (CAMERA) and Honest Reporting; publications such as *Commentary*, *The Weekly Standard* and *The New Republic*; and influential individuals such as Harvard's Alan Dershowitz, Nobel laureate Elie Wiesel, and major Republican and Democratic Party donors including gambling magnates Irving Moskowitz and Sheldon Adelson, media moguls Haim Saban, Mortimer Zuckerman and Sidney Harman, and financiers Lester Crown, Ronald Lauder and Lawrence Kadish (Figure 3).[18]

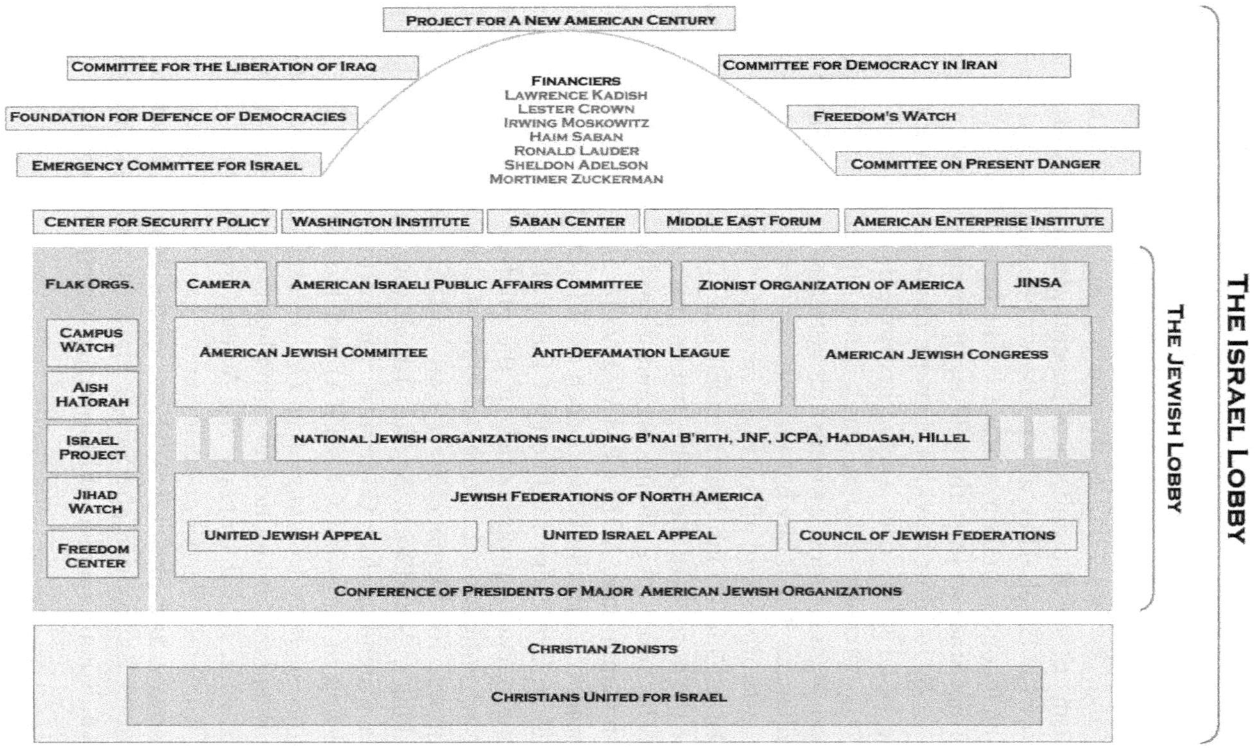

THE ISRAEL LOBBY

THE JEWISH LOBBY

COMMITTEE FOR THE LIBERATION OF IRAQ

FOUNDATION FOR DEFENCE OF DEMOCRACIES

EMERGENCY COMMITTEE FOR ISRAEL

PROJECT FOR A NEW AMERICAN CENTURY

COMMITTEE FOR DEMOCRACY IN IRAN

FREEDOM'S WATCH

COMMITTEE ON PRESENT DANGER

FINANCIERS
LAWRENCE KADISH
LESTER CROWN
IRWING MOSKOWITZ
HAIM SABAN
RONALD LAUDER
SHELDON ADELSON
MORTIMER ZUCKERMAN

CENTER FOR SECURITY POLICY

WASHINGTON INSTITUTE

SABAN CENTER

MIDDLE EAST FORUM

AMERICAN ENTERPRISE INSTITUTE

FLAK ORGS.

CAMPUS WATCH

AISH HATORAH

ISRAEL PROJECT

JIHAD WATCH

FREEDOM CENTER

CAMERA

AMERICAN ISRAELI PUBLIC AFFAIRS COMMITTEE

ZIONIST ORGANIZATION OF AMERICA

JINSA

AMERICAN JEWISH COMMITTEE

ANTI-DEFAMATION LEAGUE

AMERICAN JEWISH CONGRESS

NATIONAL JEWISH ORGANIZATIONS INCLUDING B'NAI B'RITH, JNF, JCPA, HADDASAH, HILLEL

JEWISH FEDERATIONS OF NORTH AMERICA

UNITED JEWISH APPEAL

UNITED ISRAEL APPEAL

COUNCIL OF JEWISH FEDERATIONS

CONFERENCE OF PRESIDENTS OF MAJOR AMERICAN JEWISH ORGANIZATIONS

CHRISTIAN ZIONISTS

CHRISTIANS UNITED FOR ISRAEL

Figure 3 Institutional infrastructure of the Israel lobby.

Sources of power

For Tivnan, Jewish political power in the US derives from three factors: the capacity and willingness to brand critics of Israel 'anti-Semites'; high voter turnouts; and large campaign donations.[19] The scourge of anti-Semitism has declined substantially in the post-war period according to surveys of both Europe and the US.[20] But as the Israeli film-maker Yoav Shamir has shown in his documentary *Defamation*, organisations like ADL are invested in inflating the threat to maintain Jewish support. They have done so by labelling all criticism of Israel anti-Semitism. In the early 1960s, shortly before the end of his tenure in Washington, a senior Israeli diplomat told Israeli journalist Amos Elon that his 'greatest achievement' was 'convincing Americans that anti-Zionism is anti-Semitism'.[21] Fear of opprobrium by the lobby has in turn forced many to suppress criticism of Israeli actions. Equally useful have been the invocations of the Holocaust as an ideological tool to permanently cast Israel – one of the world's leading military powers – as the victim.[22]

'The Jews are a valued electoral prize', writes J. J. Goldberg, even if their significance is overstated.[23] According to the 2008 census, Jews constitute a mere 2.2 per cent of the US population, but up to 94 per cent of them reside in large states like New York, California, Florida and Illinois, which control half of the Electoral College. They also vote in high numbers. This gives them political significance out of proportion to their numbers.[24] Writing in the Jerusalem Center for Public Affairs' newsletter, Jeffrey Helmreich observes:

> the greatest political strength of American Jewry lies in the fact that it is *a uniquely swayable bloc*. The issue of support for Israel has proven capable of spurring a sizable portion of Jews to switch parties . . . Moreover, the 'Israel swing vote' is especially open to political courtship because, unlike the interests of other minority groups, support for Israel has long been compatible with traditional Republican and Democratic agendas. By contrast, most other issues (abortion, affirmative action, etc.) cannot be embraced by Republicans or Democrats without alienating certain support bases . . . being distinctively unsupportive of Israel can significantly hurt a candidate's chances.[25]

'In a democracy,' write Mearsheimer and Walt, 'even relatively small groups can exercise considerable influence if they are strongly committed to a particular issue and the rest of the population is largely indifferent.'[26] Ralph Reed, the executive director of the Christian Coalition, concurs: according to J. J. Goldberg, he 'contends that decisions in a democracy are not necessarily made according to the beliefs of the majority, but more often according to who pushes the hardest. "Politics is a matter of intensity," Reed says.' Decisions makers are therefore able to accommodate the lobby's views without fearing penalisation by the larger electorate. Taking a principled stance on Israel's conduct, on the other hand, could potentially cost them an election.[27]

However, it is mainly through the purse that politically committed American Jews assert their power. Jews today are the most prosperous ethnic group in the US. According to a 2008 Pew survey, 46 per cent of Jewish families earn over $100,000 per annum, 28 per cent above the national average. Their social standing, education level and political participation are among the highest.[28] Declassified documents from the Ford and Carter archives show that both presidents were warned by their respective political strategists – Robert Goldwin and Hamilton Jordan – that taking positions critical of Israel would hurt them in the elections.[29] In his confidential memo, Jordan notes that 'over 50% of the money in support of the Democratic Party over the last two decades has been Jewish money'. But he adds that it was even higher in the case of specific candidates depending on their affinity for Israel: in 1972, Jews constituted 60 per cent of Nixon's largest donors; in 1968, 75 per cent of Hubert Humphrey's; and in 1976, 91 per cent of Henry 'Scoop' Jackson's.[30] According to *The Washington Post*, Democratic presidential candidates rely on Jewish donors for up to 60 per cent of their funding. Jews also contribute 25 per cent of the GOP's campaign funds.[31]

Over a third of US Jews state that they have no special attachment to Israel, but this is not the faction that dominates the American Jewish establishment. It does not have the organisation or motivation to challenge the faction for which Israel is a priority. Jewish leaders who have criticised Israel have found themselves ostracised by the American Jewish establishment.[32] Without their support, even Zionist titans like Nahum Goldmann – former president of the World Jewish Congress (WJC), the WZO and founder of the CPMAJO) and Arthur Hertzberg, former president of the American Jewish Congress and vice-president of the WJC – found themselves shunned in Washington.[33] Candidates who criticise Israel gain little – the Arab–Israeli conflict is not a US priority – but they risk seeing money flowing to their opponents. Supporting Israel on the other hand puts one in favour with a powerful constituency, aligns one's position with the generally pro-Israel orientation of US policy, and removes a potentially fatal impediment to one's career. Critics of Israel often find themselves isolated in Congress, making it impossible to caucus, diminishing their power to legislate in other areas.[34] Israel is therefore virtually immune to criticism. All legislation relating to Israel passes with virtually no opposition.[35] Despite a median household income ($37,000) that matches Britain's, at $3 billion, Israel is the largest recipient of annual US aid.[36]

Modus operandi

The lobby operates on two tracks: it targets Congress and the executive branch directly, and it attempts to shape public opinion in favour of Israel. It seeks to ensure the support of political leaders mainly through campaign contributions. Those that toe the line benefit from the lobby's largesse; those that dissent risk seeing money flowing to their opponents. As a one-issue constituency, the lobby is able to wield its financial power more flexibly than most other interest groups. This could be decisive in close races, Goldberg argues based on the evidence of presidential elections from 1916–92.[37] The default position of all candidates is therefore to support Israel uncritically, but where candidates step out of line, the lobby mobilises its resources against them as a warning to others.[38]

The lobby has relatively less influence over the executive branch. It has long relied on the personal relations of key members with the president to convey its concerns. Louis Brandeis had a close relationship with Woodrow Wilson; Abe Feinberg with Truman; Feinberg and Philip Klutznick with Kennedy; Feinberg, Abe Fortas, and Arthur and Mathilde Krimm with Johnson; Haim Saban with Clinton; and Lester Crown with Barack Obama.[39] However, in 1954, the CPMAJO was founded, as an umbrella of national Jewish organisations, specifically to lobby the executive and to present American Jewry's 'consensus support for Israel'.[40] The real check on the executive, however, was for the most part exercised through Congress, where the lobby has more clout. In 1975, when Gerald Ford threatened to 'reassess' US support for Israel and briefly withheld military aide, he received a letter drafted by AIPAC and co-signed by seventy-six senators advising him to desist.[41] Over three decades later, President Barack Obama would receive a similar ultimatum after he tried to pressure Israel to stop the expansion of illegal settlements in the Occupied Territories, also drafted by AIPAC and signed by seventy-six senators.[42] In the rare cases where presidents have chosen to act despite lobby pressure – Eisenhower after Suez, Carter after the Israeli invasion of Lebanon, Bush Sr. on loan guarantees in 1992 – they have bypassed Congressional opposition by directly appealing to the US public.[43]

Like most successful pressure groups, the lobby also influences policy by having its members appointed to government position and by manoeuvring to block appointments deemed unsympathetic to its objectives. Even before Israel's creation, it had individuals like David K. Niles serving under Roosevelt and Truman as the White House liaison to ethnic minorities. Described by Tivnan as the 'Zionists' secret weapon in the White House',[44] Niles shielded the president against a recalcitrant State Department and, along with his brother Elliot, assisted the Zionist movement.[45] According to Tivnan, Truman gave no speech on the Arab–Zionist question without Niles's approval.[46] Most presidents since then have had veterans of the Israel lobby serving in key official positions. But under Clinton, they also joined the cabinet.[47] Bush's Pentagon, OVP, NSC and DPB were likewise populated with lobby veterans. During Barack Obama's first term, aggressive lobbying purged his retinue of realists like Zbigniew Brzezinski, Robert Malley, Charles Freeman and Chuck Hagel.[48] Lobby stalwarts like Rahm Emanuel, Dennis Ross and Andrew Shapiro ,on the other hand, had little trouble securing sensitive national security portfolios. 'Every appointee to the American government', writes Natasha Mozgovaya of the Israeli daily *Haaretz*, 'must endure a thorough background check by the American Jewish community.'[49]

The lobby works sedulously to cultivate a climate of opinion favourable to Israel. This campaign is aimed as much at top decision makers as it is at civil society. The lobby also uses the media to target public opinion more directly. The editorial line of the agenda-setting press – especially *The Washington Post* and *The Wall Street Journal* – is unabashedly pro-Israel. This trend also prevails on television and radio.[50] Dissenting views appear only in the margins. According to media scholar Eric Alterman, '[f]or reasons of religion, politics, history and genuine conviction the punditocracy debate of the Middle East in America is dominated by people who cannot imagine criticizing Israel.' He lists fifty-six columnists and commentators who could be counted on to give Israel unqualified support but only five equally sympathetic towards the Palestinians (which include the late Edward Said, who was not a regular columnist).[51] He also noted the uncritical pro-Israel editorial lines of several major publications, including *The New Republic*, *Commentary*, *The Weekly Standard*, *The Wall Street Journal* and *The Atlantic Monthly*. The same generally holds true for *The Washington Post* and *The New York Times*.[52] Where journalists are seen as stepping out of line, organisations like CAMERA generate flak, organise boycotts and target advertisers.[53]

But the lobby's success is guaranteed less by its persuasive powers than by its superior command of the logistics of influence. For Israeli-American media mogul Haim Saban – who famously declared: 'I'm a one-issue guy and my issue is Israel'[54] – there are 'three ways to be influential in American politics': 'make donations to political parties, establish think tanks, and control media outlets'.[55] He has done all three: in 2002, he made the single biggest donation to the Democratic Party; he established the Saban Center for Middle East Policy at the Brookings Institution and chose former AIPAC staffer Martin Indyk as its head; and he acquired Univision and has made repeated bids to buy the *Los Angeles Times* and *Newsweek* (which in 2010 was bought by another Israel lobby stalwart, Sidney Harman).[56]

On campuses the lobby uses a phalanx of groups like Hillel, StandWithUS and the Israel on Campus Coalition (which includes organisations like ADL, American Jewish Committee and AIPAC) to train campus activists, monitor student activism, infiltrate student executive bodies and stymie anti-Zionist activism.[57] These groups also organise tours by pro-Israel speakers while lobbying against appearances by critics of Israel. Middle East Studies departments, which are seen as the potential hub of anti-Israel activity, have also been the targets of lobby activity.[58] Daniel Pipes's Campus Watch project has produced blacklists of professors it perceives as being insufficiently supportive of Israel. Lobby pressure in recent years successfully blocked the appointments of Middle East scholars like Norman Finkelstein, Juan Cole and Rashid Khalidi.[59] The lobby has also tried to introduce legislation that will allow it to control what gets taught in classrooms.[60] Jewish philanthropists have tried to bolster pro-Israel voices in academia by establishing Israel Studies departments (in addition to existing Jewish Studies programmes).[61]

Christian Zionism

The Christian Right has emerged as a key component of the Israel lobby in recent years, though the relationship itself is older.[62] Christian Zionism preceded political Zionism and Jewish leaders were courting fundamentalist Christians as far back as 1848 when American proto-Zionist Mordecai Noah sought their support for restoring Jews to 'new Judea'. Theodore Herzl appealed to the Christian Zionists and so did Chaim Weizmann and Louis Brandeis.[63] But the Christian Right's political infrastructure emerged as a formidable force only in the past four decades. The turning point was 1967, when some Christians took what seemed like Israel's 'miraculous' victory and the recovery of Jerusalem and 'Judea and Samaria' (the biblical name for the West Bank) as the fulfilment of biblical prophecy. Golda Meir actively vied for the support of influential Christian evangelist Billy Graham.[64] Shortly after the Camp David agreement, Israeli Prime Minister Menachem Begin tried to recruit evangelical leader Jerry Falwell against Jimmy Carter, inviting him to Israel and presenting him with a Learjet as a gift. Falwell formed the Moral Majority shortly afterwards, which pulled much of the evangelical vote away from Carter in the 1980 presidential election.[65]

The alliance between the Israel lobby and the Christian Right bloomed under Reagan, who was himself convinced that End Times were nigh.[66] The ranks of the coalition swelled when following his failed 1988 presidential bid, televangelist Pat Robertson formed the Christian Coalition, a lobbying organisation later turned into a political powerhouse by its executive director Ralph Reed. With Rabbi Yechiel Eckstein, Reed would go on to co-chair Stand for Israel, a 'sort of Christian AIPAC'.[67] Other groups like James Dobson's Focus on the Family and Ed McAteer's Religious Roundtable also developed a Zionist orientation. In February 2006, televangelist John Hagee established CUFI specifically to lobby for Israel.[68] At its inauguration in Washington, messages of support were read out from George Bush and the then Israeli Prime Minister Ehud Olmert.[69] Hagee also delivered a keynote address at AIPAC's 2007 annual conference; and, despite his known anti-Semitic views, became the first gentile recipient of B'nai B'rith's 'Humanitarian of the Year' award and the ZOA's Israel Award.[70] CUFI now has chapters nationwide, and it also works closely with the David Project to police academia.[71]

Christian Zionist support has given the lobby significant leverage over the Republican Party but its influence is often overstated. The Christian Right has many priorities, most of them related to domestic social issues. Support for Israel is not salient among them. Christian Zionists are a subset of the broader Christian Right, and their support is significant insofar as they shape a climate broadly supportive of Israel and hostile to the creation of a Palestinian state in the West Bank and Gaza. However, according to Mearsheimer and Walt, they do not lobby for specific policies, nor do they have the 'organizational capacity to analyze national security topics or to offer special legislative guidance on concrete foreign policy issues'.[72] In this regard, they defer to organisations such as AIPAC. They are also countered by mainline Protestant and Catholic churches which are broadly supportive of the two-state solution. The Christian Right is possessed of a network of media institutions including the Trinity Broadcasting Network,

Pat Robertson's Christian Broadcasting Network, and their vast radio and Internet affiliates.[73] However, their influence is directed more towards the masses than the policy elite. The mainstream media is less likely to turn to a Christian Right leader than an expert from Brookings, WINEP or AEI when covering issues related to the Middle East.[74] George H. W. Bush, Bill Clinton and, more recently, Barack Obama have all been able to pursue policies that ran contrary to the Christian Right's preferences.[75] The Christian Right has more influence domestically; yet on the few occasions where its interests diverged with the Jewish lobby (as they did over the issue of state-approved prayers in schools) its numerical superiority has not translated into political triumph.[76] Christian Zionists are no doubt an important Republican constituency, but their overall significance in shaping Middle East policy is exaggerated.

The 'strategic asset' myth

The claim that Israel enjoys unswerving US support because it has functioned as a 'strategic asset' is belied by evidence. Indeed, support for Israel has remained constant even when it has acted as a palpable liability. To bury this myth, an examination of the historical record is in order.

As a colonial-settler movement, Zionism was unique insofar as it had no mother country.[77] Zionist attempts to court British, French and US support by offering a future Jewish State as an imperial outpost proved futile. Britain issued the Balfour Declaration during World War I mainly to court Jewish support in getting the US to intervene on its behalf, but retreated shortly afterwards. In endorsing the Balfour Declaration, Woodrow Wilson had to shut out Secretary of State Robert Lansing, who had been opposed to Zionism because he believed it would alienate the Ottomans (whom the US had excluded from its declaration of war). Wilson's aide Col. Edward Mandel House had scribbled in his diary that British support for Zionism was 'making the [Middle East] a breeding place for future war'.[78] The King Crane Commission sent after World War I by President Woodrow Wilson to study the readiness of the former Ottoman regions for self-determination concluded that the Zionist programme was tantamount to a 'gross violation' of this principle.[79] Under Truman, the Departments of State, Defense and the military remained opposed to Zionism, seeing it as a destabilising force that undermined US interests.[80] Truman overrode the objections of all three to back the partition of Palestine and later extend recognition to Israel. His concerns were entirely domestic.[81] Secretary of State George Marshall saw the decision was 'based on domestic political considerations' and a 'transparent dodge to win a few votes'; he even threatened to vote against Truman if he persisted.[82] Secretary of Defense James Forrestal warned Truman repeatedly about 'the danger that hostile Arabs might deny us access to the petroleum treasures of their country' as a consequence of backing the Zionists.[83] Forrestal derided Truman, whom he charged would rather 'lose the United States' than lose the Jewish vote. For Loy Henderson, the head of the State Department's Office of Near East and Africa Affairs, support for Zionism was 'contrary to the interests of the United States and will eventually involve us in international difficulties ... we are forfeiting the friendship of the Arab world ... [and] incurring long-term Arab hostility toward us'.[84] Equally disappointed was George Kennan: 'US prestige in the Muslim world has suffered a severe blow, and US strategic interests in the Mediterranean and Near East have been seriously prejudiced.'[85] Even Dean Acheson, who would replace Marshall, noted that the creation of a Jewish state in Palestine 'would vastly exacerbate the political problem and imperil not only American but Western interests in the Near East'.[86]

US support for Israel subsided after its founding, even though Zionists were trying to exploit the temporary convergence in 1948 to deepen the identification and make the support irreversible.[87] In 1953, a new Republican government came to office committed to neutrality in the region, seeing its interests lying mainly with the Arabs, whose oil was necessary for the economy and for European recovery.[88] Israel, on the other hand, was seen as a nuisance: in 1953 it undermined US plans to develop the Jordan River plain by diverting water away to the Negev, forcing Secretary of State John Foster Dulles to withhold loans.[89] The

Eisenhower administration backed the Free Officers' coup against the Egyptian monarch in 1952, and both Eisenhower and Dulles saw Gamal Abdul Nasser as an anti-communist moderniser and a natural ally. However, things turned sour after the administration withheld funds for the construction of the Aswan Dam under pressure from the Israel, cotton and anti-China lobbies.[90] Nasser was forced to turn to the Soviets for assistance, and the US in turn quietly encouraged friendly states to sell arms to Israel while maintaining the façade of 'friendly impartiality'.[91] Israel tried to further sabotage US–Egypt relations by blowing up US installations in Egypt, hoping to pin the blame on Egyptian militants. The subsequent exposé of what came to be known as the Lavon Affair and Israel's raids on Gaza further infuriated Americans.[92] After the tripartite invasion in 1956, Eisenhower bucked strong lobby pressure to force the withdrawal of Israel, France and the UK from Egyptian territory.[93] However, by the time he left office, the administration's impotence in the face of constant Israeli provocations had fanned the flames of Arab nationalism.[94]

John F. Kennedy at first appeared pliant and sympathetic to the lobby's wishes. During the 1960 presidential campaign, he had quickly retreated from his promises to resolve the Palestinian refugee problem after influential Jews led by Philip Klutznick threatened to withdraw their support.[95] But Kennedy soon proved himself a thorn in the lobby's side. His Justice Department led a dogged fight to register the lobby's agents under FARA and he intensified pressure on Israel to open up its nuclear facilities for inspection. He also rebuffed Ben-Gurion's entreaties to sign a formal security treaty with Israel.[96] In August 1961, he appointed Joseph E. Johnson, the president of the Carnegie Endowment for International Peace, as his envoy to prepare recommendations for the resettlement of the Palestinian refugees. The Johnson Plan generated an intense lobby backlash, and Kennedy acquiesced to the lobby's demands to loan Israel $23 million in August 1962 to buy Hawk anti-aircraft missiles – effectively ending the arms embargo in place since the Tripartite Declaration of 25 May 1950 – hoping to secure Ben-Gurion's cooperation on the refugee issue.[97] The lobby triumphed: Israel got its weapons and the Johnson Plan vanished.[98] Following Kennedy's assassination, so, too, did the Justice Department probe into the lobby's activities.[99]

Lyndon Johnson knew little about foreign policy, and much of what he knew about the Middle East came from conversations with the suave Israeli ambassador Abba Eban. His support for Israel had come by the force of a chequebook.[100] In 1964, he lifted the arms embargo on Israel in return for Jewish financial support for his campaign against Barry Goldwater.[101] New York banker Abe Feinberg and Washington lawyer David Ginsburg along with UN ambassador Arthur Goldberg and Supreme Court Justice Abe Fortas served not only as his unofficial circuit with the Israeli leadership, but also as the 'synaptic connection between Johnson's political brain and . . . New York investment bankers and Hollywood moguls'.[102] Feinberg had already enjoyed close access to Truman and Kennedy, but according to Seymour Hersh, he had 'the greatest presidential access and influence in his twenty years as a Jewish fund-raiser and lobbyist with Lyndon Johnson'.[103] However, in the lead-up to the June war in 1967, his administration made strenuous efforts to defuse tensions, despite strong pressure from the lobby. Indeed, it was in anticipation of the Egyptian Vice President Zakaria Mohieddin's visit to Washington that Israel launched its pre-emptive war.[104] Once the war started, Johnson would shut out his own cabinet to take advice almost exclusively from his pro-Israel Jewish advisers, including James Novy, Abe Fortas, Arthur Goldberg, Walt and Eugene Rostow and John Roche; and private citizens like Arthur Krim, head of United Artists, and his wife Mathilde Krim, a former member of Irgun, the pre-state Zionist terrorist organisation.[105] During the war, Israel also launched a deliberate attack on the USS *Liberty*, a US signals vessel sailing along the Egyptian coast, without suffering consequences.[106] After the war, US Ambassador to the UN Arthur Goldberg would manipulate the language of UN Security Council resolution 242 to give Israel's land expropriation a legal cover.[107]

Israel as a stationary aircraft carrier

The notion that the US adopted Israel as a 'strategic asset' because it rendered a service in destroying the forces of Arab nationalism ignores history and inverts causation. The US had in fact backed the Free Officers' coup in Egypt – CIA agents Kermit Roosevelt and Miles Copeland, who had played an instrumental role in the overthrow of Iranian Prime Minister Mohammad Mossadegh (in Operation Ajax), were their key liaisons – and both Eisenhower and later Kennedy tried to woo Arab nationalist icon Gamal Abdul Nasser, whom they saw as an anti-communist moderniser.[108] On the other hand, despite its offer to covertly employ Jews behind the iron curtain as intelligence assets, the US did not always view Israel with favour.[109] But domestic political pressure ensured that the US remained allied with Israel, thereby alienating Arabs. Johnson was a friend of Israel, but he had no wish to see Israel waging a war that could drag US into a superpower confrontation.[110] But after the war, the conflict entered a Cold War paradigm. Outraged by Israeli aggression, Charles de Gaulle withdrew French support from Israel; and Egypt meanwhile turned to the Soviet Union to help rebuild its defences.[111] The US had joined France to put a 135-day arms ban on the region at the end of the war, but the lobby played up the Soviet role and in December Johnson lifted the arms embargo, selling Israel two squadrons of Skyhawk bombers. However, when Israel tried to use the opportunity to ask for fifty F-4 Phantom jets, both the State and Defense Departments, which were keen to de-escalate tensions in the region, opposed the sale.[112] Johnson himself wanted to use the F-4s as leverage to persuade Israel to foreswear its nuclear ambitions and sign the Nuclear Non-Proliferation Treaty, which he had championed.[113] But 1968 was an election year and AIPAC targeted both parties; it even mobilised the AFL–CIO, Americans for Democratic Action and the American Legion to endorse the sale. A policy statement issued by AIPAC in March was adopted by both houses of Congress, both party platforms and both presidential candidates.[114] Uncharacteristically, Johnson stood firm. When he eventually relented in December 1968, it had less to do with US strategic interests than the dogged persuasion of Abe Feinberg and Arthur Krim.[115] Feinberg later boasted: 'When the Phantoms were delivered to Israel, I was the only American at the airfield.'[116]

Similar myths abound about the 1973 war when under Richard

Nixon the US emphatically committed itself to arming Israel. US strategic concerns had no bearing on this decision. It was as much due to Nixon's cynical ploy to deflect pressure from the Watergate investigations, and Henry Kissinger's Machiavellian machinations, as the lobby's arm-twisting.[117] Kissinger had advanced to the position of secretary of state by repeatedly undercutting his predecessor William Rogers, who sought Israel's withdrawal from the Occupied Palestinian Territories (OPT) and, like Nixon, worried that Israeli intransigence was undermining US oil security.[118] When the war started, Nixon and Defense Secretary James Schlesinger had no intention to intervene; they argued that the US had an obligation to defend Israel but not to defend Israel's conquests. Egypt was merely trying to recover its own territory. But Kissinger – whose Zionism, according to Tyler, formed 'the bedrock of [his] view of the Middle East'[119] – raised a false alarm that other Arab armies were about to join the war against Israel and contravened Nixon, who wanted to engage the Soviets in a joint ceasefire proposal. Kissinger deliberately fomented a superpower confrontation and encouraged Israeli leaders to ignore Nixon's call for restraint to buy Israel time to secure better ceasefire terms and to finish off Egypt's besieged 3rd Army.[120] Finally, he misled Nixon about Soviet intentions and exaggerated domestic pressure to get approval for a massive arms shipment to Israel as a response to this 'Russian treachery'.[121] Tyler observes that Kissinger was manoeuvring 'as if he were a partisan for Israel's war aims' and 'his actions throughout the crisis added up to a focused advocacy more for Israel's strategic goals than for those of the United States'. 'Kissinger's duplicity was so plain', he concludes, as 'to raise questions of constitutional propriety, not to mention loyalty.'[122] After the war, Kissinger also arbitrarily raised the level of US aid to Israel to $2.2 billion – a provocation that compelled the otherwise pliant King Faisal of Saudi Arabia to announce a comprehensive oil embargo.[123] For the US the war was a disaster. Not only because it depleted US weapons stocks, leading to the near-resignation of the Chairman of the Joint Chiefs of Staff George S. Brown, but also because of its wider economic impact from which the US would take nearly a decade to recover.[124]

Gerald Ford's experience with Israel proved equally frustrating. By the time he came to office, even Henry Kissinger had lost some of his enthusiasm for the Jewish State.[125] With Kissinger's backing, Ford responded to Israeli intransigence by threatening to 'reassess' US support. He was soon forced into an embarrassing climb down after receiving a letter drafted by AIPAC and signed by seventy-six senators.[126] The lobby also challenged Jimmy Carter when he became the first US president to broach the idea of a Palestinian 'homeland'. However, he proved a more formidable adversary. Though he occasionally ceded ground, through sheer tenacity he managed to extract concessions from Israel. Following Israel's 1978 invasion of Lebanon, his threat to cut aid to Israel led Israeli Prime Minister Menachem Begin to order a withdrawal.[127] He also forced Israel to withdraw from the occupied Egyptian Sinai peninsula, despite Begin's reluctance and the opposition of the lobby.[128] Carter's wish for a comprehensive Middle East peace was frustrated by his failure to win re-election in 1980. (It has since emerged that Begin directly intervened in the US elections with the support of Likud-affiliated intelligence officers and New York Mayor Ed Koch in an attempt to ensure Carter's defeat.)[129]

Ronald Reagan, who actually believed that Israel was a strategic asset, began his presidency on a firmly pro-Israel footing. However, he found his attempts at strategic cooperation with Israel repeatedly frustrated by an intransigent Begin who, Reagan felt, was always ignoring US national interests. This tension was exploited by Reagan's Secretary of State Alexander Haig, a former Kissinger sidekick, who frequently leveraged Israeli power in his bureaucratic struggle against the president and the administration realists (mainly Vice President George H. W. Bush, Defense Secretary Caspar Weinberger and National Security Advisor William Clark).[130] Haig blocked Weinberger and Bush's attempts to penalise Israel for its attack on Iraq's Osirak reactor.[131] He also gave a green light to Israeli Defence Minister Ariel Sharon to invade Lebanon as part of the latter's plan to reshape the Middle East – an enterprise Haig would himself join without presidential authorisation.[132] Reagan ignored the realists' advice to sanction Israel and sided with the neoconservatives, who argued that the invasion benefited the US by sending a message to the 'Soviet-backed radical Arab front'.[133] The realists on the other hand maintained that 'Israeli militarism with American arms ... was hurting America's image in the Middle East' making it harder 'to build a strong anti-Soviet alliance.'[134] The US engagement in Lebanon ended in carnage with the retaliatory bombings of its embassy and Marines barracks in Beirut after its forces openly joined the conflict on the rightist Phalange's side.[135] To the neo-conservatives' great consternation, Reagan ignored their advice and ordered a withdrawal.

The lobby also became concerned about the growing influence of the Saudis, who had proved themselves Washington's dependable allies by lowering oil prices to help the teetering US economy and underwriting the US proxy wars in Afghanistan, Nicaragua and Angola.[136] The lobby's attempts to restore Israeli influence in Washington would culminate in the scandalous Iran–Contra affair.[137] Equally embarrassing was the revelation that Jonathan Pollard, a Jewish American intelligence analyst, had stolen a trove of sensitive documents for Israel, some of which were subsequently relayed to the Soviet Union as a 'gesture of goodwill' by the government of Yitzhak Shamir.[138]

The relationship between the US and Israel reached its nadir under the George H. W. Bush Administration, whose Secretary of State James Baker riled many of its supporters by telling them bluntly to 'lay aside, once and for all, the unrealistic vision of a greater Israel'.[139] Bush himself became the target of an intense Israel lobby campaign after he declared his government's firm opposition to settlements in the occupied West Bank and East Jerusalem.[140] Following the 1991 Gulf War, Bush and Baker initiated a peace process, forcing Israel to the negotiating table. Bush also withheld loan guarantees in order to force Israel to freeze new settlement construction. After the lobby mobilised its forces, Bush checkmated them by appealing directly to the US public. It proved to be his epitaph. Despite soaring approval ratings at the end of the Gulf War, Bush lost the election in 1992, in part due to the lobby's opposition.[141] His successor Bill Clinton chose to pre-empt confrontation with the lobby by handing State, Defense and the NSC to lobby alumni.[142] After claiming credit for a largely Norwegian effort at peace making, Clinton did little to hold Israel to its promises.[143] He was pushed around by both Benjamin Netanyahu and Ehud Barak (with the former at one point trying to involve Clinton in an assassination conspiracy against Palestinian leaders).[144] All his top advisers were former lobbyists for Israel who, according to one member of his negotiating team, all too often served as 'Israel's lawyers'.[145] He only returned to the issue with some conviction in the waning days of his administration, but when the negotiations failed, he singled out the Palestinians for blame.[146]

The argument that Israel serves as a bulwark for US imperial interests in the region overlooks the fact that the conditions that make its services seemingly indispensable were created by Israel itself. It is the unconditional support that Israel has received from the US since its founding that first radicalised Arab nationalists, sent them into the Soviet embrace and later inflamed Islamic fundamentalism. Critics of Mearsheimer and Walt are fond of quoting Alexander Haig's formulation that Israel serves as an unsinkable 'aircraft carrier' for the US, but they ignore the fact this was a minority view even within the Reagan Administration: Bush, Weinberger and Clark considered Israel a strategic liability (nor do they appear to know that the phrase 'immense aircraft carrier' was originally coined by US ambassador J. Rives Child in 1948 for Saudi Arabia, which he considered a 'key piece of the US front line defense' because of its strategic location).[147] In reality, whenever the US has deemed its interests at risk, it has intervened directly (as it did in Lebanon in 1958 and in Iraq in 1991). Jimmy Carter formed the Rapid Deployment Force (which would later evolve into CENTCOM) with the precise aim of intervening in the region should US interests be at risk. Also overlooked is the fact that the US already has the Fifth Fleet, which includes a Carrier Strike Group, patrolling the Persian Gulf, the Arabian Sea and the Red Sea. Indeed, far from Israel protecting its interests, the US has had to keep the Sixth Fleet permanently stationed in the Mediterranean as the ultimate guarantor of *Israel's* security.[148] In 1991, the US had to divert resources to protect Israel (causing much consternation among the military brass) lest its reaction destroy the large coalition that George H. W. Bush had assembled to evict Iraq from Kuwait.[149] The late Israel Shahak noted:

US support for Israel, when considered not in abstract but concrete detail, cannot be adequately explained as a result of American imperial interests. The strong influence wielded by the organized Jewish community in the US in support of all Israeli policies must also be taken into account in order to explain the Middle East policies of American administrations.[150]

The view is echoed by Andrew Sullivan, the former editor *The New Republic*:

Strategically, Israel is obviously a huge burden for the US, making relations with Muslim or Arab nations much harder, and undermining any attempt to portray American intervention in, say, Iraq or Afghanistan, as beneficent rather than predatory. It's a big drain on the Treasury, as Israel consumes a vast amount of military and non-military aid.[151]

Israel as the guardian of Arab oil

The claim that Israel keeps watch over the region's energy resources is also questionable. Philosopher Michael Neumann notes:

Why would American concerns about its oil supply prompt it to ally itself with the one power in the world that drives its suppliers to distraction? Were it not for that alliance, the U.S. would be able to apply much more direct and finely tuned pressure on oil-rich governments. Israel is (a) best positioned to pressure states which are not significant oil producers – Lebanon, Syria, Jordan, Egypt; (b) utterly superfluous for pressuring the very feeble Gulf states; and (c) politically unsuitable, as the Gulf Wars showed, for pressuring militarily strong producers like Iraq under Saddam Hussein and Iran. And what is true of oil is true, *mutatis mutandis*, of other U.S. economic interests: Israel is more a hindrance than a help in furthering them.[152]

Other than the oil embargoes that followed Israeli aggression, the Gulf states have never withheld their oil; it is not clear, therefore, why coercion would be necessary to secure Arab oil. The most stable and pliant ally in the region has been Saudi Arabia, with which the US has always maintained friendly relations. If there is hostility to the US in the Middle East, it is mainly due to its support for Israel. The US diplomatic and military establishments have long seen Israel as an impediment to US interests in the region. Under Eisenhower, this concern was compounded by the fact that Israel's actions were radicalising Arabs, who had hitherto seen the US as a non-imperial – indeed, anti-imperial – power.[153]

Arab hostility began with the Suez crisis in 1956, which created an anti-Western sentiment that affected many US oil companies.[154] The chastened oilmen tried to stave off the next war by engaging in diplomatic initiatives in 1967, which ultimately proved futile. Oil producers retaliated by boycotting the US and UK. Former CIA director and energy expert John McCone, writes Cole, 'saw the Johnson administration's unreserved support for Israel and Israeli expansionism as a profound threat to the position of the United States and its petroleum corporations in the Arab world'.[155]

The 1973 war was an even bigger disaster. King Faisal of Saudi Arabia and his oil minister Sheikh Yamani had both warned the Nixon Administration that because of its unstinting support for Israel, US oil companies 'would lose everything'.[156] Oil companies panicked and Exxon, Mobil and SoCal all took out ads in newspapers advising Nixon against antagonising the Arabs. Jack McCloy, the lawyer for the 'Seven Sisters', warned Kissinger before the war that 'the Administration must not think just in terms of the next New York election'.[157] Once the war started, OPEC responded by imposing a comprehensive oil embargo.[158] The price of oil jumped from $3.02 per barrel in October to $11.65 by December, and the crisis precipitated a wave of nationalisations, beginning with Saddam Hussein's confiscation of US shares in the Basra Petroleum Company.[159]

With an economy depressed by the fourfold increase in oil prices, many US companies started looking for opportunities in the lucrative Arab market. For this they had to comply with the Arab economic boycott of Israel, filing papers at the Arab Boycott Office in Damascus. This led to the biggest confrontation by far between the Israel lobby, led by the 'big three' (ADL, American

Jewish Committee and American Jewish Congress) and major US corporations represented by the BRT over an anti-boycott bill. The lobby was assisted by 'a few friendly editors at the Wall Street Journal and the New York Times', writes Goldberg, and 'opponents were in an unenviable position: in the name of pragmatism and free trade, they seemed to be defending foreign powers that discriminated against Americans'.[160] The lobby won, and in May 1977, the anti-boycott bill was signed into law.[161]

Opportunities dwindled further in the 1980s and 1990s as the US imposed sanctions first on Iran and later on Libya. The threat of new sanctions led industry majors like Texaco, Conoco, Mobil and Halliburton to join 670 other companies, trade associations and organisations from all sectors of the US economy in USA*Engage, a lobbying coalition which worked closely with the US Chamber of Commerce against sanctions on Sudan, Syria, Iran, Libya, Burma, Nigeria, India and Pakistan.[162] In 1996, despite pressure from USA*Engage, the US passed ILSA, a bill partially drafted by Steven Rosen and other AIPAC staffers.[163] By the end of the decade, even Dick Cheney was complaining about AIPAC's influence, which was keeping US business out of the lucrative Middle Eastern energy market.[164] Businesses, including oil services giant Halliburton, were fighting against sanctions as late as May 2001.[165] In 2001, even Saudi Arabia for the first time opened its oil for bidding by non-US companies following US silence over atrocities committed by Israel during the second Palestinian intifada.[166] At the time of writing, a similar battle once again pits US businesses, led by USA*Engage, against the Israel lobby. The target this time is Iran.[167]

An even bigger disaster has been the US–Israel Free Trade Agreement (USIFTA). It has allowed Israel free access to the US market without a corresponding expansion of opportunities in Israel. The treaty was itself passed, as an FBI investigation discovered, following the theft of a classified strategy document prepared by US businesses from the International Trade Commission. The document included proprietary data supplied by US industry.[168] Seventy-six major US corporations and the largest labour union, AFL–CIO, were opposed to the treaty.[169] Support came from only AIPAC and twenty-two other entities, not all of them businesses.[170] Between its passage in 1985 and 2008, the US cumulative deficit has reached $71 billion as a result, and far from expanding opportunities, the US share of Israel's import market has declined from 27 per cent in 1985 to 12 per cent in 2007. Meanwhile, the US has become the largest destination for Israeli exports. Israel's export-oriented generic drugs industry has also benefited from copying US patent-protected drug formulas, exploiting regulatory jurisdiction conflicts enabled by USIFTA.[171]

The military–industrial nexus

Another argument often marshalled to emphasise Israel's utility is that it helps to sustain US military–industrial production; or, that it serves as a testing ground for US weaponry. The prima facie plausibility of this argument is belied by the fact that where Israel receives top-drawer US weaponry for free, it ensures that similar weapons are denied to Arab states which, unlike Israel, are willing to pay for their weapons. Moreover, Israel's own military industry now competes with that of the US – often in the same markets and sometimes using US technology. True, the interests of the Israel lobby and the arms industry coincide most of the time. But where their interests do come into conflict, evidence suggests that the balance of power favours the lobby.

Here it is instructive to look at two incidents that are often cited as evidence of the lobby's relative powerlessness. The first is the 1982 battle over the sale of the AWACS to Saudi Arabia. The commonly cited version of this story elides context and consequence – beginning with the crucial fact that the Saudis had been encouraged in the first place to purchase the AWACS planes by the chairman of the US Joint Chiefs of Staff General David Jones.[172] The AWACS battle was not just about an arms sale: it was about Reagan's whole foreign policy and about a fragile economy. Reagan needed Saudi help for the recovery of the US economy and to underwrite proxy wars that Congress was unwilling to sanction. He also had the strong backing of corporate America, led by Boeing, United Technologies and Mobil.[173] Yet Reagan lost three consecutive votes on the sale during the first nine months of the confrontation with the lobby.[174] For the crucial final vote in the Senate, Reagan had to call in the support of three ex-presidents (Nixon, Ford and Carter) to personally appeal to each senator's patriotism ('Reagan or Begin?').[175] Reagan also persuaded the Saudis to accept humiliating conditions for the sale: the AWACS would be flown by a US crew, and the accompanying F-15s would not be based at Tabuk, an airfield less than 100 miles from Israel, nor would they be equipped with weapons racks or long-range fuel pods.[176] Moreover, Reagan also tried to diffuse Israeli opposition by offering Israel an additional $600 million in military credits and by relaxing the ban on the export of the controversial Kfir fighter jet, which used US technology.[177] After all the cajoling and much strong-arming by James Baker, the Senate voted 52–48 for the sale. But for AIPAC it was anything but a loss: it had emerged, according to Goldberg, as 'one of the preeminent forces in Washington politics'.[178] It had publicly demonstrated its power and, according to Tivnan, had

> hurt the President, forced him to spend more chips than he had ever expected, exposed the Administration to more scrutiny than it need during its first year in office, and tainted the White House, at least among the American Jewish community.[179]

Four years later, when King Fahd of Saudi Arabia visited Washington for the largest arms purchase in history, Reagan balked – he offered to help broker a deal with the UK rather than face AIPAC again. The US arms industry lost revenues estimated at $70 billion as a result (BAe Systems, the British beneficiary of the contract, put its real value at $225 billion).[180]

The second incident is from 2004, when US pressure stopped Israel from upgrading a batch of Harpy UAVs, which it had sold to China a decade earlier. For Chomsky, this was an attempt to 'humiliate' Israel, to make it 'very clear who runs the show'.[181] As a matter of fact, the main US objection was that Israel had illegally transferred US technology to its chief military rival China – an act that even Israel's most ingenious advocates found hard to defend. In reality, it has not been necessary for Israel to advance US interests to benefit from US munificence; it just has to avoid appearing openly *hostile* to them.

There have been few confrontations between the lobby and the arms industry, but in nearly all of them the lobby has got its way. In 1963–4, fearful of incurring the lobby's wrath, Lyndon Johnson declined a Saudi request for fighter jets, encouraging them to buy the British Lightning jet instead. The same fear gave Gerald Ford cold feet after an initial offer to sell the Saudis one hundred F-15 fighter jets; instead, he deferred the decision to his successor Jimmy Carter, who, despite his contempt for the lobby, was able to sell only sixty. In the 1980s, the lobby successfully blocked the sale of the F-20 Tigershark fighter to Arab states, costing manufacturer Northrop $1 billion in R&D losses. In 1985, the lobby blocked the sale of forty fighters, mobile anti-aircraft missiles and Stinger missiles to Jordan – despite Reagan's entreaties to AIPAC and the United Jewish Appeal – leading the Jordanians to instead sign a contract with the French.[182] During the Iran–Iraq war, AIPAC prevented a sale of Lance missiles to the Saudis, leading them to instead purchase longer-range missiles from China.[183] In 1986, the lobby blocked a $1 billion sale of Stinger, Harpoon and Sidewinder missiles, Blackhawk helicopters and advanced electronic equipment, which eventually led to a diminished sale of $265 million in equipment which the Saudis already had. AIPAC also blocked the sale of the Stinger missile to Qatar. In the lead-up to the Gulf War in 1990, the US sold Saudis $7 billion worth of weapons as part of a $20 billion contract; but once the war was over, AIPAC induced Congress to indefinitely postpone the remainder.[184] A similar battle was resolved in 2007 when the lobby dropped its earlier opposition to a sale of $20 billion worth of weapons to Saudi Arabia after the administration withheld top-of-the line weaponry and increased arms hand-outs to Israel by 20 per cent – $30 billion over the next ten years.[185]

Israel also has a long history of military–industrial espionage.[186] According to a 2007 Defense Security Service study and reports in *Air Force Magazine*, Israel was one of the leading offenders when it came to military–industrial espionage.[187] It has taken US arms systems, developed its own variants and often sold them to rivals. The HAVE-NAP missile system became POPEYE; US cruise missile systems became the STAR cruise missile; the Sidewinder air-to-air missile became the Python-3 and Shafrir-2; the TOW-2 anti-tank missile became Mapatz. Patriot anti-missile system information was leaked to China in return for sensitive intellectual property; and US thermal imaging systems were integrated by Israel–Dutch firm Delft into tank sights and sold to China (which subsequently sold them to Iraq). Israel is today a leading competitor for the US military industry in the international arms market; Israel also enjoys a special status whereby its arms companies are allowed to bid directly for US defence contracts.[188]

Commerce is a potential bridge between the US and the resource-rich Middle East. But the Israel lobby has successfully pre-empted opportunities for trade with bills such as ILSA and by engendering an environment hostile to the region and its people. The effect of the lobby's relentless demonisation of Arabs and Muslims was most evident during the 2006 Dubai Ports scandal, when a legitimate Middle East business was denied commission following lurid fear-mongering about Arabs controlling US ports.[189] These attitudes have alienated the region and robbed US businesses of a vast potential market.[190]

In Marxist analysis the US elite and the Israel lobby are often treated as mutually exclusive entities. The restricted focus on structures and processes allows individual actors to be ignored. Sheldon Adelson, Haim Saban, Lester Crown, Irving Moskowitz and Mortimer Zuckerman are among the largest individual donors to the Republican and Democratic parties. Only the rigid categories of ideology could force critics of the lobby thesis to exclude them from the ranks of the US elite. Few would dispute that the board members and CEOs of major pharmaceutical and oil companies should be counted as part of the elites. Yet Israel lobby-backed initiatives like USIFTA and ILSA have passed despite the opposition of the business elites. If the two factions are indeed mutually exclusive, then at a minimum a reconsideration of the balance of power is in order. The examples of ILSA, the Iraq war and the lobby-backed legislation against Iran also suggest that the lobby's power is not limited to the Israel–Palestine conflict alone, but since at least the Jackson–Vanik amendment, has extended to US Middle East policy in general.[191]

Conclusion

In the debate over the Israel lobby's significance and its clout over US Middle East policy, part of the confusion is conceptual, stemming from a defective understanding of the concept and function of social power. At its simplest, power is social relation between a paramount and a subordinate agent which can be identified with reference to the former's interests.[192] If A is the principal and B the subaltern, then, 'A has power over B, if A affects B in a manner contrary to B's interests.'[193] This does not mean, however, that B has no alternatives; indeed, it is by making B follow A's preferences while B could potentially choose otherwise that A exercises power. A's power lies in restricting B's choices. Power requires a cause but not necessarily the intention to produce an effect. Indeed, it does not always have to be exercised to bring about a desired result: it is in essence a capacity. If B reacts in a manner contrary to its own interests to avoid the anticipated adverse reaction from A, then this, according to sociologist John Scott, is 'an effect of a principal's power, even though he or she does nothing directly to make this power effective'.[194] Since an actor's reputation can often be as important as its actual power, it leads most actors to cultivate exaggerated perceptions of their power in order to enhance it.

But power does not manifest itself only in visible instances of conflict involving decision making. It is also at work when actors are able to pre-empt conflict in the first place by excluding contentious issues from arising through their capacity to define the scope of legitimate political debate. Power is exercised, as it were, when 'A devotes his energies to creating or reinforcing social and political values and institutional practices that limit the scope of the political process to public consideration of only those issues that are comparatively innocuous to A.'[195]

However, beyond the Weberian conception of power which presupposes observable conflict, overt or covert, there is also another more effective and insidious form of power where a principal is able to prevent conflict from arising in the first place by 'influencing, shaping, and determining' the subaltern's very wants. If the second face of power focused on a principal's capacity to exclude *actual* issues from the agenda, this view focuses on the capacity to exclude *potential* issues.[196]

Critics often reject or criticise Mearsheimer and Walt's thesis on the basis of the pluralist, one-dimensional view of power. Turning to what Lukes calls the two- and three-dimensional views, Mearsheimer and Walt's thesis is virtually unassailable. If instances of overt conflict between the Israel lobby and the US government have been few and far between, it is because the lobby has successfully pre-empted any debate on issues inimical to its interests as this chapter has demonstrated. Moreover, the Israel lobby in general and the neoconservatives in particular have long tried (though not always successfully) to redefine US interests in a manner that would make them indistinguishable from Israel's. This allows them to pursue Israeli ends while passing them off as US interests. As one analyst sympathetic to the neoconservatives remarked, 'There is no conflict of interest because they [the neocons] define the interest.'[197]

Beyond political and financial constraints, power also operates as persuasive influence through appeals to reason, by either drawing subalterns into the principal's interpretive frame or by according a normative character to the principal's views.[198] The Israel lobby's neoconservative spearhead has been instrumental in dominating the discourse on national security through its network of think tanks which are used to mint its ideologues as authoritative voices dispensing defence expertise.

The aim here was to present an overview rather than an exhaustive account of the lobby's actions and composition. The degree to which Israeli interests have embedded themselves into US Middle East policy cannot be explained without reference to the lobby. And no single faction of the lobby has done more to appropriate the totems of US nationalism and its military pre-eminence in the service of an Israeli expansionist agenda than the neoconservatives.

Notes

Introduction

1 Karon, 'What to Do about Iran?'
2 Hagopian, et al., 'Mortality in Iraq'.
3 Stiglitz, 'The War Costs'; Stiglitz and Bilmes, '$3 Trillion May Be too Low'.
4 Ricchiardi, 'Whatever Happened to Iraq?'
5 Brzezinski, 'Hegemonic Quicksand'; Tyler, *A World of Trouble*, p. 129; Lieven, *America Right or Wrong*, pp. 189–90.
6 Tivnan, *The Lobby*; Tyler, *A World of Trouble*, p. 120.
7 See for example Chomsky, *Fateful Triangle*; Zunes, 'The Israel Lobby' *Tikkun*.
8 See for example: Mearsheimer and Walt, *The Israel Lobby*; Heilbrunn, *They Knew They Were Right*; Unger, *The Fall of the House of Bush*; Packer, *The Assassins' Gate*; Kaplan, *Daydream Believers*; Sniegoski, *The Transparent Cabal*; Lieven, *America Right or Wrong*; Bamford, *A Pretext for War*; Mann, *Rise of the Vulcans*; Halper and Clarke, *America Alone*.
9 Packer, *The Assassins' Gate*.
10 Shavit, 'White Man's Burden'.
11 J. Klein, 'Surge Protection'. The comments drew a predictable backlash, and Klein responded by recounting the neoconservatives' and ADL's attempts to get him fired from *Time*, adding: 'There is a small group of Jewish neoconservatives who unsuccessfully tried to get Benjamin Netanyahu to attack Saddam Hussein in the 1990s, and then successfully helped provide the intellectual rationale for George Bush to do it in 2003. Their motivations involve a confused conflation of what they *think* are Israel's best interests with those of the United States. They are now leading the charge for war with Iran.' J. Klein, 'When Extremists Attack'. Klein's

Jewishness and his passionate devotion to Israel did not protect him from the lethal charge of anti-Semitism. Klein dismissed the charges and declared himself merely 'anti-neoconservative'. Luban and Lobe, 'Neocon Flap Highlights Jewish Divide'.

12 Dreyfuss, 'The Pentagon Muzzles the CIA'.
13 Kuttner, 'Neo-Cons Have Hijacked US Foreign Policy'.
14 Isikoff and Corn, *Hubris*, pp. 21–5.
15 Rice, *No Higher Honor*; Rumsfeld, *Known and Unknown*.
16 'Remarks of President Barack Obama'.
17 Wedel, *Shadow Elite*, p. 1.
18 Ibid. pp. 7, 8.
19 Ibid. p. 20.
20 Ibid. pp. 78–9.
21 Ibid. p. 20.
22 Ibid. pp. 47–91.
23 Mearsheimer and Walt, *The Israel Lobby*, pp. 175–8; Harper and Clarke, *America Alone*, pp. 47–8; G. F. Smith, *Foreign Agents*, pp. 114–24; Flynn, 'Surge of Think Tanks – Part 1'; Flynn, 'Surge of Think Tanks – Part 2'.
24 Abelson, *A Capitol Idea*, p. 119.
25 Ibid. pp. 117–22.
26 Slater, 'The Two Books'; Abelson, *A Capitol Idea*, pp. 156–9.
27 Abelson, *A Capitol Idea*, pp. 156, 157.
28 Michael Dolny, 'The Incredible Shrinking Think Tank'.
29 McClellan, *What Happened*.
30 Miller and Dinan, *Century of Spin*, p. 177.
31 Moore, *The Opinion Makers*, pp. 103–5.
32 Ibid. pp. 103–5.
33 Moore, *The Opinion Makers*, p. 7.
34 Ibid. p. 103.
35 Publius, 'Federalist No. 49: Method of Guarding against the Encroachments of Any One Department of Government by Appealing to the People through a Convention', The Library of Congress, 1788.
36 Moore, *The Opinion Makers*, p. 2.
37 Ibid. p. 104.

Chapter 1

1 Nordland, 'Rebuilding Its Economy'; Cockburn, 'Iraq Looks to Spectacular Oil Boom'; Alexander Cockburn, 'Thank You, Glen Beck!'; Carlisle, 'Iraq Awards Contract for Giant Field'.
2 Bertrand, 'ExxonMobil's Iraq Oil Field Contract'.
3 Kramer, 'In Rebuilding Iraq's Oil Industry'.
4 Arango and Krauss, 'China Is Reaping Biggest Benefits'.
5 Burbach, 'Bush Ideologues Trump Big Oil Interests'.
6 Lefton, 'Big Oil's Long History'; Jeffrey Goldberg, 'Real Insiders'.
7 P. H. Stone, 'Big Oil's Overseas Push'. Big Business's opposition to sanctions remains consistent to this day. 'Business Urges Obama Resist'.
8 Brady, 'Rogue States'; Wayne, 'Companies Used to Getting Their Way'.
9 Cheney, 'Defending Liberty'; Cole, *Engaging the Muslim World*, pp. 136–8; Brady, 'Rogue States'.
10 Cave, 'The United States of Oil'.
11 Brady, 'Rogue States'.
12 Ivanovich, 'Conoco's Chief Blasts Sanctions'. See also P. H. Stone, 'Big Oil's Overseas Push'.
13 S. F. Cohen, 'The New American Cold War'.
14 Sampson, 'Oilmen Don't Want Another Suez'.
15 Cave, 'Oily Waters'.
16 Woodward, *State of Denial*, pp. 45, 75–6.
17 Sampson, 'Oilmen Don't Want Another Suez'.
18 Seib, 'Exxon Mobil Breaks Its Own Profit Record'.
19 Wallace, 'Oil Prices Are All Speculation'.
20 Coleman and Levin, 'The Role of Market Speculation'.
21 Kellner, 'The Law Catches Up to Oil'.
22 Quoted in Herrick, 'US Oil Wants to Work in Iraq'.
23 Sadowski, 'No War for Whose Oil?'
24 Parrish, 'There Is No War on Terror'.
25 Klare, *Blood and Oil*.
26 Harvey, *The New Imperialism*, pp. 18–19, 22–3.
27 Ibid. p. 33.
28 Brzezinski, 'Hegemonic Quicksand', quoted in Chomsky, *Failed States*, p. 36.
29 Ibid. pp. 36–7.
30 Klare, *Blood and Oil*, pp. 32–3.
31 Brzezinski, 'Iraq in the Strategic Context'.

32 Eisele, 'George Kennan Speaks Out'.

33 Ibid.; Brzezinski, 'Hegemonic Quicksand'.

34 Chomsky, 'It's the Oil, Stupid!'.

35 Packer, *The Assassins' Gate*, p. 147.

36 Cited in Sniegoski, *The Transparent Cabal*, pp. 340–2.

37 Schmitt and Brinkley, 'State Dept. Study Foresaw Trouble'; National Security Archives (17 August 2005); Packer, *The Assassins' Gate*, pp. 120–3.

38 Quoted in Pincus, 'Memo'. See also Tenet, *At the Center of the Storm*, pp. 308–9; Woodward, *State of Denial*.

39 Cohen and O'Driscoll, 'The Road to Economic Prosperity'; Kiernan, 'Iraq's Oil'.

40 Sadowski, 'No War for Whose Oil?'

41 Sampson, 'Oilmen Don't Want Another Suez'.

42 Keller, 'The Sunshine Warrior'.

43 Schmitt and Brinkley, 'State Dept. Study Foresaw Trouble'. It was as a result of these bleak predictions that post-war planning was taken over by the Pentagon. Pincus, 'Ex-Cia Official Faults Use of Data on Iraq'; Crane and Terrill, *Reconstructing Iraq*; Gerth, 'Report Offered Bleak Outlook'. All cited in Sniegoski, *The Transparent Cabal*.

44 Gerth, 'Report Offered Bleak Outlook'.

45 Becker, 'Why War with Iraq Is Not About the Oil'.

46 A common logical fallacy: Denying the Antecedent. If A, then B. Not A. Therefore, not B. E.g., if I am in Glasgow, I am in Scotland. If I'm not in Glasgow, I'm not in Scotland (I could be in Edinburgh).

47 The overthrow of Mossadegh is often cited as an early example of US policy of regime change for oil; however, in this case the motivation for the Eisenhower Administration was anti-communism, rather than oil. It was the British who wanted their control of Iranian oil restored, and they had convinced the Eisenhower Administration that Mossadegh was turning to communism. See Kinzer, *All the Shah's Men*.

48 Cole, *Engaging the Muslim World*, pp. 136–40.

49 Cave, 'Oily Waters'.

50 Brzezinski, *Power and Principle*, p. 444.

51 Morse and Jaffe, 'Strategic Energy Policy Challenges'.

52 MacKay, 'Officials'.

53 Brzezinski, *Power and Principle*, p. 444.

54 Stokes, 'Blood for Oil?'

55 Binnendijk, et al., *Strategic Assessment 1999*, cited in R. Goldstein, 'Oil Wars'. It bears noting that the report's chapter on energy policy is written by neoconservative 'defence expert' Patrick Clawson.

56 Quoted in R. Goldstein, 'Oil Wars'.

57 Harvard historian and Russia expert Richard Pipes (of Team B fame) told *The New York Times* that the Soviet invasion of Afghanistan was a prelude to larger conquests. 'Russians do not seize territories that have no strategic importance,' he said. 'Afghanistan has no natural resources of importance, and the risk of antagonizing the West is very high for a bit of mountainous territory with a primitive economy, with a population that has never been subdued by any colonial power.' He therefore asserted that the ultimate Soviet objective was to seize control of Persian Gulf oil, something Carter could prevent. Quoted in Bacevich, 'The Colors Run Red'.

58 N. Smith, *The Endgame of Globalization*.

59 N. Klein, *The Shock Doctrine*, p. 7.

60 Ibid.

61 Miliband, *The State in Capitalist Society*, p. 23. Also cited in Stokes, 'Blood for Oil?'

62 Holmes, 'Free-Marketeering'.

63 Stiglitz and Bilmes, '$3 Trillion May Be too Low'.

64 Lieven, *America Right or Wrong*, p. 14.

65 D. R. Baker, 'Bechtel Pulling Out'.

66 Risen and Williams, 'US Looks for Blackwater Replacement'.

67 Lind, 'How Neoconservatives Conquered Washington'; Cutler, 'Beyond Incompetence'.

68 Brzezinski, 'Why Unity Is Essential'.

69 Kaiser, 'US Risks Isolation'.

70 Scowcroft, 'Don't Attack Saddam'.

71 Purdum and Tyler, 'Top Republicans Break with Bush'; Lobe, 'Washington Goes to War'. Even Kissinger initially told *The New York Times*, 'I am viscerally opposed to a prolonged occupation of a Muslim country at the heart of the Muslim world by Western nations who proclaim the right to re-educate that country'. Sanger and Schmitt, 'US Has a Plan'. A seasoned weathervane, however, he would dispel doubts in time to join the war party.

72 Woodward, *State of Denial*, pp. 114–15; Woodward, *Plan of Attack*, p. 160; Unger, *Fall of the House of Bush*, pp. 242–4; Wilson, *The Politics of Truth*, p. 297. Bush Sr. likewise earned neoconservative opprobrium for believing, according to *The*

Weekly Standard, that 'many of our problems in the Islamic world relate to our support for Israel'. Bell, 'Bush I Vs. Bush II'.

73 Isikoff and Corn, *Hubris*, pp. 21–5.

74 Lobe, 'Anti-empire Forces Strike Back'.

75 Wilson, *The Politics of Truth*, pp. 290–1. See also Wilson, 'How Saddam Thinks'; Wilson, 'Republic or Empire'; Wilson, 'What I Didn't Find in Africa'; Wright, 'Letter of Resignation'; Kiesling, 'U.S. Diplomat's Letter of Resignation'.

76 Sniegoski, *The Transparent Cabal*, p. 347.

77 Ricks, *Fiasco*; Ricks, 'Some Top Military Brass'.

78 Zinni, 'Speech'; Thompson and Duffy, 'Pentagon Warlord'; Raimondo, 'Listen Up, Soldier'.

79 Roberts, *The Collapse of Fortress Bush*, p. 141.

80 Sniegoski, *The Transparent Cabal*, p. 346.

81 Graham, 'Officers'.

82 Though Myers emerged as a trusted sidekick to Rumsfeld in the years preceding and following the war, in private he remained disdainful of the bullying defence secretary. According to Woodward, he frequently referred to Rumsfeld as an 'asshole' and a 'son of a bitch'. Woodward, *State of Denial*, p. 73.

83 Ricks, *Fiasco*, p. 48.

84 Thompson and Duffy, 'Pentagon Warlord'.

85 Lieven, 'We Do Not Deserve These People'.

86 See for example Johnson, *The Sorrows of Empire* and *Nemesis*; Bacevich, *The New American Militarism*; Vest, 'The Men from JINSA and CSP'; and the films *Why We Fight* and *Hijacking Catastrophe*. JINSA alumni who have gone on to play key roles in promoting the Iraq war include Dick Cheney, John Bolton, Douglas Feith, James Woolsey, Richard Perle, Michael Ledeen and David Wurmser.

87 Barstow, 'Behind TV Analysts'; Barstow, 'One Man's Military–Industrial Media Complex'.

88 C. Johnson, *Blowback*; C. Johnson, *The Sorrows of Empire*; C. Johnson, *Nemesis*.

89 C. Johnson, *The Sorrows of Empire*, pp. 233–8. Oddly, in support of his argument that oil was a factor in the war, Johnson quotes Anthony Sampson who, as shown earlier, in fact argued the opposite.

90 Ibid. p. 236.

91 Vest, 'The Men from JINSA and CSP'.

92 C. Johnson, *The Sorrows of Empire*, p. 241.

93 Ibid. p. 253.

94 A proponent of the old Zionist dictum that force is the only language an Arab understands, Kagan dismissed adverse Arab reactions to the use of US power noting: 'Well, I see that the Arab street has gotten very, very quiet since we started blowing things up.' Quoted in Bookman, 'Bush's Real Goal'.

95 Transcript: Deputy Secretary Wolfowitz Interview with Sam Tannenhaus, Vanity Fair, Department of Defense, 9 May 2003. In the interview Wolfowitz disingenuously highlighted the US presence in Saudi Arabia as the key grievance driving Osama bin Laden but left out the fact that his other two grievances were the US role in Iraq and in the Israel–Palestine conflict.

96 P. Cockburn, 'America Concedes'.

97 Sharansky had been introduced to Bush through the machinations of Richard Perle. Perle had arranged for Sharansky to meet Cheney, who promised to share his ideas with Bush. Four days later when Bush laid out his 'roadmap' for the Israeli–Palestinian conflict, his choice of words led an overjoyed Perle to call Sharansky to relay the news: 'He was speaking your words.' Quoted in Kaplan, *Daydream Believers*. Sharansky expanded his ideas into a book, *The Case for Democracy*. Bush was so taken with it that he invited Sharansky for a personal audience at the White House. Many phrases from the book would eventually end up verbatim in Bush's second inaugural speech, partly written by William Kristol and Charles Krauthammer. Kaplan, *Daydream Believers*, pp. 127–31; Avnery, 'Bush's Guru'.

98 Lacey, 'Turkey Rejects Criticism'.

Chapter 2

1 'Study: Paying for Lobbyists – Pays Off'.

2 Jeffrey Goldberg, 'Real Insiders'.

3 The Center for Responsive Politics' *Opensecrets.org* website maintains a database of individuals who have passed through the 'revolving door' from lobbying into government positions or vice versa. See <http://www.opensecrets.org/revolving/>.

4 Black, 'Rebirth of the Right'.

5 Ibid.

6 Naomi Klein, for example, sees 'neoconservative' as merely an American label for what the rest of the world calls 'neoliberal'. N. Klein, *The Shock Doctrine*, p. 253.

7   Brown, 'American Nightmare'.
8   Steger and Roy, *Neoliberalism.*
9   Harvey, *A Brief History*, pp. 41–2.
10 N. Smith, *The Endgame of Globalization.*
11 Mirowski and Plehwe, *The Road from Mont Pèlerin*, p. 426.
12 Harvey, 'Neo-Liberalism'.
13 Ibid.
14 The Chicago School was itself founded by the Austrian Hayek
    and Henry Simon, who succeeded in establishing the Free Market
    Project through generous grants from the Volker Fund. Mirowski
    and Plehwe, *The Road from Mont Pèlerin.*
15 Ibid. p. 432.
16 Ibid. pp. 430–2.
17 Cockett, *Thinking the Unthinkable.* It needs pointing out here that
    MPS members stopped using the term 'neoliberal' around the late
    1950s. See Mirowski and Plehwe, *The Road from Mont Pèlerin*,
    p. 427.
18 Harvey, *A Brief History*, pp. 12–13.
19 Ibid. p. 15.
20 L. Powell, 'Attack'.
21 Carey, *Taking the Risk out of Democracy*, p. 92; Harvey, *A Brief
    History*, p. 43.
22 Harvey, 'Neo-Liberalism'.
23 Indeed, from Hayek to Friedman, political rights have been sec-
    ondary to market imperatives. For Hayek, democracy itself could
    be an enemy of liberalism. The imprint of Hitler's crown jurist
    Carl Schmitt's anti-democratic principles is also palpable on his
    protégé Leo Strauss. Drury, *Leo Strauss and the American Right.*
24 Brown, 'American Nightmare'.
25 Harrington, 'The Welfare State'.
26 Saunders, *Who Paid the Piper?*
27 Once an opponent of the war, Podhoretz would later go on to write
    a retrospective justification of the Vietnam war as a 'moral' enter-
    prise. Podhoretz, *Why We Were in Vietnam*; Gerson, 'Norman's
    Conquest'.
28 Heilbrunn, *They Knew*; Friedman, *Neoconservative Revolution.*
29 Heilbrunn, *They Knew*, p. 68.
30 Ibid.; S. Blumenthal, *The Rise of the Counter-Establishment*;
    J. J. Goldberg, *Jewish Power*, p. 159.
31 Kristol, 'The Neoconservative Persuasion'.
32 Ibid.

33 Bellow credits Irving Kristol for helping the neophyte neoconservative's career by launching him in the publishing world through an introduction to Erwin Glikes of Free Press: 'Glikes was a major force in American publishing and a four-star general in the culture war . . . [he] had been brought into publishing in 1969 by Kristol himself, when the latter was running Basic Books. There he had also worked with Midge Decter, who's married to Norman Podhoretz. In short, Glikes was a member of that group of New York Jewish intellectuals who used to be known as "The Family." . . . When I began to make the rounds as Glikes's protégé, I felt like a returning long-lost relative.' A. Bellow, 'My Escape'.

34 Kristol, 'The Neoconservative Persuasion'.

35 Judt, 'The Way We Live Now'.

36 J. Klein, 'Mccain's Foreign Policy Frustration'.

37 S. Blumenthal, *The Rise of the Counter-Establishment*, p. 110.

38 Judis, 'Trotskyism to Anachronism'.

39 Kristol's *The Public Interest* had emerged as a leading cheerleader for business, and Robert Bartley, the neoconservative editor of *The Wall Street Journal*, had opened the paper's editorial pages to Kristol and other neoconservatives. S. Blumenthal, *The Rise of the Counter-Establishment*, p. 134; see also p. 139.

40 Ibid. p. 141.

41 Harvey, *A Brief History*, p. 46.

42 Wanniski, 'The Mundell–Laffer Hypothesis'. These ideas were anathema to traditional 'balanced-budget' conservatives such as George H. W. Bush, who dismissed supply side economics as 'voodoo economics' during the 1980 election campaign. Economist J. K. Galbraith disparaged it as 'the horse-and-sparrow theory': 'If you feed the horse enough oats, some will pass through to the road for the sparrows.' Galbraith, 'Recession Economics'.

43 Kristol, *Neoconservatism*, p. 35.

44 Quoted in S. Blumenthal, *The Rise of the Counter-Establishment*, p. 134.

45 Ibid. ch. 7.

46 Lieven, 'Book Review'.

47 Harvey, *A Brief History*, pp. 49–50 Here as well, their views are not free of contradiction: though in the early 1980s Podhoretz was blaming the 'prominence of homosexuals in the literary world' for the 'culture of appeasement' under Jimmy Carter, today the absence of gay rights is one of the key planks in the neoconservative case for intervention against Iran. Allan Bloom – Wolfowitz's

mentor and author of the influential *The Closing of the American Mind* – was himself gay though he kept this fact under wraps. This fact is also revealed in *Ravelstein*, Saul Bellow's thinly disguised tribute to his late friend. Sleeper, 'Allan Bloom'.

48 Harvey, *A Brief History*, pp. 49–50, 82. On the contradiction between Kristol's own secularism and his advocacy of traditional religion for its functional role in legitimising 'bourgeois society' see Glazer, 'The Interested Man'.
49 Frank, *What's the Matter with Kansas?*
50 Bloom was forthright in blaming the proponents of free-market capitalism for the decline of liberal education and religious belief. See Bloom, *The Closing of the American Mind*.
51 Kristol, *Reflections of a Neoconservative*, p. xii.
52 'The War Party', BBC.
53 S. Blumenthal, *The Rise of the Counter-Establishment*, chs 3–4.
54 Kristol, *Neoconservatism*, p. 25.
55 Kristol, 'The Neoconservative Persuasion'.
56 Ibid.; Kristol, *Neoconservatism*, p. 25.
57 Bacevich, *The New American Militarism*, pp. 73–8. See also Podhoretz, 'Making the World Safe'; Podhoretz, *Breaking Ranks*; Podhoretz, 'The Neo-Conservative Anguish'; Podhoretz, 'Appeasement by any other Name'.
58 Stelzer, *The Neocon Reader*.
59 Harvey makes the same observation about the conflict between neoliberalism in practice and in principle. Harvey, 'Neoliberalism'.
60 McCarthy, 'Kristol Reflections'; Judis, 'Trotskyism to Anachronism'. Kristol has more accurately described neoconservative foreign policy approach as 'global unilateralism'. Kristol, 'Foreign Policy'.
61 Podhoretz, *Breaking Ranks*, p. 336.
62 Friedman, *Neoconservative Revolution*, p. 147.
63 Ginsberg, *The Fatal Embrace*, p. 231.
64 Lieber, 'The Left's Neocon Conspiracy Theory'; Brooks, 'The Era of Distortion'; Dana Milbank, 'Prince of Darkness'; Raimondo, 'Neocons in Denial'.
65 Vaïsse, *Neoconservatism*, p. 273.
66 Friedman, *Neoconservative Revolution*; M. Phillips, 'The Politics of Progress'.
67 Blumenthal, *The Rise of the Counter-Establishment*, p. 111.
68 J. J. Goldberg, *Jewish Power*, p. 160.
69 Beckerman, 'The Neoconservative Persuasion'.

70 Heilbrunn, *They Knew*, p. 11.

71 Ibid. pp. 10–13.

72 Weiss, 'The Long Fuse'. However, once success was at hand, the same neoconservatives developed a hostile attitude towards the inclusion of other excluded groups. Norman Podhoretz and other neoconservatives opposed affirmative action mainly because it was not 'good for the Jews'. Podhoretz, 'Is It Good for the Jews?'; J. J. Goldberg, *Jewish Power*, p. 321; Greenberg, *Troubling the Waters*, ch. 6.

73 In an interview with the *Paris Review* (No. 36, Winter 1966) Saul Bellow confesses the degree to which his earlier writing was constrained by fear that he will not be taken seriously unless he paid homage to the holy cows of the WASP literary establishment.

74 Quoted in Lobe, 'From Holocaust to Hyperpower'. Moynihan's defection from neoconservatism had started already in the 1980s over Central American. Ehrman, *The Rise of Neoconservatives*, pp. 166–70, 190.

75 S. Phillips, 'When Is a Neocon Not a Neocon?'

76 Lobe 'What Is a Neo-Conservative Anyway?'; Lobe, 'From Holocaust to Hyperpower.

77 'The War Party', BBC.

78 R. A. Clarke, *Against All Enemies*; Heilbrunn, *They Knew*, p. 12.

79 Isikoff and Corn, *Hubris*, p. 109; Heilbrunn, *They Knew*, p. 256.

80 The 10 December 1969 issue of *The New York Times*, for example, carries a letter by fifteen-year-old Douglas Feith denouncing efforts by Secretary of State William Rogers to secure Israel's withdrawal from the OPT. Cited in Heilbrunn, *They Knew*, p. 255.

81 Jeffrey Goldberg, 'A Little Learning'.

82 Noah, 'Fathers and Sons'.

83 Frum and Perle, *An End to Evil*.

84 Explaining his own break with liberalism, Donald Kagan, father of Robert and Frederick Kagan, cites an episode during the 1960s when Cornell University administration agreed to negotiate with black student activists who were demanding the institution of a black studies programme. 'Watching administrators demonstrate all the courage of Neville Chamberlain had a great impact on me,' Kagan confessed, assigning black students the role of the Nazis in the analogy, 'and I became much more conservative.' Quoted in Unger, *Fall of the House of Bush*, p. 39n.

85 Novick, *The Holocaust in American Life*; Finkelstein, *The Holocaust Industry*.

86 Finkelstein, 'How the Arab–Israeli War'.
87 Finkelstein, *The Holocaust Industry*, pp. 24–7.
88 Rogan and Shlaim, *The War for Palestine*.
89 G. F. Smith, *America's Defense Line*.
90 Chomsky, *Middle East Illusion*, p. 99. Israeli generals and the CIA estimated that it would take Israel a week at most to prevail over her combined enemies. Finkelstein, *Image and Reality*; Oren, *Six Days of War*.
91 As evidence of the neoconservatives' belated attachment to Israel, Finkelstein adduces Norman Podhoretz's memoir: 'Although already editor of the leading American Jewish periodical, *Commentary*, his memoir includes only one fleeting allusion to Israel.' Finkelstein, *The Holocaust Industry*, p. 15. But the book Finkelstein cites is about Podhoretz's literary career (or in his own words 'a frank bid for literary distinction, fame, and money all in one package'). Podhoretz, *Making It*, p. 356. The archives of *Commentary*, however, tell a different story. Between Israel's founding in May 1948 and the war of June 1967, the periodical published a total of 864 articles on Israel. An archive search for the keyword 'Israel' yield 1,393 results, of which 864 are articles filed under 'Israel, Jews and Judaism'. Many of these are written by neoconservative luminaries such as Leo Strauss, Daniel Bell, Walter Laqueur, Irving Kristol and his brother-in-law Milton Himmelfarb. As regards Podhoretz's attachment to Israel, his daughter Ruthie Blum Leibowitz is actually an Israeli citizen and during the 1991 Gulf War, Podhoretz himself went to stay with her as a gesture of solidarity.
92 Quoted in 'The Israel Lobby'; Sherman, 'The Rebirth'.
93 Heilbrunn, *They Knew*, p. 11.
94 Quoted in ibid.
95 Quoted in Podhoretz, *Breaking Ranks*, p. 335.
96 Halper and Clarke, *America Alone*, p. 19.
97 Ibid. pp. 17–19.
98 For more on AVOT, see Beinin, 'The New American McCarthyism'.
99 Sullivan, 'A False Premise'. Opprobrium predictably followed. *The New Republic*'s literary editor Leon Wieseltier went so far as to write a 4,500-word essay denouncing Sullivan, suggesting that there was something 'much darker' beneath the surface of Sullivan's criticism. Sullivan's years of service as a stalwart defender of Israel failed to protect him from the charge of anti-Semitism. See Wieseltier, 'Something Much Darker'.

100 Mearsheimer and Walt, *The Israel Lobby*, p. 132.

101 J. J. Goldberg, *Jewish Power*, p. 160.

102 G. F. Smith, *Deadly Dogma*, pp. 105–17.

103 Gottfried, 'Cryptic Fascist?'

104 Horton, 'The Letter'; Heilbrunn, *They Knew*, pp. 90–7.

105 Cited in Friedman, *Neoconservative Revolution*, p. 60.

106 It is worth noting here that neoconservatism is *not* Straussianism. In his acclaimed documentary series 'The Power of Nightmares', Adam Curtis mistakenly elevates one strain of neoconservative thought as the whole of the ideology. Drury, 'Leo Strauss and the American Imperial Project'.

107 Abrams, *Faith or Fear*, p. 181.

108 David, 'The Apprentice'.

109 Heilbrunn, *They Knew*, p. 224.

110 Podhoretz, 'The Neo-Conservative Anguish'.

111 Gerson, 'Norman's Conquest'.

112 Heilbrunn, *They Knew*, pp. 139–41, 170–4.

113 Wedel, *Shadow Elite*, pp. 148–9; Heilbrunn, *They Knew*, p. 186; Green, 'Serving Two Flags'.

114 Giraldi, 'Saving Feith'.

115 Bamford, 'Iran: The Next War'. Some of the information Pollard passed on to Israel was subsequently relayed to the Soviet Union and Apartheid South Africa. Naylor, *Economic Warfare*, pp. 163–4.

116 Bamford, 'Iran: The Next War'. Rhode, a Hebrew speaker, is also close to Zionist Orientalist Bernard Lewis, who dedicated his post-9/11 best-seller *What Went Wrong?* to him.

117 Heilbrunn, *They Knew*; Lind, 'How Neoconservatives Conquered Washington'. Though the takeover itself did not last long, bureaucratic inertia ensured that its impact on US foreign policy persists, even in the face of later attempts to reverse it.

118 Bacevich, *The New American Militarism*.

119 Heilbrunn, *They Knew*; A. Blumenthal, *The Rise of the Counter-Establishment*.

120 Andrew Cockburn, *Rumsfeld*, p. 42; Heilbrunn, *They Knew*, p. 146.

121 Abella, *Soldiers of Reason*, pp. 88–92.

122 Wohlstetter, 'The Delicate Balance of Terror' – published earlier as a working paper by RAND in December 1958.

123 Abella, *Soldiers of Reason*, p. 118.

124 The groundwork for RMA was in fact laid down by Wohlstetter and his associate Andrew Marshall during the Reagan Administration.

Both are credited with providing the intellectual scaffolding for the MIC. See K. Silverstein, 'The Man from ONA'.

125 Abella, *Soldiers of Reason*, p. 121.

126 Ibid. p. 196. Another Wohlstetter charge William Luti was to play a key role in manufacturing the propaganda used to sell the Iraq war as the head of the OSP. See Heilbrunn, *They Knew*, pp. 232–3.

127 Abella, *Soldiers of Reason*, p. 93. In a fawning tribute, Wanniski hailed Wohlstetter's genius and suggested that his influence was not limited to the US. 'Maggie Thatcher didn't make a move on national security unless it was cleared by Albert,' he boasted. Quoted in Unger, *Fall of the House of Bush*, p. 42.

128 In a language that anticipates neoconservative formulations about the 'Islamic threat', the report described the Soviet Union as 'animated by a new fanatic faith, antithetical to our own, and seeks to impose its absolute authority over the rest of the world'. Nitze, 'NSC-68'.

129 Quoted in Kaplan, *Wizards of Armageddon*, p. 140.

130 After Truman received NSC-68 on 7 April 1950, he gave a copy to his chief domestic adviser Charles Murphy. Kaplan writes: 'It scared him so much that he didn't go to the office the next day, but just sat at home, reading the memorandum over and over.' Kaplan, *Wizards of Armageddon*, pp. 138–40.

131 Heilbrunn, *They Knew*, p. 119.

132 Quoted in Herbert, 'A Tragic Mistake'.

133 Ibid.

134 Abella, *Soldiers of Reason*, p. 109.

135 Ibid. ch. 7; Kaplan, *Wizards of Armageddon*, chs 8–9.

136 Nitze, 'Deterrence and Survival'.

137 Following a formal meeting with Committee members, he asked: 'You recommend spending a billion dollars for something in there. You know how much a billion dollars is? Why, it's a stack of ten-dollar bills as high as the Washington Monument.' Quoted in Abella, *Soldiers of Reason*, p. 113. See also Kaplan, *Wizards of Armageddon*.

138 Kaplan, *Wizards of Armageddon*, chs 8–9; Abella, *Soldiers of Reason*, ch. 7.

139 Kaplan, *Wizards of Armageddon*, ch. 10; Abella, *Soldiers of Reason*, p. 114.

140 Abella, *Soldiers of Reason*, p. 115.

141 Kaplan, *Wizards of Armageddon*, ch. 19; Abella, *Soldiers of Reason*, pp. 164–5.

142 Heilbrunn, *They Knew*, pp. 119–22.

143 Kaplan, 'Paul Nitze'.

144 The hawks were supported by another LHO, the Citizens Committee for Peace and Security, headed by future CIA director William Casey. Heilbrunn, *They Knew*, pp. 121–2.

145 Buruma, 'Lost in Translation'.

146 J. J. Goldberg, *Jewish Power*, pp. 167–72. In 1973, Nixon even tried to buy Israeli Prime Minister Golda Meir's cooperation by selling her F-4 Phantom jets in return for trying to rein in the neo-conservatives. Tyler, *A World of Trouble*, pp. 114–15.

147 AFL–CIO has historically maintained close ties with the Israel lobby, going so far during the 1982 invasion of Lebanon as to take out a full page ad in *The New York Times* which read: 'We Are Not Neutral. We Support Israel!' The ad was reportedly paid for by an Israel lobbyist with a Park Avenue address. Blankfort, 'Damage Control'.

148 Heilbrunn, *They Knew*, p. 130.

149 Ibid. p. 125. The charge was unfair: Kissinger was in fact very much committed to Israel. By 1973, Tyler notes, 'Israeli leaders considered Kissinger their most important asset in the Nixon administration.' According to the then ambassador to Washington Yitzhak Rabin, 'deep in his heart, [Kissinger] comes from here' – pointing to his heart –'the Holocaust and he's a very warm Jew and for him it is a mission to defend us'. He had risen in the Nixon Administration by derailing a nascent attempt to secure Israel's withdrawal from the OPT. It was under his advice that Nixon abandoned his earlier concern about alienating 'oil states' by too closely allying with Israel. During the first Palestinian Intifada, Kissinger advised Yitzhak Rabin to suppress it 'brutally and rapidly'. He also prescribed a media blackout: 'The first step should be to throw out television, a la [Apartheid] South Africa.' Quoted in Tyler, *A World of Trouble*, p. 344. See also pp. 337, 136.

150 Podhoretz, 'Making the World Safe'.

151 Andrew Cockburn, *Rumsfeld*, pp. 29–31; Abella, *Soldiers of Reason*, p. 234; Mann, *Rise of the Vulcans*, pp. 65–9.

152 Abella, *Soldiers of Reason*, pp. 230–43.

153 Wohlstetter, 'Is There a Strategic Arms Race?'; Wohlstetter, 'Is There a Strategic Arms Race? (II)'; Wohlstetter, 'Clocking the Strategic Arms Race'; Wohlstetter, 'Optimal Ways to Confuse Ourselves'; Wohlstetter, 'The Uncontrolled Upward Spiral'.

154 Abella, *Soldiers of Reason*, pp. 238–44.
155 Ibid. pp. 238–44; Wedel, *Shadow Elite*, pp. 158–61. Significantly, it included William van Cleave, the defence analyst who would later direct the Likud-linked, Jerusalem-based Institute for Advanced Strategic and Political Studies, the think tank that published the neoconservatives' infamous 'A Clean Break' paper in 1996.
156 Warnke, 'The B Team'.
157 Abella, *Soldiers of Reason*, pp. 243–5.
158 Cahn, *Killing Detente*, p. 163. For a fuller account of the report's conclusions see chapter 9 of the book.
159 Ibid. pp. 178–9.
160 Cited in Abella, *Soldiers of Reason*, pp. 245–6.
161 Heilbrunn, *They Knew*, pp. 142–3.
162 Abella, *Soldiers of Reason*, p. 245.
163 To be sure, this language was also resented by administration hard-liners such as Zbigniew Brzezinski.
164 The committee was founded on 11 November 1976 and included such figures as Rumsfeld, Podhoretz, Perle, Pipes and Saul Bellow.
165 It was also here that the pre-emption doctrine later to emerge as Bush's 2002 National Security Strategy was first articulated. In 2004, the neoconservatives would once again revive CPD. In each incarnation, CPD 'leveraged fear in attempts to increase military budgets, to mobilize the country for war, and to beat back isolationist, anti-interventionist, and realist forces in American politics'. Barry, 'US: Danger, Danger Everywhere'.
166 Vest, 'The Men from JINSA and CSP'.
167 Tivnan, *The Lobby*, pp. 102–4, 120. They were even less thrilled when in 1979 Carter was quoted as saying that the Palestinian issue was like 'the civil rights movement here in the United States'. Ibid. p. 131. Tyler, *A World of Trouble*, pp. 178, 182.
168 Tivnan, *The Lobby*, p. 133; Terry, *U.S. Foreign Policy*, pp. 116–17; Cockburn and Cockburn, *Dangerous Liaison*, pp. 313–19.
169 Tyler, *A World of Trouble*, pp. 178–203, 229–40. In 1979, it occasioned a particularly scathing attack in the Heritage Foundation's *Policy Review* from future Undersecretary of Defense Douglas Feith, then working for neoconservative Max Kampelman's Washington law firm, in which he denounced Carter for demanding Israeli withdrawal from 'Judaea and Samaria' (the biblical name for the West Bank preferred by Likud supporters). Heilbrunn, *They Knew*, pp. 150–1.
170 Heilbrunn, pp. 142–55.

171 Kirkpatrick, 'Dictatorships and Double Standards'. Kirkpatrick was drawing on Hannah Arendt's distinction between totalitarianism and authoritarianism, filtered through the writings of Nathan Glazer, Maurice Cranston, Raymond Aron, Carl Gershman and Peter Berger. Ehrman, *The Rise of Neoconservatism*, pp. 115–17.

172 Heilbrunn, *They Knew*, p. 153.

173 Ibid. pp. 154–5.

174 Core neoconservatives who had served under Democratic Senator Henry Jackson, including Perle, Wolfowitz, Ledeen, Gaffney, Abrams and Feith, would all join the Reagan Administration, though none in a cabinet position.

175 Heilbrunn, *They Knew*, p. 171.

176 Ehrman, *The Rise of Neoconservatism*, p. 140. According to the Committee's financial statement for 1981, it had generated $449,000 in revenues, spent $405,000 and pocketed a $44,000 surplus.

177 Ibid. p. 141.

178 Podhoretz, 'Appeasement by any other Name'.

179 On the AWACs battle see Tivnan, *The Lobby*, pp. 137–61; J. J. Goldberg, *Jewish Power*, pp. 197–202; Findley, *They Dare*, pp. 103–4, 154–5 (on strategic leaks), pp. 203–6 (pressure on think tanks); Ball and Ball, *The Passionate Attachment*, pp. 213–15.

180 Tyler, *A World of Trouble*, pp. 252–5.

181 Podhoretz also blamed the Saudis for refusing to join a de facto alliance to unite the 'moderate Arab states' and Israel. Podhoretz, 'The Neo-Conservative Anguish'.

182 Tyler, *A World of Trouble*, pp. 309–10, 313. The deal was eventually signed with the UK's BAe Systems, broadened to include the construction of two air bases; the final cost was estimated at £225 billion. Ball and Ball, *The Passionate Attachment*.

183 Tyler, *A World of Trouble*, p. 307.

184 Parsi, *Treacherous Alliance*, p. 110. Ledeen would continue to lobby for rapprochement with Iran throughout Reagan's presidency, but after helping foment the invasion of Iraq in 2003, he would reinvent himself as the chief proponent of regime change in Iran.

185 Wawro, *Quicksand*, pp. 402–4; Tyler, *A World of Trouble*, p. 326.

186 Milstein, 'Washington Institute for Near East Policy'.

187 On 4 August 2005, Rosen would be indicted under the Espionage Act on charges of spying for Israel. However, after much legal wrangling, intense lobbying and delay, the charges were eventually

dropped once the trial was rigged in a manner that made conviction impossible. Rosen in turn sued AIPAC for libel and slander
because he maintained all his actions were known to the lobby
group (which had distanced itself).

188   Tivnan, *The Lobby*, p. 180.
189   G. F. Smith, *Foreign Agents*, pp. 115–24; Beinin, 'The Israelization';
      Halsell, 'Clinton's Indyk Appointment'. US Internal Revenue
      Code 501(c)3 grants tax-exempt, non-profit status to 'Religious,
      Educational, Charitable, Scientific, Literary, Testing for Public Safety,
      to Foster National or International Amateur Sports Competition, or
      Prevention of Cruelty to Children or Animals Organizations'.
190   Former AIPAC staffer M. J. Rosenberg describes the scene of its
      creation where 'Steve Rosen announced his plan for an AIPAC
      cutout that would do AIPAC's work but appear independent.'
      M. J. Rosenberg, 'Steve Walt'; M. J. Rosenberg, 'Does PBS Know?'
191   Halsell, 'Clinton's Indyk Appointment'.
192   Cited in Beinin, 'The Israelization'.
193   Ibid.
194   Sniegoski, *Transparent Cabal*, pp. 65–73; Heilbrunn, *They Knew*,
      pp. 202–5; Bacevich, *The New American Militarism*, p. 163;
      Mann, *Rise of the Vulcans*, pp. 184–9.
195   Heilbrunn, *They Knew*, p. 204.
196   Stauber and Rampton, *Toxic Sludge*, pp. 169–71; MacArthur,
      Second Front, pp. 63–77.
197   Lobe, 'New Champions '.
198   Ironically, Lantos was one of the biggest critics of Amnesty and
      Human Rights Watch for being 'overly critical of Israel'. The
      Kuwaitis donated $50,000 in thanks to HRC. Amnesty retracted
      the story after the war. Stauber and Rampton, *Toxic Sludge*,
      pp. 167–74.
199   Ibid. pp. 167–74.
200   Tyler, *A World of Trouble*, pp. 377–84; Heilbrunn, *They
      Knew*, p. 205; Sniegoski, *The Transparent Cabal*, pp. 77–80;
      Morris, *Righteous Victims*, pp. 612–16; Shlaim, *The Iron Wall*,
      pp. 484–92.
201   Beinin, 'The Israelization'; Fisk, *The Great War*, pp. 469–76;
      Pappe, 'Clusters of History', pp. 18–19.
202   J. J. Goldberg, *Jewish Power*, pp. xv–xxiv; Frankel, 'A Beautiful
      Friendship?'
203   Heilbrunn, *They Knew*, pp. 205–7.
204   Heilbrunn, *They Knew*, pp. 206–7. Woolsey was rewarded for his

efforts with an appointment as Director of Central Intelligence.

205 Ehrman, *The Rise of Neoconservatism*, pp. 194–5.

206 So total was Clinton's surrender to the Israel lobby that it led former National Security Advisor Zbigniew Brzezinski, an ally, to opine: 'We've got a president who's not interested in foreign policy, so domestic lobbies are decisive when foreign policy issues arrive.' Quoted in Mann, *Rise of the Vulcans*, p. 288.

207 Michael Tracy Thomas, *American Policy Towards Israel*, p. 160.

208 Jeffrey Goldberg, 'Real Insiders'.

209 A report by in Israel's major daily *Ma'ariv* proudly reported that in 'the National Security Council, 7 out of 11 top staffers are Jews. Clinton had especially placed them in the most sensitive junctions in the U.S. security and foreign administrations', and that the President's office is 'full of warm Jews'. Bar-Yosef, 'The Jews Who Run Clinton's Court'.

210 Beinin, 'The Israelization'.

211 While working at the Pentagon during the Carter Administration, Ross and Wolfowitz co-authored a study that laid the germs of the policy which eventually led to the invasion of Iraq. The study stressed the US stake in the security of the region's oil resources because 'events in the Persian Gulf affect the Arab–Israeli conflict'. It gave particular attention to Iraq, which it said had 'become militarily pre-eminent in the Persian Gulf, a worrisome development because of Iraq's radical-Arab stance, its anti-Western attitudes, its dependence of Soviet arms sales, and its willingness to foment trouble in other local nations.' Quoted in Mann, *Rise of the Vulcans*, p. 79. According Mann, the project would play 'a groundbreaking role in changing American military policy toward the Persian Gulf over the coming decades' (p. 80).

212 Beinin, 'The Israelization'.

213 Gause, 'The Illogic of Dual Containment'.

214 A. D. Miller, *The Much Too Promised Land*, p. 75.

215 During this period, AIPAC vice president Harvey Friedman was forced to resign after he was overheard calling Israel's Deputy Foreign Minister Yossi Beilin a 'little slime ball' for participating in the 'peace process'. Yitzhak Rabin in turn simply refused to meet lobby officials during his visits to the US. See Thomas, *American Policy Towards Israel*, p. 160.

216 Abrams, 'Words of War'.

217 Saunders, *Who Paid the Piper?*

Chapter 3

1 Israel is the largest recipient of US foreign aid. By 2007 it had received over $140 billion in direct aid, but Stauffer calculates the total cost of the alliance to US taxpayers at $3 trillion. See Stauffer, 'The Costs to American Taxpayers'; Sharp, *U.S. Foreign Aid to Israel*; McArthur, 'A Conservative Estimate'.

2 Kojève, from whom Fukuyama borrowed the notion of 'end of history', was a major influence on Bloom.

3 Fukuyama, 'The End of History?' See also Fukuyama, *The End of History and the Last Man.* The thesis has been criticised by Jacques Derrida and Perry Anderson among others. See Derrida, *Specters of Marx*; P. Anderson, *A Zone of Engagement.* Fukuyama himself retreats from it in a later book. Fukuyama, *Our Posthuman Future.*

4 Heilbrunn, *They Knew*, pp. 196–7.

5 Ehrman, *The Rise of Neoconservatism*, pp. 179–80; On the neo-conservative migration to DC with the express aim of influencing policy see Kristol, *Neoconservatism*, pp. 37–9.

6 Quoted in 'Forced Urbanization'.

7 Crozier, et al., *The Crisis of Democracy.*

8 Huntington, 'The Clash of Civilizations?'

9 Kennan, 'The Sources of Soviet Conduct'. Though, as noted earlier, Kennan's containment policy was immediately superseded by Nitze's policy of confrontation.

10 Abrahamian, 'The US Media, Huntington and September 11'; Said, 'The Clash of Ignorance'.

11 Nafissi, 'Before and Beyond'. For one, the thesis failed to account for the fact that the closest ally the US has in the Middle East is Saudi Arabia, whose culture could not be more different; for another, empirical studies have shown that more conflict has happened within civilisations than across them. For refutations of the clash thesis see Henderson and Tucker, 'Clear and Present Strangers'; Henderson, 'Mistaken Identity'; Henderson, 'Not Letting Evidence Get in the Way of Assumptions'; Fox, 'State Failure and the Clash of Civilisations'; Fox, 'Paradigm Lost'; Bonney, *False Prophets*, pp. 33–51; Alam, *Israeli Exceptionalism*, pp. 25–39.

12 E. A. Cohen, 'World War IV'; Podhoretz, 'How to Win World War IV?'; Podhoretz, 'World War IV: How It Started'; Podhoretz, *World War IV: The Long Struggle.*

13 Bonney, *False Prophets*, pp. 39–40. On differences with neocon-
    servatives see ibid. pp. 42–7.

14 Where 'the end of history' started as a speech Fukuyama deliv-
    ered at the University of Chicago's Olin Center, 'clash' began as a
    speech at AEI based on Huntington's research for Harvard's Olin
    Institute. Allan Bloom headed Chicago's John M. Olin Center
    for Inquiry into the Theory and Practice of Democracy (<http://
    olincenter.uchicago.edu>) and Hungtington headed Harvard's
    John M. Olin Institute for Strategic Studies (<http://www.wcfia.
    harvard.edu/olin>). See J. J. Miller, 'Foundation's End'.

15 B. Lewis, 'The Roots of Muslim Rage'.

16 Glass, 'Lewis of Arabia'.

17 Steinberger, 'Interview'.

18 Huntington, 'Religion, Culture and International Conflict'.

19 These include Golda Meir, Ariel Sharon and Benjamin Netanyahu
    among others. Meir's infamous statement denying the existence of
    Palestinians as a nation was reportedly inspired by an article Lewis
    wrote for *Commentary* (which, according to Amnon Cohen, she
    made required reading for her cabinet). More recently, Netanyahu
    invoked Lewis's authority at AIPAC's annual gathering to argue
    for regime change in Iran. According to Israeli experts, it was also
    Lewis's contacts with Turkish generals and politicians that helped
    cement Israeli–Turkish military ties. According to Waldman, he also
    formed 'lasting ties with several young Jackson and Moynihan aides
    who went on to apply his views to Iraq'. These included Wolfowitz,
    Abrams, Gaffney, Perle and Rhode. Waldman, 'Containing Jihad'.
    Massing, 'The Storm over the Israel Lobby'.

20 Quoted in Waldman, 'Containing Jihad'.

21 B. Lewis, *What Went Wrong?* Amongst others in a long career of
    tendentious claims is a recent one by the 'prophet from Princeton'
    that Muslims are taking over Europe (*Jerusalem Post*, 29 January
    2007), and another in 2006 predicting that according to his eso-
    teric understanding of Islamic theology, the president of Iran
    would launch an apocalyptic attack on Israel and the Western
    world on 22 September 2006. See also Kimmerling, 'Thus Spoke
    Bernard Lewis'. Massing, 'The Storm over the Israel Lobby'.

22 Hirsh, 'Bernard Lewis Revisited'.

23 Quoted in Waldman, 'Containing Jihad'. See also B. Lewis, 'A
    War of Resolve'.

24 Hirsh, 'Bernard Lewis Revisited'. Lewis had allegedly first advo-
    cated redrawing the map of the Middle East at a meeting of

the secretive Bilderberg Group in 1979. Dreyfuss and LeMarc, *Hostage to Khomeini*, p. 157.

25   The Israeli historian Ilan Pappe has warned that by following Lewis's advice, the US is priming itself for a disaster similar to that which befell Israel in Lebanon. Quoted in Waldman, 'Containing Jihad'.

26   In Powell's own words: 'I believe in the bully's way of going to war.' Quoted in Mann, *Rise of the Vulcans*, p. 221.

27   Quoted in Bacevich, *The New American Militarism*, p. 157.

28   Heilbrunn, *They Knew*, p. 223. In his 2006 book *The Good Fight*, liberal hawk Peter Beinart would advise liberals to wrest defence away from conservatives as an election winner by celebrating World War II and the fight against Stalin and forgetting Vietnam. Bacevich, 'The American Political Tradition'.

29   Quoted in Bacevich, *The New American Militarism*, pp. 163–4; Wohlstetter started campaigning for further intervention to overthrow Hussein immediately after the war. See Wohlstetter and Hoffman, 'The Bitter End'.

30   Bacevich, *The New American Militarism*, p. 169; Strobel, 'The CNN Effect'.

31   For an account of the close coordination between the media and the Pentagon see MacArthur (1992). According to MacArthur, many of the press censorship and pooling ideas followed the British example in the Falklands war. See also Fisk, *The Great War*, p. 853.

32   These ironies are best captured in Baudrillard, *The Gulf War Did Not Take Place*.

33   Quoted in Rogin, 'Sucking Up'.

34   Bacevich, *The New American Militarism*, pp. 19–23. The truth about the failure of the 'precision weaponry' only emerged after the war. See MacArthur, *Second Front*. On new technological enablers of war see Singer, *Wired for War*.

35   Quoted in Gongora, 'The Revolution in Military Affairs'.

36   K. Silverstein, 'The Man from ONA'; Abella, *Soldiers of Reason*.

37   Quoted in Bacevich, *The New American Militarism*, p. 161.

38   Ibid. pp. 161–2.

39   Bransford, 'U.S. Defence Spending'.

40   Dobbs, 'With Albright, Clinton Accepts New U.S. Role'.

41   Bacevich, *American Empire*, pp. 147–62. On PMCs see Singer, *Corporate Warriors*; Scahill, *Blackwater*; C. Johnson, *The Sorrows of Empire*, ch. 5; Chatterjee, *Iraq, Inc.*, ch. 3.

42 Bacevich, *The New American Militarism*, p. 54.

43 Quoted in Bacevich, *American Empire*, pp. 142–3.

44 Mutua, 'Savages, Victims, and Saviors'.

45 Caldwell, '"Communiste et Rastignac."'; Traub, 'A Statesman without Borders'.

46 UN General Assembly Resolution 43/131, 'Humanitarian assistance to victims of natural disasters and similar emergency situations', 75th Plenary Meeting, 8 December 1988.

47 Caldwell, '"Communiste et Rastignac."'

48 According to Jean-Maurice Ripert, France's ambassador to the UN, Kouchner persuaded George H. W. Bush to send US troops to Somalia. Traub, 'A Statesman without Borders'.

49 Quoted in N. Clarke, 'If the World Is his Oyster'.

50 Levy, like his fellow *nouveaux philosophes*, is a committed Zionist. Shortly after Israel's twenty-two-day assault on Gaza, killing 1,400, mostly civilians, Lévy visited Israel to show solidarity and wrote an article presenting Israel as the victim. He would follow the feat in June 2010 joining André Glucksmann to defend Israel's massacre of nine peace activists aboard a flotilla of ships trying to break the siege of Gaza. In June 2008, criticism of Israel led Pascal Bruckner to call for the dissolution of the UN Human Rights Council. In the case of Alain Finkielkraut, the hostility towards Palestinians extends to Arabs in general. In an 18 November 2005 interview with *Haaretz*, he stirred controversy by making racist comments about North African immigrants and celebrating French colonialism for civilising 'the savages'. He later apologised.

51 Quoted in Caldwell, '"Communiste et Rastignac."'

52 Traub, 'A Statesman without Borders'.

53 In Caldwell, '"Communiste et Rastignac."'

54 Beeston, 'Prepare for War with Iran'.

55 Judt, *Reappraisals*, p. 389.

56 Ibid. pp. 389–90.

57 Lieven, *America Right or Wrong*, pp. 76–9; Asmus, et al., 'Progressive Internationalism'.

58 Heilbrunn, *They Knew*, pp. 195–6.

59 Cushman, *A Matter of Principle*. Interestingly, Berman was not always so sanguine about philanthropic warfare. 'The line between liberating the world and enslaving the world is amazingly thin', he wrote in his 1997 book *A Tale of Two Utopias* (p. 217).

60 Brown, '"The Most We Can Hope For . . ."'.

61 Mamdani, 'Responsibility to protect', p. 126.

62 Mamdani, *Saviors and Survivors*, pp. 273–4.

63 Powell took the extraordinary step (for the chairman of the Joint Chiefs of Staff) of penning an op-ed for *New York Times* arguing against intervention in Bosnia. Mann, *Rise of the Vulcans*, p. 221.

64 Packer notes with satisfaction: 'During the Congressional debates on the war resolution, it was just about impossible to hear an argument in favor of the administration without the words "Munich" and "Chamberlain." The words "Tonkin" and "Johnson" were far rarer, which tells you something about the relative acceptability of World War II and Vietnam – appeasement and quagmire – as historical precedents.' Packer, 'The Liberal Quandary over Iraq'.

65 Heilbrunn, *They Knew*, p. 222.

66 Rademaker, a former Abrams employee at the State Department, is the husband of AEI vice president Danielle Pletka. Ibid. p. 225. Lobe, 'New Champions'.

67 Public Law 107–243 – OCT. 16, 2002, <http://www.c-span.org/resources/pdf/hjres114.pdf>.

68 Madeleine Albright justified the US right to intervene thus: 'If we have to use force, it is because we are America. We are the indispensable nation. We stand tall and we see further into the future.' Quoted in T. Smith, 'It's Uphill for the Democrats'.

69 In a *New York Times Magazine* feature, Ignatieff summoned the White Man to pick up 'The Burden' and gushed: 'empire has become a precondition for democracy'. His defence of torture appeared in the paper the day the Abu Ghraib story broke. Ignatieff, 'The Burden'; Ignatieff, 'Lesser Evils'.

70 P. Berman, *Terror and Liberalism*; Elshtain, *Just War against Terror*; Pollack, *The Threatening Storm*.

71 Packer, *The Fight Is for Democracy*.

72 Packer, 'The Liberal Quandary over Iraq'.

73 On Pollack see Fisk, *The Great War*, pp. 1138–40; on Goldberg see J. Cole, 'Cpl. Jeffrey Goldberg'.

74 Reinhart, *Israel/Palestine*.

75 Parsi, *Treacherous Alliance*, pp. 21–2; Cockburn and Cockburn, *Dangerous Liaison*, pp. 99–100. The doctrine is also referred to in Mahler's *Israel after Begin* as 'erosion of the Periphery Theory' (p. 138). In a memo dated 25 September 1969, Henry Kissinger apprised Richard Nixon of the possible motivations behind Israeli attacks on Nasser, of whose weakness they had no doubt: 'It seems more likely – and some Israelis admit this – that Israel's purpose is to surround itself with weak Arab governments so that it can

weather prolonged tension behind its present borders.' Quoted in Tyler, *A World of Trouble*, p. 558n1. In addition, Israel also sponsored a secessionist movement in South Sudan against the country's Arab–Muslim government. Cockburn and Cockburn, *Dangerous Liaison*, p. 113.

76 Tyler, *A World of Trouble*, pp. 27–9. Others had their eyes even further afield. In 1973, Israeli Airforce General and future President Ezer Weizmann told officers that he wished 'Israel had bases on the Euphrates'. Quoted in Cooley, *An Alliance against Babylon*, p. 76.

77 The idea of pre-emption had found its way into the Bush Doctrine (NSS2002) via the PNAC's 'Rebuilding America's Defenses'. Not known for his bibliophilia, George W. Bush was seen reading Israeli-American historian (and present Israeli ambassador to the US) Michael Oren's book on the June 1967 war, *Six Days of War*. Fineman, 'Bush Studied '67 Pre-Emptive Strike'.

78 Peleg, *Begin's Foreign Policy, 1977–1983*, p. 47, quoted in Sniegoski, *The Transparent Cabal*, p. 49.

79 According to Peleg, the article was 'an authentic mirror' of the Israeli right's thinking under Begin reflecting its sense of 'unlimited and unrestrained power.' Quoted in Sniegoski, *The Transparent Cabal*, p. 50.

80 Yinon, 'A Strategy for Israel in the 1980s'.

81 Ibid.

82 Chomsky, *Fateful Triangle*, p. 457.

83 Tyler, *A World of Trouble*, pp. 249, 255.

84 Chomsky, *Fateful Triangle*, p. 455. More recently, US Congresswoman Jane Harman, who in April 2009 was revealed to maintain clandestine contact with Israeli intelligence, proposed a similar solution for Iran. She told an audience: 'The Persian population in Iran is not a majority, it is a plurality. There are many different, diverse, and disagreeing populations inside Iran and an obvious strategy, which I believe is a good strategy, is to separate those populations.' Rep. Jane Harman at the AIPAC annual conference (3 May 2009).

85 During one phone call, Reagan reportedly responded to the Israeli prime minister's prevarications about his military's actions by shouting: 'Don't lie to me, I am watching it on CNN.' Quoted in Tyler, *A World of Trouble*, p. 272.

86 Ibid. pp. 272–5, 574n51. Haig would later try to deny that he had given Sharon a green light: Haig, 'Caveat'.

87 Quoted in Sniegoski, *The Transparent Cabal*, p. 55.

88 Kaplan, *Daydream Believers*, p. 130.

89 Tripp, 'Iraq and the 1948 War'.

90 Abdel-Jawwad, 'Israel'; Cooley, *An Alliance against Babylon*, pp. 137, 142–4.

91 Huggler, 'Palestinians Mourn Fall of Their Hero'.

92 Cockburn and Cockburn, *Dangerous Liaison*, pp. 104–5. Israeli liaisons with the Kurds included David Kimche, Aryeh Eliav and Yacov Nimrodi, who was also overseeing Israeli training of the Shah of Iran's SAVAK.

93 Cooley, *An Alliance Against Babylon*, pp. 76–92, esp. p. 84.

94 Minasian, 'The Israeli–Kurdish Relations'.

95 Marshall, et al., *The Iran–Contra Connection*, p. 169, cited in Minasian, 'The Israeli–Kurdish Relations', p. 23.

96 Parsi, *Treacherous Alliance*, pp. 102–9.

97 Ball and Ball, *The Passionate Attachment*, pp. 112–4; Cooley, *An Alliance against Babylon*, pp. 159–62. The incident also led to the third invocation of the AECA by a US government to penalise Israel but, as on the two previous occasions (under Carter), it was quashed by Congress. Bobby Inman, the deputy CIA director who tried to limit Israel's access to satellite imagery in the aftermath, paid the price thirteen years later when the lobby mobilised to deny him appointment as Clinton's Secretary of Defense. Cooley, *An Alliance against Babylon*, p. 163.

98 Cockburn and Cockburn, *Dangerous Liaison*, pp. 301–6. Earlier, Bull had helped the Israelis and South Africans extend their artillery range by 25 per cent. Hersh, *The Samson Option*, p. 216.

99 Cooley, *An Alliance against Babylon*, pp. 151–3, 156. Months later on 17 December, it also occasioned the first of Donald Rumsfeld's two trips to seal the rapprochement. Tyler, *A World of Trouble*, pp. 296–7. Western support for Iraq intensified as the war dragged on and Iran consolidated its gains. For US–UK military support for Iraq see Cooley, *An Alliance Against Babylon*, pp. 168–71.

100 Tyler, *A World of Trouble*, pp. 301–3, 314–15.

101 Tyler, *A World of Trouble*, pp. 321–6; Kornbluh and Byrne, *The Iran–Contra Scandal*; declassified record at the National Security Archives (2006); Wawro, *Quicksand*, pp. 402–4; Parsi, *Treacherous Alliance*, pp. 116–26.

102 Mann, *Rise of the Vulcans*, pp. 184–6; Tyler, *A World of Trouble*, pp. 358–9, 363–4; Sniegoski, *The Transparent Cabal*, p. 72; DeYoung, *Soldier*, pp. 191–200.

103 Mann, *Rise of the Vulcans*, pp. 186–8. On the neocons' enthusiasm for war in general see Heilbrunn, *They Knew*, pp. 202–5.

104 Dionne, 'A Question of Tactics'. This alignment also occasioned Patrick Buchanan's infamous comment on NBC's *The McLaughlin Group* (26 August 1990): 'There are only two groups that are beating the drums for war in the Middle East – the Israeli Defense Ministry and its amen corner in the United States.'

105 Gause, 'The Illogic of Dual Containment'.

106 Still in his early twenties, Wurmser in 1985 had produced a study titled *Hydra of Carnage*, with the express aim of influencing policy in the manner of George Kennan's 'Long Telegram' or of NSC-68. Feith contributed a chapter. Gellman, *Angler*, p. 223.

107 Wurmser, et al., 'A Clean Break'.

108 Wurmser, et al., 'Coping with Crumbling States'.

109 Eldar, 'Perles of Wisdom'.

110 In a display of astonishing ignorance, Wurmser, the neocons' inhouse Iraq expert, adds that the 'Shia retain strong ties to the Hashemites: the Shia venerate foremost the Prophet's family, the direct descendants of which . . . is King Hussein.' As a matter of fact, the Sunni Hashemites have little influence over the Shia, and a decade later would be issuing dark warnings about the threat of a 'Shia crescent'. Wurmser, et al., 'Coping with Crumbling States'.

111 Beinin, 'The Israelization'; Unger, *Fall of the House of Bush*, p. 148.

112 Wurmser, 'Iraq Needs a Revolution'.

113 Wurmser, *Tyranny's Ally*. The 'ally' in the title refers to the US government for refusing to bring down Saddam Hussein. In the book's acknowledgements, Wurmser lists as influences Perle, Ledeen, Feith, Woolsey, Harold Rhode and Ahmad Chalabi amongst others. He also thanks Irving Moskowitz, a gambling tycoon and long-time funder of Israel's extremist settlement movement, for funding his work at AEI.

114 Ibid. pp. 73–4.

115 Ibid. pp. 74–6. The doctrine of *Wilayat al-Faqih* – rule of the religious jurist, preached in the Iranian city of Qom – served as the ideological underpinning of the 1979 Islamic Revolution in Iran. 'It grants absolute authority over all matters – religious, social, and political – to a *marja* who has earned the title of *mujtahid*, a blend of judge and theologian.' Blanford, 'Iran, Iraq, and Two Shiite Visions'.

116 Wurmser, *Tyranny's Ally*, pp. 78–9, 107, 110.

117 Quoted in Blanford, 'Iran, Iraq, and Two Shiite Visions'.
118 Gerecht, 'Liberate Iraq'; Gerecht, 'Regime Change in Iran?'
119 Ledeen, 'One Battle in a Wider, Longer War'.
120 Buchta, *Who Rules Iran?*, p. 89.
121 Feith, *War and Decision*, p. 201.
122 Frum and Perle, *An End to Evil*, p. 141.
123 Cutler, 'Beyond Incompetence'.
124 Cockburn, *Muqtada Al-Sadr*.
125 Wurmser, et al., 'A Clean Break' (original emphasis).
126 Reagan's decision was made under the influence of the hawkish High Frontier and the Heritage Foundation, despite the reservations of his Secretaries of State and Defense. Abelson, *A Capitol Idea*, pp. 185–7.
127 Vest, 'The Men from JINSA and CSP'.
128 Quoted in P. H. Stone, 'Ice-Cold Warrior'.
129 Johnson, *Nemesis*, p. 210.
130 AVOT is a spinoff from William Bennett's Empower America; it identifies post-9/11 'external' and 'internal' threats, which include former President Jimmy Carter, *Harper's* magazine editor Lewis Lapham and Representative Maxine Waters. BICOM is a London-based group that provides daily and weekly briefings on media coverage of Israel; arranges junkets to Israel for friendly journalists; and works to cultivate relationships with decision makers and media leaders in Europe with a view to influencing them. It equates reportage or commentary critical of Zionism with anti-Semitism. According to former Director Daniel Shek, it works with AIPAC in order to develop 'grassroots networks in Britain and with organizing pro-Israel events similar to AIPAC's conference'. 'European Media Is Questioning Israel's Right to Exist'; Oborne and Jones 'The Pro-Israel Lobby in Britain'; Vest, 'The Men from JINSA and CSP'.
131 Hartung and Ciarrocca, 'Star Wars II'; Hartung and Ciarrocca, 'The Military–Industrial–Think Tank Complex'; Isaacs, 'Spinning to the Right'; C. Johnson, *Nemesis*, p. 212.
132 Committee for Peace and Security in the Gulf, 'Open Letter to the President', 19 February 1998.
133 Schmitt, 'The Rumsfeld Commission'.
134 Gronlund and Wright, 'The Rumsfeld Report'.
135 Although Clinton questioned the efficacy of NMD, he did not veto it. Instead he deferred the decision to his successor.
136 Andrew Cockburn, *Rumsfeld*, pp. 91–2; C. Johnson, *Nemesis*,

pp. 210–13; Mann, *Rise of the Vulcans*, pp. 240–2. Encouraged by the success, Rumsfeld pushed for the creation of another commission, the Cox Committee, to investigate US business relations with China which ensured employment for Libby and a lucrative sinecure for Wolfowitz. Mann, *Rise of the Vulcans*, p. 243.

137 Israeli allegations of technology transfers between Moscow and Tehran had become the basis of a series of Congressional hearings beginning in 1997, and in June 1998 had led to the passage of the Iran Missile Proliferation Sanctions Act, immediately vetoed by Clinton. Dobbs, 'How Politics Helped Redefine Threat'.

138 Rumsfeld, et al., 'Report of the Commission to Assess United States National Security Space Management and Organization'.

139 Vest, 'The Men from JINSA and CSP'.

140 Vest, 'The Men from JINSA and CSP'. Amitay presents a good example of the alphabet soup of think tanks, 'citizens' initiatives' and letterhead organisations through which the Israel lobby and its neoconservative vanguard operate. Besides AIPAC, CSP and JINSA, Amitay also played a leading role in CPD, CDM, the Committee for a Democratic Iran, the Washington Public Affairs Council and the Washington Kurdish Institute. A member of AEI and CFR, he was also a leading booster of PNAC.

141 Jinsa.org

142 Vest, 'The Men from JINSA and CSP'.

143 B. R. Cole, 'War for Peace'; Vest, 'The Men from JINSA and CSP'.

144 Quoted in Vest, 'The Men from JINSA and CSP'.

145 Ibid.

146 Heilbrunn, *They Knew*, pp. 213–14, 210–11.

147 Kristol and Kagan, 'Toward a Neo-Reaganite Foreign Policy'.

148 Parry, 'Iran–Contra's "Lost Chapter"'.

149 PNAC Statement of Principles.

150 Although signatories to this letter also included Francis Fukuyama and Richard Armitage, both defected from the war party in the lead-up to the invasion.

151 Solarz's obituary stated: 'When he was elected to the House in 1974, Mr. Solarz finagled a seat on the Foreign Affairs Committee with the idea that he could appeal to his largely Jewish district by attending to the needs of Israel.' Martin, 'Stephen J. Solarz'. The same concern also motivated his successors Tom Lantos and Howard Berman in chairing the committee. Guttman, 'New Foreign Affairs Committee Chairman'.

152 Andrew Cockburn, *Rumsfeld*, pp. 91, 146.

153 Heilbrunn, *They Knew*, p. 225; Isikoff and Corn, *Hubris*, p. 78; Bacevich, *The Limits of Power*, p. 56.

154 Kagan and Kristol, *Present Dangers*; Halper and Clarke, *America Alone*, p. 19.

155 Wolfowitz and Khalilzad, 'Overthrow Him'.

156 Mann, *Rise of the Vulcans*, pp. 227–8, 231.

157 Wolfowitz, 'Clinton's Bay of Pigs'.

158 Ledeen, 'Bill Clinton's Bay of Pigs'.

159 Wolfowitz, 'The United States and Iraq', 111, cited in Mann, *Rise of the Vulcans*, pp. 235–7.

160 Andrew Cockburn, *Rumsfeld*, p. 148.

161 Halper and Clarke, *America Alone*, p. 101.

162 Wolfowitz, 'Statement before the House National Security Committee'.

163 Testimony to the Senate Armed Forces Committee, 28 September 1998; Ricks, *Fiasco*, pp. 22–3.

164 Mann, *Rise of the Vulcans*, p. 238.

165 Ibid. p. 287.

166 Members included Richard Perle, Dov Zakheim, Stephen Hadley, Robert Zoellick, Robert Blackwill and Richard Armitage. Mann, *Rise of the Vulcans*, pp. 251–2, 274.

167 Powell and Persico, *My American Journey*, p. 540.

168 Wolfowitz in turn had cooperated with books aimed at puncturing Powell's mystique, particularly his role in Gulf '91. Mann, Rise of the *Vulcans*, p. 260.

169 Lang, 'Drinking the Kool-Aid'.

170 Rice, 'Campaign 2000'.

171 Andrew Cockburn, *Rumsfeld*, p. 101.

172 Mann, *Rise of the Vulcans*, p. 225.

173 Ibid. pp. 273, 275, 290.

174 Suskind, *The Price of Loyalty*, pp. 70–5.

175 Ricks, *Fiasco*, pp. 27–8.

176 Ibid. p. 28.

177 Feith, *War and Decision*, pp. 203–11.

178 Woodward, *State of Denial*, pp. 28–9.

179 Kagan and Kristol, 'A National Humiliation'. See also Mann, *Rise of the Vulcans*, pp. 282–5.

180 Heilbrunn, *They Knew*, p. 234. See also Ricks, *Fiasco*, p. 27.

181 According to Feith, though Armitage had signed the PNAC letter on Iraq, he had such disdain for his former friend Wolfowitz that

he had even refuse to meet him. Feith, *War and Decision*, pp. 203–5.

182 Press conference in Cairo, 24 February 2001.

183 Feith, *War and Decision*, pp. 209–11. Rumsfeld, *Known and Unknown*.

184 Andrew Cockburn, *Rumsfeld*, p. 149.

185 Gramsci, *A Gramsci Reader*, p. 209.

Chapter 4

1 The imminence of the threat was always implied rather than stated, which suggests the administration was strictly adhering to legal advice so it could maintain deniability. Bugliosi, *The Prosecution of George W. Bush*.

2 Blitzer, 'Search for the "Smoking Gun"'; Isikoff and Corn, *Hubris*, p. 35.

3 Duelfer, 'Comprehensive Report'.

4 Andrew Cockburn, *Rumsfeld*, pp. 145–6. Kamel was subsequently lured back and killed by Saddam Hussein. Cockburn and Cockburn, *Saddam Hussein*.

5 Mann, *Rise of the Vulcans*, p. 259.

6 The only prominent individual from the UN inspections programme who did not share this view was David Kay; however, his employment with SAIC, a corporation which had secured major reconstruction contracts in anticipation of the war, presented a conflict of interests.

7 Porter, 'How Tenet Betrayed the CIA'; Suskind, *The Way of the World*; Risen, *State of War*.

8 Kean, et al., 'The 9/11 Commission Report', p. 66; Woods and Lacey, 'Iraqi Perspectives Project'; Strobel, 'Exhaustive Review Finds No Link'.

9 Hersh, 'A Case Not Closed'.

10 Kirk, 'The Dark Side'.

11 'Poll: 70% Believe Saddam, 9-11 Link'.

12 Lieven, *America Right or Wrong*, p. 25.

13 'U.S. Troops in Iraq'.

14 While this commission was presented as a bipartisan initiative, it was conceived by the Bush Administration, which also dictated its composition, for the express aim of whitewashing the administration's pre-war conduct, writes Woodward in *State of Denial*.

15 Feith, *War and Decision*, p. 354.

16 Mylroie, *Study of Revenge*. One article appeared just two weeks before 9/11. Laurie Mylroie, 'Usama and Country'.

17 Mylroie, 'The Baghdad Alternative'.

18 Pipes and Mylroie, 'Back Iraq'.

19 Isikoff and Corn, *Hubris*, pp. 68–9.

20 Perle has since revised his position from 'wholly convincing' to 'not everything she says is convincing'. See Tanenhaus, 'Bush's Brain Trust'.

21 According to one longtime Wolfowitz friend, the Deputy Defense Secretary was convinced of Iraqi involvement based on alleged telephone logs, and Timothy McVeigh's website, because it 'said there was nothing worse than the suffering of Iraqi children under the sanctions'. Tanenhaus, 'Bush's Brain Trust'.

22 R. A. Clarke, *Against All Enemies*, pp. 30, 95, 232.

23 Bergen, 'Armchair Provocateur'.

24 Ibid.

25 At the very first deputy secretarial level meeting on terrorism on 30 April, Wolfowitz had invoked Mylroie's research to claim that Iraq was behind various acts of terror during the 1990s. R. A. Clarke, *Against All Enemies*, pp. 30, 231–2.

26 Andrew Cockburn, *Rumsfeld*, p. 9.

27 Ken Adelman has since claimed that in 1995 Rumsfeld once kept him up till 3 a.m. 'giving him an earful how badly the elder Bush had screwed up', by not toppling Saddam. Quoted in Woodward, *State of Denial*, p. 77. But considering that Adelman only made this claim at a time when the neoconservatives were turning on Rumsfeld to wash their hands of the responsibility for the war, it is best taken with a grain of salt.

28 This fact was highlighted most acutely in a Bush-era memo to Douglas Feith which came to light in 2011. See Donald Rumsfeld to Douglas Feith, 'Issues w/Various countries', <http://bit.ly/scF2px>.

29 Dick Cheney was equally suspicious of Chalabi, according to Heilbrunn, *They Knew*, p. 250.

30 Andrew Cockburn, *Rumsfeld*, p. 149; Wedel, *Shadow Elite*, pp. 175–6.

31 Fitchett, 'For Washington, a Modern Pearl Harbor'.

32 Quoted in Unger, *Fall of the House of Bush*, p. 215.

33 In his memoir of service in the Bush Administration, Frum claims full credit for this shift in policy. Frum, *The Right Man*, pp. 142–4;

see also Kirk, 'Bush's War'. According to the PBS documentary, Bush was asked by Condoleezza Rice whether he wanted to keep this line in the speech. Bush chose to do so. Even though Bush reiterated this point on 20 September, he still advised patience on Iraq. Woodward, *Bush at War*, p. 107.

34 Sciolino and Tyler, 'Some Pentagon Officials and Advisors'.

35 Quoted in ibid.

36 Woolsey and Ijaz, 'Revenge Is a Dish Best Served Cold'; Mylroie, 'Who Is to Blame?'; Krauthammer, 'To War, Not to Court'. Krauthammer returned to the theme in another article days later, arguing that the 'overriding aim of the war on terrorism is changing regimes'. Krauthammer, 'The War: A Roadmap'. He advised that Afghanistan must only be stage one, followed by stage two, Syria, and stage three, Iraq and Iran. A week later he used the panic caused by anthrax mailed to key journalists and politicians to once again press for invading Iraq. (It turned out that the attacks originated in a research lab in the US.) He called again for invading Iraq in his 30 November column. It had remained the subject of every one of his weekly columns since September 11. By the end of the year, the Iraq–Al-Qaeda link was well established in the public mind. Krauthammer, 'Victory Changes Everything . . . '; Krauthammer, 'A War on Many Fronts . . . '.

37 Hoagland, 'Hidden Hand of Terror'.

38 Mylroie, 'The Iraqi Connection'; Woolsey, 'Blood Baath'; Gove, 'Be Warned'.

39 Kim, 'Gingrich Says'.

40 'Special Report: America United'.

41 Mylroie, 'Familiar Rogue'; Woolsey, 'Saddam May Be Target Americans Are Looking for'.

42 R. A. Clarke, *Against All Enemies*, p. 32; see also p. 30.

43 'Blair Warned Bush against Iraq Push after 9/11: Advisor'.

44 Suskind, *The One Percent Doctrine*, pp. 23–4.

45 Bamford, 'The Man Who Sold the War'. Rendon Group would receive a new contract in autumn 2001, this time from the Pentagon to sell the new war. It would be associated with the Office of Strategic Influence, which was shut down after drawing media attention, though Rendon retained its contract.

46 Isikoff and Corn, *Hubris*, p. 54.

47 Woolsey, 'The Iraq Connection'.

48 Hoagland, 'What About Iraq?'

49 Safire, 'Essay; Advance the Story'. See also the following arti-

cles by Safire: 'The Ultimate Enemy'; 'The Turkey Card'; 'Prague Connection'; 'To Fight Freedom's Fight'; 'The Inspection Ploy'; 'Protecting Saddam'; 'Saddam's Offensive'; 'Tenet's Palestine'; 'What Else is Missing?'; 'Of Turks and Kurds'; 'Relying on Saddam'; 'Saddam's Last Ploy'; 'In Material Breach'; 'On Playing Hunches'; 'Clear Ties of Terror'; 'Irrefutable and Undeniable'.

50   Kirk, 'Gunning for Saddam'.
51   Rose, 'Spies and Their Lies'.
52   Rose's alleged training camps recall scenes from an Ian Fleming novel: 'People who are judged to have failed tests in this training course will become victims, basically targets for live ammunition practice next time around. They are people who are completely inured to the taking and losing of human life.'
53   Rose, 'Inside Saddam's Terror Regime'; Roase, 'Iraq's Arsenal of Terror'; Rose, 'An Inconvenient Iraq'; Rose, 'Baghdad's Cruel Princes'.
54   Rose, 'The Iraqi Connection'. See also Rose and Vulliamy, 'Iraq "Behind US Anthrax Outbreaks"'; Rose, 'The Case for Tough Action against Iraq'; Rose, 'A Blind Spot Called Iraq'; Rose, 'Spain Links Suspect in 9/11 Plot to Baghdad'.
55   Rose, 'A Blind Spot Called Iraq'.
56   Official Charter, Director of Administration and Management.
57   These included Woolsey, Kenneth Adelman, Eliot Cohen, Newt Gingrich, Richard Allen, Ruth Wedgwood and Devon Gaffney Cross, a PNAC director and sister of CSP head Frank Gaffney. Cross would later serve as an advisor to the PR firm Lincoln Group, tasked with placing war propaganda in the Iraqi press, and head the Pentagon's Policy Forum. The neoconservatives' numbers were buttressed in 2002 by the appointment of eight Fellows from the right-wing Hoover Institution.
58   Verloy and Politi, 'Advisors of Influence'.
59   Tenet incorrectly recorded the date of the encounter as 12 September, which he now admits may have been a few days off. Perle denies that he made such a statement to Tenet; however, it is consistent with public statements he was making throughout this period. Tenet, *At the Center of the Storm*, p. xix.
60   Asked by host Tim Russert if there was any evidence 'linking Saddam Hussein or Iraqis to this operation', Cheney answered with a categorical 'No'. He added: 'Saddam Hussein's bottled up, at this point, but clearly, we continue to have a fairly tough policy where the Iraqis are concerned.' 'Meet the Press'.

61 'Richard Perle discusses US defense'.

62 Whitaker, 'Conflict and Catchphrases'; Whitaker, 'US Thinktanks Give Lessons in Foreign Policy'.

63 Conrad Black is married to Barbara Amiel, a hard-line Zionist columnist. He has since resigned his positions at Hollinger following accusations of receiving millions in unauthorised payments from company funds. In 2007, he was convicted in the US federal court on three counts of mail and wire fraud and one count of obstruction of justice, and sentenced to seventy-eight months in prison. On 24 March 2005, *Bloomberg News* reported that the 'Securities and Exchange Commission has warned a former Pentagon adviser, Richard N. Perle, that it might sue him for his role in the suspected looting of Hollinger International.' A 2004 investigation at the behest of Hollinger stockholders would label Perle a 'faithless fiduciary' and demand millions of dollars back. Andrew Cockburn, *Rumsfeld*, p. 104. Its flagship publications are known for their intolerance of views critical of Israel. According to a letter of complaint from three distinguished contributors, William Dalrymple, A. N. Wilson and Piers Paul Read, 'under Black's proprietorship, serious, critical reporting of Israel is no longer tolerated in the Telegraph Group'. Wells, 'The Black Arts'.

64 See Robert Greenwald's *Outfoxed: Rupert Murdoch's War on Journalism*.

65 Page, 'Showdown with Saddam'.

66 Chalabi touted his long-standing proposal for an insurgency under his command which, under US air cover and with Special Forces advisers, would easily topple Saddam. The military had long been sceptical of Chalabi and saw his plan as an attempt to drag the US military in support of his own ambitions. Zinni, Senate Testimony, 28 September 1998. See also Andrew Cockburn, *Rumsfeld*, p. 150; Heilbrunn, *They Knew*, pp. 250–1.

67 Hirsh, 'Bernard Lewis'.

68 Quoted in E. R. Goldstein, '"Osama bin Laden Made Me Famous"'. A decade later, Lewis would try implausibly to argue that he was actually opposed to the war. Ibid.

69 Hirsh, 'Bernard Lewis'; Frum, *The Right Man*, pp. 170–1.

70 Frum, *The Right Man*, pp. 170–6.

71 B. Lewis, 'The Revolt of Islam'; B. Lewis, 'Time for Toppling'; B. Lewis, 'A War of Resolve'.

72 Quoted in Waldman, 'Containing Jihad'. Perle also acknowledges Lewis's significance to the shift in policy, calling him 'the single

most important intellectual influence countering the conventional wisdom on managing the conflict between radical Islam and the West'. For Lewis, says Perle, 'a big part of the problem is failed societies on the Arab side is very important. That is not the point of view of the diplomatic establishment.' Ibid.

73 Hirsh, 'Bernard Lewis'. Cheney's former friend Brent Scowcroft credits his transformation from a conservative to a radical to the influence of Bernard Lewis. See Jeffrey Goldberg, 'Breaking Ranks'. See also Heilbrunn, *They Knew*, p. 242.
74 Waldman, 'Containing Jihad'.
75 Andrew Cockburn, *Rumsfeld*, pp. 150–1.
76 Heilbrunn, *They Knew*, p. 250.
77 Rumsfeld, 'Saddam Hussein'.
78 Kristol, et al., 'Letter to President Bush'. The letter also bore the signatures of liberal Zionists like Leon Wieseltier of *The New Republic*.
79 Sciolino and Tyler, 'Some Pentagon Officials and Advisors'.
80 Tanenhaus, 'Bush's Brain Trust'. Ehrman, *The Rise of Neoconservatism*, p. 141.
81 *Fox News*, 17, 25, 30 October and 15 November 2001; CNN, 29 October, 1, 2, 9, 21, 29 November, 6, 10, 21 December and 11 January 2001; CTV, 3 December 2001.
82 Adelman, 'Cakewalk in Iraq'. On the same night, in a debate with Scott Ritter on Fox News, Adelman dismissed warnings about the violations of international law and the potentially disastrous consequences of war by declaring the former weapons inspector 'one of the naysayers and dooms-painters'. He quoted INC-man Khidir Hamza to reject the potential of weapons inspectors to disarm Iraq.
83 Adelman, 'The Ankle Biters'.
84 Adelman, 'Saddam's State of Terror'.
85 Adelman, 'No, Let's Not Waste Any Time'.
86 Adelman, 'Cakewalk Revisited'.
87 Woodward, *Plan of Attack*, pp. 409–12. According to Woodward, participants took turns poking fun at sceptics such as Brent Scowcroft, Lawrence Eagleburger, James Baker and Colin Powell.
88 Dreyfuss, 'The Pentagon Muzzles the CIA'; Lang, 'Drinking the Kool-Aid'.
89 Woodward, *State of Denial*, pp. 83–5.
90 Gerecht, 'With Support, Iraq's Opposition Would Have a Chance'; Gerecht, 'The Coalition Delusion'; Gerecht, 'Crushing Al Qaeda

Is Only a Start'; Gerecht, 'Appeasing Arab Dictators'; Gerecht, 'Better to Be Feared Than Loved, Cont.'; Gerecht, 'Liberate Iraq'; Gerecht, 'Hardly Intelligent'; Gerecht, 'An Iraq War Won't Destabilize the Mideast'; Gerecht, 'While Clinton Slept'.

91 Gerecht, 'Iran Plays the Waiting Game'; Gerecht, 'On to Iran!'; Gerecht, 'Regime Change in Iran?'

92 Cohen, 'World War IV'.

93 Podhoretz, 'How to Win World War IV?'

94 Borger, 'The Spies Who Pushed for War'; Lobe, 'Pentagon Office'.

95 Hersh, *Chain of Command*, pp. 189–92. For his efforts in revealing the shady business deals, Perle branded Hersh the 'closest thing American journalism has to a terrorist'. *Late Edition with Wolf Blitzer*, CNN, 9 March 2003. In March 2003, *The New York Times* reported that Perle was to earn $725,000 (including a staggering fee of $600,000 contingent on the success of the deal) helping telecommunications giant Global Crossing overcome FBI and Pentagon opposition to the sale of its assets to Hong Kong-based Hutchison Whampoa, a company linked to China's People's Liberation Army, ignoring the concerns of the military brass, who feared that the transaction could compromise national security. Labaton, 'Democrat Seeks Inquiry'. In 1997 he had told *The Washington Post* that China was 'laying the foundations for an aggressive claim to pre-eminence in the Pacific', which, he emphasised, was 'a catastrophe for all of us, and could foreshadow a Cold War as bad as the last'. Quoted in Shafer, 'Richard Perle Libel Watch'. He also joined anti-China hawks to sign a PNAC–Heritage Foundation statement calling for the defence of Taiwan against China. Feulner, et al., 'Statement on the Defense of Taiwan'.

96 Labaton, 'Democrat Seeks Inquiry'; Lobe, 'Perle: "Prince of Darkness" in the Spotlight'.

97 According to Woolsey, INC was the DPB's primary source of information. 'A lot of what is useful with respect to what's going on in Iraq is coming from defectors', who according to Woolsey, 'have often come through an organization [the INC] that neither State nor the CIA likes very much'. Quoted in Dreyfuss, 'The Pentagon Muzzles the CIA'.

98 Andrew Cockburn, *Rumsfeld*, pp. 146–7; Another post-September 11 coup was for Cheney–Rumsfeld to wrest Middle East policy away from the State Department and White House to the Pentagon and OVP, with Wolfowitz, Feith and Libby granted a seat at the

interagency discussions on the Middle East. Halper and Clarke, *America Alone*, p. 153.

99 Mann, *Rise of the Vulcans*, pp. 77–82; 'Paul Wolfowitz, Velociraptor'.

100 'Paul Wolfowitz, Velociraptor'.

101 Keller, 'The Sunshine Warrior'.

102 Woodward, *Bush at War*, pp. 60–1.

103 Rice, *No Higher Honor*.

104 Woodward, *Plan of Attack*, pp. 21–2.

105 Woodward, *Bush at War*, p. 91.

106 Woodward, *Plan of Attack*, p. 25.

107 Tanenhaus, 'Bush's Brain Trust'. In the interview, Wolfowitz concurred with this assessment.

108 Kean, et al., 'The 9/11 Commission Report', pp. 335–6.

109 Page, 'Showdown with Saddam'.

110 Andrew Cockburn, *Rumsfeld*, p. 149.

111 R. A. Clarke, *Against All Enemies*, p. 95.

112 Dreyfuss, 'The Pentagon Muzzles the CIA'.

113 Lang, 'Drinking the Kool-Aid'.

114 Woodward, *State of Denial*, pp. 83–5. He adds: 'Asking a think tank if it would be willing to strategize for top policy-makers in a time of extraordinary crisis was like asking General Motors if they would be willing to sell a million more cars.' Ibid.

115 Clemons, 'Did Secret Wolfowitz Meeting Violate Federal Advisory Committee Act?'

116 Woodward, *State of Denial*, pp. 83–5. The group also included 'Bush's favourite columnist' Fareed Zakaria and journalist Robert Kaplan, though it appears their inclusion was more to give the initiative a fig leaf of legitimacy since Zakaria claims he only attended one brainstorming session and was not told a report would be published. Bosman, 'Secret Iraq Meeting'.

117 Woodward, *State of Denial*, p. 85.

118 Heilbrunn, *They Knew*, p. 200; Keller, 'The Sunshine Warrior'.

119 Curtiss, 'I. Lewis ("Scooter") Libby'.

120 David, 'The Apprentice'.

121 Unger, *Fall of the House of Bush*, pp. 199–200. See also Gellman, *Angler*, pp. 41–4.

122 Woodward, *Plan of Attack*, pp. 48–9. Libby also has relations with another DPB member, George Shultz, for whom he had served as a speech writer in the 1980s. Curtiss, 'I. Lewis ("Scooter") Libby'. See also Woodward, *Bush at War*, pp. 83–5.

123 Gellman, *Angler*, p. 44.

124 Woodward, *State of Denial*, pp. 456–7.

125 Bumiller and Eric Schmitt, 'On the Job and at Home'.

126 Nir, 'Libby Played Leading Role'.

127 Wheatcroft, 'A State Like No Other'.

128 Weisman, 'White House Is Pressing Israelis'.

129 Lobe, 'The Bush Doctrine in Embryo'.

130 Lang, 'Drinking the Kool-Aid'; David, 'The Apprentice'.

131 In between, Libby found time to pen *The Apprentice*, a 'sex shocker' with graphic descriptions of bestiality, paedophilia, necrophilia and incest. In 2002 when the book came out in paperback, Cheney threw a lavish party at his home. Collins, 'Scooter's Sex Shocker'.

132 Unger, *The Fall of the House of Bush*, p. 216n.

133 Tenet, *At the Center of the Storm*, p. 342.

134 Kirk, 'Bush's War'.

135 Tenet, *At the Center of the Storm*, p. 310.

136 Bamford, *A Pretext for War*, p. 336; Isikoff and Corn, *Hubris*, pp. 3–6; Unger, *Fall of the House of Bush*, p. 263; Borger, 'The Spies Who Pushed for War'.

137 Suskind, *The One Percent Doctrine*, pp. 189–91; Tenet, *At the Center of the Storm*, p. 302.

138 Borger, 'The Spies Who Pushed for War'; Hamburger and Wallstein, 'Cheney, CIA Long at Odds'.

139 Burrough, et al., 'The Path to War'.

140 Risen, *State of War*, pp. 72–3. On Wolfowitz's and other neoconservatives' history of liaising with Israeli intelligence see Green, 'Serving Two Flags'; Wedel, *Shadow Elite*, pp. 147–9.

141 Feith, *War and Decision*, pp. 26–7.

142 Isikoff and Korn, *Hubris*, p. 109. Feith would later reward his benefactors by hiring Richard Perle to his consultancy, International Advisors, Inc., and John Lehman's brother Chris to his OSP.

143 Bamford, *A Pretext for War*, pp. 287–90; Gellman, *Angler*, pp. 222–5.

144 Wilkerson, et al., 'An Oversight Hearing on Pre-War Intelligence'.

145 'As far as we're concerned we've been entirely successful,' he told *The Daily Telegraph*. 'That tyrant Saddam is gone and the Americans are in Baghdad. What was said before is not important.' 'We are heroes in error,' he declared. Fairweather and La Guardia, 'Chalabi Stands by Faulty Intelligence'; Michael Smith, 'Ministers Were Told'.

146 Uhler, '"Fixed" Intelligence'.

147 Risen, 'How Pair's Finding'.
148 Ibid.; Gellman, *Angler*, pp. 222–4.
149 Bamford, *A Pretext for War*, p. 289.
150 Dreyfuss and Vest, 'The Lie Factory'.
151 Schmitt and Shanker, 'A CIA Rival'.
152 Ibid.
153 Unger, *Fall of the House of Bush*, p. 250. In 2004, Wurmser was one of the people targeted by the FBI's counterintelligence investigators in their probe into the espionage case involving Israel and AIPAC. According to *The Washington Post*, agents asked current and former officials whether 'certain people', including Perle and Wurmser, 'would spy for Israel and pass secret information'. Wright and Eggen, 'Leak Inquiry Includes Iran Experts'.
154 Bamford, *A Pretext for War*, p. 289. This story appears more complicated. El-Hage, according to James Risen of *The New York Times*, was being used by the Iraqi government as a conduit for relaying its list of concessions to the Bush Administration in order to avert war. It is not clear, however, whether this offer was ever relayed to the principals. Risen, 'Iraq Said to Have Tried to Reach Last-Minute Deal'.
155 Risen, 'How Pair's Finding'.
156 Waas, 'Key Bush Intelligence Briefing Kept From Hill Panel'.
157 Andrew Cockburn, *Rumsfeld*, p. 151.
158 Wilkerson, Pillar, et al., 'An Oversight Hearing on Pre-War Intelligence.
159 Gellman, *Angler*; Nichols, *Dick*; Senator Chuck Hagel, a Nebraska Republican on the Foreign Relations Committee, describes Cheney's powers: 'This is a vice president who's a prime minister, a senior counsellor, a chief of staff, whatever he wants to be.' Quoted in Bumiller and Schmitt, 'On the Job and at Home'. In 2000, when Bush tasked Cheney with selecting his running mate, he proposed himself. Woodward, *State of Denial*, p. xiii.
160 Lobe, 'Cheney as Extremist'.
161 Gellman, *Angler*. Cheney has amassed so much power that some joke George W. Bush is 'a heartbeat away from the presidency'. Dreyfuss, 'Vice Squad'.
162 Cheney, who keeps a 'man-size' safe in his office, also had the satellite image of his home blurred on Google Earth. See Gellman and Becker, '"A Different Understanding With the President"' in *The Washington Post* series on Cheney, <http://blog.washingtonpost.com/cheney/>.

163 Gellman, *Angler*. Addington has been a Cheney sidekick since the 1980s. In 2002, he helped draft the 'torture memos', which said that the president has the authority to sidestep the Geneva Conventions in the 'war on terror'. He also led efforts to undermine Congress's attempt to draft stringent rules governing the treatment of detainees. He played a key role in blocking the release of essential documents to the Senate Intelligence Committee regarding its investigation into pre-war intelligence, and to the General Accounting Office investigating Cheney's energy plan. His disdain for due process is also noted within the administration: according to Powell, Addington 'doesn't care about the Constitution'. According to Jane Mayer, Addington's 'New Paradigm' rests 'on a reading of the Constitution that few legal scholars share – namely, that the president, as commander-in-chief, has the authority to disregard virtually all previously known legal boundaries, if national security demands it'. According to one former administration lawyer, the administration's legal positions were, to a remarkable degree, 'all Addington'. All quotes from Mayer, 'The Hidden Power'. See also Mayer, *Dark Side*. For an analysis of this legal exceptionalism and its historical precedents see Levinson, 'Preserving Constitutional Norms'; Levinson, 'Torture in Iraq'.
164 Quoted in Dreyfuss, 'Vice Squad'.
165 Ibid.
166 Unger, *Fall of the House of Bush*, p. 250.
167 Suskind, *The One Percent Doctrine*, pp. 25–6.
168 Unger, *Fall of the House of Bush*, p. 250.
169 Jeffrey Goldberg, 'Breaking Ranks'. Already in the first Bush presidency, James Baker had warned Bush to watch out for the 'kooks' working under Cheney. See Unger, *Fall of the House of Bush*, p. 117.
170 Hersh, 'Watching Lebanon'.
171 Mann, *Rise of the Vulcans*, p. 192.
172 Unger, *Fall of the House of Bush*, pp. 182–3.
173 Mann, *Rise of the Vulcans*, pp. 270, 273–4; Gellman, *Angler*, pp. 36–40.
174 Unger, *Fall of the House of Bush*, pp. 187–8.
175 Lobe, 'Cheney as Extremist'.
176 Unger, 'How Cheney Took Control'.
177 Schmitt, 'Cheney Assembles Formidable Team'.
178 Dreyfuss, 'Vice Squad'.

179 Blumenthal, *Rise of Counter-establishment*, pp. ix–xviii.

180 Woodward, *Plan of Attack*, p. 292.

181 Dreyfuss, 'Vice Squad'. Others in Cheney's orbit included Eric Edelman, who would later replace Feith at the Pentagon. In between the two jobs he served as an ambassador to Turkey, where he earned the distinction, according to Turkish columnist Ibrahim Karagul, of becoming the 'least-liked and trusted American ambassador in Turkish history' for acting 'like a colonial governor'. Quoted in Singh, 'U.S.–Turkish Relations Go Wobbly'. Aaron Friedberg, another deputy national security adviser, is a PNAC signatory and a China expert who contributed a chapter to *Present Dangers*. According to Dreyfuss, Stephen Yates and Samantha Ravich formed the fulcrum of Cheney's foreign policy outlook which linked 'energy, China, Iraq, Israel, and oil in the Middle East'. Ravich would play a crucial role in promoting the war and serving as a liaison to the Iraqi opposition. Edelman was replaced by Victoria Nuland, who is married to PNAC co-founder Robert Kagan. Her brother-in-law Frederick Kagan would later author the administration's 'Surge' policy.

182 Gellman, *Angler*, pp. 189, 376–7; Isikoff and Corn, *Hubris*, p. 5.

183 Quoted in Dreyfuss, 'Vice Squad'.

184 These also included Robert Joseph at the NSC and some staffers at the CIA's WINPAC (the arms control shop). See Dreyfuss, 'Vice Squad'.

185 Hamburger and Wallstein, 'Cheney, CIA Long at Odds'.

186 Risen, *State of War*; Hersh, *Chain of Command*, pp. 177–8.

187 Unger, *Fall of the House of Bush*, p. 250.

188 Hersh, *Chain of Command*, p. 178.

189 *The New Republic* quoted in Mearsheimer and Walt, *The Israel Lobby*, p. 167.

190 Lobe, 'Bush's Trusty New Mideast Point Man'.

191 Lobe, 'Pentagon Office Home to Neo-Con Network'.

192 Bruck, 'Back Roads'.

193 Kaiser, 'Bush and Sharon'.

194 Bruck, 'Back Roads'; Guttman, 'From Clemency to a Senior Post'. His new responsibilities included the Israel–Palestine conflict and he would go on to use his base at the NSC to change long-standing US policy on issues such as the 'Jerusalem Law'; to derail the so-called 'roadmap' being pursued by the Quartet; to back a coup attempt against the elected government; and to undermine future

attempts at peacemaking by the Saudi king and later by Rice. Mearsheimer and Walt, *The Israel Lobby*, p. 224; Lobe, 'Bush's Trusty New Point Man'.

195 Quoted in Lobe, 'Bush's Trusty New Point Man'.
196 Quoted in ibid.
197 Quoted in Bruck, 'Back Roads'.
198 Ritter, 'Dinner with Ahmed'.
199 Zamora, 'N. M. Tech, SAIC to Sign Agreement'.
200 Barstow, 'Behind TV Analysts'.
201 In 2006 he was awarded the annual 'Defender of Israel Award' by ZOA for undermining the 'Zionism is Racism' declaration at the United Nations Anti-Racism conference in Durban, South Africa. Senate staffers investigating Bolton also found that he prevented from reaching Powell's desk a State Department memo accusing Israel of violating US arms-export laws prohibiting the 'non-defensive' use of US-supplied weapons. In 2005 when Bush's appointment of Bolton as the ambassador to the UN met resistance in Congress, the Israel lobby pushed hard on his behalf. In May 2006, the Israeli ambassador to the UN jokingly described Bolton as 'a secret member of Israel's own team at the United Nations'. We 'really are not just five diplomats,' he added. 'We are at least six including John Bolton.' Quoted in Mearsheimer and Walt, *The Israel Lobby*, p. 240. Bolton is also a long-time activist with the right wing Federalist Society. Bolton also has admirers among Christian Zionists: the late, notoriously racist Senator Jesse Helms, who had helped Bolton's entry to the Reagan Administration, told an AEI gathering that Bolton 'is the kind of man with whom I would want to stand at Armageddon.' Barry, 'Israel's Man at the UN'.
202 'UNSCOM "Infiltrated by Spies"'.
203 Bustani subsequently challenged the decision and was vindicated by International Labour Organisation Tribunal. Bolton would later also try to oust Muhammad ElBaradei, the head of IAEA, for refusing to declare Iran in breach of its treaty obligations.
204 Williams, 'John Bolton in Jerusalem'; Williams, 'John Bolton's Greatest Hits'.
205 Linzer, 'Bolton Often Blocked Information'.
206 Dreyfuss, 'The Commissar's in Town'.
207 According to one former deputy assistant secretary at NEA, the bureau was offered the choice of either Elizabeth Cheney or Danielle Pletka, the hard-line neoconservative vice president of AEI. Not keen on either, Powell ultimately settled for the lesser of

the two evils. Dreyfuss, 'The Commissar's in Town'.

208 Ibid. After the war, Elizabeth Cheney would work closely with Hannah and Wurmser, in an initiative brokered by Wurmser's wife Meyrav, to shore up Syrian exile Farid Ghadry (described by some as Chalabi's 'mini-me', Ghadry has close ties to the Israel lobby) for possible regime change in Syria. Cheney, who oversaw the State Department's 'freedom' and 'democracy promotion' initiative, secured millions in dollars to bolster the opposition groups in both Syria and Iran.

209 Quoted in Dreyfuss, 'The Pentagon Muzzles the CIA'.

210 Quoted in Dreyfuss, 'The Commissar's in Town'.

211 Suskind, *The One Percent Doctrine*, p. 62.

212 Woodward, *Plan of Attack*, p. 292.

Chapter 5

1 Andrew Cockburn, *Rumsfeld*, p. 167.

2 Jeffrey Goldberg, 'The Great Terror'.

3 Trilling, 'Fighting Word'.

4 Cockburn and St. Clair, *End Times*, pp. 217–19; Burke, 'The Missing Link'.

5 Jeffrey Goldberg, 'Should the US Invade Iraq?'

6 K. Silverstein, 'Goldberg's War'.

7 Jeffrey Goldberg, 'The Unknown'. For a critique of Goldberg see Ackerman, 'Fast and Loose with the Facts'.

8 Pollack, 'Next Stop Iraq?'

9 Pollack, *The Threatening Storm*.

10 It makes 'the best case possible for an invasion of Iraq'. Matlock, 'Deterring the Undeterrable'. It makes 'the best and strongest case that can be made for invading Iraq'. Bernstein, 'Making a Case'.

11 Keller, 'The I-Can't-Believe-I'm-a-Hawk Club'.

12 For a comprehensive critique see Friel and Falk, *The Record of the Paper*, pp. 47–50.

13 Pollack, 'Why Iraq Can't Be Deterred'; Pollack and Indyk, 'How Bush Can Avoid'; Pollack, 'A Last Chance to Stop Iraq'. See also Friel and Falk, *Record of the Paper*, p. 49; Massing, 'The War Expert'.

14 He misidentified the play as *Henry V*. The actual quote from *Julius Caesar* (III, i, 273) is 'Cry havoc and let slip the dogs of war!' ABC was so taken with Koppel's erudition that it would repeat the

segment on various occasions in its coverage. Other sources were likewise struck with admiration. *Voice of America*, 8 April 2003 (VOA also misidentified the play).

15 Pollack, 'Saddam's Bombs?'

16 Pollack and O'Hanlon, 'A War We Just Might Win'.

17 Powell focused on the need to acquire UN authorisation, but the intention was clear: he knew the UN would not approve. See Woodward, *Plan of Attack*, pp. 332–3; Feith, *War and Decision*, pp. 221–3.

18 Woodward, *Plan of Attack*, p. 344. In his memoir, Cheney does not mention Powell, but insists that he 'became concerned' that Rice and Blair were pushing the president towards following a UN track. Cheney, *In My Time*.

19 Woodward, *Plan of Attack*, p. 164.

20 Suskind, *The One Percent Doctrine*, p. 168; Tenet, *At the Center of the Storm*, pp. 315–16.

21 Bush writes: '[Cheney] made it sound like my decision had been made. But I was still considering my options. I asked Condi [Rice] to make clear to Dick [Cheney] that he had gotten out in front of my position.' Bush, *Decision Points*, p. 91.

22 Woodward, *Plan of Attack*, p. 163; DeYoung, *Soldier*, pp. 407–8.

23 Polls from before and after the war aggregated in AEI's 'Public Opinion on the War with Iraq'.

24 Ironically, Carney was later elected to Congress in the 2006 mid-term election; and though he ran as a Democrat, his fund-raising effort was assisted by Richard Perle; and first to congratulate him was Douglas Feith. Carney ended an interview with *The New York Times* after the election thus: 'Let's win the war first, then maybe look at how we got into it.' Quoted in Risen, 'A New House Democrat'.

25 Tenet, *At the Center of the Storm*, pp. 347–8. In a curious defence of her role, Shelton insisted that there was indeed a link between Iraq and Al-Qaeda and that the title of her presentation was actually *Assessing the Relationship Between Iraq and al-Qa'ida*. Shelton, 'Iraq, Al-Qaeda, and Tenet's Equivocation'.

26 Bamford, *A Pretext for War*, p. 317.

27 Tenet, *At the Center of the Storm*, p. 348.

28 G. Miller, 'Special Pentagon Unit'.

29 'Interview with Vice President Dick Cheney'.

30 The letter is signed by CIA Deputy Director John McLaughlin for George Tenet. Shelton, 'Iraq, Al-Qaeda, and Tenet's Equivocation'.

31 Although the Senate Select Committee on Intelligence report places the date OSP went into operation as October 2002, according to Lt Col Karen Kwiatkowski, it had been in operation since at least August 2002. Kwaitkowski, 'The New Pentagon Papers'.

32 Woodward, *Plan of Attack*, p. 292.

33 DeYoung, *Soldier*, pp. 356, 388.

34 Hersh, *Chain of Command*, p. 207.

35 Lang, 'Drinking the Kool-Aid'.

36 Hersh, *Chain of Command*, pp. 215, 227–8.

37 Quoted in Borger, 'The Spies Who Pushed for War'. See also Lang, 'Drinking the Kool-Aid'; Suskind, *The One Percent Doctrine*, p. 189; Unger, *Fall of the House of Bush*, p. 263.

38 Scheer, et al., *The Five Biggest Lies*, p. 18; Hersh, *Chain of Command*, p. 224.

39 Quoted in Porter, 'Burnt Offering'. See also Dreyfuss and Vest, 'Lie Factory'.

40 Unger, *Fall of the House of Bush*, p. 200.

41 Lang, 'Drinking the Kool-Aid'.

42 Kwaitkowski quoted in ibid.

43 Quoted in Lang, 'Drinking the Kool-Aid'. The confirmation for this came from Cheney himself, who told the *Rocky Mountain News* that the best source for the Saddam–Al-Qaeda link was an article in *The Weekly Standard*, which instead was based on a leaked fifty-point memo sent by Feith to the Senate Select Committee on Intelligence on 27 October 2003 making the case. See Hayes, 'The U.S. Government's Secret Memo'.

44 Kwaitkowski, 'The New Pentagon Papers'. See for example Krauthammer, 'We Can't Blow it Again'; Krauthammer, 'The Obsolescence of Deterrence'.

45 Lobe, 'Pentagon Office'.

46 Kwaitkowski, 'The New Pentagon Papers'; Lang, 'Drinking the Kool-Aid'.

47 Schulman, 'Meet the "Whack Iran" Lobby'.

48 The book was promoted by fellow neoconservative Eliot A. Cohen with a laudatory review in *Foreign Affairs* in which he wrote that it was '[s]imply the best primer on intelligence now and for some time to come.' E. A. Cohen, 'Silent Warfare'.

49 Schmitt and Shulsky, 'Leo Strauss and the World of Intelligence'.

50 Following the invasion, Rubin would continue his propaganda efforts as a member of the Coalition Provisional Authority in Iraq. According to Juan Cole, 'The Pentagon hired the Lincoln

Group which in turn deployed secret agents for someone like Michael Rubin of AEI to manufacture sermons and other material and attribute them to Iraqis. So then the analysts read Rubin in Arabic translation and report him back to their bosses as Iraqi public opinion! Then Rubin defended this sort of thing to the NYT without revealing his links to Lincoln.' J. Cole, 'McCain'.

51 Based on his subsequent reaction, Rozen and Vest speculate that classified documents may have been passed with Rubin's consent to help enlist the support of AIPAC to push an anti-Iran policy on a hesitant administration. Rozen and Vest, 'Cloak and Swagger'.

52 Recognising that Franklin could 'serve as a useful spy', Bamford writes, AIPAC officials had earlier plotted 'to plant him in the White House – specifically in the National Security Council, the epicenter of intelligence and national-security policy'. Bamford, 'Iran: the Next War'.

53 Borger, 'The Spies Who Pushed for War'

54 Other lesser appointees included Chris Straub, a former Senate Intelligence Committee staffer; Yousef Aboul-Enein, an Egyptian-born naval officer tasked with poring over Arabic media and CIA transcripts of radio broadcasts to find evidence linking Al-Qaeda and Saddam Hussein; a DIA officer named John Trigilio; Kevin Jones, an Air Force officer; and Ladan Archin, an Iranian-American protégé of Paul Wolfowitz. Lobe, 'Pentagon Office'; Herman, 'A Whole New Ballgame Overseas'; Kwaitkowski, 'The New Pentagon Papers'

55 Kwaitkowski, 'The New Pentagon Papers'; Lang, 'Drinking the Kool-Aid'; Borger, 'The Spies Who Pushed for War'.

56 Borger, 'The Spies Who Pushed for War'.

57 The operation continued well after the invasion. Months into the occupation of Iraq, a story was floated by 'unnamed senior US officials' suggesting that the reason no WMDs were discovered in Iraq was that they had been smuggled to Syria ahead of invasion. The source, once again, was the Israeli prime minister's intelligence unit. Ibid.; Lobe, 'Pentagon Office'.

58 Dreyfuss, 'The Pentagon Muzzles the CIA'; Mayer, 'The Manipulator'.

59 Dreyfuss, 'The Pentagon Muzzles the CIA'.

60 Harding, 'Germans accuse US'; Vest, 'Big Lies, Blind Spies, and Vanity Fair'.

61 Kwaitkowski, 'The New Pentagon Papers'.

62 Hersh, *Chain of Command*, p. 177; Dreyfuss and Vest, 'Lie Factory';

Porter, 'Burnt Offering'; Kwaitkowski, 'The New Pentagon Papers'. One key supporter of the OSP was Roy Godson, the head of the Consortium for the Study of Intelligence, a long-time colleague of Shulsky, and brother of British neoconservative Dean Godson, who runs the far-right Policy Exchange. He told *The American Prospect* he hoped the OSP 'might turn out to be a David' against CIA's 'Goliath'. Quoted in Dreyfuss, 'The Pentagon Muzzles the CIA'.

63   Suskind, *The Way of the World*, pp. 371–80; Giraldi, 'Suskind Revisited'; Suskind and Goodman, 'The Way of the World'. Following the US invasion, sources told investigative journalist Larisa Alexandrovna that the OSP tried to solve the problem of the non-existent WMDs through an 'off-book' operation, deploying 'several extra-legal and unapproved task force missions prior to and after combat operations began'. Alexandrovna, 'Secretive Military Unit'. The four- to five-man team operated from summer through the autumn of 2003 interviewing former Iraqi intelligence officers, encouraging them to help the US, embarrassed by the absence of Iraqi WMDs. The claims were also corroborated by one of Scott Ritter's Iraqi sources, who was asked by a Pentagon intelligence unit (most likely the aforementioned OSP operation) if he could assist with planting WMDs to help the president, who was 'in trouble'. Ritter, 'Where Are the Weapons of Mass Destruction?'

64   Lobe, 'Pentagon Office'.

65   Quoted in Unger, *Fall of the House of Bush*, p. 231.

66   Edsall and Milbank, 'White House's Roving Eye for Politics'.

67   Feith, *War and Decision*, p. 29.

68   Bamford, *A Pretext for War*, p. 415.

69   Ibid.; Unger, *Fall of the House of Bush*, pp. 232–6.

70   First, to derail Jimmy Carter's presidential bid by placing defamatory articles about his brother's connections to the PLO, and then to allege that the KGB was behind the assassination attempt on Pope John Paul II. The story was soon discredited. Herman and Chomsky, *Manufacturing Consent*, pp. 133–56.

71   Unger, 'The War They Wanted'; Parsi, *Treacherous Alliance*, pp. 116–26; Tyler, *A World of Trouble*, pp. 321–5.

72   Senate Select Committee on Intelligence, 'Report on Intelligence Activities Relating to Iraq', p. 4.

73   Unger, 'The War They Wanted'.

74   Whitaker, 'Conflict and Catchphrases'.

75   Bumiller, 'Bush Aides Set Strategy'; Rampton and Stauber, *Weapons of Mass Deception*, p. 37.

76   Gellman and Pincus, 'Depiction of Threat Outgrew Supporting Evidence'.
77   Isikoff and Corn, *Hubris*, p. 35.
78   Bamford, *A Pretext for War*, p. 325.
79   Miller and Gordon, 'U.S. Says Saddam Hussein Intensifies Quest'.
80   Isikoff and Corn, *Hubris*, p. 35.
81   Said, 'A Devil Theory of Islam'; Said, *Covering Islam*.
82   Jackson, 'Miller's Latest Tale Questioned'.
83   Both writers are represented by the same publicist: neoconservatives favourite Benador Associates. The book also got a boost from Bernard Lewis's glowing review in *The New York Review of Books*. Lewis, 'At Stake in the Gulf'.
84   Quoted in Kurtz, 'Intra-Times Battle over Iraqi Weapons'.
85   Bamford, 'The Man Who Sold the War'.
86   J. Miller, 'Iraqi Tells of Renovations'.
87   Miller and Gordon, 'White House Lists Iraq Steps'.
88   J. Miller, 'Verification Is Difficult at Best'.
89   J. Miller, 'CIA Hunts Iraq Tie to Soviet Smallpox'.
90   J. Miller, 'Defectors Bolster US Case against Iraq'.
91   J. Miller, 'Illicit Arms Kept Till Eve of War'.
92   For more on Miller's journalistic malpractices see Massing, 'Now They Tell Us'; Friel and Falk, *Record of the Paper*, pp. 104–20; Shafer, 'The Times Scoops that Melted'; R. Baker, '"Scoops" and Truth at the Times'; Layton, 'Miller Brouhaha'; MacArthur, 'The Lies We Bought'.
93   The paper's position in this regard is telling: unlike Miller, Gordon or Thomas Friedman, who suffered no consequences for their public advocacy in support of the war, veteran Middle East correspondent Chris Hedges was formally reprimanded by the paper after he made an anti-war speech two weeks into the war. 'Media Matters with Bob McChesney'.
94   Lewis and Reading-Smith 'Iraq: The War Card'.
95   Dreyfuss, 'The Pentagon Muzzles the CIA'; Risen, *State of War*, pp. 11–12, 17, 20.
96   Risen, *State of War*, p. 20.
97   Ibid. pp. 20, 62–8; S. Blumenthal, 'Bush's War on Professionals'. For one CIA official, Tenet 'was a pussy,' who 'just wanted people to like him'. For another, Tenet was 'a cheer leader, not a leader'. Risen, *State of War*, pp. 66–7.
98   Risen, *State of War*, p. 69.
99   Ibid. p. 71–3.

100 Schmitt and Shanker, 'A CIA Rival'.
101 Quoted in Dreyfuss, 'The Pentagon Muzzles the CIA'.
102 Quoted in ibid.
103 Risen, *State of War*, pp. 109, 110–11.
104 Ibid. pp. 87, 112.
105 Indeed, Paul Pillar, the national intelligence officer for the Near East and South Asia from 2000–5, has revealed that the first request his office received from any administration policy maker for any intelligence assessment on any aspect of Iraq was a year into the war. Senate Democratic Policy Committee Hearing, 26 June 2006.
106 Bob Graham, 'What I Knew Before'.
107 McGovern, 'A Disingenuous Tour de Force'; Gumbel, 'Case for War Confected'.
108 Quoted in Kirk, 'Bush's War'.
109 Ibid.
110 Suskind, *The One Percent Doctrine*, p. 173.
111 Graham, 'What I Knew Before'. See also Unger, *Fall of the House of Bush*, p. 266.
112 'Iraq's Continuing Programs'.
113 Bob Graham, 'What I Knew Before'. See also Isikoff and Corn, *Hubris*, pp. 138–9; 'CIA Whites out Controversial Estimate'.
114 Interviewed in Kirk, 'Bush's War'. See also Isikoff and Corn, *Hubris*, pp. 139–40.
115 Wilkerson, et al., 'An Oversight Hearing on Pre-War Intelligence'. See also Pillar, 'Intelligence, Policy, and the War in Iraq'.
116 Tenet, *At the Center of the Storm*; Prados, 'PR Push for Iraq War'.
117 Priest, 'Congressional Oversight of Intelligence Criticized'; Raju, et al., 'Few Senators Read Iraq NIE Report'.
118 Isikoff and Corn, *Hubris*, p. 137.
119 Suskind, *The Way of the World*, p. 179.
120 S. Blumenthal, 'Bush Knew'.
121 Drumheller, *On the Brink*; Suskind, *The Way of the World*, pp. 180–1.
122 Quoted in Suskind, *The Way of the World*, p. 181.
123 Ibid.
124 Ibid. pp. 181–2.
125 Risen, *State of War*, p. 88.
126 Ibid. p. 90.
127 Ibid. p. 106.
128 Ibid. p. 107. Charmelot, 'The CIA Operation'.

129 Suskind, *The Way of the World*, p. 364.
130 Quoted in ibid. p. 366.
131 Ibid. p. 366.
132 S. Blumenthal, 'Bush's War on Professionals'.
133 Suskind, *The Way of the World*, pp. 366–9.
134 Borger, Whitaker and Dodd, 'Saddam's Desperate Offers'.
135 Ibid.
136 Suskind, *The Way of the World*, pp. 362–6; Bamford, *A Pretext for War*, p. 289; Borger, Whitaker and Dodd, 'Saddam's Desperate Offers'.
137 Maalouf's Pentagon security clearance would later be revoked over his ties to el-Hage, who was under federal investigation for arms trafficking. Bamford, *A Pretext for War*, p. 289.
138 Borger, Whitaker and Dodd, 'Saddam's Desperate Offers'. The final attempt, made in early April as the war was already under-way, floundered when a proposed meeting between Habbush and former CIA official Robert Baer was pre-empted by the fall of Baghdad. The proposal this time included 'a promise to hold free elections supervised by France and the US'. On 9 April, six precision-guided bombs obliterated the house in which the meeting was to take place in two days. Ibid.
139 Landay, 'Bush Gets Intelligence Data'.
140 Ibid.
141 McLaughlin and Tenet, 'DCI Memo'.
142 Woodward, *Plan of Attack*, p. 249. In his memoir, Tenet offers a novel defence: he avers he did not suggest that the case against Iraq would be a 'slam dunk', but rather selling it to the US public would be so. Tenet, *At the Center of the Storm*.
143 Woodward, *Plan of Attack*, pp. 269–73.
144 Ibid. pp. 288–92.
145 Unger, *Fall of the House of Bush*, pp. 275–6.
146 Quoted in Woodward, *Plan of Attack*, p. 291.
147 Ibid.
148 Burrough, et al., 'The Path to War'.
149 Woodward, *Plan of Attack*, p. 292. See also Drogin, *Curveball*, p. 152.
150 Unger, *Fall of the House of Bush*, p. 278.
151 'Fact Sheet'; Thomas, et al., 'Where Are Iraq's WMDs?'.
152 Bolton was considerably less forgiving towards his own subordi-nates: he tried to oust Rexon Ryu – a young career official who had been instrumental in getting the most controversial allegations

out of Powell's UN speech – accusing him of insubordination. Carl Ford, Jr., the former assistant secretary of state for intelligence and research, has described Bolton as a 'kiss-up, kick-down sort of guy' and a 'serial abuser' of analysts who disagreed with him. Wayne White, the former deputy director, mentioned Bolton's 'harassment of a friend, Bureau of Intelligence & Research (INR) analyst Christian Westermann' as an example of the attempt by administration officials to ensure conformity. Greg Thielmann, who was detailed as the daily intelligence liaison to Bolton, told Seymour Hersh, 'Bolton seemed to be troubled because INR was not telling him what he wanted to hear.' Thielmann found himself shut out of Bolton's early-morning staff meetings as a consequence because, he was told, the undersecretary wants to 'keep this in the family'. Bolton instead demanded and acquired direct access to raw intelligence, thus bypassing the checks and balances of the intelligence services. See Hersh, *Chain of Command*, pp. 222–3.

153 Drogin, *Curveball*, p. 151; Woodward, *Plan of Attack*, pp. 288–92. Subsequent to Powell's UN speech, Tenet would once more have to intervene to prevent Cheney from repeating the allegation. Woodward, *State of Denial*, p. 135.

154 Quoted in Unger, *Fall of the House of Bush*, p. 280.

155 Unger, 'The War They Wanted'.

156 Ibid.; Tenet, *At the Center of the Storm*, pp. 449–50.

157 Gellman and Linzer, 'A "Concerted Effort"'.

158 Unger, *Fall of the House of Bush*, pp. 269–71. See also Milbank and Pincus, 'Bush Aides Disclose Warnings from CIA'.

159 Milbank and Pincus, 'Bush Aides Disclose Warnings from CIA'. See also McClellan, *What Happened*, p. 177.

160 Erich Follath, John Goetz, Marcel Rosenbach, and Holger Stark, 'The Real Story of 'Curveball': How German Intelligence Helped Justify the US Invasion of Iraq,' *Der Spiegel*, 22 March 2008.

161 Isikoff and Corn, *Hubris*, p. 179.

162 Quoted in Thomas, et al., 'Where Are Iraq's WMDs?'

163 Drogin, *Curveball*, pp. 148, 154–5, 158.

164 Risen, *State of War*; Woodward, *State of Denial*, p. 216.

165 Drogin, *Curveball*; Drumheller, *On the Brink*.

166 Drogin, *Curveball*.

167 In 2006, Wippl was relieved from that position as well. Suskind, *The Way of the World*, pp. 176–9.

168 Ibid. pp. 141–50.

169 Ibid. p. 156.

170 Risen, *State of War*, pp. 115–19; Drumheller, *On the Brink*; Follath, et al., 'The Real Story of "Curveball"'.
171 Quoted in Burrough, et al., 'The Path to War'.
172 DeYoung, *Soldier*, p. 442; Woodward, *Plan of Attack*, p. 291.
173 Drogin, *Curveball*, p. 159; Unger, *Fall of the House of Bush*, p. 286.
174 Drogin, *Curveball*, p. 159.
175 The Bush Administration responded by dispatching John Wolf, an assistant secretary of state, to confront Blix in his UN office with information obtained through US surveillance about Blix and his team's work. 'I resented that,' Blix later told *Vanity Fair*. Quoted in Burrough, et al., 'The Path to War'. But the attempts to vilify the inspectors did not abate. The Murdoch press chimed in with *The Times* (London) running a headline suggesting Blix should turn the smoking gun on his own head.
176 Perle, 'Take Out Saddam'.
177 Dreyfuss, 'Just the Beginning'.
178 Unger, *Fall of the House of Bush*, pp. 289–90.
179 Ricks, *Fiasco*, p. 97.
180 Ibid. p. 97.
181 Burrough, et al., 'The Path to War'.
182 Schieffer, 'Interview with Condoleezza Rice'.
183 Beaumont, et al., 'Revealed: US Dirty Tricks'.
184 Woodward, *Plan of Attack*, pp. 357–63.
185 Brzezinski, 'Terrorized by "War on Terror"'.
186 Kuttner, 'Neo-Cons Have Hijacked US Foreign Policy'; Gellman, *Angler*, pp. 227–32.
187 Gellman, *Angler*, pp. 227–32.
188 Ibid. pp. 231–2.
189 John Simpson, 'How Predictions for Iraq Came True,' *BBC News*, 9 April 2006.
190 Roy, 'Europe Won't Be Fooled Again'.
191 Ibid.

Conclusions

1 Rice, 'Campaign 2000'.
2 Indeed Bush's evangelical Christian beliefs disposed him favourably enough towards Israel to repeatedly state that he would intervene militarily should its existence be at stake. See Nir, 'Groups to Bush'.

3   Bruce Fein, a former neoconservative and an associate deputy
     attorney general in the Reagan Justice Department, argues that
     the notion of US exceptionalism is itself a political construct
     which was explicitly rejected by the founding fathers of the US
     in Federalist Nos 10, 51 and 75. Moreover, he notes, the US's
     chequered moral record at home in itself suffices to undermine any
     claims to moral superiority. Fein, 'American Exceptionalism'.
4   For a discussion of the political uses of the loaded binaries see
     Bacevich, *American Empire*, p. 8.
5   Wedel, *Shadow Elite*, pp. 1–2.
6   Though the Iraq war policy originated in the executive branch, it
     cannot be explained simply as a failure of constitutional checks
     and balances. The war happened with the full complicity of
     Congress, which is by no means subservient to the executive.
     Marginalised in times of crisis, Congress is frequently able to
     reassert once the crisis was over. It did so even after the Iraq
     fiasco, holding hearings and launching multiple inquiries. If it
     has failed to hold anyone to account, this has less to do with its
     capacity than its willingness to indict top officials. Under Barack
     Obama, the relationship between Congress and the executive has
     been adversarial, even where both houses have been dominated by
     the Democrats. Yet, the national security discourse has remained
     by and large identical to that of the Bush Administration. None
     of this is inexplicable if one refers back to Michael Mann's
     argument that politics is merely one of the three overlapping
     networks which constitute social power. Ideology and economics
     also matter. All played a part in defusing the potential resistance
     of Congress. The Congressional debate took place in the shadow
     of 9/11, and the war had the support of the Israel lobby. With
     an upcoming election in which the Republican political strate-
     gists were determined to play the national security card and the
     neoconservatives were eager to brand any hesitation on part of a
     Congressperson as a mark of cowardice or lack of patriotism, few
     could dissent.
7   Marx, *The 18th Brumaire*, p. 15.
8   Bourdieu, *Outline of a Theory of Practice*; Berger and Luckmann,
     The Social Construction of Reality; Giddens, *The Constitution of
     Society*.
9   Archer, *Realist Social Theory*.
10   Scott, *Power*, pp. 16–25.
11   Lukes, *Power*, ch. 1.

12 Carey, *Taking the Risk out of Democracy*, p. 90.
13 Laumann and Knoke, *The Organisational State*.
14 Mann, *The Sources of Social Power*, p. 1.

Appendix

1 Mearsheimer and Walt, *The Israel Lobby*, pp. 230–1,
2 Ibid. p. 253.
3 Slater, 'The Two Books'; Kovel, 'Mearsheimer and Walt Revisited'; Lieberman, '"Israel Lobby" and American Politics'; Bacevich, 'Review: The Israel Lobby'.
4 Mearsheimer and Walt, *The Israel Lobby*, p. 112.
5 Judt, 'In Defence of Academic Freedom'.
6 Tivnan, *The Lobby*, p. 13.
7 Ibid. pp. 23–4.
8 Ibid. pp. 26–8; Snetsinger, *Truman*, chs 9–12. Zionists in the US government had also ensured the appointment of James MacDonald, an ardent Zionist, as the US envoy, who coaxed the US government into delivering a guaranteed loan through the Import–Export Bank to David Ben-Gurion's Mapai Party in order to deny victory to the Leftist Mapam in Israel's first general elections. Cockburn and Cockburn, *Dangerous Liaison*, p. 30.
9 G. F. Smith, *Foreign Agents*; G. F. Smith, *America's Defense Line*; G. F. Smith, *Spy Trade*.
10 Dershowtiz, *Chutzpah*, p. 16.
11 Mearsheimer and Walt, *The Israel Lobby*, p. 6.
12 See for example Massing, 'The Storm over the Israel Lobby'.
13 J. J. Goldberg, *Jewish Power*, pp. xvi–xvii, 152–3; Tivnan, *The Lobby*, pp. 40–1.
14 J. J. Goldberg, *Jewish Power*, pp. 105, 125–8.
15 Tivnan, *The Lobby*; Alam, *Israeli Exceptionalism*, p. 225n12; Trice, 'Domestic Interest Groups and the Arab–Israeli Conflict', pp. 121–2.
16 Tivnan, *The Lobby*, p. 76.
17 Mearsheimer and Walt, *The Israel Lobby*, p. 120.
18 Mearsheimer and Walt, *The Israel Lobby*, ch. 4; Findley, *They Dare*; Tivnan, *The Lobby*; J. J. Goldberg, *Jewish Power*.
19 Tivnan, *The Lobby*, pp. 54–5.
20 'A Year after Iraq War'; 'Poll: Anti-Semitic Views'. For an

extended discussion of how definitions and statistics are manipulated to claim that there has been a resurgence of anti-Semitism see Finkelstein, *Beyond Chutzpah*, pp. 66–85.

21 Quoted in Judt, 'Amos Elon'. A similar view was also expressed by Abba Eban, who noted that 'one of the chief tasks of any dialogue with the Gentile world is to prove that the distinction between anti-Semitism and anti-Zionism is not a distinction at all'. Quoted in Chomsky, *Necessary Illusions*, p. 316.

22 Finkelstein, *The Holocaust Industry*; Novick, *The Holocaust in American Life*.

23 J. J. Goldberg, *Jewish Power*, p. xxi.

24 Ibid. pp. 30–1; Steven Windmueller, 'Are American Jews Becoming Republican?'

25 Helmreich, 'The Israel Swing Vote' (original emphasis).

26 Mearsheimer and Walt, *The Israel Lobby*, p. 140.

27 J. J. Goldberg, *Jewish Power*, pp. 62–3.

28 *US Religious Landscape Survey*.

29 Terry, *U.S. Foreign Policy*, pp. 10–12.

30 Jordan [Confidential File] (June 1977).

31 Edsall and Cooperman, 'GOP Uses Remarks to Court Jews'. According to journalist Glenn Frankel, 'Pro-Israel interests have contributed $56.8 million in individual, group and soft money donations to federal candidates and party committees since 1990. By contrast, Arab/Muslims contributed less than $800,000 during the same period.' Frankel, 'A Beautiful Friendship?'; Mearsheimer and Walt, *The Israel Lobby*, p. 157.

32 In 2010 this led to a notable dissent by Peter Beinart, one of the lobby's most influential young voices. Beinart, 'The Failure of the American Jewish Establishment'.

33 Tivnan, *The Lobby*.

34 A. Berman, 'AIPAC's Hold'.

35 Ibid.; Massing, 'The Israel Lobby'; Mearsheimer and Walt, *The Israel Lobby*, pp. 152–62.

36 Frankel, 'A Beautiful Friendship?' Income figures are from Israel's Central Bureau of Statistics for the year 2006. According to the CIA *World Fact Book*, Israel's GDP per capita for the year 2008 was $28,900.

37 J. J. Goldberg, *Jewish Power*, pp. 29–35; Mearsheimer and Walt, *The Israel Lobby*, pp. 163–4.

38 Mearsheimer and Walt, *The Israel Lobby*, pp. 156–60; Findley, *They Dare*, ch. 3; J. J. Goldberg, *Jewish Power*, pp. 269–71.

39 Hersh, *The Samson Option*, pp. 93, 96–7; Tivnan, *The Lobby*, ch. 2; Snetsinger, *Truman*; Tyler, *A World of Trouble*.

40 Tivnan, *The Lobby*, pp. 40–1; J. J. Goldberg, *Jewish Power*.

41 Rubenberg, *Israel and the American National Interest*, p. 207.

42 B. Smith, '76 Senators'; B. Smith, 'US Senators Press Obama'.

43 Tyler, *A World of Trouble*, pp. 58–9; Wawro, *Quicksand*, p. 218; Mearsheimer and Walt, *The Israel Lobby*; Tivnan, *The Lobby*.

44 Tivnan, *The Lobby*, p. 26.

45 Green, *Taking Sides*, p. 54. Lt Col Elliot A. Niles, who had previously served as a high official of the B'nai B'rith, was found by US Army Intelligence illegally providing Adjutant General's Office records of US military personnel to Zionist organisations for the identification of potential candidates for recruitment to the Haganah. For more on David Niles's Zionism and influence see McKinzie, 'Oral History Interview with Edwin M. Wright'.

46 Tivnan, *The Lobby*, pp. 26–7.

47 Beinin, 'The Israelization'; Bar-Yosef, 'The Jews Who Run Clinton's Court'.

48 Dreyfuss, 'The Freeman Affair'; B. Smith, 'Freeman Hits "Israel Lobby"'. According to the Israeli daily *Haaretz*, 'Every appointee to the American government must endure a thorough background check by the American Jewish community.' See Mozgovaya, 'American Jews'.

49 Mozgovaya, 'American Jews'.

50 Friel and Falk, *Israel–Palestine on Record*; Abunimah and Ibish, 'The US Media and the New Intifada'.

51 Alterman, 'Intractable Foes, Warring Narratives'.

52 Friel and Falk, *Israel–Palestine*; Abunimah and Ibish, 'The US Media'.

53 Jurkowitz, 'Blaming the Messenger'; Mearsheimer and Walt, *The Israel Lobby*, p. 173; J. J. Goldberg, *Jewish Power*, pp. 296–7; Fisk, 'The Internet Threat'; Jones, 'Pro-Israel Groups Take Aim'; Farago, 'Israel Backed by Army of Cyber Soldiers'. For an insight into the lobby's intimidation tactics see article by former AIPAC opposition researcher Gregory D. Slabodkin, 'The AIPAC Politics of Smear'.

54 Sorkin, 'Schlepping to Moguldom'.

55 Bruck, 'The Influencer'.

56 Ibid.

57 Roy, 'Intimidation'; Findley, *They Dare*, pp. 180–6.

58 Roy, 'Short Cuts'.

59 R. Silverstein, 'Pro-Israel Campaign'.

60 Roy, 'Short Cuts'.

61 Karni, 'Pro-Israel Group'; Jaschik, 'A Call to Defend'; Mearsheimer and Walt, *The Israel Lobby*, pp. 178–85; Findley, *They Dare*, pp. 310–11.

62 Pappe, 'Clusters of History'.

63 Alam, *Israeli Exceptionalism*, pp. 129–36.

64 Graham admired Israelis but looked less favourably upon Jews at home. In tapes released of his conversations with Nixon, Graham is heard saying: '[Jews] swarm around me and are friendly to me, because they know that I am friendly to Israel and so forth, but they don't know how I really feel about what they're doing to this country.' See Nixontapes.org.

65 Bonney, *False Prophets*, p. 116.

66 Ostling, et al., 'Religion'; J. C. Rosenberg, 'Ezekiel 38–39 FAQ'.

67 Bonney, *False Prophets*, p. 120.

68 Rosner, 'US Christians Create Umbrella Organization'.

69 Berkowitz, 'Christian Right Steps Up'.

70 Founded in 1843, B'nai B'rith (literally 'sons of the covenant') is the oldest Jewish service organisation. It founded the ADL in 1913. Siegel and Guttman, 'AIPAC Conference'; M. Blumenthal, 'AIPAC Cheers'; M. Blumenthal, 'Pastor Hagee'.

71 Mearsheimer and Walt, *The Israel Lobby*, pp. 178–9.

72 Mearsheimer and Walt, *The Israel Lobby*, pp. 138–9.

73 TBN is the world's largest religious network, co-founded by Paul and Jan Crouch, and Jim and Tammy Faye Bakker in 1973. In 2010, it was ranked the third-largest over-the-air station group in the US, with CBS, FOX and NBC holding the fourth, fifth and sixth place, according to *TV News Check* (Haim Saban's Univision ranked number 2). 'Top Station Groups Stay the Course'0.

74 Mearsheimer and Walt, *The Israel Lobby*, p. 139.

75 Indeed, Obama was able to lift a ban on gays openly serving in the military, a subject which provokes far more passions than Israel (Christian Zionists being a subset of the Christian Right). Both Bush Sr. and Clinton ignored Christian Zionist protestations to pursue a peace process aimed at some form of a two-state solution for the Israeli–Palestinian conflict.

76 The three Jewish defence agencies – the ADL, the American Jewish Committee and the American Jewish Congress – joined civil rights groups to defeat an amendment introduced by the powerful Senator Jesse Helms. J. J. Goldberg, *Jewish Power*, pp. 21–2.

77 Piterberg, *The Returns of Zionism*; Alam, *Israeli Exceptionalism*, pp. 31–7.
78 Quoted in Alam, *Israeli Exceptionalism*, p. 113.
79 Ibid. p. 150.
80 Kenen himself admits that among his adversaries were 'the State Department Arabists; the anti-Zionists – both Jews and non-Jews; the oil and defense lobbies, which had always influenced FDR; and the missionaries who regarded the Jews as interlopers'. Kenen, *All My Causes*, p. 66.
81 Cockburn and Cockburn, *Dangerous Liaison*, pp. 25–7; Snetsinger, *Truman*.
82 Memorandum of Conversation by Secretary of State, 12 May 1948, *Foreign Relations of the United States 1948*, p. 975.
83 Quoted in Alam, *Israeli Exceptionalism*, p. 162; Cockburn and Cockburn, *Dangerous Liaison*, p. 24.
84 Quoted in Alam, *Israeli Exceptionalism*, p. 163.
85 Quoted in ibid. p. 163.
86 A friend of the influential Supreme Court Justices Louis Brandeis and Felix Frankfurter, Acheson lamented that 'in urging Zionism as an American government policy they had allowed, so I thought, their emotion to obscure the totality of American interests'. Acheson, *Present at the Creation*, p. 169.
87 During his first official visit to the US in May 1951, David Ben-Gurion held a meeting with CIA Director Walter Bedell Smith and his deputies Allan Dulles and James Jesus Angleton in which he offered to enlist the Israeli spy agency in the service of the CIA. Cockburn and Cockburn, *Dangerous Liaison*, p. 41.
88 Hersh, *The Samson Option*, p. 22; Tyler, *A World of Trouble*, p. 37.
89 Green, *Taking Sides*, pp. 77–93; Cockburn and Cockburn, *Dangerous Liaison*, pp. 50–1. Ben-Gurion duly imputed an anti-Semitic motive to Dulles.
90 Tyler, *A World of Trouble*, p. 47.
91 Tal, 'Symbol Not Substance?', pp. 304–17.
92 Hersh, *The Samson Option*, p. 34; Tivnan, *The Lobby*, pp. 42–3.
93 Ball and Ball, *The Passionate Attachment*, pp. 47–8. An attempt by Republican Senate minority leader William Knowland to lobby Eisenhower's State Department drew this retort from Dulles: 'I am aware how almost impossible it is in this country to carry out a foreign policy not approved by the Jews. Marshall and Forrestal learned that. I am going to try to have one.'

94 Tivnan, *The Lobby*; Tyler, *A World of Trouble*.

95 Tivnan, *The Lobby*, pp. 52–3.

96 G. F. Smith, *America's Defense Line*, pp. 137–54; Hersh, *The Samson Option*, pp. 120–1; Cockburn and Cockburn, Dangerous Liaison, p. 91.

97 Ball and Ball, *The Passionate Attachment*, pp. 50–1; Hersh, *The Samson Option*, p. 110; Tal, 'Symbol Not Substance?', pp. 315–16; Tivnan, *The Lobby*, pp. 56–8; Cockburn and Cockburn, *Dangerous Liaison*, p. 126.

98 Hersh, *The Samson Option*, p. 114; Tivnan, *The Lobby*, pp. 57–8. Kennedy was also frustrated in his attempts to check Israel's nuclear ambitions. He would later complain to his friend Charles Bartlett that the 'Israeli sons of bitches lie to me constantly about their nuclear capability'. Quoted in Hersh, *The Samson Option*, p. 117.

99 Tivnan, *The Lobby*; G. F. Smith, *America's Defense Line*. In an interview about his stint in Kennedy's Defense Department, Paul Nitze would later relate how the Secretary of Defense Robert MacNamara was cowed by bullying from Abe Feinberg. See Hersh, *The Samson Option*, pp. 108–9.

100 Tivnan, pp. 59–60; Tyler, pp. 57–8, 64–6. Johnson's ambassador to Israel Walworth Barbour once explained to Deputy Chief of Mission William N. Dale: 'I'm here under orders from Johnson, who told me, "I don't care a thing about what happens to Israel, but your job is to keep the Jews off my back."' Quoted in Hersh, *The Samson Option*, p. 161.

101 Freeman, 'Is Israel a Strategic Asset or Liability?'

102 Tyler, *A World of Trouble*, pp. 65, 77.

103 Hersh, *The Samson Option*, p. 192. According to Hersh, Feinberg's cash was often delivered directly to Johnson's personal aide Walter W. Jenkins. The scale of these gifts has only become known because Jenkins was arrested on 16 October 1964 in the bathroom of a Washington YMCA on charges of homosexual solicitation and Johnson sent his aides Bill Moyers and Myer Feldman to clear up Jenkins's safe of potentially damaging material. Among other things, Moyers and Feldman found a briefcase from Feinberg containing $250,000 in cash. Ibid. p. 193.

104 Tyler, *A World of Trouble*, pp. 86, 94, 95. For a picture of the Israeli concerns about Muhieddin's visit see Oren, *Six Days of War*, pp. 145–60.

105 Tyler, pp. 63, 100–1. Johnson took pains to keep his close relationship with the Krims from the media. Ibid. p. 67.

106 Tyler, *A World of Trouble*, pp. 97–8; Ball and Ball, *The Passionate Attachment*, pp. 57–8; Finkelstein, *Image and Reality*, pp. 196–7. For Egyptian attempts to forestall the coming war see the declassified State Department document 'Document 148'.

107 Ball and Ball, *The Passionate Attachment*, pp. 61–3; Tyler, *A World of Trouble*, p. 102.

108 Tyler, *A World of Trouble*, pp. 23–4, 39–40, 64–5, 102; Cockburn and Cockburn, *Dangerous Liaison*, pp. 52–3. The CIA would later subcontract the ex-Nazi Reinhard Gehlen's organisation to train Egypt's new military intelligence.

109 Cockburn and Cockburn, *Dangerous Liaison*, p. 54. The exception was CIA's KK Mountain programme, which relied on Israeli intelligence to penetrate regions that it could not otherwise. Ibid. p. 100.

110 Tyler, *A World of Trouble*, pp. 68–9.

111 Polakow-Suransky, *The Unspoken Alliance*, pp. 53–7.

112 Hersh, *The Samson Option*, pp. 183, 186, 189–90.

113 Ibid. pp. 183–4, 186; Tyler, *A World of Trouble*, pp. 102–3.

114 Tivnan, *The Lobby*, pp. 66–7.

115 Ibid. pp. 67–8; Hersh, *The Samson Option*, pp. 190–4.

116 Quoted in Tivnan, *The Lobby*, p. 68; Paul Nitze would later recall being visited by a representative of the Jewish Relief Agency, who would tell him that the Pentagon could not block the delivery. The visitor, a certain 'Mr Finkelstein', threatened to take the matter to the president. Soon afterwards Nitze was overruled. Cockburn and Cockburn, *Dangerous Liaison*, pp. 75–6.

117 Tyler, *A World of Trouble*; J. J. Goldberg, *Jewish Power*, pp. 239–43; Ball and Ball, *The Passionate Attachment*, p. 77.

118 J. J. Goldberg, *Jewish Power*, pp. 244–6; Tyler, *A World of Trouble*, pp. 108, 129, 136. In the early days of his presidency Nixon had dispatched William Scranton, the former Pennsylvania governor, to study the prospect for diplomacy. Scranton's recommendation of 'even-handedness' outraged the lobby and he was unceremoniously dropped by Nixon; but Nixon recognised that the Israel–Palestine conflict was at the centre of US troubles in the Middle East. Tyler, pp. 109–10, 113, 118.

119 Quoted in Tyler, *A World of Trouble*, pp. 120–1. Tyler also notes that Nixon saw US Middle East policy in strictly domestic terms and made his compromises accordingly. Ibid. Kissinger himself invoked his family's experience during the Holocaust to explain why he opposed pressuring Israel. Ibid. p. 177. On Nixon's dis-

trust of Kissinger over the Middle East see J. J. Goldberg, *Jewish Power*, pp. 238–9.

120 Transcripts of telephone conversations obtained by the National Security Archives: Telcon: Kissinger–Dinitz, 2:09 a.m., 25 October 1973; Telcon: Kissinger–Lord Cromer, 1:03 a.m., 25 October 1973. See also Tyler, *A World of Trouble*, pp. 163–4, 166–7.

121 In Tyler, *A World of Trouble*, pp. 147, 153. For full discussion see pp. 136–47, 156–64.

122 Ibid. pp. 166–70. Later Kissinger would also try to sabotage Carter's attempts to engineer peace between Israel and the Arabs by advising the Israeli ambassador Simcha Dinitz to mobilise Israel and the lobby against the peace plan. Cockburn and Cockburn, *Dangerous Liaison*, p. 314.

123 J. J. Goldberg, *Jewish Power*, pp. 245–6; Yergin, *The Prize*, p. 608.

124 Brown's outspoken comments about the lobby's grip over US Congress also led to pressure on him from Gerald Ford to resign. 'Brown's Bomb'; Crooke and Perry 'Winning the Ground War'. On the economic and political consequences of the embargo see Yergin, *The Prize*, pp. 613–30; Ball and Ball, *The Passionate Attachment*, pp. 78–80.

125 Tyler, pp. 86–7.

126 Rubenberg, *Israel and the American National Interest*, p. 207; Tivnan, *The Lobby*, pp. 87–90.

127 Cockburn and Cockburn, *Dangerous Liaison*, pp. 314–15; Tyler, *A World of Trouble*, pp. 186–7, 192.

128 Ball and Ball, *The Passionate Attachment*, pp. 102–3; Tyler, *A World of Trouble*, pp. 200–3.

129 Cockburn and Cockburn, *Dangerous Liaison*, pp. 313–14; Parry, 'The CIA/Likud Sinking'.

130 Tyler, *A World of Trouble*, pp. 251–61.

131 Cooley, *An Alliance against Babylon*, pp. 163–4; Tyler, *A World of Trouble*, pp. 251–2. Unusually, however, the US joined a Third World-led resolution which 'strongly condemned' the Israeli attack. Tivnan, *The Lobby*, p. 151.

132 Tyler, *A World of Trouble*, pp. 267–71, 272, 574n51.

133 Ibid. p. 273.

134 Ibid. p. 273.

135 Fisk, *Pity the Nation*, pp. 359–400.

136 Tyler, *A World of Trouble*, pp. 254, 307, 314–15; for a fuller discussion, see ibid. ch. 8.

137 Ibid. pp. 314–15, 321–6; Kornbluh and Byrne, *The Iran–Contra*

Scandal; declassified record at the National Security Archives (2006); Wawro, *Quicksand*, pp. 402–4.

138 Quoted in Hersh, *The Samson Option*, p. 286. See also Cockburn and Cockburn, *Dangerous Liaison*, pp. 85, 203–9; Hersh, 'The Traitor'.

139 Quoted in J. J. Goldberg, *Jewish Power*, p. xviii. See also ibid. pp. xv–xxiv; Arens, *Broken Covenant*, ch. 3; Frankel, 'A Beautiful Friendship?'

140 Aruri, *Dishonest Broker*, pp. 128–35.

141 Ibid.; Carter, *Palestine*, pp. 131–2; J. J. Miller, *The Much Too Promised Land*, pp. 223–8.

142 Beinin, 'The Israelization'.

143 Carter, *Palestine*, p. 134.

144 Tyler, *A World of Trouble*, p. 482.

145 J. J. Miller, *The Much Too Promised Land*, p. 75.

146 Tyler, *A World of Trouble*, p. 515. Also, according to Tyler, before leaving office, Clinton was 'duped and bribed' by people who were 'closely connected to the Israeli intelligence agency Mossad' to grant a pardon to the fugitive financier and Mossad asset Marc Rich. Ibid. pp. 510–11; G. F. Smith, *Spy Trade*, pp. 116–17; Isikoff and Corn, *Hubris*, p. 237.

147 Quoted in Wawro, *Quicksand*, p. 72.

148 Tyler, *A World of Trouble*, p. 109; Wawro, *Quicksand*, p. 256. It was also expanded and deployed to the eastern Mediterranean by Nixon during the 'Black September' uprising in Jordan to deter an anticipated Syrian intervention. Wawro, *Quicksand*, p. 305.

149 Mearsheimer and Walt, *The Israel Lobby*, p. 53

150 Shahak, *Jewish History, Jewish Religion*, p. 103.

151 Sullivan, 'America, Stop Sucking Up to Israel'.

152 Neumann, *The Case against Israel*, pp. 178–9. This view is also echoed in Brzezinski, 'Hegemonic Quicksand'.

153 Khalidi, *Resurrecting Empire*, pp. 30–4; Said, *Culture and Imperialism*, p. 291.

154 Yergin, *The Prize*, pp. 491–2.

155 J. Cole, *Engaging the Muslim World*, pp. 16–17. McCone had resigned from his post as CIA director in 1965 over Johnson's refusal to press the Israelis on their nuclear programme. Hersh, *The Samson Option*, pp. 150–1.

156 Wawro, *Quicksand*, p. 313.

157 Ibid. p. 313.

158 Yergin, *The Prize*, pp. 555–7, 606–9.

159 Wawro, *Quicksand*, pp. 311–13.

160 J. J. Goldberg, *Jewish Power*, pp. 176–80.

161 Ibid. Ironically, the pro-Israel Lyndon Johnson had vetoed a similar bill after it passed Congress in 1965, but a decade later things had moved so far that the lobby even managed to get Jimmy Carter's support, whose Jewish campaign aide Stuart Eizenstat inserted a promise into his notes briefing favouring the anti-boycott bill.

162 Lefton, 'Big Oil's Long History'.

163 Jeffrey Goldberg, 'Real Insiders'.

164 J. Cole, *Engaging the Muslim World*, pp. 136–8.

165 Brady, 'Rogue States'.

166 Cave, 'Oily Waters'.

167 Ramsey, 'The Winners and Losers'.

168 G. F. Smith, *Spy Trade*, pp. 57–61.

169 These included Dow Chemicals, Ethyl Corporations, Monsanto, Sunkist, various farm federations and AFL–CIO.

170 These included American Israel Chamber of Commerce and the Jewish War Veterans of the United States.

171 G. F. Smith, *Spy Trade*, pp. 93, 97, 105–8.

172 Ball and Ball, *The Passionate Attachment*, p. 273.

173 Tivnan, *The Lobby*, p. 153.

174 Though its public face was AIPAC, the campaign, according to Goldberg, was 'waged by a board consortium under the umbrella of NCRAC working with AIPAC and the Presidents Conference. The Presidents Conference oversaw the efforts of the national agencies to flood the media, forge interfaith coalitions, and create a national mood of urgency. NCRAC delivered its armies of local community leaders to call their representatives and talk tough. AIPAC did what it had always done: it lobbied.' J. J. Goldberg, *Jewish Power*, p. 198.

175 Ibid. pp. 156–60.

176 Tivnan, *The Lobby*, ch. 5; Tyler, *A World of Trouble*, ch. 8; Ball and Ball, *The Passionate Attachment*, pp. 213–15, 273, 278. The Pentagon would go on to quietly ignore the restrictions. Tyler, *A World of Trouble*, p. 309.

177 Tivnan, *The Lobby*, p. 145; Cockburn and Cockburn, *Dangerous Liaison*, p. 193.

178 J. J. Goldberg, *Jewish Power*, p. 197.

179 Tivnan, *The Lobby*, p. 160. Moreover, AIPAC's Executive Director Thomas Dine used the sale as a basis for a recruitment drive emphasising the Jewish State's vulnerability, which resulted

in the lobby group's membership expanding fivefold during his tenure. J. J. Goldberg, *Jewish Power*, pp. 198–202.

180 Ball and Ball, *The Passionate Attachment*, pp. 273–5; Tyler, *A World of Trouble*, pp. 309–10, 313.

181 Aksan and Bailes, 'On Media'.

182 Ball and Ball, pp. 272–3, 266, 277; Gwertzman, 'Cancellation of Jordan Arms Sale'.

183 Ball and Ball, p. 276. The lobby tried to get the US government to compel the Chinese to stop the sale, until it was revealed that the missiles had actually been built with Israeli assistance based on technology stolen from the US.

184 Ibid. pp. 273–4, 276–7.

185 Lake, 'Bush Urged to Place Rules'.

186 G. F. Smith, *Spy Trade*, pp. 75–85.

187 Cited in Richardson and Luchsinger, 'Strategic Marketing Implications'. For more on Israel's military–industrial espionage see Cockburn and Cockburn, *Dangerous Liaison*; Hersh, *The Samson Option*.

188 G. F. Smith, *Spy Trade*, p. 83; G. F. Smith, *America's Defense Line*.

189 R. Silverstein, 'Dubai Ports Deal'.

190 Smith and Hus, *Visa Denied*.

191 Tivnan, *The Lobby*, p. 77.

192 Scott, *Power*. But as Lukes notes, these interests could themselves be the products of the paramount agent's power. Lukes, *Power*.

193 Lukes, *Power*, p. 30.

194 Scott, *Power*, p.4.

195 Scott, *Power*, p. 58.

196 Lukes, *Power*, p. 28. There is also a more expansive definition of power put forth by French philosopher Michel Foucault which sees power as diffuse, not reducible to armies and parliaments. It is rather an intangible network of forces which weaves itself into the very being of an individual to constitute it as a subject. However, it is not clear if there is anything to be gained analytically from such an expansive definition. If power is so diffuse that it makes subjects of all, then the sharp divide in US public opinion over the Iraq war shows that it must be flexible enough to allow citizens to be both pro- or anti-war. Foucault's power was evidently agnostic to the political choices of its subjects. Foucault, *Discipline and Punish*.

197 Quoted in Wedel, *Shadow Elite*, p. 19.

198 Scott, *Power*, pp. 16–25.

Bibliography

Abdel-Jawwad, Saleh, 'Israel: The Ultimate Winner', *Al-Ahram Weekly*, 17–23 April 2003.

Abella, Alex, *Soldiers of Reason: The Rand Corporation and the Rise of the American Empire* (Orlando and London: Harcourt, 2008).

Abelson, Donald E., *A Capitol Idea: Think Tanks and US Foreign Policy* (Montreal and London: McGill-Queen's University Press, 2006).

Abrahamian, Ervand, 'The US Media, Huntington and September 11', *Third World Quarterly*, 24:3 (2003), pp. 529–44.

Abrams, Elliott, *Faith or Fear: How Jews Can Survive in a Christian America* (New York: Free Press, 1997).

Abrams, Elliott, 'Words of War: Why Sanctions Are Necessary', *Weekly Standard*, 27 July 1998.

Abunimah, Ali, and Hussein Ibish, 'The US Media and the New Intifada', in Roane Carey (ed.), *The New Intifada: Resisting Israel's Apartheid* (London and New York: Verso, 2001), pp. 233–56.

Acheson, Dean, *Present at the Creation: My Years in the State Department* (New York: Norton, 1969).

Ackerman, Spencer, 'Fast and Loose with the Facts: How Two Leading Journalists Played the Public to Help Bush Sell His War', *Washington Independent*, 19 March 2008.

Adelman, Kenneth, 'The Ankle Biters', *Fox News*, 10 July 2002.

Adelman, Kenneth, 'Cakewalk in Iraq', *Washington Post*, 13 February 2002.

Adelman, Kenneth, 'Cakewalk Revisited', *Washington Post*, 10 April 2003.

Adelman, Kenneth, 'No, Let's Not Waste Any Time', *Time*, 14 October 2002.

Adelman, Kenneth, 'Saddam's State of Terror', *The Wall Street Journal*, 28 August 2002.

Ahrari, Mohammed E., *Ethnic Groups and US Foreign Policy* (New York: Greenwood Press, 1987).

Aksan, Cihan, and Jon Bailes, 'On Media: An Interview with Noam Chomsky', *State of Nature*, 30 August 2006.

Alam, M. Shahid, *Israeli Exceptionalism: The Destabilizing Logic of Zionism* (New York: Palgrave Macmillan, 2009).

Alexandrovna, Larisa, 'Secretive Military Unit Sought to Solve Political WMD Concerns Prior to Securing Iraq, Intelligence Sources Say', *The Raw Story*, 5 January 2006.

Alterman, Eric, 'Intractable Foes, Warring Narratives', *Alternet*, 2 April 2002.

Altheide, D. L., and J. N. Grimes, 'War Programming: The Propaganda Project and the Iraq War', *Sociological Quarterly*, 46:4 (2005), pp. 617–43.

Anderson, Benedict R. O., *Imagined Communities: Reflections on the Origin and Spread of Nationalism* (London: Verso, 1983).

Anderson, Perry, *A Zone of Engagement* (London: Verso, 1992).

Arango, Tim, and Clifford Krauss, 'China Is Reaping Biggest Benefits of Iraq Oil Boom', *The New York Times*, 2 June 2013.

Archer, Margaret Scotford, *Realist Social Theory: The Morphogenetic Approach* (Cambridge: Cambridge University Press, 1995).

Arens, Moshe, *Broken Covenant: American Foreign Policy and the Crisis between the U.S. and Israel* (New York and London: Simon and Schuster, 1995).

Aruri, Naseer Hasan, *Dishonest Broker: The U.S. Role in Israel and Palestine* (Cambridge, MA: South End Press, 2003).

Asmus, Ronald D., Kurt Campbell, Michele A. Flournoy, Larry Diamond, Philip Gordon, Bob Kerrey, Michael McFaul, Kenneth M. Pollack, and Jeremy Rosner, 'Progressive Internationalism: A Democratic National Security Strategy' (Washington, DC: Progressive Policy Institute, 2003).

Avnery, Uri, 'Bush's Guru', *Counterpunch.org*, 10 March 2005.

Bacevich, Andrew, *American Empire: The Realities and Consequences of U.S. Diplomacy* (Cambridge, MA: Harvard University Press, 2002).

Bacevich, Andrew, 'The American Political Tradition', *The Nation*, 17 July 2006.

Bacevich, Andrew, 'The Colors Run Red', *The American Conservative*, 1 October 2009.

Bacevich, Andrew, *The Limits of Power: The End of American Exceptionalism* (New York: Metropolitan Books, 2008).

Bacevich, Andrew, *The New American Militarism: How Americans Are Seduced by War* (New York: Oxford University Press, 2005).

Bacevich, Andrew, 'Review: *The Israel Lobby and U.S. Foreign Policy*', *Diplomacy & Statecraft*, 19:4 (2008), pp. 787–95.

Bachrach, P, and M. S. Baratz, 'Decisions and Nondecisions: An Analytical Framework', *The American Political Science Review*, 57:3 (1963), pp. 632–42.

Bachrach, P, and M. S. Baratz, 'Two Faces of Power', *The American Political Science Review*, 56:4 (1962), pp. 947–52.

Baker, David R., 'Bechtel Pulling Out after 3 Rough Years of Rebuilding Work', *San Francisco Chronicle*, 1 November 2006.

Baker, Russ, '"Scoops" and Truth at the Times', *The Nation*, 23 June 2003.

Ball, George W., and Douglas B. Ball, *The Passionate Attachment: America's Involvement with Israel, 1947 to the Present* (New York and London: Norton, 1992).

Bamford, James, 'Iran: The Next War', *Rolling Stone*, 26 July 2006.

Bamford, James, 'The Man Who Sold the War', *Rolling Stone*, 17 November 2005.

Bamford, James, *A Pretext for War: 9/11, Iraq, and the Abuse of America's Intelligence Agencies* (New York and London: Doubleday, 2004).

Bard, Mitchell, *The Arab Lobby: The Invisible Alliance that Undermines America's Interests in the Middle East* (New York: Harper, 2010).

Bard, Mitchell, 'The Israeli and Arab Lobbies', Jewish Virtual Library, <http://www.jewishvirtuallibrary.org/jsource/US-Israel/lobby.html>.

Barry, Tom, 'Israel's Man at the UN', International Relations Center, 26 July 2006.

Barry, Tom, 'US: Danger, Danger Everywhere', *Asia Times*, 23 June 2006.

Barstow, David, 'Behind TV Analysts, Pentagon's Hidden Hand', *The New York Times*, 20 April 2008.

Barstow, David, 'One Man's Military–Industrial Media Complex', *The New York Times*, 29 November 2008.

Bar-Yosef, Avinoam, 'The Jews Who Run Clinton's Court', *Ma'ariv*, 2 September 1994.

Baudrillard, Jean, *The Gulf War Did Not Take Place* (Bloomington: Indiana University Press, 1995).

Baumgartner, F. R., and B. L. Leech, *Basic Interests: The Importance of Groups in Politics and in Political Science* (Princeton: Princeton University Press, 1998).

Baumgartner, F. R., and B. L. Leech, 'Interest Niches and Policy Bandwagons: Patterns of Interest Group Involvement in National Politics', *The Journal of Politics*, 63:4 (2008), pp. 1191–213.

Becker, Gary S., 'Why War with Iraq Is Not About the Oil', *Business Week*, 17 May 2003.

Beckerman, Gal, 'The Neoconservative Persuasion', *Forward*, 6 January 2006.

Beeston, Richard, 'Prepare for War with Iran, France Warns', *The Times*, 17 September 2007.

Beinart, Peter, 'The Failure of the American Jewish Establishment', *The New York Review of Books*, 10 June 2010.

Beinin, Joel, 'The Israelization of American Middle East Policy Discourse', *Social Text*, 21:275 (2003), p. 125.

Beinin, Joel, 'The New American McCarthyism: Policing Thought about the Middle East', *Race & Class*, 46:1 (2004), p. 101.

Beinin, Joel, 'US: The Pro-Sharon Thinktank', *Le Monde Diplomatique*, July 2003.

Bell, Jeffrey, 'Bush I vs. Bush II', *Weekly Standard*, 13 October 2003.

Bellow, Adam, 'My Escape from the Zabar's Left', *New York Magazine*, 21 May 2005.

Bellow, Saul, *To Jerusalem and Back: A Personal Account* (New York: Viking Press, 1976).

Bellow, Saul, *Ravelstein* (New York: Viking, 2000).

Bergen, Peter, 'Armchair Provocateur; Laurie Mylroie: The Neocons' Favorite Conspiracy Theorist', *Washington Monthly*, December 2003.

Berger, Peter L., and Thomas Luckmann, *The Social Construction of Reality: A Treatise in the Sociology of Knowledge* (London: Allen Lane, 1966).

Berkowitz, Bill, 'Christian Right Steps Up Pro-Israel Lobbying', *Inter Press Service*, 27 July 2006.

Berman, Ari, 'AIPAC's Hold', *The Nation*, 14 August 2006.

Berman, Paul, *Terror and Liberalism* (New York: Norton, 2003).

Berman, Paul, *A Tale of Two Utopias: The Political Journey of the Generation of 1968* (New York: W. W. Norton, 1997).

Bernays, Edward L., 'The Engineering of Consent', *The Annals of the American Academy of Political and Social Science*, 250:1 (1947), p. 113.

Bernays, Edward L., *Public Relations* (Norman: University of Oklahoma Press, 1952).

Bernstein, Richard, 'Making a Case for a U.S. Invasion of Iraq', *The New York Times*, 22 October 2002.

Bertrand, Pierre, 'ExxonMobil's Iraq Oil Field Contract Could Go to Lukoil, Shell', *International Business Times*, 30 November 2011.

Beaumont, Peter, Martin Bright, and Ed Vulliamy, 'Revealed: US Dirty Tricks to Win Vote on Iraq War', *The Observer*, 2 March 2003.

Binnendijk, Hans, Richard L. Kugler, Charles B. Shotwell, and Kori Schake, *Strategic Assessment 1999: Priorities for a Turbulent World* (Washington, DC: National Defense University, 1999).

Black, Conrad, 'Rebirth of the Right – with Brains', *The Globe and Mail (Canada)*, 7 June 1979.

'Blair Warned Bush against Iraq Push after 9/11: Advisor', *AFP*, 30 November 2009.

Blanford, Nicholas, 'Iran, Iraq, and Two Shiite Visions', *Christian Science Monitor*, 20 February 2004.

Blankfort, Jeffrey, 'Damage Control', *Left Curve*, June 2006.

Blitzer, Wolf, 'Search for the "Smoking Gun"', *CNN*, 10 January 2003.

Bloom, Allan, *The Closing of the American Mind: How Higher Education Has Failed Democracy and Impoverished the Souls of Today's Students* (New York: Simon and Schuster, 1987).

Blumenthal, Max, 'AIPAC Cheers an Anti-Semitic Holocaust Revisionist (and Abe Foxman Approves)', *MaxBlumenthal.com*, 14 March 2007.

Blumenthal, Max, 'Pastor Hagee: The Antichrist Is Gay, "Partially Jewish, as Was Adolph Hitler" (Paging Joe Lieberman!)', *The Huffington Post*, 2 June 2008.

Blumenthal, Sidney, 'Bush Knew Saddam Had No Weapons of Mass Destruction', *Salon*, 6 September 2007.

Blumenthal, Sidney, 'Bush's War on Professionals', *Salon*, 5 January 2006.

Blumenthal, Sidney, *The Rise of the Counter-Establishment: The Conservative Ascent to Political Power* (New York: Union Square, 2008).

Bonney, Richard, *False Prophets: The 'Clash of Civilizations' and the Global War on Terror* (Oxford: Peter Lang, 2008).

Bookman, Jay, 'Bush's Real Goal in Iraq', *Atlanta Journal-Constitution*, 29 September 2002.

Borger, Julian, 'Special Investigation: The Spies Who Pushed for War', *The Guardian*, 17 July 2003.

Borger, Julian, Brian Whitaker, and Vikram Dodd, 'Saddam's Desperate Offers to Stave Off War', *The Guardian*, 7 November 2003.

Bosman, Julian, 'Secret Iraq Meeting Included Journalists', *The New York Times*, 9 October 2006.

Bourdieu, Pierre, *Outline of a Theory of Practice*, trans. Richard Nice (Cambridge: Cambridge University Press, 1977).

Bourke, Richard, John Dunn, and Raymond Geuss, *Political Judgement Essays for John Dunn* (Cambridge: Cambridge University Press, 2009).

Brady, Rose, 'Rogue States: Why Washington May Ease Sanctions', *Business Week*, 7 May 2001.

Bransford, Amanda, 'U.S. Defence Spending Far Outpaces Rest of the World', *Inter Press Service*, 28 May 2010.

Brom, Shlomo, 'The War in Iraq: An Intelligence Failure', *Strategic Assessment*, 6:3 (2003), pp. 8–16.

Brooks, David, 'The Era of Distortion', *The New York Times*, 6 January 2004.

Brown, Wendy, 'American Nightmare: Neoliberalism, Neoconservatism, and De-Democratization', *Political Theory*, 34:6 (2006), p. 690.

Brown, Wendy, '"The Most We Can Hope For . . .": Human Rights and the Politics of Fatalism', *South Atlantic Quarterly*, 103:2–3 (2004), p. 451.

'Brown's Bomb', *Time*, 25 November 1974.

Bruck, Connie, 'Back Roads: How Serious Is the Bush Administration about Creating a Palestinian State?', *New Yorker*, 15 December 2003.

Bruck, Connie, 'The Influencer', *New Yorker*, 10 May 2010.

Brzezinski, Zbigniew, 'A Dangerous Exemption: Why Should the Israel Lobby Be Immune from Criticism?', *Foreign Policy*, 155 (2006), pp. 63–4.

Brzezinski, Zbigniew, 'Hegemonic Quicksand', *The National Interest*, 74 (2003), p. 4.

Brzezinski, Zbigniew, 'Iraq in the Strategic Context', Testimony to the Senate Foreign Relations Committee, 1 February 2007.

Brzezinski, Zbigniew, *Power and Principle: Memoirs of the National Security Advisor 1977–1981* (London: Weidenfeld and Nicholson, 1983).

Brzezinski, Zbigniew, 'Terrorized by "War on Terror"', *Washington Post*, 25 March 2007.

Brzezinski, Zbigniew, 'Why Unity Is Essential', *Washington Post*, 19 February 2003.

Buchta, Wilfried, *Who Rules Iran?: The Structure of Power in the Islamic Republic* (Washington, DC: Washington Institute for Near East Policy, 2000).

Bugliosi, Vincent, *The Prosecution of George W. Bush for Murder* (New York: Vanguard Press, 2008).

Bumiller, Elisabeth, 'Bush Aides Set Strategy to Sell Policy on Iraq', *The New York Times*, 7 September 2002.

Bumiller, Elisabeth, and Eric Schmitt, 'On the Job and at Home, Influential Hawks' 30-Year Friendship Evolves', *The New York Times*, 11 September 2002.

Buruma, Ian, 'Lost in Translation: The Two Minds of Bernard Lewis', *The New Yorker*, 14 June 2004.

Burawoy, Michael, 'For Public Sociology', *American Sociological Review*, 70:1 (2005), pp. 4–28.

Burbach, Roger, 'Bush Ideologues Trump Big Oil Interests in Iraq', *Alternatives*, 30 September 2003.

Burke, Jason, 'The Missing Link', *The Observer*, 9 February 2003.

Burnham, Gilbert, Riyadh Lafta, Shannon Doocy, and Les Roberts, 'Mortality after the 2003 Invasion of Iraq: A Cross-Sectional Cluster Sample Survey', *The Lancet*, 368:9545 (2006), pp. 1421–8.

Burrough, Bryan, Evgenia Peretz, David Rose, and David Wise, 'The Path to War. Special Report: The Rush to Invade Iraq: The Ultimate Inside Account', *Vanity Fair*, May 2004, pp. 228–45.

Bush, George W., *Decision Points* (London: Random House, 2011).

'Business Urges Obama Resist Iran Sanctions Bill', *Reuters*, 26 January 2010.

Butler, Richard, *Saddam Defiant: The Treat of Weapons of Mass Destruction and the Crisis of Global Security* (London: Weidenfeld and Nicolson, 2000).

Buttigieg, Joseph A., 'The Contemporary Discourse on Civil Society: A Gramscian Critique', *Boundary 2*, 32:1 (2005), p. 33.

Buttigieg, Joseph A., 'Gramsci on Civil Society', *Boundary 2*, 22:3 (1995), pp. 1–32.

Byman, Daniel, Kenneth Pollack, and Gideon Rose, 'The Rollback Fantasy', *Foreign Affairs*, January/February 1999.

Cahn, Anne Hessing, *Killing Detente: The Right Attacks the CIA* (University Park, PA: Pennsylvania State University Press, 1998).

Caldwell, Christopher, '"Communiste et Rastignac." Review of *Le Monde Selon K.*, by Pierre Péan', *London Review of Books*, 9 July 2009, pp. 7–10.

Calhoun, Craig, 'Social Science for Public Knowledge', (Brooklyn: Social Science Research Council: Public Spheres, 2009).

Calhoun, R. D., 'Arming David: The Haganah's Illegal Arms Procurement Network in the United States, 1945–1949', *Journal of Palestine Studies*, 36:4 (2007), pp. 22–32.

Carey, Alex, *Taking the Risk out of Democracy: Corporate Propaganda*

Versus Freedom and Liberty (Urbana: University of Illinois Press, 1995).

Carlisle, Tamsin, 'Iraq Awards Contract for Giant Field', *The National*, 12 December 2010.

Carter, Jimmy, *Palestine: Peace Not Apartheid* (New York and London: Simon and Schuster, 2006).

Cave, Damien, 'The United States of Oil', *Salon*, 19 November 2001.

Cave, Damien, 'Oily Waters', *Salon*, 21 November 2001.

Chandrasekaran, Rajiv, *Imperial Life in the Emerald City: Inside Iraq's Green Zone* (New York: Alfred A. Knopf, 2006).

Charmelot, Jacques, 'The CIA Operation that Should Have Prevented the Iraq War', *AFP*, 4 February 2008.

Chatterjee, Pratap, *Iraq, Inc.: A Profitable Occupation* (New York: Seven Stories, 2004).

Cheney, Richard B., 'Defending Liberty in a Global Economy', speech delivered at Collateral Damage Conference, Cato Institute, 23 June 1998.

Cheney, Richard B., *In My Time: A Personal and Political Memoir* (New York: Simon and Schuster, 2011).

Chomsky, Noam, *Failed States: The Abuse of Power and the Assault on Democracy* (London: Hamish Hamilton, 2006).

Chomsky, Noam, *Fateful Triangle: The United States, Israel, and the Palestinians* (London: Pluto Press, 1999).

Chomsky, Noam, *Hegemony or Survival: America's Quest for Global Dominance* (New York: Metropolitan Books, 2003).

Chomsky, Noam, 'It's the Oil, Stupid!', *Khaleej Times*, 8 July 2008.

Chomsky, Noam, *Middle East Illusions: Including Peace in the Middle East?: Reflections on Justice and Nationhood* (Lanham, MD and Oxford: Rowman and Littlefield, 2003).

Chomsky, Noam, *Necessary Illusions: Thought Control in Democratic Societies* (London: Pluto, 1989).

Christison, Kathleen, *Perceptions of Palestine: Their Influence on U.S. Middle East Policy* (Berkeley: University of California Press, 1999).

'CIA Whites Out Controversial Estimate on Iraq Weapons', National Security Archive, 9 July 2004.

Cigler, Allan J., and Burdett A. Loomis, *Interest Group Politics*, 3rd edn (Washington, DC: CQ Press, 1991).

Clarke, Neil, 'If the World Is his Oyster', *The Guardian*, 21 May 2007.

Clarke, Richard A., *Against All Enemies: Inside America's War on Terror* (New York: Free Press, 2004).

Clemons, Steve, 'Did Secret Wolfowitz Meeting Violate Federal Advisory Committee Act?', *WashingtonNote.com*, 9 October 2006.

Cockburn, Alexander, and Jeffrey St. Clair, *End Times: The Death of the Fourth Estate* (Edinburgh: AK Press, 2007).

Cockburn, Alexander, 'Thank You, Glen Beck!', *Counterpunch.org*, 27–9 August 2010.

Cockburn, Andrew, *Rumsfeld: An American Disaster* (London: Verso, 2007).

Cockburn, Andrew, and Leslie Cockburn, *Dangerous Liaison: The Inside Story of the U.S.–Israeli Covert Relationship* (New York: HarperCollins, 1991).

Cockburn, Andrew, and Patrick Cockburn, *Saddam Hussein: An American Obsession* (London: Verso, 2002).

Cockburn, Patrick, 'America Concedes', *London Review of Books*, 18 December 2008.

Cockburn, Patrick, 'Iraq Looks to Spectacular Oil Boom to Revive Its Political Fortunes', *The Independent*, 1 July 2010.

Cockburn, Patrick, *Muqtada Al-Sadr and the Fall of Iraq* (London: Faber and Faber, 2008).

Cockburn, Patrick, *The Occupation: War and Resistance in Iraq* (London: Verso, 2007).

Cockett, Richard, *Thinking the Unthinkable: Think-Tanks and the Economic Counter-Revolution 1931–1983* (London: HarperCollins, 1994).

Cohen, Ariel, and Gerald O'Driscoll, 'The Road to Economic Prosperity for a Post-Saddam Iraq', *The Heritage Foundation*, 25 September 2002.

Cohen, Eliot A., 'Silent Warfare: Understanding the World of Intelligence', *Foreign Affairs*, May/June 1994.

Cohen, Eliot A., 'World War IV: Let's Call the Conflict What It Is', *The Wall Street Journal*, 20 November 2001.

Cohen, Stephen F., 'The New American Cold War', *The Nation*, 21 June 2006.

Cole, Benjamin R., 'War for Peace: Neoconservative Networks, Strategic Issue Framing, and the Making of a War', *New Voices in Public Policy*, 3:1 (2008), pp. 1–30.

Cole, David, 'Enemy Aliens', *Stanford Law Review*, 54:5 (2002), pp. 953–1004.

Cole, David, and James X. Dempsey, *Terrorism and the Constitution: Sacrificing Civil Liberties in the Name of National Security* (London: New Press, 2006).

Cole, Juan, 'Cpl. Jeffrey Goldberg, Guarding the Prison of the Nationalist Mind', *Informed Comment*, 17 March 2010.

Cole, Juan, *Engaging the Muslim World* (Basingstoke: Palgrave Macmillan, 2009).

Cole, Juan, 'McCain, the Retired Military "Analysts" and the Myth of Al-Qaeda in Iraq', *Informed Comment*, 20 April 2008.

Coleman, Norm, and Carl Levin, 'The Role of Market Speculation in Rising Oil and Gas Prices: A Need to Put the Cop Back on the Beat', Permanent Subcommittee on Investigations of the Committee on Homeland Security and Governmental Affairs United States Senate (Washington, DC: US Government Printing Office, 2006).

Collins, Lauren, 'Scooter's Sex Shocker', *New Yorker*, 7 November 2005.

Cooley, John K., *An Alliance against Babylon: The U.S., Israel, and Iraq* (London: Pluto Press, 2005).

Crane, Conrad C., and W. Andrew Terrill, *Reconstructing Iraq: Insights, Challenges, and Missions for Military Forces in a Post-Conflict Scenario* (Carlisle, PA: Strategic Studies Institute, U.S. Army War College, 2003).

Crooke, Alastair, and Mark Perry, 'Winning the Ground War', *Asia Times*, 13 October 2006.

Crossley, Nick, 'Social Networks and Extraparliamentary Politics', *Sociology Compass*, 1:1 (2007), pp. 222–36.

Crozier, Michel, *The Bureaucratic Phenomenon* (Chicago: University of Chicago Press, 1964).

Crozier, Michel, Samuel P. Huntington, and Joji Watanuki, *The Crisis of Democracy: On the Governability of Democracies* (New York: New York University Press, 1975).

Curtiss, Richard H., 'I. Lewis ("Scooter") Libby: The Nexus of Washington's Neocon Network', *Washington Report on Middle East Affairs*, September 2004.

Cushman, Thomas (ed.), *A Matter of Principle: Humanitarian Arguments for War in Iraq* (Berkeley and London: University of California Press, 2005).

Cutler, Jonathan, 'Beyond Incompetence: Washington's War in Iraq', *ZNet*, 30 April 2006.

David, Anthony, 'The Apprentice', *The American Prospect*, 5 June 2007.

Defamation, documentary film, directed by Yoav Shamir (Israel: Cinephil, 2009).

Dekmejian, Hrair, and Angelos Themelis, 'Ethnic Lobbies in US Foreign Policy: A Comparative Analysis of the Jewish, Greek, Armenian and

Turkish Lobbies', Occasional Research Paper 13 (Athens: Institute of International Relations, Panteion University of Social and Political Sciences, 1997).

Derrida, Jacques, *Specters of Marx* (London: Routledge, 1994).

Dershowitz, Alan, *The Case for Israel* (Hoboken, NJ: John Wiley and Sons, 2003).

Dershowitz, Alan, *Chutzpah* (London: Touchstone, 1991).

Deudney, D., 'Geopolitics as Theory: Historical Security Materialism', *European Journal of International Relations*, 6:1 (2000), pp. 77.

DeYoung, Karen, *Soldier: The Life of Colin Powell* (New York: Knopf, 2006).

Dionne, E. J., 'A Question of Tactics – Gulf Scrambles Left and Right Wings of Democratic Party', *Washington Post*, 3 January 1991.

Dobbs, Michael, 'How Politics Helped Redefine Threat', *Washington Post*, 14 January 2002.

Dobbs, Michael, 'With Albright, Clinton Accepts New U.S. Role', *Washington Post*, 8 December 1996.

'Document 148: Minutes of the Ninth Meeting of the Middle East Control Group, Washington, June 4, 1967, 11 a.m.', in Harriet Dashiell Schwar (ed.), *Foreign Relations of the United States, 1964–1968, Vol. XIX, Arab–Israeli Crisis and War, 1967* (Washington, DC: United States Government Printing Office, 2004).

Dolan, J. A., and D. H. Rosenbloom, *Representative Bureaucracy: Classic Readings and Continuing Controversies* (Armonk, NY: M. E. Sharpe, 2003).

Dolny, Michael, 'The Incredible Shrinking Think Tank', *Extra!*, March/April 2008.

Donnelly, Thomas, 'Rebuilding America's Defenses: Strategy, Forces and Resources for a New Century', Project for a New American Century, 2000.

Dreyfuss, Robert, 'The Commissar's in Town', *The American Prospect*, 21 May 2006.

Dreyfuss, Robert, 'The Freeman Affair', *TomDispatch.com*, 15 March 2009.

Dreyfuss, Robert, 'Just the Beginning', *The American Prospect*, 14 March 2003.

Dreyfuss, Robert, 'The Pentagon Muzzles the CIA', *The American Prospect*, 16 December 2002.

Dreyfuss, Robert, 'Vice Squad', *The American Prospect*, 17 April 2006.

Dreyfuss, Robert, and Thierry LeMarc, *Hostage to Khomeini* (New York: New Benjamin Franklin House, 1980).

Dreyfuss, Robert, and Jason Vest, 'The Lie Factory', *Mother Jones*, January/February 2004.

Drogin, Bob, *Curveball: Spies, Lies, and the Con Man Who Caused a War* (New York: Random House, 2007).

Drumheller, Tyler, *On the Brink: An Insider's Account of How the White House Compromised American Intelligence* (New York: Carroll and Graf Publishers, 2006).

Drury, Shadia B., 'Leo Strauss and the American Imperial Project', *Political Theory*, 35:1 (2007), pp. 62–7.

Drury, Shadia B., *Leo Strauss and the American Right* (New York: St. Martin's Press, 1997).

Duelfer, Charles, 'Comprehensive Report of the Special Advisor to the DCI on Iraq's WMD', Iraq Survey Group, 2004.

Eagleton, Terry, *Ideology: An Introduction* (London: Verso, 2007).

Edsall, Thomas B., and Alan Cooperman, 'GOP Uses Remarks to Court Jews', *Washington Post*, 13 March 2003.

Edsall, Thomas, and Dana Milbank, 'White House's Roving Eye for Politics', *Washington Post*, 10 March 2003.

Ehrman, J., *The Rise of Neoconservatism: Intellectuals and Foreign Affairs, 1945–1994* (New Haven, CT: Yale University Press, 1995).

Eisele, Albert, 'George Kennan Speaks Out About Iraq', *The Hill*, 26 September 2002.

Eldar, Akiva, 'Perles of Wisdom for the Feithful', *Haaretz*, 1 October 2002.

Elshtain, Jean Bethke, *Just War against Terror: The Burden of American Power in a Violent World* (New York: Basic Books, 2003).

'European Media Is Questioning Israel's Right to Exist', *European Jewish Press*, 10 March 2006.

Evans, G., 'The Responsibility to Protect: An Idea Whose Time Has Come ... And Gone?', *International Relations*, 22:3 (2008), p. 283.

'Fact Sheet: Illustrative Examples of Omissions from the Iraqi Declaration to the United States Security Council' (Washington, DC: Office of the Spokesman, 2002).

Fairweather, Jack, and Anton La Guardia, 'Chalabi Stands by Faulty Intelligence that Toppled Saddam's Regime', *The Daily Telegraph*, 19 February 2004.

Farago, Yonit, 'Israel Backed by Army of Cyber Soldiers', *The Times*, 28 July 2006.

Fein, Bruce, 'American Exceptionalism Is Un-American', *The Huffington Post*, 17 December 2010.

Feith, Douglas J., *War and Decision: Inside the Pentagon at the Dawn of the War on Terrorism* (New York: Harper, 2008).

Feulner, Edwin J., Jr., et al., 'Statement on the Defense of Taiwan', Heritage Foundation and Project for the New American Century, 20 August 1999.

Findley, Paul, 'Paul Findley: Congress and the Pro-Israel Lobby', *Journal of Palestine Studies*, 15:1 (1985), pp. 104–13.

Findley, Paul, *They Dare to Speak Out: People and Institutions Confront Israel's Lobby* (Westport, CT: Lawrence Hill, 1985).

Fineman, Howard, 'Bush Studied '67 Pre-Emptive Strike', *Newsweek*, 9 October 2002.

Finkelstein, Norman G., *Beyond Chutzpah: On the Misuse of Anti-Semitism and the Abuse of History* (Berkeley: University of California Press, 2005).

Finkelstein, Norman G., *The Holocaust Industry: Reflection on the Exploitation of Jewish Suffering* (London: Verso, 2000).

Finkelstein, Norman G., 'How the Arab–Israeli War of 1967 Gave Birth to a Memorial Industry', *London Review of Books*, 6 January 2000.

Finkelstein, Norman G., *Image and Reality of the Israel–Palestine Conflict*, 2nd edn (London: Verso, 2003).

Finkelstein, Norman G., *The Rise and Fall of Palestine: A Personal Account of the Intifada Years* (Minneapolis: University of Minnesota Press, 1996).

Finkelstein, Norman G., *This Time We Went too Far: Truth and Consequences of the Gaza Invasion* (New York: OR Books, 2010).

Fishman, B., 'The 'Israel Lobby': A Realistic Assessment', *Orbis*, 52:1 (2008), pp. 159–80.

Fisk, Robert, *The Great War for Civilisation: The Conquest of the Middle East* (New York: Alfred A. Knopf, 2005).

Fisk, Robert, 'The Internet Threat to Truly Honest Reporting', *The Independent*, 28 May 2001.

Fisk, Robert, *Pity the Nation: Lebanon at War* (Oxford: Oxford University Press, 1991).

Fitchett, Joseph, 'For Washington, a Modern Pearl Harbor', *International Herald Tribune*, 12 September 2001.

Flynn, Michael, 'Surge of Think Tanks Blurs U.S. Policy Lines – Part 1', *Inter Press Service*, 17 June 2010.

Flynn, Michael, 'Surge of Think Tanks Blurs U.S. Policy Lines – Part 2', *Inter Press Service*, 18 June 2010.

Follath, Erich, John Goetz, Marcel Rosenbach, and Holger Stark, 'The

Real Story of "Curveball": How German Intelligence Helped Justify the US Invasion of Iraq', *Der Spiegel*, 22 March 2008.

Foucault, Michel, *Discipline and Punish: The Birth of the Prison* (London: Allen Lane, 1977).

Fox, Jonathan, 'Paradigm Lost: Huntington's Unfulfilled Clash of Civilizations Prediction into the 21st Century', *International Politics*, 42:4 (2005), pp. 428–57.

Fox, Jonathan, 'State Failure and the Clash of Civilisations: An Examination of the Magnitude and Extent of Domestic Civilisational Conflict from 1950 to 1996', *Australian Journal of Political Science*, 38:2 (2003), pp. 195–213.

Foxman, Abraham H., *The Deadliest Lies: The Israel Lobby and the Myth of Jewish Control* (New York: Palgrave Macmillan, 2007).

Frank, Thomas, *What's the Matter with Kansas?: How Conservatives Won the Heart of America* (New York: Henry Holt, 2004).

Frankel, Glenn, 'A Beautiful Friendship?', *The Washington Post*, 16 July 2006.

Freeman, Chas W., 'Is Israel a Strategic Asset or Liability for the United States?' (Washington, DC: Nixon Center, 20 July 2010).

Friedman, Murray, *The Neoconservative Revolution: Jewish Intellectuals and the Shaping of Public Policy* (Cambridge: Cambridge University Press, 2005).

Friel, Howard, and Richard A. Falk, *Israel–Palestine on Record: How the* New York Times *Misreports Conflict in the Middle East* (London and New York: Verso, 2007).

Friel, Howard, and Richard A. Falk, *The Record of the Paper: How the* New York Times *Misreports US Foreign Policy* (London: Verso, 2004).

Frum, David, *The Right Man: An Inside Account of the Bush White House* (New York: Random House Trade Paperbacks, 2003).

Frum, David, and Richard Norman Perle, *An End to Evil: How to Win the War on Terror* (New York: Random House, 2003).

Fukuyama, Francis, *After the Neocons: America at the Crossroads* (London: Profile, 2006).

Fukuyama, Francis, 'The End of History?', *The National Interest*, Summer (1989).

Fukuyama, Francis, *The End of History and the Last Man* (London: Hamilton, 1992).

Fukuyama, Francis, *Our Posthuman Future: Consequences of the Biotechnology Revolution* (London: Profile, 2002).

Galbraith, John Kenneth 'Recession Economics', *The New York Review of Books*, 14 February 1982.

Gause, F. Gregory, 'The Illogic of Dual Containment', *Foreign Affairs*, March/April 1994.

Geertz, Clifford, *The Interpretation of Cultures: Selected Essays* (London: Fontana, [1973] 1993).

Gellman, Barton, *Angler: The Shadow Presidency of Dick Cheney* (London: Allen Lane, 2008).

Gellman, Barton, and Dafna Linzer, 'A "Concerted Effort" to Discredit Bush Critic', *Washington Post*, 9 April 2006.

Gellman, Barton, and Walter Pincus, 'Depiction of Threat Outgrew Supporting Evidence', *Washington Post*, 10 August 2005.

Gerecht, Reuel Marc, 'Appeasing Arab Dictators; the Road to Peace in the Middle East Runs through Baghdad, Not the Arab League', *The Weekly Standard*, 8 April 2002.

Gerecht, Reuel Marc, 'Better to Be Feared than Loved, Cont.; Especially in the Middle East', *Weekly Standard*, 29 April 2002.

Gerecht, Reuel Marc, 'The Coalition Delusion; Friends Aren't Necessary to Gain Respect in the Middle East. Power Is', *Weekly Standard*, 1 October 2001.

Gerecht, Reuel Marc, 'Crushing Al Qaeda Is only a Start', *The Wall Street Journal*, 19 December 2001.

Gerecht, Reuel Marc, 'Hardly Intelligent: How the CIA Unintentionally Aids Terrorism in the Middle East', *Weekly Standard*, 10 June 2002.

Gerecht, Reuel Marc, 'Iran Plays the Waiting Game', *The New York Times*, 13 March 2003.

Gerecht, Reuel Marc, 'An Iraq War Won't Destabilize the Mideast', *The New York Times*, 26 November 2002.

Gerecht, Reuel Marc, 'Liberate Iraq', *Weekly Standard*, 14 May 2001.

Gerecht, Reuel Marc, 'On to Iran!', *Weekly Standard*, 18 February 2002.

Gerecht, Reuel Marc, 'Regime Change in Iran? Applying George W. Bush's "Liberation Theology" to the Mullahs', *Weekly Standard*, 5 August 2002.

Gerecht, Reuel Marc, 'While Clinton Slept: How Osama and Saddam Got Away with It', *Weekly Standard*, 10 February 2003.

Gerecht, Reuel Marc, 'With Support, Iraq's Opposition Would Have a Chance', *The New York Times*, 18 January 1999.

Gerson, Mark, 'Norman's Conquest: A Commentary on the Podhoretz Legacy', *Policy Review*, 74 (1995), pp. 64–8.

Gerth, Jeff, 'Report Offered Bleak Outlook about Iraq Oil', *The New York Times*, 5 October 2003.

Geuss, Raymond, *The Idea of a Critical Theory: Habermas and the Frankfurt School* (Cambridge: Cambridge University Press, 1981).

Giddens, Anthony, *The Constitution of Society: Outline of the Theory of Structuration* (Cambridge: Polity, 1984).

Ginsberg, Benjamin, *The Fatal Embrace: Jews and the State* (Chicago and London: University of Chicago Press, 1993).

Giraldi, Philip, 'Saving Feith', *The American Conservative*, 12 March 2007.

Giraldi, Philip, 'Suskind Revisited', *The American Conservative*, 7 August 2007.

Glantz, Aaron, *How America Lost Iraq* (New York: Jeremy P. Tarcher/ Penguin, 2005).

Glass, Charles, 'Lewis of Arabia', *The Nation*, 26 August 2004.

Glazer, Nathan, 'The Interested Man', *The New Republic*, 22 October 2009.

Goldberg, Jeffrey, 'Breaking Ranks', *The New Yorker*, 31 October 2005.

Goldberg, Jeffrey, 'Deputy Secretary Wolfowitz Interview with the New Yorker Festival', *New Yorker Festival*, 21 September 2003.

Goldberg, Jeffrey, 'The Great Terror', *The New Yorker*, 25 March 2002.

Goldberg, Jeffrey, 'A Little Learning', *New Yorker*, 9 May 2005.

Goldberg, Jeffrey, 'Real Insiders', *The New Yorker*, 4 July 2005.

Goldberg, Jeffrey, 'Should the US Invade Iraq?', *Slate*, 3 October 2002.

Goldberg, Jeffrey, 'The Unknown', *New Yorker*, 10 February 2003.

Goldberg, J. J., *Jewish Power: Inside the American Jewish Establishment* (Reading, MA: Addison-Wesley, 1996).

Goldstein, Evan R., '"Osama bin Laden Made Me Famous": Bernard Lewis Looks Back', *Chronicle of Higher Education*, 22 April 2012.

Goldstein, Ritt, 'Oil Wars Pentagon's Policy since 1999', *Sydney Morning Herald*, 20 May 2003.

Gongora, Thierry, 'The Revolution in Military Affairs: What Should the CF Do about It?', presentation made at the Security and Defence Forum conference, Ottawa, 29–30 April 1998.

Gottfried, Paul, 'Cryptic Fascist?', *The American Conservative*, 6 January 2011.

Gove, Michael, 'Be Warned: Drawing a Single Tooth Will Not Stop a Mad Dog', *The Times*, 13 September 2001.

Graham, Bob, 'What I Knew Before the Invasion', *The Washington Post*, 20 November 2005.

Graham, Bradley, 'Officers: Iraq Could Drain Terror War', *Washington Post*, 1 September 2002.

Gramsci, Antonio, *A Gramsci Reader: Selected Writings, 1916–1935*, ed. David Forgacs (London: Lawrence and Wishart, 1999).

Gramsci, Antonio, Quintin Hoare, and Geoffrey Nowell-Smith, *Selections from the Prison Notebooks* (London: Lawrence and Wishart, 1971).

Gray, John, *Black Mass: Apocalyptic Religion and the Death of Utopia* (London: Allen Lane, 2007).

Green, Stephen, 'Serving Two Flags: Neo-Cons, Israel and the Bush Administration', *Counterpunch*, 28 February 2004.

Green, Stephen, *Taking Sides: America's Secret Relations with a Militant Israel* (New York: W. Morrow, 1984).

Greenberg, Cheryl Lynn, *Troubling the Waters: Black–Jewish Relations in the American Century* (Princeton: Princeton University Press, 2006).

Gronlund, Lisbeth, and David Wright, 'The Rumsfeld Report: What they Didn't Do', *The Bulletin of the Atomic Scientists*, 54:6 (1998), pp. 46–51.

Gumbel, Andrew, 'Case for War Confected, Say Top Us Officials', *The Independent*, 9 November 2003.

Guttman, Nathan, 'From Clemency to a Senior Post', *Haaretz*, 16 December 2002.

Guttman, Nathan, 'New Foreign Affairs Committee Chairman Draws Praise from All Sides', *Forward*, 2 May 2008.

Gwertzman, Bernard, 'Cancellation of Jordan Arms Sale: U.S. Policy Adrift?', *The New York Times*, 22 March 1984, p. A08.

Haas, Peter M., 'Introduction: Epistemic Communities and International Policy Coordination', *International Organization*, 46:1 (1992), pp. 1–35.

Haas, Peter M., and E. Adler, 'Conclusion: Epistemic Communities, World Order, and the Creation of a Reflective Research Program', *International Organization*, 46:1 (2009), pp. 367–90.

Habermas, Jürgen, *The Structural Transformation of the Public Sphere: An Inquiry into a Category of Bourgeois Society* (Cambridge: Polity, 1989).

Habermas, Jürgen, S. Lennox, and F. Lennox, 'The Public Sphere: An Encyclopedia Article (1964)', *New German Critique*, 3 (1974), pp. 49–55.

Hagopian, A., A. D. Flaxman, T. K. Takaro, S. A. Esa Al Shatari, J. Rajaratnam, et al. 'Mortality in Iraq Associated with the 2003–2011 War and Occupation: Findings from a National Cluster Sample

Survey by the University Collaborative Iraq Mortality Study', *PLoS Med* 10(10) (2013).

Haig, Alexander, 'Caveat: Realism, Reagan and Foreign Policy (Excerpt)', *Time*, 9 April 1984.

Hall, Richard L., and Alan V. Deardorff, 'Lobbying as Legislative Subsidy', *American Political Science Review*, 100:1 (2006), pp. 69–84.

Hall, Richard L., and Frank W. Wayman, 'Buying Time: Moneyed Interests and the Mobilization of Bias in Congressional Committees', *The American Political Science Review*, 84:3 (1990), pp. 797–820.

Halper, Stefan, and Jonathan Clarke, *America Alone: The Neo-Conservatives and the Global Order* (Cambridge: Cambridge University Press, 2004).

Halsell, Grace, 'Clinton's Indyk Appointment One of Many from Pro-Israel Think Tank', *Washington Report on Middle East Affairs*, March 1993.

Hamburger, Tom, and Peter Wallstein, 'Cheney, CIA Long at Odds', *Los Angeles Times*, 20 October 2005.

Haney, Patrick J., and Walt Vanderbush, 'The Role of Ethnic Interest Groups in US Foreign Policy: The Case of the Cuban American National Foundation', *International Studies Quarterly*, 43:2 (1999), pp. 341–61.

Harding, Luke, 'Germans Accuse US over Iraq Weapons Claim', *The Guardian*, 2 April 2004.

Harrington, Michael, 'The Welfare State and Its Neoconservative Critics', *Dissent*, 20:4 (1973), pp. 435–54.

Hartung, William D., and Michelle Ciarrocca, 'The Military–Industrial–Think Tank Complex, Corporate Think Tanks and the Doctrine of Aggressive Militarism', *The Multinational Monitor*, 24:1–2 (2003).

Hartung, William D., and Michelle Ciarrocca, 'Star Wars II: Here We Go Again', *The Nation*, 19 June 2000.

Harvey, David, *A Brief History of Neoliberalism* (Oxford and New York: Oxford University Press, 2005).

Harvey, David, 'Neo-Liberalism as Creative Destruction', *The Annals of the American Academy of Political and Social Science*, 610:1 (2007), pp. 21–44.

Harvey, David, *The New Imperialism* (Oxford: Oxford University Press, 2003).

Hayes, Stephen, 'The U.S. Government's Secret Memo Detailing Cooperation between Saddam Hussein and Osama Bin Laden', *Weekly Standard*, 24 November 2003.

Hedges, Chris, *American Fascists: The Christian Right and the War on America* (New York and London: Free Press, 2007).

Hedges, Chris, *War Is a Force that Gives Us Meaning* (New York: Public Affairs, 2002).

Heilbrunn, Jacob, *They Knew They Were Right: The Rise of the Neocons* (New York: Doubleday, 2008).

Helmreich, Jeffrey, 'The Israel Swing Vote: How the American Jewish Vote Influences US Elections', *Jerusalem Letter Viewpoints*, 15 January 2001.

Henderson, Errol A., 'Mistaken Identity: Testing the Clash of Civilizations Thesis in Light of Democratic Peace Claims', *British Journal of Political Science*, 34:3 (2004), pp. 539–54.

Henderson, Errol A., 'Not Letting Evidence Get in the Way of Assumptions: Testing the Clash of Civilizations Thesis with More Recent Data', *International Politics*, 42:4 (2005), pp. 458–69.

Henderson, Errol A., and Richard Tucker, 'Clear and Present Strangers: The Clash of Civilizations and International Conflict', *International Studies Quarterly*, 45:2 (2001), pp. 317–38.

Herbert, Bob, 'A Tragic Mistake', *The New York Times*, 1 December 2009.

Herman, Edward S., and Gerry O'Sullivan, *The 'Terrorism' Industry: The Experts and Institutions that Shape Our View of Terror* (New York: Pantheon Books, 1989).

Herman, Jack, 'A Whole New Ballgame Overseas', *St. Louis Post-Dispatch*, 20 February 1989.

Herrick, Thaddeus, 'US Oil Wants to Work in Iraq, Firms Discuss How to Raise Nation's Output after a Possible War', *The Wall Street Journal*, 16 January 2003.

Hersh, Seyour M., 'A Case Not Closed', *The New Yorker*, 1 November 1993.

Hersh, Seymour M., *Chain of Command: The Road from 9/11 to Abu Ghraib* (New York: HarperCollins, 2004).

Hersh, Seymour M., *The Samson Option: Israel's Nuclear Arsenal and American Foreign Policy* (New York: Random House, 1991).

Hersh, Seymour M., 'The Traitor', *New Yorker*, 18 January 1999.

Hersh, Seymour M., 'Watching Lebanon', *New Yorker*, 21 August 2006.

Hijacking Catastrophe: 9/11, Fear & the Selling of American Empire, film, directed by Jeremy Earp and Sut Jhall (USA: Media Education Foundation, 2004).

Hiro, Dilip, *Secrets and Lies: The True Story of the Iraq War* (London: Politico's, 2005).

Hirsh, Michael, 'Bernard Lewis Revisited', *Washington Monthly*, November 2004.

Hoagland, Jim, 'Hidden Hand of Terror', *Washington Post*, 12 September 2001.

Hoagland, Jim, 'What About Iraq?', *Washington Post*, 12 October 2001.

Holmes, Stephen, 'Free-Marketeering', *London Review of Books*, 8 May 2008.

Horton, Scott, 'The Letter', *Balkinization*, 16 July 2006.

Hossein-zadeh, Ismael, 'Shell Games: Are They Really Oil Wars?', in Institute of Chartered Financial Analysts of India (ed.), *The OPEC Story* (Hyderabad: ICFAI University Press, 2008).

Huggler, Justin, 'Palestinians Mourn Fall of Their Hero Saddam after Flow of Dollars for "Martyrs" Dries Up', *The Independent*, 7 May 2003.

Huntington, Samuel P., 'The Clash of Civilizations?', *Foreign Affairs*, 72:3 (1992), pp. 22–49.

Huntington, Samuel P., 'Religion, Culture and International Conflict after September 11', *Center Conversations*, 14 (2002), pp. 1–16.

Ignatieff, Michael, 'The Burden', *The New York Times Magazine*, 1 May 2003.

Ignatieff, Michael, 'Lesser Evils', *The New York Times Magazine*, 2 May 2004.

'Interview with Vice President Dick Cheney', NBC *Meet the Press*, 8 September 2002.

'Iraq's Continuing Programs for Weapons of Mass Destruction', National Intelligence Estimate (redacted) (Langley, VA: Central Intelligence Agency, 2002).

Isaacs, John, 'Spinning to the Right', *The Bulletin of the Atomic Scientists*, 53:6 (1997).

Isikoff, Michael, and David Corn, *Hubris: The Inside Story of Spin, Scandal, and the Selling of the Iraq War* (New York: Crown Publishers, 2006).

'The Israel Lobby', television programme in the 'Tegenlicht' series, directed by Marije Meerman (Netherlands: VPRO Television, 2007).

Ivanovich, David, 'Conoco's Chief Blasts Sanctions', *Houston Chronicle*, 12 February 1997.

Jackson, Jr., William E., 'Miller's Latest Tale Questioned', *Editor & Publisher*, 2 October 2003.

Jamail, Dahr, *Beyond the Green Zone: Dispatches from an Unembedded Journalist in Occupied Iraq* (Chicago: Haymarket Books, 2007).

Jaschik, Scott, 'A Call to Defend Academic Freedom', *Inside Higher Ed*, 23 October 2007.

Johnson, Chalmers, *Blowback: The Costs and Consequences of American Empire* (London: Time Warner, 2002).

Johnson, Chalmers, *Nemesis: The Last Days of the American Republic* (New York: Metropolitan Books, 2006).

Johnson, Chalmers, *The Sorrows of Empire: Militarism, Secrecy, and the End of the Republic* (New York: Metropolitan Books, 2004).

Johnson, Teresa Pelton, 'Writing for International Security: A Contributor's Guide', *International Security*, 16:2 (1991), pp. 171–80.

Jones, Tim, 'Pro-Israel Groups Take Aim at U.S. News Media', *Chicago Tribune*, 26 May 2002.

Jordan, Hamilton, 'Confidential File: Foreign Policy/Domestic Politics Memo, HJ Memo, 6/77' (Atlanta, GA: Jimmy Carter Library, 1977).

Judis, John B., 'Trotskyism to Anachronism: The Neoconservative Revolution', *Foreign Affairs*, 74 (1995), p. 123.

Judt, Tony, 'Amos Elon (1926–2009)', *The New York Review of Books*, 2 July 2009.

Judt, Tony, 'A Lobby, Not a Conspiracy', *The New York Times*, 19 April 2006.

Judt, Tony, 'In Defence of Academic Freedom', conference speech, University of Chicago, 12 October 2007,

Judt, Tony, *Reappraisals: Reflections on the Forgotten Twentieth Century* (New York and London: Penguin Press, 2008).

Judt, Tony, 'The Way We Live Now', *The New York Review of Books*, 27 March 2003.

Jurkowitz, Mark, 'Blaming the Messenger', *Boston Globe*, 23 February 2003.

Kagan, Robert, and William Kristol, 'A National Humiliation', *Weekly Standard*, 16 April 2001.

Kagan, Robert, and William Kristol, *Present Dangers: Crisis and Opportunity in American Foreign and Defense Policy* (San Francisco: Encounter Books, 2000).

Kaiser, Robert G., 'Bush and Sharon Nearly Identical on Mideast Policy', *Washington Post*, 9 February 2003, p. A01.

Kaiser, Robert, 'US Risks Isolation, Breakdown of Old Alliances in Case of War', *Washington Post*, 16 March 2003.

Kaplan, Fred, *Daydream Believers: How a Few Grand Ideas Wrecked American Power* (Hoboken, NJ: John Wiley and Sons, 2008).

Kaplan, Fred, 'Paul Nitze: The Man Who Brought Us the Cold War', *Slate*, 31 October 2004.

Kaplan, Fred, *Wizards of Armageddon* (New York: Simon and Schuster, 1983).

Karni, Annie, 'Pro-Israel Group Puts Emissaries on Campuses', *New York Sun*, 10 December 2007.

Karon, Tony, 'What to Do about Iran?' *Time*, 22 July 2004.

Kean, Thomas H., Lee H. Hamilton, Richard Ben-Veniste, Bob Kerrey, Fred F. Fielding, John F. Lehman, Jamie S. Gorelick, Timothy J. Roemer, Slade Gorton, and James R. Thompson, 'The 9/11 Commission Report', The National Commission on Terrorist Attacks Upon the United States, 2004.

Keller, Bill, 'The I-Can't-Believe-I'm-a-Hawk Club', *The New York Times*, 8 February 2003.

Keller, Bill, 'The Sunshine Warrior', *The New York Times Magazine*, 22 September 2002.

Kellner, Irwin, 'The Law Catches Up to Oil', *Market Watch*, 4 August 2008.

Kenen, I. L., *All My Causes: An 80-Year Life Span in Many Lands and for Many Causes, Some We Won and Some We Lost but We Never Gave Up* (Washington, DC: Near East Research, 1985).

Kenen, I. L., *Israel's Defense Line: Her Friends and Foes in Washington* (Buffalo, NY: Prometheus Books, 1981).

Kennan, George, 'The Sources of Soviet Conduct', *Foreign Affairs*, 25:4 (1947), p. 582.

Kennedy, E., '"Ideology" from Destutt De Tracy to Marx', *Journal of the History of Ideas*, 40:3 (1979), pp. 353–68.

Khalidi, Rashid, 'The Past and Future of Democracy in the Middle East', *Macalester International*, 14:1 (2004), p. 8.

Khalidi, Rashid, *Resurrecting Empire: Western Footprints and America's Perilous Path in the Middle East* (London: I. B. Tauris, 2004).

Kiernan, Peter, 'Iraq's Oil: A Neo-Con Dream Gone Bust', *Asia Times*, 17 May 2006.

Kiesling, John Brady, 'U.S. Diplomat's Letter of Resignation', *The New York Times*, 27 February 2003.

Kim, Ahan, 'Gingrich Says US Must Go Beyond Targeting Terrorists', *Cox News Service*, 14 September 2001.

Kimmerling, Baruch, 'Thus Spoke Bernard Lewis', *Haaretz*, 25 September 2006.

King, David, and Miles Pomper, 'The US Congress and the Contingent Influence of Diaspora Lobbies: Lessons from US Policy toward Armenia and Azerbaijan', *Journal of Armenian Studies*, 3:1 (2004).

Kinzer, Stephen, *All the Shah's Men: An American Coup and the Roots of Middle East Terror* (Hoboken, NJ: John Wiley and Sons, 2003).

Kirk, Michael, 'Bush's War', *PBS Frontline*, 2008.

Kirk, Michael, 'The Dark Side', *PBS Frontline*, 2006.

Kirk, Michael, 'Gunning for Saddam', *PBS Frontline*, 2001.

Kirkpatrick, Jeane, 'Dictatorships and Double Standards', *Commentary*, November 1979, pp. 34–45.

Kirkpatrick, Jeane, 'The Myth of Moral Equivalence', *Imprimis*, 15:1 (1986).

Kissinger, Henry, *Years of Upheaval* (Boston: Little, Brown, 1982).

Klare, Michael T., *Blood and Oil: The Dangers and Consequences of America's Growing Petroleum Dependency* (New York: Metropolitan Books, 2004).

Klein, Joe, 'Mccain's Foreign Policy Frustration', *Time*, 23 July 2008.

Klein, Joe, 'Surge Protection', *Time (Swampland)*, 24 June 2008.

Klein, Joe, 'When Extremists Attack', *Time (Swampland)*, 29 July 2008.

Klein, Naomi, *The Shock Doctrine: The Rise of Disaster Capitalism* (New York: Metropolitan Books/Henry Holt, 2007).

Kollman, Ken, 'Inviting Friends to Lobby: Interest Groups, Ideological Bias, and Congressional Committees', *American Journal of Political Science*, 41:2 (1997), pp. 519–44.

Kollman, Ken, *Outside Lobbying: Public Opinion and Interest Group Strategies* (Princeton: Princeton University Press, 1998).

Kornbluh, P., and M. Byrne, *The Iran–Contra Scandal: The Declassified History* (New York: New Press, 1993).

Kovel, Joel, 'Mearsheimer and Walt Revisited', *Socialism and Democracy*, 23:2 (2009), pp. 129–37.

Kramer, Andrew, 'In Rebuilding Iraq's Oil Industry, U.S. Subcontractors Hold Sway', *The New York Times*, 16 June 2011.

Krauthammer, Charles, 'The Obsolescence of Deterrence', *Weekly Standard*, 29 November 2002.

Krauthammer, Charles, 'Victory Changes Everything . . . ', *Washington Post*, 30 November 2001.

Krauthammer, Charles, 'A War on Many Fronts . . . ', *Washington Post*, 5 October 2001.

Krauthammer, Charles, 'To War, Not to Court', *Washington Post*, 12 September 2001.

Krauthammer, Charles, 'The War: A Roadmap', *Washington Post*, 28 September 2001.

Krauthammer, Charles, 'We Can't Blow it Again', *Washington Post*, 19 April 2002.

Kristol, Irving, 'Foreign Policy in an Age of Ideology', *The National Interest*, Fall 1985.

Kristol, Irving, *Neoconservatism: The Autobiography of an Idea* (New York and London: Free Press, 1995).

Kristol, Irving, 'The Neoconservative Persuasion', *The Weekly Standard*, 25 August 2003.

Kristol, Irving, *Reflections of a Neoconservative: Looking Back, Looking Ahead* (New York: Basic Books, 1983).

Kristol, William, and Robert Kagan, 'Toward a Neo-Reaganite Foreign Policy', *Foreign Affairs*, 75:4 (1996), pp. 18–32.

Kristol, William, and Lawrence Kaplan, *The War over Iraq: Saddam's Tyranny and America's Mission* (San Francisco: Encounter Books, 2003).

Kristol, William, et al., 'Letter to President Bush on the War on Terrorism', Project for the New American Century, 20 September 2001.

Kuhn, Thomas S., *The Structure of Scientific Revolutions*, enlarged 2nd edn (Chicago: University of Chicago Press, 1970).

Kull, Steven, Clay Ramsay, and Evan Lewis, 'Misperceptions, the Media, and the Iraq War', *Political Science Quarterly*, 118:4 (2003), pp. 569–98.

Kumamoto, Robert D., *International Terrorism & American Foreign Relations, 1945–1976* (Boston: Northeastern University Press, 1999).

Kundnani, Arun, 'Islamism and the Roots of Liberal Rage', *Race & Class*, 50:2 (2008), pp. 40–68.

Kurtz, Howard, 'Intra-Times Battle over Iraqi Weapons', *The Washington Post*, 26 May 2003.

Kuttner, Robert, 'Neo-Cons Have Hijacked US Foreign Policy', *Boston Globe*, 10 September 2003.

Kwaitkowski, Karen, 'The New Pentagon Papers', *Salon*, 10 March 2004.

Labaton, Stephen, 'Democrat Seeks Inquiry on Bankrupt Firm's Adviser', *The New York Times*, 25 March 2003.

Lacey, Marc, 'Turkey Rejects Criticism by U.S. Official over Iraq', *The New York Times*, 8 May 2003.

Lake, Eli, 'Bush Urged to Place Rules on $20B Saudi Arms Sale', *New York Sun*, 15 November 2007.

Landay, Jonathan, 'Bush Gets Intelligence Data Lawmakers Do Not: A Study Called into Question His Assertion that Democratic Critics Saw the Same Iraq Reports He Did', *Philadelphia Inquirer*, 16 December 2005.

Landy, M., 'Zealous Realism: Comments on Mearsheimer and Walt', *The Forum*, 4:1 (2006), pp. 1–10.

Lang, W. Patrick, 'Drinking the Kool-Aid', *Middle East Policy*, 11:2 (2004), pp. 39–60.

Laumann, Edward O., and David Knoke, *The Organizational State: Social Choice in National Policy Domains* (Madison: University of Wisconsin Press, 1987).

Layton, Charles, 'Miller Brouhaha', *American Journalism Review*, August/September 2003.

Ledeen, Michael, 'Bill Clinton's Bay of Pigs', *Weekly Standard*, 7 October 1996.

Ledeen, Michael, 'One Battle in a Wider, Longer War', *New York Sun*, 19 March 2003.

Lefton, Rebecca, 'Big Oil's Long History of Compromising National Security for Profit', *Think Progress*, 12 August 2010.

Levinson, Sanford, 'Preserving Constitutional Norms in Times of Permanent Emergencies', *Constellations*, 13:1 (2006), pp. 59–73.

Levinson, Sanford, 'Torture in Iraq & the Rule of Law in America', *Daedalus*, 133 (2004), pp. 5–9.

Lewis, Bernard, 'The Revolt of Islam', *The New Yorker*, 19 November 2001.

Lewis, Bernard, 'The Roots of Muslim Rage', *The Atlantic Monthly*, September 1990.

Lewis, Bernard, 'At Stake in the Gulf', *The New York Review of Books*, 20 December 1990.

Lewis, Bernard, 'Time for Toppling', *The Wall Street Journal*, 28 September 2002.

Lewis, Bernard, 'A War of Resolve', *The Wall Street Journal*, 26 April 2002.

Lewis, Bernard, *What Went Wrong?: The Clash between Islam and Modernity in the Middle East* (London: Weidenfeld and Nicolson, 2002).

Lewis, Charles, and Mark Reading-Smith, 'Iraq: The War Card – Orchestrated Deception on the Path to War' (Washington, DC: Center for Public Integrity, 2008).

Lewis, Neil A., 'Anti-Terrorism Bill: Blast Turns a Snail into a Race Horse', *The New York Times*, 21 April 1995.

Lexington, 'Taming Leviathan', *The Economist*, 15 March 2007.

Lieber, Robert J., 'The Left's Neocon Conspiracy Theory', *Chronicle of Higher Education*, 29 April 2003.

Lieberman, Robert C., 'The 'Israel Lobby' and American Politics', *Perspectives on Politics*, 7:2 (2009), pp. 235–57.

Lieberman, Robert C., 'Rejoinder to Mearsheimer and Walt', *Perspectives on Politics*, 7:2 (2009), pp. 275–81.

Lieven, Anatol, *America Right or Wrong: An Anatomy of American Nationalism* (London: HarperCollins, 2004).

Lieven, Anatol, 'Book Review: Neoconservatism by Justin Vaïsse', *New Humanist*, July–August 2010.

Lieven, Anatol, 'We Do Not Deserve These People', *London Review of Books*, 20 October 2005.

Lilienthal, Alfred, 'Still, What Price Israel?', *Washington Report on Middle East Affairs*, August/September 1992.

Lind, Michael, 'The American Creed: Does It Matter? Should It Change?', *Foreign Affairs*, 75:2 (1996), pp. 135–9.

Lind, Michael, 'Distorting US Foreign Policy: The Israel Lobby and American Power', *Washington Report on Middle East Affairs*, May 2002.

Lind, Michael, 'How Neoconservatives Conquered Washington – and Launched a War', *Salon*, 9 April 2003.

Lind, Michael, 'The Israel Lobby', *Prospect*, 20 April 2002.

Linzer, Dafna, 'Bolton Often Blocked Information, Officials Say', *Washington Post*, 18 April 2005.

Lippmann, Walter, *Public Opinion* (London: Allen and Unwin, 1922).

Lipset, Seymour Martin, *American Exceptionalism: A Double-Edged Sword* (New York and London: Norton, 1996).

Lobe, Jim, 'Anti-empire Forces Strike Back', *Asia Times*, 18 October 2003.

Lobe, Jim, 'The Bush Doctrine in Embryo', *Lobelog.com*, 29 February 2008.

Lobe, Jim, 'Bush's Trusty New Mideast Point Man', *Asia Times*, 19 December 2002.

Lobe, Jim, 'Cheney as Extremist', *IPS News*, 29 September 2003.

Lobe, Jim, 'From Holocaust to Hyperpower', *Inter Press Service*, 26 January 2005.

Lobe, Jim, 'New Champions of the War Cause', *Asia Times*, 6 November 2002.

Lobe, Jim, 'Pentagon Office Home to Neo-Con Network', *IPS News*, 7 August 2003.

Lobe, Jim, 'Perle: "Prince of Darkness" in the Spotlight', *Asia Times*, 25 March 2003.

Lobe, Jim, 'Washington Goes to War over War', *Asia Times*, 21 August 2002.

Lobe, Jim, 'What Is a Neo-Conservative Anyway?', *Asia Times*, 13 August 2003.

Luban, Daniel, and Jim Lobe, 'Neocon Flap Highlights Jewish Divide', *IPS News*, 30 July 2008.

Lukes, Steven, *Power: A Radical View*, 2nd edn (New York: Palgrave Macmillan, 2005).

MacArthur, John, 'The Lies We Bought', *Columbia Journalism Review*, May/June 2003.

MacArthur, John, *Second Front: Censorship and Propaganda in the Gulf War* (New York: Hill and Wang, 1992).

MacKay, Neil, 'Officials: US Oil at the Heart of Iraq Crisis', *Sunday Herald*, 6 October 2002.

Mahler, Gregory S., *Israel after Begin* (Albany, NY: State University of New York Press, 1990).

Mamdani, Mahmood, 'Responsibility to Protect, Right to Punish', in Philip Cunliffe (ed.), *Critical Perspectives on the Responsibility to Protect* (Oxon: Routledge, 2011).

Mamdani, Mahmood, *Saviors and Survivors: Darfur, Politics, and the War on Terror* (New York: Pantheon Books, 2009),

Mann, James, *Rise of the Vulcans: The History of Bush's War Cabinet* (New York and London: Viking, 2004).

Mann, Michael, *Incoherent Empire* (London and New York: Verso, 2003).

Mann, Michael, *The Sources of Social Power. Volume I: A History of Power from the Beginning to AD 1760* (Cambridge: Cambridge University Press, 1986).

Marshall, Jonathan, Peter Dale Scott, and Jane Hunter, *The Iran–Contra Connection: Secret Teams and Covert Operations in the Reagan Era* (Boston: South End Press, 1987).

Martin, Douglas, 'Stephen J. Solarz, Former N.Y. Congressman, Dies at 70', *The New York Times*, 29 November 2010.

Marx, Karl, *The 18th Brumaire of Louis Bonaparte* (Rockville, MD: Wildside Press, 2008).

Massing, Michael, 'The Israel Lobby', *The Nation*, 10 June 2002.

Massing, Michael, 'Now They Tell Us', *The New York Review of Books*, 51:3 (2004).

Massing, Michael, 'The Storm over the Israel Lobby', *The New York Review of Books*, 8 June 2006.

Massing, Michael, 'The War Expert', *Columbia Journalism Review*, 26 November 2007.

Mathias, Charles M., 'Ethnic Groups and Foreign Policy', *Foreign Affairs*, 59:5 (1981), p. 975.

Matlock, Jack F., 'Deterring the Undeterrable', *The New York Times*, 20 October 2002.

Mayer, Jane, *Dark Side: The Inside Story of How the War on Terror Turned into a War on American Ideals* (New York and London: Doubleday, 2008).

Mayer, Jane, 'The Hidden Power', *New Yorker*, 3 July 2006.

Mayer, Jane, 'The Manipulator', *New Yorker*, 7 June 2004.

McArthur, Shirl, 'A Conservative Estimate of Total Direct U.S. Aid to Israel: Almost $114 Billion', *Washington Report on Middle East Affairs*, November 2008.

McCarthy, Daniel, 'Kristol Reflections', *The American Conservative*, 1 December 2009.

McClellan, Scott, *What Happened: Inside the Bush White House and Washington's Culture of Deception* (New York: PublicAffairs, 2008).

McConnell, Scott, 'The Weekly Standard's War', *The American Conservative*, 21 November 2005.

McGann, James G., 'Academics to Ideologues: A Brief History of the Public Policy Research Industry', *PS: Political Science and Politics*, 25:4 (1992), pp. 733–40.

McGann, James G., 'The Global "Go to Think Tanks". The Leading Public Policy Research Organizations in the World' (Philadelphia: Think Tanks and Civil Societies Program, Foreign Policy Research Institute, 2008).

McGann, James G., and R. Kent Weaver, *Think Tanks and Civil Societies: Catalysts for Ideas and Action* (New Brunswick, NJ: Transaction Publishers, 2002).

McGarvey, Ayelish, 'Carter's Crusade: Jimmy Carter Explains How the Christian Right Isn't Christian at All', *The American Prospect*, 5 April 2004.

McGovern, Ray, 'A Disingenuous Tour de Force', *Counterpunch.org*, 12 February 2004.

McKinzie, Richard D., 'Oral History Interview with Edwin M. Wright' (Independence, MO: Harry S. Truman Library, 1977).

McLaughlin, John, and George Tenet, 'DCI Memo to Chairman of the Select Committee on Intelligence', Central Intelligence Agency, 2002.

Mead, Walter Russell, 'Jerusalem Syndrome – Decoding the Israel Lobby', *Foreign Affairs*, 86 (2007), p. 160.

Mearsheimer, J., 'Conversations in International Relations: Interview with John J. Mearsheimer (Part I)', *International Relations*, 20:1 (2006), pp. 105–23.

Mearsheimer, J., 'Hans Morgenthau and the Iraq War: Realism Versus Neo-Conservatism', *openDemocracy*, 18 May 2005.

Mearsheimer, J. J., and S. M. Walt, 'The Blind Man and the Elephant in the Room: Robert Lieberman and the Israel Lobby', *Perspectives on Politics*, 7:2 (2009), pp. 259–73.

Mearsheimer, J. J., and S. M. Walt, 'Can Saddam Be Contained? History Says Yes', *Foreign Policy Bulletin*, 14:1 (2003), pp. 219–24.

Mearsheimer, J. J., and S. M. Walt, 'Is It Love or the Lobby? Explaining America's Special Relationship with Israel', *Security Studies*, 18:1 (2009), pp. 58–78.

Mearsheimer, J. J., and S. M. Walt, *The Israel Lobby and U.S. Foreign Policy* (New York: Farrar, Straus and Giroux, 2007).

Mearsheimer, J. J., and S. M. Walt, 'Setting the Record Straight: A Response to Critics of "the Israel Lobby"', 12 December 2006, < http://mearsheimer.uchicago.edu/pdfs/A0043.pdf>.

'Media Matters with Bob McChesney', radio programme (USA: WILL-AM, 17 May 2009).

'Meet the Press', television programme (USA: NBC, 16 September 2001).

Michaels, Seth, 'Kristol, Krauthammer Lauded Bush Inauguration Speech without Disclosing Their Role as Consultants', *Media Matters for America*, 24 January 2005.

Milbank, Dana, 'Prince of Darkness Denies Own Existence', *Washington Post*, 20 February 2009.

Milbank, Dana, and Walter Pincus, 'Bush Aides Disclose Warnings from CIA: Oct. Memos Raised Doubts on Iraq Bid', *Washington Post*, 23 July 2003.

Miliband, Ralph, *The State in Capitalist Society* (London: Weidenfeld and Nicolson, 1969).

Miller, Aaron David, *The Much Too Promised Land: America's Elusive Search for Arab–Israeli Peace* (New York: Bantam Books, 2008).

Miller, David, and William Dinan, *A Century of Spin: How Public Relations Became the Cutting Edge of Corporate Power* (London: Pluto Press, 2009).

Miller, Greg, 'Special Pentagon Unit Left CIA out of the Loop', *Los Angeles Times*, 10 March 2004.

Miller, John J., 'Foundation's End: The Last Days of John M. Olin's Conservative Fortune', *National Review*, 6 April 2005.

Miller, Judith, 'CIA Hunts Iraq Tie to Soviet Smallpox', *The New York Times*, 3 December 2002.

Miller, Judith, 'Defectors Bolster US Case against Iraq, Officials Say', *The New York Times*, 24 January 2003.

Miller, Judith, 'Illicit Arms Kept Till Eve of War, an Iraqi Scientist Is Said to Assert', *The New York Times*, 21 April 2003.

Miller, Judith, 'Iraqi Tells of Renovations at Sites for Chemical and Nuclear Arms', *The New York Times*, 20 December 2001.

Miller, Judith, 'Verification Is Difficult at Best, Say the Experts, and Maybe Impossible', *The New York Times*, 18 September 2002.

Miller, Judith, and Michael Gordon, 'U.S. Says Saddam Hussein Intensifies Quest for A-Bomb Parts', *The New York Times*, 8 September 2002.

Miller, Judith, and Michael Gordon, 'White House Lists Iraq Steps to Build Banned Weapons', *The New York Times*, 13 September 2002.

Miller, Judith, and Laurie Mylroie, *Saddam Hussein and the Crisis in the Gulf* (New York: Times Books, 1990).

Mills, C. Wright, *The Power Elite* (New York: Oxford University Press, 1956).

Mills, C. Wright, *Power, Politics, and People; the Collected Essays of C. Wright Mills* (New York: Oxford University Press, 1963).

Mills, C. Wright, *The Sociological Imagination* (New York: Oxford University Press, 1959).

Milstein, Mark H., 'Washington Institute for Near East Policy: An AIPAC "Image Problem"', *Washington Report on Middle East Affairs*, July 1991.

Minasian, Sergey, 'The Israeli–Kurdish Relations', *21st Century*, 1 (2007), pp. 21–2.

Mirowski, Philip, and Dieter Plehwe (eds), *The Road from Mont Pèlerin: The Making of the Neoliberal Thought Collective* (Cambridge, MA: Harvard University Press, 2009).

Moore, David W., *The Opinion Makers: An Insider Exposes the Truth Behind the Polls* (Boston: Beacon, 2008).

Morris, Benny, *Righteous Victims: A History of the Zionist–Arab Conflict, 1881–1999* (New York: Knopf, 1999).

Morse, Edward L., and Amy Myers Jaffe, 'Strategic Energy Policy Challenges for the 21st Century', in *Report of an Independent Task Force cosponsored by the James A. Baker III Institute for Public Policy of Rice University and the Council on Foreign Relations* (New York: Council on Foreign Relations Press, 2001).

Moyers, Bill, 'Buying the War', *PBS* (2007).

Moynihan, Daniel P., 'The United States in Opposition', *Commentary*, 59 (1975), pp. 31–44.

Mozgovaya, Natasha, 'American Jews Eye Obama's "Anti-Israel" Appointees', *Haaretz*, 4 December 2009.

Mutua, Makau, 'Savages, Victims, and Saviors: The Metaphor of Human Rights', *Harvard International Law Journal*, 42:1 (2001), p. 201.

Mylroie, Laurie, 'The Baghdad Alternative', *Orbis*, 32:3 (1988), pp. 339–64.

Mylroie, Laurie, 'Familiar Rogue', *National Review*, 17 September 2001.

Mylroie, Laurie, *The Future of Iraq* (Washington, DC: Washington Institute for Near East Policy, 1991).

Mylroie, Laurie, 'The Iraqi Connection: Did Osama bin Laden Act Alone? Not Likely', *The Wall Street Journal*, 13 September 2001.

Mylroie, Laurie, *Study of Revenge: Saddam Hussein's Unfinished War against America* (Washington, DC: AEI Press, 2000).

Mylroie, Laurie, 'Usama and Country', *Weekly Standard*, 27 August 2001.

Mylroie, Laurie, 'Who Is to Blame?', *Globe and Mail*, 12 September 2001.

Nafissi, Mohammad R., 'Before and Beyond the Clash of Civilizations', *ISIM Review*, 19 (2007), pp. 46–7.

Naylor, R. T., *Economic Warfare: Sanctions, Embargo Busting, and Their Human Cost* (Boston, MA: Northeastern University Press, 2001).

Nelson, Keith LeBahn, *The Making of Détente: Soviet-American Relations in the Shadow of Vietnam* (Baltimore and London: Johns Hopkins University Press, 1995).

Netanyahu, Benjamin, 'The Case for Toppling Saddam', *The Wall Street Journal*, 20 September 2002.

Neumann, Michael, *The Case against Israel* (Petrolia: CounterPunch/AK Press, 2005).

Neumann, Michael, 'Libby Played Leading Role on Foreign Policy Decisions', *Forward*, 4 November 2005.

Nichols, John, *Dick: The Man Who Is President* (New York: New Press, 2004).

Nir, Ori, 'Groups to Bush: Drop Iran–Israel Linkage', *Forward*, 12 May 2006.

Nir, Ori, 'Libby Played Leading Role on Foreign Policy Decisions', *Forward*, 4 November 2005.

Nitze, Paul, 'Deterrence and Survival in the Nuclear Age' (Washington, DC: Security Resources Panel of the Science Advisory Committee [Gaither Commission], 1957).

Nitze, Paul, 'NSC-68: United States Objectives and Programs for National Security' (Washington, DC: National Security Council, 1950).

Noah, Timothy, 'Fathers and Sons', *The New York Times*, 13 January 2008.

Nordhaus, W. D., 'The Economic Consequences of a War in Iraq', *NBER Working Paper* (Cambridge, MA: National Bureau of Economic Research, 2002).

Nordland, Rod, 'Rebuilding Its Economy, Iraq Shuns U.S. Businesses', *The New York Times*, 12 November 2009.

Novak, Robert, 'Sharon's War?', *CNN*, 26 December 2002.

Novick, Peter, *The Holocaust in American Life* (Boston: Houghton Mifflin, 1999).

Oborne, Peter, and James Jones, 'The Pro-Israel Lobby in Britain', *openDemocracy*, 13 December 2009.

Oren, Michael B., *Six Days of War: June 1967 and the Making of the Modern Middle East* (Oxford: Oxford University Press, 2002).

Ostling, Richard N., Michael P. Harris, and James Castelli, 'Religion: Armageddon and the End Times', *Time*, 5 November 1984.

O'Tuathail, Gearóid, 'Pleasures of the Polemic', *Public Culture*, 20:3 (2008), p. 561.

Outfoxed: Rupert Murdoch's War on Journalism, documentary film, directed by Robert Greenwald (USA: Carolina Productions, 2004).

Packer, George, *The Assassins' Gate: America in Iraq* (New York: Farrar, Straus and Giroux, 2005).

Packer, George (ed.), *The Fight Is for Democracy: Winning the War of Ideas in America and the World* (New York: Harper Perennial, 2003).

Packer, George, 'The Liberal Quandary over Iraq', *The New York Times Magazine*, 8 December 2002.

Page, Susan, 'Showdown with Saddam: The Decision to Act', *USA Today*, 11 September 2002.

Palast, Greg, *Armed Madhouse* (London: Allen Lane, 2006).

Pappe, Ilan, 'Clusters of History: US Involvement in the Palestine Question', *Race & Class*, 48:3 (2007), pp. 1–28.

Parenti, Christian, *The Freedom: Shadows and Hallucinations in Occupied Iraq* (New York and London: New Press, 2004).

Parmar, Inderjeet, 'Catalysing Events, Think Tanks and American Foreign Policy Shifts: A Comparative Analysis of the Impacts of Pearl Harbor 1941 and 11 September 2001', *Government and Opposition*, 40:1 (2005), pp. 1–25.

Parmar, Inderjeet, 'Foreign Policy Fusion: Liberal Interventionists,

Conservative Nationalists and Neoconservatives – the New Alliance Dominating the US Foreign Policy Establishment', *International Politics*, 46:2 (2009), pp. 177–209.

Parmar, Inderjeet, *Think Tanks and Power in Foreign Policy: A Comparative Study of the Role and Influence of the Council on Foreign Relations and the Royal Institute of International Affairs, 1939–1945* (New York: Palgrave Macmillan, 2004).

Parrish, Geov, 'There Is No War on Terror (Interview with Noam Chomsky)', *Alternet*, 14 February 2006.

Parry, Robert, 'The CIA/Likud Sinking of Jimmy Carter, *Consortiumnews. com*, 24 June 2010.

Parry, Robert, 'Iran–Contra's "Lost Chapter"', *Consortiumnews.com*, 30 June 2008.

Parsi, Trita, *Treacherous Alliance: The Secret Dealings of Israel, Iran, and the United States* (New Haven, CT and London: Yale University Press, 2007).

'Patterns of Global Terrorism 2000' (Washington, DC: US Department of State, 2001).

Paul, James A., 'Oil Companies in Iraq', paper presented at Global Policy Forum Conference in Berlin on Corporate Accountability, 25–6 November 2003.

'Paul Wolfowitz, Velociraptor', *The Economist*, 7 February 2002.

Payne, R. A., 'Neorealists as Critical Theorists: The Purpose of Foreign Policy Debate', *Perspectives on Politics*, 5: (2007), pp. 503–14.

Peleg, Ilan, *Begin's Foreign Policy, 1977–1983: Israel's Move to the Right* (New York and London: Greenwood, 1987).

Perelman, Marc, 'Washington Seeking to Reduce Number of Anti-Israel Votes at UN', *Forward*, 14 November 2003.

Perle, Richard, 'Take Out Saddam – It's the Only Way', *News of the World*, 23 February 2003.

Perry, George L., 'The War on Terrorism, the World Oil Market and the US Economy', Analysis Paper 7 (Washington, DC: Brookings Institution, 2001).

Peters, Joan, *From Time Immemorial: The Origins of the Arab–Jewish Conflict over Palestine* (New York: Harper and Row, 1984).

Petras, James F., *The Power of Israel in the United States* (Atlanta: Clarity Press, 2006).

Phillips, Melanie, 'The Politics of Progress', *Jewish Chronicle*, 31 December 2004.

Phillips, Stephen, 'When Is a Neocon Not a Neocon?', *Times Higher Education Supplement*, 21 March 2006.

Pillar, Paul R., 'Intelligence, Policy, and the War in Iraq', *Foreign Affairs*, March/April 2006.

Pincus, Walter, 'Ex-CIA Official Faults Use of Data on Iraq', *Washington Post*, 10 February 2006.

Pincus, Walter, 'Memo: U.S. Lacked Full Postwar Iraq Plan', *Washington Post*, 12 June 2005.

Pipes, Daniel, 'Review of "Tyranny's Ally: America's Failure to Defeat Saddam Hussein"', *Middle East Quarterly*, 6:3 (1999).

Pipes, Daniel, and Laurie Mylroie, 'Back Iraq: It's Time for a U.S. "Tilt"', *The New Republic*, 27 April 1987.

Piterberg, Gabriel, *The Returns of Zionism: Myths, Politics and Scholarship in Israel* (London: Verso, 2008).

Podhoretz, Norman, 'Appeasement by any other Name', *Commentary*, July 1983, p. 29.

Podhoretz, Norman, *Breaking Ranks: A Political Memoir* (New York: Harper and Row, 1979).

Podhoretz, Norman, 'How to Win World War IV?', *Commentary*, February 2002, pp. 19–29.

Podhoretz, Norman, 'Is It Good for the Jews?', *Commentary*, February 1972, pp. 7–12.

Podhoretz, Norman, *Making It* (New York: Random House, 1967).

Podhoretz, Norman, 'Making the World Safe for Communism', *Commentary*, April 1976, pp. 33–41.

Podhoretz, Norman, 'The Neo-Conservative Anguish over Reagan's Foreign Policy', *The New York Times Magazine*, 2 May 1982, pp. 88–94.

Podhoretz, Norman, *Why We Were in Vietnam* (New York: Simon and Schuster, 1982).

Podhoretz, Norman, *World War IV: The Long Struggle against Islamofascism* (New York: Doubleday, 2007).

Podhoretz, Norman, 'World War IV: How It Started, What It Means, and Why We Have to Win', *Commentary*, September 2004, pp. 17–54.

Polakow-Suransky, Sasha, *The Unspoken Alliance: Israel's Secret Relationship with Apartheid South Africa* (New York: Pantheon Books, 2010).

'Poll: Anti-Semitic Views in the U.S. at a Historic Low', *Reuters*, 29 October 2009.

'Poll: 70% Believe Saddam, 9-11 Link', *USA Today*, 6 September 2003.

Pollack, Kenneth M., 'A Last Chance to Stop Iraq', *The New York Times*, 21 February 2003.

Pollack, Kenneth M., 'Next Stop Iraq?', *Foreign Affairs*, March–April 2002.

Pollack, Kenneth M., 'Saddam's Bombs? We'll Find Them', *The New York Times*, 20 June 2003.

Pollack, Kenneth M., *The Threatening Storm: The Case for Invading Iraq* (New York: Random House, 2002).

Pollack, Kenneth M., 'Why Iraq Can't Be Deterred', *The New York Times*, 26 September 2002.

Pollack, Kenneth M., Martin Indyk, 'How Bush Can Avoid the Inspections Trap', *The New York Times*, 27 January 2003.

Pollack, Kenneth M., and Michael O'Hanlon, 'A War We Just Might Win', *The New York Times*, 30 July 2007.

Porath, Yehoshua, 'Mrs. Peters's Palestine', *The New York Review of Books*, 16 January 1986.

Porter, Gareth, 'Burnt Offering', *The American Prospect*, 21 May 2006.

Porter, Gareth, 'How Tenet Betrayed the CIA on WMD in Iraq', *IPS News*, 8 August 2008.

Powell, Colin, 'The International Campaign against Terrorism' (Washington, DC: US Senate Committee on Foreign Relations, 2001).

Powell, Colin, and Joseph E. Persico, *My American Journey* (New York: Random House, 1995).

Powell, Lewis, 'Attack on American Free Enterprise System', Memo to Eugene B. Sydnor, Jr., Chairman, Education Committee, US Chamber of Commerce, 23 August 1971.

'The Power of Nightmares: The Rise of the Politics of Fear', television documentary series, directed by Adam Curtis (UK: BBC, 2004).

Prados, John, 'PR Push for Iraq War Preceded Intelligence Findings: "White Paper" Drafted before NIE Even Requested', in *National Security Archive Electronic Briefing Book No. 254*, 2008.

Pratt, Julius W., 'The Origin of "Manifest Destiny"', *American Historical Review*, 32:4 (1927), pp. 795–8.

Price, Joyce Howard, 'Peres Encourages U.S. Action on Iraq', *Washington Times*, 12 May 2002, p. A02.

Priest, Dana, 'Congressional Oversight of Intelligence Criticized', *Washington Post*, 27 April 2004, p. A01.

'Public Opinion on the War with Iraq', in 'AEI Public Opinion Studies' series (Washington, DC: American Enterprise Institute, 2008).

Purdum, Todd, and Patrick Tyler, 'Top Republicans Break with Bush on Iraq Strategy', *The New York Times*, 16 August 2002.

Raimondo, Justin, 'Listen Up, Soldier', *Antiwar.com*, 20 January 2003.

Raimondo, Justin, 'Neocons in Denial', *Antiwar.com*, 30 April 2003.

Raju, Manu, Elana Schor, and Ilan Wurman, 'Few Senators Read Iraq NIE Report', *The Hill*, 19 June 2007.

Rampton, Sheldon, and John Stauber, *Weapons of Mass Deception: The Uses of Propaganda in Bush's War on Iraq* (New York: Jeremy P. Tarcher/Penguin, 2003).

Ramsey, Jasmin, 'The Winners and Losers of US Policy on Iran', *Al Jazeera*, 23 December 2011.

Reinhart, Tanya, *Israel/Palestine: How to End the War of 1948* (New York: Seven Stories Press, 2005).

'Remarks of President Barack Obama: Responsibly Ending the War in Iraq' (Washington, DC: The White House, 27 February 2009).

Ricchiardi, Sherry, 'Whatever Happened to Iraq?', *American Journalism Review*, June/July 2008.

Rice, Condoleezza, 'Campaign 2000: Promoting the National Interest', *Foreign Affairs*, 79:1 (2000), pp. 45–62.

Rice, Condoleezza, *No Higher Honor: A Memoir of My Years in Washington* (London: Simon and Schuster, 2011).

Rich, A., *Think Tanks, Public Policy, and the Politics of Expertise* (Cambridge: Cambridge University Press, 2004).

'Richard Perle Discusses US Defense', *CNN* , 16 September 2001.

Richardson, Lee, and Vince Luchsinger, 'Strategic Marketing Implications in Competitive Intelligence and the Economic Espionage Act of 1996', *Journal of Global Business Issues*, 1:2 (2007).

Ricks, Thomas, *Fiasco: The American Military Adventure in Iraq* (London: Allen Lane, 2006).

Ricks, Thomas, 'Some Top Military Brass Favor Status Quo in Iraq', *Washington Post*, 28 July 2002.

Risen, James, 'How Pair's Finding on Terror Led to Clash on Shaping Intelligence', *The New York Times*, 28 April 2004.

Risen, James, 'Iraq Said to Have Tried to Reach Last-Minute Deal to Avert War', *The New York Times*, 6 November 2003.

Risen, James, 'A New House Democrat with an Insiders' View of Iraq', *The New York Times*, 28 November 2006.

Risen, James, *State of War: The Secret History of the CIA and the Bush Administration* (New York: Free Press, 2006).

Risen, James, and Timothy Williams, 'US Looks for Blackwater Replacement in Iraq', *The New York Times*, 30 January 2009.

Ritter, Scott, 'Dinner with Ahmed', *TruthDig.org*, 17 March 2008.

Ritter, Scott, *Iraq Confidential: The Untold Story of America's Intelligence Conspiracy* (London: I. B. Tauris, 2005).

Ritter, Scott, *Target Iran: The Truth About the White House's Plans for Regime Change* (New York: Nation Books, 2006).

Ritter, Scott, 'Where Are the Weapons of Mass Destruction?', *TruthDig.com*, 11 August 2008.

Roberts, Alasdair, *The Collapse of Fortress Bush: The Crisis of Authority in American Government* (New York: New York University Press, 2008).

Rogan, Eugene L., and Avi Shlaim (eds), *The War for Palestine: Rewriting the History of 1948* (New York: Cambridge University Press, 2001).

Rogin, Michael, 'Sucking Up', *London Review of Books*, 12 May 1994.

Rose, David, 'Baghdad's Cruel Princes', *Vanity Fair*, May 2003.

Rose, David, 'A Blind Spot Called Iraq', *The Observer*, 13 January 2002.

Rose, David, 'The Case for Tough Action against Iraq', *The Observer*, 2 December 2001.

Rose, David, 'An Inconvenient Iraq', *Vanity Fair*, January 2003.

Rose, David, 'Inside Saddam's Terror Regime', *Vanity Fair*, February 2002.

Rose, David, 'The Iraqi Connection', *The Observer*, 11 November 2001.

Rose, David, 'Iraq's Arsenal of Terror', *Vanity Fair*, May 2002.

Rose, David, 'Spain Links Suspect in 9/11 Plot to Baghdad', *The Observer*, 16 March 2003.

Rose, David, 'Spies and Their Lies', *New Statesman*, 27 September 2007.

Rose, David, and Ed Vulliamy, 'Iraq "Behind US Anthrax Outbreaks"', *The Observer*, 14 October 2001.

Rosenberg, Joel C., 'Ezekiel 38–39 FAQ', *Joel C. Rosenberg (Blog)*, accessed 5 January 2014.

Rosenberg, M. J., 'Steve Walt Exposes Winep/Aipac's Satloff', *TMPCafe*, 10 April 2010.

Rosenberg, M. J., 'Does PBS Know that "the Washington Institute" Was Founded by AIPAC?', *Huffington Post*, 12 April 2010.

Rosner, Shmuel, 'US Christians Create Umbrella Organization to Lobby for Israel', *Haaretz*, 23 February 2006.

Rothfield, Lawrence, *The Rape of Mesopotamia: Behind the Looting of the Iraq Museum* (Chicago and London: University of Chicago Press, 2009).

Roy, Olivier, 'Europe Won't Be Fooled Again', *The New York Times*, 13 May 2003.

Roy, Sara, 'Intimidation', *London Review of Books*, 17 February 2005.

Roy, Sara, 'Short Cuts', *London Review of Books*, 1 April 2004.

Rozen, Laura, and Jason Vest, 'Cloak and Swagger', *The American Prospect*, 1 November 2004.

Rubenberg, Cheryl A., *Israel and the American National Interest: A Critical Examination* (Urbana: University of Illinois Press, 1986).

Rumsfeld, Donald, *Known and Unknown: A Memoir* (London: Penguin, 2012).

Rumsfeld, Donald, 'Saddam Hussein', *The Rumsfeld Papers*, 21 September 2001, *Rumsfeld.com*.

Rumsfeld, Donald, et al., 'Report of the Commission to Assess United States National Security Space Management and Organization' (Washington, DC: Department of Defense, 2001).

Sadowski, Yahya, 'No War for Whose Oil?', *Le Monde Diplomatique*, April 2003.

Safire, William, 'Clear Ties of Terror', *The New York Times*, 27 January 2003.

Safire, William, 'Essay; Advance the Story', *The New York Times*, 22 October 2001.

Safire, William, 'To Fight Freedom's Fight', *The New York Times*, 31 January 2002.

Safire, William, 'The Inspection Ploy', *The New York Times*, 4 March 2002.

Safire, William, 'In Material Breach', *The New York Times*, 28 October 2002.

Safire, William, 'Irrefutable and Undeniable', *The New York Times*, 6 February 2003.

Safire, William, 'On Playing Hunches', *The New York Times*, 31 October 2002.

Safire, William, 'Prague Connection', *The New York Times*, 12 November 2001.

Safire, William, 'Protecting Saddam', *The New York Times*, 18 March 2002.

Safire, William, 'Relying on Saddam', *The New York Times*, 16 September 2002.

Safire, William, 'Saddam's Last Ploy', *The New York Times*, 7 October 2002.

Safire, William, 'Saddam's Offensive', *The New York Times*, 8 April 2002.

Safire, William, 'Tenet's Palestine', *The New York Times*, 15 April 2002.

Safire, William, 'The Turkey Card', *The New York Times*, 5 November 2001.

Safire, William, 'Of Turks and Kurds', *The New York Times*, 26 August 2002.

Safire, William, 'The Ultimate Enemy', *The New York Times*, 24 September 2001.

Safire, William, 'What Else Is Missing?', *The New York Times*, 6 June 2002.

Said, Abdul Aziz, *Ethnicity and US Foreign Policy* (New York: Praeger, 1981).

Said, Edward, 'The Clash of Ignorance', *The Nation*, 4 October 2001.

Said, Edward, *Covering Islam: How the Media and the Experts Determine How We See the Rest of the World* (London: Vintage, 1997).

Said, Edward, *Culture and Imperialism* (London: Chatto and Windus, 1993).

Said, Edward, 'A Devil Theory of Islam', *The Nation*, 25 July 2000.

Said, Edward, *Orientalism* (Harmondsworth: Penguin, [1978] 1985).

Said, Edward, *The Question of Palestine* (New York: Times Books, 1979).

Sampson, Anthony, 'Oilmen Don't Want Another Suez', *The Observer*, 22 December 2002.

Sampson, Anthony, *The Seven Sisters: The Great Oil Companies and the World They Made*, 3rd edn (London: Coronet, 1993).

Sanger, David, and Eric Schmitt, 'US Has a Plan to Occupy Iraq, Officials Report', *The New York Times*, 11 October 2002.

Saunders, Frances Stonor, *Who Paid the Piper?: The CIA and the Cultural Cold War* (London: Granta Books, 1999).

Scahill, Jeremy, *Blackwater: The Rise of the World's Most Powerful Mercenary Army* (London: Serpent's Tail, 2007).

Scheer, Christopher, Robert Scheer, and Lakshmi Chaudhry, *The Five Biggest Lies Bush Told Us About Iraq* (Lahore: Vanguard Books, 2004).

Schieffer, Bob, 'Interview with Condoleezza Rice', *Face the Nation*, 9 March 2003.

Schmitt, Eric, 'Cheney Assembles Formidable Team', *The New York Times*, 3 February 2001.

Schmitt, Eric, and Joel Brinkley, 'State Dept. Study Foresaw Trouble Now Plaguing Iraq', *The New York Times*, 19 October 2003.

Schmitt, Eric, and Thomas Shanker, 'A CIA Rival; Pentagon Sets up Intelligence Unit', *The New York Times*, 28 October 2002.

Schmitt, Gary, 'The Rumsfeld Commission and Ballistic Missile Defense', Project for the New American Century, 16 July 1998.

Schmitt, Gary J., and Abram N. Shulsky, 'Leo Strauss and the World of Intelligence (by Which We Do Not Mean Nous)', in Kenneth L. Deutsch and John A. Murley (eds), *Leo Strauss, the Straussians, and the American Regime* (New York: Rowman and Littlefield, 1999).

Schulman, Daniel, 'Meet the "Whack Iran" Lobby', *Mother Jones*, 6 October 2006.

Schumpeter, Joseph, *Social Classes: Imperialism: Two Essays* (New York: Meridian Books, 1951).

Sciolino, Elaine, and Patrick Tyler, 'Some Pentagon Officials and Advisors Seek to Oust Iraq's Leader in War's Next Phase', *The New York Times*, 12 October 2001.

Scott, John, *A Matter of Record: Documentary Sources in Social Research* (Cambridge: Polity, 1990).

Scott, John, *Power: Key Concepts* (Cambridge: Polity, 2001).

Scowcroft, Brent, 'Don't Attack Saddam', *The Wall Street Journal*, 15 August 2002.

Seib, Christine, 'Exxon Mobil Breaks Its Own Profit Record', *The Times*, 30 January 2009.

Senate Select Committee on Intelligence, 'Report on Intelligence Activities Relating to Iraq Conducted by the Policy Counterterrorism Evaluation Group and the Office of Special Plans within the Office of the Under Secretary of Defense for Policy' (Washington, DC: US Government Printing Office, June 2008).

Shafer, Jack, 'Richard Perle Libel Watch, Week 4', *Slate*, 2 April 2003.

Shafer, Jack, 'The Times Scoops that Melted', *Slate*, 25 July 2003.

Shahak, Israel, *Jewish History, Jewish Religion: The Weight of Three Thousand Years* (London: Pluto Press, 1994).

Shain, Yossi, 'Ethnic Diasporas and US Foreign Policy', *Political Science Quarterly*, 109:5 (1994), pp. 811–41.

Sharp, Jeremy M., *U.S. Foreign Aid to Israel* (Washington, DC: Congressional Research Service, 2009).

Shatz, Adam, 'Obsession with Islam', *London Review of Books*, 9 October 2008.

Shavit, Ari, 'White Man's Burden', *Haaretz*, 5 April 2003.

Sheffer, Gabriel, *Diaspora Politics: At Home Abroad* (Cambridge: Cambridge University Press, 2003).

Shelton, Christina, 'Iraq, Al-Qaeda, and Tenet's Equivocation', *Washington Post*, 30 June 2007.

Sherman, Scott, 'The Rebirth of the NYRB', *The Nation*, 20 May 2004.

Shlaim, Avi, *The Iron Wall: Israel and the Arab World* (New York and London: W. W. Norton, 2000).

Shulsky, Abram N., and Gary J. Schmitt, *Silent Warfare: Understanding the World of Intelligence* (Washington, DC: Brassey's, 2002).

Siegel, Jennifer, and Nathan Guttman, 'AIPAC Conference: Pastor Hailed, Bibi Dissed, Pollard Rejected, while Politicians Preen', *Forward*, 16 March 2007.

Silverstein, Ken, 'Goldberg's War', *Harpers*, 30 June 2006.

Silverstein, Ken, 'The Man from ONA', *The Nation*, 25 October 1999.

Silverstein, Richard, 'Dubai Ports Deal', *Tikun Olam*, 18 March 2006.

Silverstein, Richard, 'Pro-Israel Campaign to Deny Nadia Abu El-Haj Tenure', *Tikun Olam*, 17 August 2007.

Simpson, John, 'How Predictions for Iraq Came True', *BBC News*, 9 April 2006.

Singer, Peter W., *Corporate Warriors: The Rise of the Privatized Military Industry* (Ithaca, NY and London: Cornell University Press, 2003).

Singer, Peter W., *Wired for War: The Robotics Revolution and Conflict in the Twenty-First Century* (New York: Penguin Press, 2009).

Singh, Gajendra, 'U.S.–Turkish Relations Go Wobbly Now over Syria', *Al Jazeerah*, 23 March 2005.

Slabodkin, Gregory D., 'The AIPAC Politics of Smear: The Secret Section in Israel's U.S. Lobby that Stifles American Debate', *Washington Report on Middle East Affairs*, July 1992.

Slater, Jerome, 'The Two Books of Mearsheimer and Walt', *Security Studies*, 18:1 (2009), pp. 4–57.

Sleeper, Jim, 'Allan Bloom and the Conservative Mind', *The New York Times*, 4 September 2005.

Smith, Ben, 'Freeman Hits "Israel Lobby" on Way Out', *Politico*, 10 March 2009.

Smith, Ben, '76 Senators Sign on to Israel Letter', *Politico*, 13 April 2010.

Smith, Ben, 'US Senators Press Obama on "Risk" for Israel', *AFP*, 19 May 2010.

Smith, Grant F., *America's Defense Line: The Justice Department's Battle to Register the Israel Lobby as Agents of a Foreign Government* (Washington, DC: Institute for Research, Middle Eastern Policy, 2008).

Smith, Grant F., *Deadly Dogma: How Neoconservatives Broke the Law to Deceive America* (Washington, DC: Institute for Research, Middle Eastern Policy, 2006).

Smith, Grant F., *Foreign Agents: The American Israel Public Affairs Committee from the 1963 Fulbright Hearings to the 2005 Espionage Scandal* (Washington, DC: Institute for Research, Middle Eastern Policy, 2007).

Smith, Grant F., *Spy Trade: How Israel's Lobby Undermines America's Economy* (Washington, DC: Institute for Research, Middle Eastern Policy, 2009).

Smith, Grant F., and Tanya C. Hus, *Visa Denied: How Anti-Arab Visa Policies Destroy US Exports, Jobs and Higher Education* (Washington, DC: Institute for Research, Middle Eastern Policy, 2006).

Smith, James A., *The Idea Brokers: Think Tanks and the Rise of the New Policy Elite* (New York: Free Press, 1993).

Smith, Martin A., 'US Bureaucratic Politics and the Decision to Invade Iraq', *Contemporary Politics*, 14:1 (2008), pp. 91–105.

Smith, Michael, 'Ministers Were Told Premier Was Seen as Stooge', *The Daily Telegraph*, 23 September 2004.

Smith, Neil, *The Endgame of Globalization* (New York: Routledge, 2005).

Smith, Tony, *Foreign Attachments: The Power of Ethnic Groups in the Making of American Foreign Policy* (London: Harvard University Press, 2000).

Smith, Tony, 'It's Uphill for the Democrats', *Washington Post*, 11 March 2007.

Snetsinger, John, *Truman, the Jewish Vote, and the Creation of Israel* (Stanford, CA: Hoover Institution Press, 1974).

Sniegoski, Stephen J., *The Transparent Cabal: The Neoconservative Agenda, War in the Middle East, and the National Interest of Israel* (Norfolk, VA: Enigma Editions, 2008).

Sorkin, Andrew Ross, 'Schlepping to Moguldom', *The New York Times*, 5 September 2004.

'Special Report: America United', television programme in 'The O' Reilly Factor' series, presented by Bill O'Reilly (USA: Fox, 14 September 2001).

Stauber, John, and Sheldon Rampton, *Toxic Sludge is Good For You: Lies, Damn Lies and the Public Relations Industry* (Monroe, ME: Common Courage Press, 2002).

Stauffer, Thomas R., 'The Costs to American Taxpayers of the Israeli–Palestinian Conflict: $3 Trillion', *Washington Report on Middle East Affairs*, June 2003.

Steger, Manfred B., and Ravi K. Roy, *Neoliberalism: A Very Short Introduction* (Oxford and New York: Oxford University Press, 2010).

Steinberger, Michael, 'Interview: So, Are Civilisations at War?', *Observer*, 21 October 2001.

Steinfels, Peter, *The Neoconservatives: The Men Who Are Changing America's Politics* (New York: Simon and Schuster, 1979).

Stelzer, Irwin M., *The Neocon Reader* (New York: Grove Press, 2004).

Stiglitz, Joseph, 'The War Costs and Costs and Costs', *The Guardian*, 13 March 2008.

Stiglitz, Joseph, and Linda Bilmes, '$3 Trillion May Be too Low', *The Guardian*, 6 April 2008.

Stiglitz, Joseph, and Linda Bilmes, *The Three Trillion Dollar War: The True Cost of the Iraq Conflict* (New York: W. W. Norton, 2008).

Stokes, Doug, 'Blood for Oil? Global Capital, Counter-Insurgency and the Dual Logic of American Energy Security', *Review of International Studies*, 33:2 (2007), pp. 245–64.

Stone, Diane, *Capturing the Political Imagination: Think Tanks and the Policy Process* (London: Frank Cass, 1996).

Stone, Diane, 'Old Guard Versus New Partisans: Think Tanks in Transition', *Australian Journal of Political Science*, 26:2 (1991), pp. 197–215.

Stone, Peter H., 'Big Oil's Overseas Push', *The National Journal*, 28 April 2001.

Stone, Peter H., 'Ice-Cold Warrior', *The National Journal*, 23 December 1995.

Strobel, Warren P., 'The CNN Effect', *American Journalism Review*, 18 (1996).

Strobel, Warren P., 'Exhaustive Review Finds No Link between Saddam and Al Qaida', *McClatchy Newspapers*, 10 March 2008.

'Study: Paying for Lobbyists – Pays Off', *Associated Press*, 9 April 2009.

Sullivan, Andrew, 'America, Stop Sucking Up to Israel', *The Atlantic (The Daily Dish)*, 2 November 2009.

Sullivan, Andrew, 'A False Premise', *The Atlantic (The Daily Dish)*, 5 February 2009.

Sundström, Mikael, 'A Brief Introduction: What Is an Epistemic Community?', PSU.edu (2000), pp. 1–8.

Suskind, Ron, *The One Percent Doctrine: Deep inside America's Pursuit of its Enemies since 9/11* (New York and London: Simon and Schuster, 2006).

Suskind, Ron, *The Price of Loyalty: George W. Bush, the White House, and the Education of Paul O'Neill* (New York and London: Simon and Schuster, 2004).

Suskind, Ron, *The Way of the World: A Story of Truth and Hope in an Age of Extremism* (New York: Harper, 2008).

Suskind, Ron, and Amy Goodman, 'The Way of the World', *Democracy Now!*, 13 August 2008.

Tal, David, 'Symbol Not Substance? Israel's Campaign to Acquire

Hawk Missiles, 1960–1962', *The International History Review*, 22:2 (2000), pp. 304–17.

Tanenhaus, Sam, 'Bush's Brain Trust', *Vanity Fair*, July 2003.

Tenet, George, *At the Center of the Storm: My Years at the CIA* (London: HarperPress, 2007).

Terry, Janice J., *U.S. Foreign Policy in the Middle East: The Role of Lobbies and Special Interest Groups* (London and Ann Arbor, MI: Pluto Press, 2005).

Thomas, Evan, Richard Wolffe, and Michael Isikoff, 'Where Are Iraq's WMDs?', *Newsweek*, 9 June 2003.

Thomas, Michael Tracy, *American Policy Towards Israel: The Power and Limits of Beliefs* (London: Routledge, 2007).

Thompson, Mark, and Michael Duffy, 'Pentagon Warlord', *Time*, 19 January 2003.

Tivnan, Edward, *The Lobby: Jewish Political Power and American Foreign Policy* (New York: Simon and Schuster, 1987).

'Top Station Groups Stay the Course', *TVNewsCheck*, 7 April 2010.

Traub, James, 'A Statesman without Borders', *The New York Times Magazine*, 3 February 2008.

Trice, Robert H., 'The American Elite Press and the Arab–Israeli Conflict', *The Middle East Journal*, 33:3 (1979), pp. 304–25.

Trice, Robert H., 'Domestic Interest Groups and the Arab–Israeli Conflict: A Behavioral Analysis', in Abdul Aziz Said (ed.), *Ethnicity and US Foreign Policy* (New York: Praeger, 1981), pp. 117–38.

Trice, Robert H., 'Foreign Policy Interest Groups, Mass Public Opinion and the Arab–Israeli Dispute', *Political Research Quarterly*, 31: (1978), p. 238.

Trice, Robert H., *Interest Groups and the Foreign Policy Process: US Policy in the Middle East* (Beverly Hills: Sage, 1976).

Trilling, Roger, 'Fighting Word', *Village Voice*, 30 April 2002.

Tripp, Charles, 'Iraq and the 1948 War: Mirror of Iraq's Disorder', in Eugene L. Rogan and Avi Shlaim (eds), *The War for Palestine: Rewriting the History of 1948* (New York: Cambridge University Press, 2001), pp. 125–49.

Tyler, Patrick, *A World of Trouble: The White House and the Middle East – from the Cold War to the War on Terror* (New York: Farrar, Straus and Giroux, 2009).

Uhler, Walter C., '"Fixed" Intelligence from Feith's "Gestapo Office," the CIA and the Bush Administration's Impeachable Lies about Iraq's Prewar Links to Al Qaeda', *walter-c-uhler.com*, 20 January 2006.

Unger, Craig, *The Fall of the House of Bush: The Untold Story of How* a Band of True Believers Seized the Executive Branch, Started the Iraq War, and Still Imperils America's Future (New York: Scribner, 2007).

Unger, Craig, House of Bush, House of Saud: The Hidden Relationship between the World's Two Most Powerful Dynasties (London: Gibson Square Books, 2004).

Unger, Craig, 'How Cheney Took Control of Bush's Foreign Policy', Salon, 9 November 2007.

Unger, Craig, 'The War They Wanted, the Lies They Needed', Vanity Fair, July 2006.

'UNSCOM "Infiltrated by Spies"', BBC News, 23 March 1999.

US Religious Landscape Survey (Pew Forum on Religion and Public Life, 2008, <http://religions.pewforum.org/comparisons>).

'U.S. Troops in Iraq: 72% Say End War in 2006', Zogby International, 28 February 2006.

Vaïsse, Justin, Neoconservatism: The Biography of a Movement (Cambridge, MA: Harvard University Press, 2010).

Van Evera, Stephen, Guide to Methods for Students of Political Science (Ithaca, NY: Cornell University Press, 1997).

Verloy, Andre, and Daniel Politi, 'Advisors of Influence: Nine Members of the Defense Policy Board Have Ties to Defense Contractors' (Washington, DC: Center for Public Integrity, 2003).

Vest, Jason, 'Big Lies, Blind Spies, and Vanity Fair: Quick Lessons from the WMD Report', Village Voice, 5 April 2005.

Vest, Jason, 'The Men from JINSA and CSP', The Nation, 2 September 2002.

Waas, Murray, 'Key Bush Intelligence Briefing Kept from Hill Panel', National Journal, 22 November 2005.

Waldman, Peter, 'Containing Jihad: A Historian's Take on Islam Steers U.S. in Terrorism Fight', The Wall Street Journal, 3 February 2004.

Wallace, Ed, 'Oil Prices Are All Speculation', Bloomberg Businessweek, 27 June 2008.

Wallace, William, 'Between Two Worlds: Think Tanks and Foreign Policy', in Christopher Hill and Pamela Beshoff (eds), Two Worlds of International Relations (London: Routledge, 1994), pp. 139–63.

Walt, Stephen M., Taming American Power: The Global Response to U.S. Primacy (New York and London: W. W. Norton, 2005).

Waltz, K. N., Man, the State, and War: A Theoretical Analysis (New York: Columbia University Press, 2001).

Wanniski, Jude, 'The Mundell–Laffer Hypothesis: A New View of the World Economy', The Public Interest, 39 (1975), pp. 31–52.

War Made Easy: How Presidents & Pundits Keep Spinning Us to Death, documentary film, directed by Loretta Alper and Jeremy Earp (USA: Media Education Foundation, 2007).

Warnke, Paul C., 'The B Team: Paul C. Warnke Reviews Killing Detente: The Right Attacks the CIA', *The Bulletin of the Atomic Scientists*, 55:1 (1999), p. 70.

'The War Party', television programme, produced by Mike Rudin, reporter Steve Bradshaw (UK: BBC, 18 May 2003).

Wawro, Geoffrey, *Quicksand: America's Pursuit of Power in the Middle East* (New York: Penguin Press, 2010).

Waxman, D., 'From Jerusalem to Baghdad? Israel and the War in Iraq', *International Studies Perspectives*, 10:1 (2009), pp. 1–17.

Wayne, Leslie, 'Companies Used to Getting Their Way', *The New York Times*, 4 December 1998.

Wedel, Janine R., *Shadow Elite: How the World's New Power Brokers Undermine Democracy, Government, and the Free Market* (New York: Basic Books, 2009).

Weisberg, Jacob, *The Bush Tragedy* (New York: Random House, 2008).

Weisman, Steven R., 'White House Is Pressing Israelis to Take Initiatives in Peace Talks', *The New York Times*, 17 April 2003.

Weiss, Philip, 'Ferment over "the Israel Lobby"', *The Nation*, 15 May 2006.

Weiss, Philip, 'The Long Fuse to the Iraq War', *The American Conservative*, 28 January 2008.

Wells, Matt, 'The Black Arts Leave Writers Riled', *The Guardian*, 16 March 2001.

Wheatcroft, Geoffrey, 'A State Like No Other', *New Statesman*, 25 April 2005.

Whitaker, Brian, 'Conflict and Catchphrases', *The Guardian*, 24 February 2003.

Whitaker, Brian, 'US Thinktanks Give Lessons in Foreign Policy', *The Guardian*, 19 August 2002.

Why We Fight, film, directed by Michael Moore (USA: Arte, 2005).

Wieseltier, Leon, 'Something Much Darker', *The New Republic*, 8 February 2009.

Wilkerson, Lawrence, Paul Pillar, Carl Ford, Wayne White, Rod Barton, Michael Smith, and Joseph Cirincione, 'An Oversight Hearing on Pre-War Intelligence Relating to Iraq', paper presented at the Senate Democratic Policy Committee Hearing, 26 June 2006.

Williams, Ian, 'John Bolton in Jerusalem: The New Age of Disarmament Wars', *Foreign Policy in Focus*, 20 February 2003.

Williams, Ian, 'John Bolton's Greatest Hits', *The Nation*, 18 December 2006.

Wilson, Joseph, 'How Saddam Thinks', *San Jose Mercury News*, 13 October 2002.

Wilson, Joseph, *The Politics of Truth: Inside the Lies that Led to War and Betrayed My Wife's CIA Identity: A Diplomat's Memoir* (New York: Carroll and Graf Publishers, 2004).

Wilson, Joseph, 'Republic or Empire', *The Nation*, 13 February 2003.

Wilson, Joseph, 'What I Didn't Find in Africa', *The New York Times*, 6 July 2003.

Windmueller, Steven, 'Are American Jews Becoming Republican? Insights into Jewish Political Behavior', *Jerusalem Viewpoints*, 15 December 2003.

Wohlstetter, Albert, 'Between an Unfree World and None: Increasing Our Choices', *Foreign Affairs*, 63:5 (1985), pp. 962–94.

Wohlstetter, Albert, 'Clocking the Strategic Arms Race', *The Wall Street Journal*, 24 September 1974.

Wohlstetter, Albert, 'The Delicate Balance of Terror', *Foreign Affairs*, 37:2 (1959), pp. 211–33.

Wohlstetter, Albert, 'Is There a Strategic Arms Race?', *Foreign Policy*, 15 (1974), pp. 3–20.

Wohlstetter, Albert, 'Is There a Strategic Arms Race? (II): Rivals but No "Race"', *Foreign Policy*, 16 (1974), pp. 48–92.

Wohlstetter, Albert, 'Optimal Ways to Confuse Ourselves', *Foreign Policy*, 20 (1975), pp. 170–98.

Wohlstetter, Albert, 'Strength, Interest and New Technologies', opening address of the 9th Annual Conference of the Institute of Strategic Studies on Military Technology in the 1970's, Elsinore, 27 September 1967.

Wohlstetter, Albert, 'Threats and Promises of Peace: Europe and America in the New Era', *Orbis*, 17 (1974), p. 1124.

Wohlstetter, Albert, 'The Uncontrolled Upward Spiral', *Strategic Review*, 3 (1975), pp. 71–86.

Wohlstetter, Albert, 'The Uses of Irrelevance', *New York Times*, 25 February 1979.

Wohlstetter, Albert, and Fred S. Hoffman, 'The Bitter End: The Case for Re-Intervention in Iraq', *The New Republic*, 29 April 1991, pp. 20–4.

Wolfowitz, Paul, 'Clinton's Bay of Pigs', *The Wall Street Journal*, 27 September 1996.

Wolfowitz, Paul, 'Deputy Secretary Wolfowitz Q&A Following IISS

Asia Security Conference (Transcript)' (Washington, DC: Department of Defense, 2003).

Wolfowitz, Paul, 'Statement before the House National Security Committee', Project for the New American Century, 1998.

Wolfowitz, Paul, 'The United States and Iraq', in John Calabrese (ed.), *The Future of Iraq* (Washington, DC: Middle East Institute, 1997), pp. 107–13.

Wolfowitz, Paul, and Zalmay Khalilzad, 'Overthrow Him', *The Weekly Standard*, 1 December 1997.

Wolfowitz, Paul, and Sam Tanenhaus, 'Transcript: Deputy Secretary Wolfowitz Interview with Sam Tannenhaus, Vanity Fair' (Washington, DC: Department of Defense, 2003).

Woods, Kevin M., and James Lacey, 'Iraqi Perspectives Project. Saddam and Terrorism: Emerging Insights from Captured Iraqi Documents (Redacted)' (Alexandria, VA: Department of Defense, Institute for Defense Analyses, 2007).

Woodward, Bob, *Bush at War* (New York: Simon and Schuster, 2002).

Woodward, Bob, *Plan of Attack* (New York: Simon and Schuster, 2004).

Woodward, Bob, *State of Denial* (New York: Simon and Schuster, 2006).

Woodward, Bob, *Veil: The Secret Wars of the CIA, 1981–1987* (New York: Simon and Schuster, 1987).

Woodward, Bob, *The War Within: A Secret White House History, 2006–2008* (New York: Simon and Schuster, 2008).

Woolsey, R. James, 'Blood Baath', *The New Republic*, 24 September 2001 [first published online, 13 September 2001].

Woolsey, R. James, 'The Iraq Connection', *The Wall Street Journal*, 18 October 2001.

Woolsey, R. James, 'Saddam May Be Target Americans Are Looking for', *The Daily Telegraph*, 17 September 2001.

Woolsey, R. James and Mansoor Ijaz, 'Revenge Is a Dish Best Served Cold', *Los Angeles Times*, 12 September 2001.

The World Fact Book (Washington, DC: Central Intelligence Agency, 2009).

Wright, Ann Mary, 'Letter of Resignation to US Secretary of State Colin Powell', *TruthOut.org*, 19 March 2003.

Wright, Robin, and Dan Eggen, 'Leak Inquiry Includes Iran Experts in Administration', *Washington Post*, 4 September 2004.

Wurmser, David, 'Iraq Needs a Revolution', *The Wall Street Journal*, 12 November 1997.

Wurmser, David, 'The Rise and Fall of the Arab World', *Strategic Review*, 21:3 (1993), pp. 33–46.

Wurmser, David, *Tyranny's Ally: America's Failure to Defeat Saddam Hussein* (Washington, DC: AEI Press, 1999).

Wurmser, David, Richard Perle, James Colbert, Jr. Charles Fairbanks, Douglas Feith, Robert Loewenberg, Jonathan Torop, and Meyrav Wurmser, 'A Clean Break: A New Strategy for Securing the Realm' (Jerusalem: Institute for Advanced Strategic and Political Studies, 1996).

Wurmser, David, Richard Perle, James Colbert, Jr. Charles Fairbanks, Douglas Feith, Robert Loewenberg, Jonathan Torop, and Meyrav Wurmser, 'Coping with Crumbling States: A Western and Israeli Balance of Power Strategy for the Levant' (Jerusalem: Institute for Advanced Strategic and Political Studies, 1997).

'A Year after Iraq War: Mistrust of America in Europe Ever Higher, Muslim Anger Persists' (Washington, DC: The Pew Research Center for the People & the Press, 2004).

Yergin, Daniel, *The Prize: The Epic Quest for Oil, Money, and Power* (London: Simon and Schuster, 1991).

Yinon, Oded, 'A Strategy for Israel in the 1980s', trans. Israel Shahak, *Kivunim* (1982), pp. 1–17.

Zinni, Anthony, 'Speech given at the Middle East Institute Annual Conference', *Middle East Institute*, 10 October 2002.

Zamora, George, 'N. M. Tech, SAIC to Sign Agreement', *New Mexico Tech*, 9 January 2003.

Žižek, Slavoj, *Iraq: The Borrowed Kettle*, 'Wo Es War' series (London and New York: Verso, 2004).

Zunes, Stephen, 'The Israel Lobby: A Progressive Response to Mearsheimer and Walt'. *Tikkun*, November/December 2007.

Index